Big Water, Little Boats

Moulty Fulmer and the First Grand Canyon Dory
on the Last of the Wild Colorado River

Tom Martin

First Edition

ISBN 978-0-9795055-6-0

Front cover photos: Palisades of the Desert with three replica boats, 2011, Tom Martin photo, and Moulty Fulmer and Guy Taylor in the *Gem* at Deer Creek Falls, 1958, courtesy Joe Szep.

Back cover photos: Tommy Cox, Moulty Fulmer at the oars, and Carl Pederson seated behind Moulty on the *Gem* near Kanab Creek, 1955, courtesy Fulmer Collection, reproduced by permission, Utah State Historical Society, all rights reserved, and Tom Martin in *Gem* replica below Deer Creek, 2011, courtesy Rick Demarest.

Cover design: Sandra Kim Muleady
Map Courtesy Jeff Jenness, www.jennessent.com

Vishnu Temple Press, LLC
P O Box 30821
Flagstaff AZ 86003-0821
(928) 556 0742
www.vishnutemplepress.com

Dedicated to

Priss Becker and Joe Szep,

with thanks

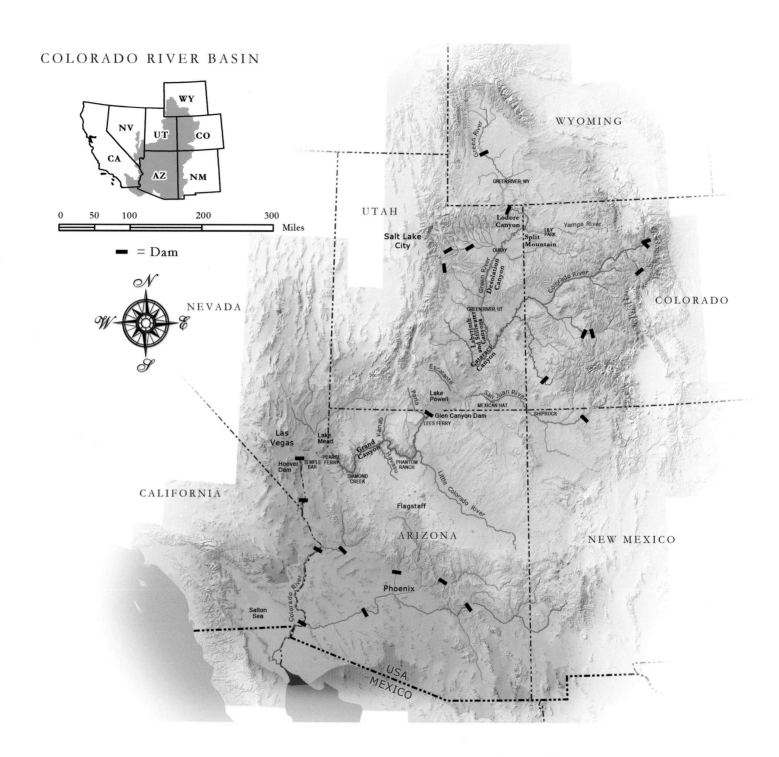

COLORADO RIVER BASIN

= Dam

WY
NV
UT
CO
CA
AZ
NM

0   50   100   200   300
Miles

N
W   E
S

WYOMING

Green River

GREEN RIVER, WY

UTAH

Lodore
Canyon

Salt Lake
City

OURAY

Split
Mountain

BR.Y
PARK

Yampa River

COLORADO

Green River

Desolation
Canyon

GREEN RIVER, UT

Colorado River

NEVADA

Labyrinth,
Stillwater,
and Canyons

Cataract
Canyon

Escalante

Lake
Powell

Paria

San Juan River

MEXICAN HAT

SHIPROCK

Glen Canyon Dam

LEES FERRY

Kanab

Las
Vegas

Lake
Mead

Grand
Canyon

PEARCE
FERRY

TEMPLE
BAR

Havasu

PHANTOM
RANCH

Hoover
Dam

DIAMOND
CREEK

Little Colorado River

CALIFORNIA

Flagstaff

ARIZONA

NEW MEXICO

Phoenix

Colorado River

Salton
Sea

USA
MEXICO

Contents

Foreword 7
Prologue 11
1. The *Gem* in God's Pocket (1964) 13
2. The Midget Champion (1906-1941) 15
3. The River Bug Bites (1942) 21
4. Indiana Boating in a *Tub* (1942-1943) 25
5. The Boating Soldier Meets a Boat Builder (1944-1945) . . 29
6. Eating Sand Waves with the *Moja* (1945-1947). . . . 35
7. The Grand at Last (1948) 41
8. Tragedy and Gasoline (1949-1950) 55
9. More Practice and the *Gem* (1951-1952) 67
10. A Hell of a Good Time (1953). 79
11. The Trip that Never Left Lee's Ferry (1954) 89
12. Only One Flip (1955) 99
13. The Perfect Run, Almost (1956) 121
14. To Phantom on 126,000 cfs and We're Hiking Out (1957) . 139
15. A Race to Temple Bar Without Boats (1958) . . . 159
16. The Sinking of the Reilly Fleet (1959) 175
17. New Boats, a New Dam and a New River (1960 and beyond) . 189
Epilogue 205
Acknowledgements 213
Citation Key 215
Notes 215
Index 231
About the author 240

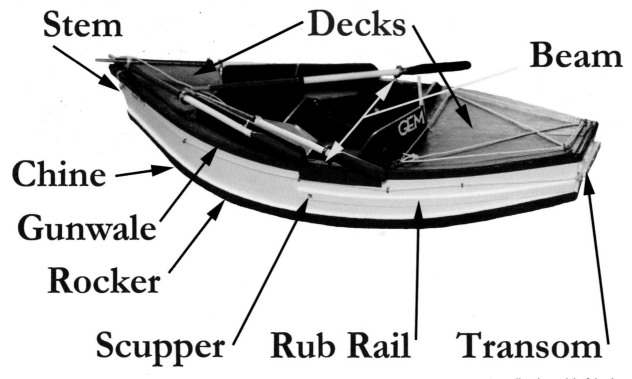

Stem   **Decks**   **Beam**

Chine

Gunwale

Rocker

Scupper   **Rub Rail**   **Transom**

A small scale model of the dory *Gem*, 2009.
Tom Martin photo

The Making of a Grand Canyon Dory

A Grand Canyon dory is a fully decked McKenzie River dory hull, with watertight chambers for river gear, and is tradionally brightly painted.

Terms used to describe a dory include:

Beam: width of the boat at the widest point, usually at the oarlocks

Chine: edge where the side of the boat meets the bottom of the boat

Deck: sturdy, watertight, integral cover which allows for gear storage below and seating above.

Gunwale: edge where the top of the boat meets the side of the boat

Rocker: also mistakenly called rake by river runners in this book, rocker is the curve of the boat's floor from bow to stern

Rub rail: an additional protective strip of wood added to the side of the boat

Scupper: a drain hole in the side of a boat above the normal water line

Stem: a pointed end of the boat

Transom: the small flat end of a boat

Foreword

In the writing of *Big Water, Little Boats*, Tom Martin fills a huge gap in the history of Grand Canyon river running, a gap that should have been articulated a long time ago. Even the popular book by David Lavender, *River Runners of the Grand Canyon*, failed to mention the name of Moulty Fulmer and his wooden dory *Gem*. This is especially true as the McKenzie River (Oregon) whitewater wood dory has received a high degree of attention for about six decades now.

In fact, Lavender's book leaves the impression that the emergence of the whitewater wooden dory on the Grand Canyon boating scene is the contribution of P. T. Reilly and Martin Litton. The reader of *Big Water, Little Boats* will discover the Reilly-Litton connection is only an incidental truth. The history of river running in Grand Canyon is more complete and Moulty finally gets full credit for the introduction of this craft not only to the Grand Canyon but to the Colorado River basin. This book is therefore a major contribution to the history of river running in Grand Canyon.

Not only do we learn about the rich heritage of the McKenzie River dory, but Tom Martin also brings forth Moulty Fulmer's character. Moulty shines as an unassuming individual who is ever polite and helpful on the many river trips he participated in, especially when the chips were down. It is interesting to note that Moulty never asserted himself to be a trip leader on those big water Grand Canyon expeditions mentioned in this book, but was usually positioned as the last boat in the running order. In the group culture of whitewater boating, the last boat, or "sweep" position, is generally given to the individual who is most likely to solve whatever dire circumstance the group might get into, and therefore it is a tacit position of skill and wisdom.

I can't help but think that Moulty would have acquired more innovation in the techniques of running big water rapids sooner had he only followed his heart to run Hance Rapid and Lava Falls head on, instead of lining or portaging. Individual river runners approach big water differently and according to a combination of one's personality and the depth of their previous experience. As an example, the 1914 big water adventure of Bert Loper and Charles S. Russell in Cataract Canyon included two fabricated metal boats each dragging a heavy chain in the current to slow the boats down a bit. Loper preferred to stay in the main current, while Russell preferred the margins where there were whirling eddies choked with driftwood. The end result included the sinking of Russell's boat and, after caching Loper's boat on high ground, a long walk overland to Hite, Utah, with the transformation of an initial friendship into acute bitterness.

For those who have not experienced the thrill of running big rapids when the Colorado River is swollen with snowmelt and driftwood, I would like to think that the majority of us don't feel inclined anymore to drag chains, portage, or line our boats. That is because we stand on the shoulders of those who ran before us, like Loper and Fulmer. Through repetition and acquired skills, based on decades of knowledge and experience, river running has matured to the point where most of us take that big water on as a privilege.

Even though it is true that the Colorado River in Grand Canyon does not swell with snowmelt and driftwood anymore, because of closing the gates of Glen Canyon Dam in 1963, the big water experience still remains present in the canyons above Lake Powell. And despite the truncation of the fifty-seven dams above Lee's Ferry, Arizona, the river will one day again see flows exceeding 200,000 cubic feet per second (cfs). When it does, river runners will once more have to reinvent their skills and knowledge—so will the U.S. Bureau of Reclamation, which presently manages all the large dams in the Colorado River basin.

While Moulty Fulmer and Pat Reilly were perfecting the wooden boat approach to running rapids in Grand Canyon, others were simultaneously augmenting the approach with gasoline-powered motor boats and increased flotation. Georgie White-Clark was floating upwards of thirty people on about 900 square feet of neoprene rubber, while using an outboard motor for steerage. Martin recounts their stories along with those of Ed Hudson, Otis "Dock" Marston, and others who were implementing outboard and inboard motors to not only roar down the rapids, but also to roar up them.

A restraint for these kinds of mechanized devices, and egregious litter bugging and privy practices, occurred when the National Park Service decided to make enforceable regulations about what is, and what is not, appropriate for the river corridor within Grand Canyon National Park. Georgie benefited from these regulations immensely and would prosper as a commercial outfitter until 1992. The up-runner Dock Marston did not, but he adjusted very quickly and pioneered, with Bill Belknap, a one-person, plastic oar boat called a Sportyak--and loved his return to simplicity.

Most of the negative changes happening in the river corridor were the result of constructing Glen Canyon Dam, and help explain how the contrarian nickname, "The Ditch," came about to describe what the Grand Canyon had become, essentially a conduit of clear and cold water running between Lake Powell and Lake Mead, the two largest artificial reservoirs in the United States. With annual flushes from melting snow now contained in Lake Powell, the beaches of the Grand Canyon became the common denominator of accumulating filth, trash, and driftwood-burning charcoal. It was getting pretty disgusting back then. Now, even with low-impact regulations well-established and faithfully abided by, occasional outbreaks of serious intestinal disorders still occur on river and backpacking trips.

Martin also documents the loss of sediment along the river as a result of Glen Canyon Dam. In 1965 the Bureau of Reclamation intentionally sent high volumes of crystal clear water racing through the various outlets of the dam for about two months (releases peaked at 60,200 cfs on June 15). This began the removal of sediment from the river corridor. The 1965 flow stripped the equivalent of about 267,000 metric tons of sediment per mile from the Colorado above Phantom Ranch. Later flows would continue the trend. Low-lying driftwood piles were sent downstream into Lake Mead to ferment into greenhouses gases, instead of fertilizing the riparian ecosystem in a time-released fashion.

The remaining perched sediment along the river has been creeping toward the river ever since and exposing, ironically, federally protected Native American cultural properties that include ancient burial sites. In Lake Powell the opposite situation is occurring, because the inundated archaeology there is being covered by ever-thickening deposits of silt and sand transported by the flowing Colorado River upstream.

While some river runners felt the changes enforced by the National Park Service were beneficial and appropriate, others felt the management directives did not go far enough and were unfair to the commons. Some were completely outraged—especially toward the recalcitrant Bureau of Reclamation and the timid National Park Service. That outrage was successful enough to keep two dams from being built in Grand Canyon, and led to expansion of the park to 1.2 million acres in 1975.

Big Water, Little Boats clearly documents how it came to pass that the lion's share of river running permits were given arbitrarily to the commercial outfitters, and during the prime season of fair weather. That Park Service policy has resulted in river access chaos. Today, unless you become a commercial river guide or concession owner, the chances of a do-it-yourself river runner obtaining a permit to run a river trip in the summer months of the year means accepting a situation where waiting to win the permit lottery can take a very long time—sometimes the better parts of two decades.

Those who were the most outraged about the building of Glen Canyon Dam were not necessarily river runners at all, at least not in the sense that they owned and operated their own boats. These were citizen activists like David Brower and Jeff Ingram of the Sierra Club. But even the water establishment was not necessarily enthralled about Glen Canyon Dam either, such as the attorney Northcutt Ely who represented the Colorado River Board of California. These gentlemen thought the existing Glen Canyon Dam, as well as the dams proposed in Grand Canyon in the 1960s (Marble Canyon Dam and Bridge Canyon Dam), were a fixation of grandiosity and unbridled greed.

First, they proclaimed in whole, or in part, that water was more precious than electricity, and that redundant reservoirs in desert climes evaporated huge amounts of a very limited water supply; second, inundating superlative scenery and destroying vibrant ecosystems was not only controversial but unnecessary, and; third, the more technology and growth that the dominant society inserted into our daily lives, the more we as a people abandoned the wildness that lives in each and every human spirit. This characteristic is why we find it so very necessary to get a boat, float down the river, and hike up the side canyons as far as we dare. To feel truly alive and vibrant it is absolutely necessary to get wet, hot, cold, windblown, clawed, abraded, and scratched. We also need measures of disappointment, joy, heavy-breathing, naps, hunger, satiation, friendships, and time to be alone in silence.

The campaign activists succeeded on every point but one—gaining a motor-free wilderness designation established by Congress through the Wilderness Act of 1964. Ironically, it was the river concessionaires themselves in 1980 that obstructed this outcome for a river that was incrementally beaten down into an industrialized water park with a helicopter ride thrown in as the encore. Many observers refer to this transformation as the "Disneyfication" of our national park system.

However, as David Brower was fond of saying, "If you can't save the Grand Canyon, you can't save anything." While we know the river will be restored in the scope of geologic time, what is important is that this restoration is implemented by those who did the installation of the current working model that changed what Moulty was so privileged to see and enjoy. This is why *Big Water, Little Boats* it so important. Tom Martin has documented not only what a free-flowing Colorado River in Grand Canyon was like before Glen Canyon Dam, but how river running was transformed into what we see today.

John Weisheit
Conservation Director, Living Rivers

Prologue

As a young child I was lucky enough to accompany my father, the Pleistocene ecologist Paul S. Martin, on many a hiking trip in the Grand Canyon. Paul was looking for remains of the last megafauna in the Canyon's dry caves, remains that were 13,000 years old or older. A victim of polio in his twenties, Paul would "explore" by sending me and his students scrambling all over the rugged terrain, looking into the Canyon's many caves. It seemed natural that we would expand our explorations of the Canyon to include river travel, and in 1969 my dad brought me along for a one-week hitchhiking river trip from Diamond Creek to Temple Bar.

My parents sent me on another Grand Canyon river trip in 1971, and on that river trip I heard stories of some early river runners. One of those stories involved watching a run-away boat float into Lava Falls on very high water before the construction of Glen Canyon Dam. I thought nothing of it at the time.

Two decades later, under the watchful eye of Larry Stevens and Paul "Zeke" Lauck, I rowed a fourteen-foot raft through the Canyon as a technician on a Glen Canyon Dam Environmental Studies trip. That year, I also spent over 250 days on the river, and came to learn that while I knew a lot about Grand Canyon, there was a lot more about it that I didn't know.

The next two years I enjoyed working summers as a river guide. Occasionally I rowed a support raft for trips where the passengers rode in colorful wooden or aluminum dories. I had no idea where these boats originated. All the while, I could see remnants of what the river was like before the dam. Giant tree trunks lay quietly parked on rocks way above the present river level, ever so slowly rotting in the hot sun. Mud deposits would surprise me as I found them far up above the river. These clues whispered of that seemingly mythical time when the Colorado was silt-red big-water with lots of driftwood and hardly anybody floating down it.

But a few people had floated the river before the dam. Small groups of friends, often with homemade boats, traveled "Big Red" without the assistance of river guides or big motor boats. I discovered the various pleasures of running the river with friends on a thirty-day do-it-yourself river trip in January of 1993. That trip was magical. It rained almost every day, and we ran Lava Falls on 30,000 cubic feet per second.

By this time I was well aware that do-it-yourself river runners, also called self-guided river runners, private or non-commercial boaters, had little voice in river management. I had also learned that the highest level of federal protection available to a landscape of Grand Canyon caliber, congressionally designated wilderness, had been derailed by the very river concessions I had worked for as a guide.

It seemed logical then to form a group dedicated to wilderness protection for the Grand Canyon, including the Colorado River, with equitable river access to same. My first endeavor in this direction, the formation of the Grand Canyon Private Boaters Association in 1996, ended in spectacular failure when a slim majority of the board of directors voted to put river runner access ahead of wilderness and resource protection in 2002.

With the assistance of Jo Johnson and John Weisheit, in 2002 we formed River Runners for Wilderness. Litigation ensued in 2006 over the commercialization and motorization of the Colorado River in Grand Canyon. Four groups, River Runners for Wilderness, Living Rivers, Rock the Earth and Wilderness Watch were on one side; the NPS, the river concessionaires trade association, and the private boaters association on the other. We lost in court. The resource lost, and river runners lost… for the time being anyway.

As we made our way over this long and winding journey through the rugged badlands of broken friendships, new friendships, park planning, congressional and court visits, I became more and more acquainted with a river runner no one seemed to know much about. And yet he seemed to have done some amazing river running over a span of almost forty years. More importantly, he tied together the stories I had heard as a child, with the history of hard-hulled boats and what running the wild Colorado was all about. With litigation and river management planning subsided for the moment, it was finally time to explore the life of Moulton Fulmer.

This book contains the stories of an incredibly rich array of self-guided river runners in Grand Canyon, based on their trip logs, letters, photos, and personal recollections. Some of these accounts have been paraphrased to improve flow, with inclusion of the actual text to stress the occasional point. *Big Water, Little Boats* is intended to accompany anyone who travels by watercraft on the Colorado River in Grand Canyon. Many of the historic photos used in the book can be matched on the river today, and the stories can be read, especially around the camp circle after dinner, while the river softly purrs in the background.

Traveling on little boats through the immensity of Grand Canyon honors the "can-do" spirit that makes this a great country. To do so allows Grand Canyon to challenge one's very core. To not be an expert or authority, to stand in awe, inspired by such a big and powerful place, to try your best, and see what happens, on the Canyon's terms and the River's speed, honors the greatness that Grand Canyon is, and still has to offer us today. Our wilderness national parks do the country proud by allowing this type of self-directed discovery.

It is with utmost respect and humility that I offer to you the story of Moulty Fulmer, a Grand Canyoneer.

Tom Martin

1

The *Gem* in God's Pocket

1964

Late September 1964 was a wonderful time to be on Lake Mead. Calm days made powerboat travel easy, and the blast furnace heat of summer had abated. The National Park Service patrol boat slowly explored the base of steep limestone cliffs along the west side of Driftwood Bay, far up in the headwaters of the lake. Rumor had it that the wreck of a boat was resting in a crack somewhere along the west edge of the bay in a place called God's Pocket.

Extremely low water in the reservoir had exposed the wreck. With the closing of the floodgates of Glen Canyon Dam on the Colorado River 300 miles upstream the year before, Lake Mead was experiencing its second lowest water level since it started to fill in the 1930s. The reservoir level would start rising once more in 1965 and would not be this low again until 2008. Had the boat sunk another fifty feet to the east, it would still have been under water on that mild fall day in 1964. Had it not been recovered then, it would be completely buried under sediment today.

Ted Whitmoyer, Chief Naturalist for Lake Mead National Recreation Area, surveyed the steep hillsides at the mouth of God's Pocket. One deep gully after another ran down into the water, as if a giant mountain lion had clawed the west side of Iceberg Canyon from the high ridgeline above, all the way down to the water's edge. As Whitmoyer eased the patrol boat along the rocky shore, he suddenly saw it: the fifteen-foot-long hulk of a boat resting uncomfortably in a mass of driftwood, jammed tight in one of the gullies.

Bill Belknap, a good friend of Whitmoyer's and owner of Belknap Photographic Services in nearby Boulder City, Nevada, stepped carefully onto the

Bill Belknap, left, and Ted Whitmoyer with the *Gem* in God's Pocket, 1964. Courtesy Marston Collection, reproduced by permission, the Huntington Library, San Marino, California. This image also found in the Bill Belknap Collection, Cline Library, Northern Arizona University

steep rock from the patrol boat and climbed up into the cool shade where the remains lay. Belknap snapped a few pictures of Whitmoyer and the wreck. Finding an empty can resting nearby in the drift, he filled the can with water and climbed up to the boat's bow. As he poured a trickle of water onto the hulk, a thin layer of mud softened and fell away. A letter painted on the side of the boat emerged from under the mud, then another, and another. G….E….M. This was it! Moulty Fulmer's *Gem* was found at last!

The whereabouts of the *Gem* had remained a mystery for six years. Belknap, a seasoned Grand Canyon river runner himself, had heard the stories about the *Gem*, one of a trio of little boats that ran the big water of the Colorado River through the Grand Canyon year after year in the 1950s.

Indeed, Belknap had rendezvoused with Moulty Fulmer and Pat Reilly's river trip when they exited the Grand Canyon in 1955. It had been a hot July afternoon and there had been three oar boats. Two of the boats, which belonged to Pat, were fiberglass cataract designs. The third boat, the *Gem*, was an odd duck—a wooden boat based on the McKenzie River design. Belknap had towed all three boats the thirty miles across the lake to Temple Bar. And that Fulmer fellow had done a headstand on the deck of the *Gem* as they motored across the lake.

Were there ever stories about this boat! As Belknap took a few more photos of the wreck, did he recall the high water, no, the *highest* water anyone had run in recorded history? This boat had been on that water, in 1957. And it had survived Horn Creek where Fulmer had flipped it in 1955. Then there was the time Moulty and Pat had stood at the top of Lava Falls in 1958, contemplating whether or not to run the raging rapid. They had already lost one of Pat's boats. The group took a vote, and only Moulty voted to run Lava Falls. The group had hiked out instead. The two remaining boats, including the *Gem*, had been set free on the river to make their way to Lake Mead. While Pat recovered his two boats, the *Gem* had not been found. The next year, Pat had flipped one of his boats and then had sunk them both in mid-trip. All three of the boats Belknap had towed to Temple Bar in 1955 had been written off as gone for good.

But here it was, Fulmer's *Gem*, sitting in a tight cleft of rock in 1964 looking completely mangled. God had certainly put the *Gem* in his pocket. There would be people to notify about this discovery. A few in particular would want to know about this one, right away.

2

The Midget Champion

1906-1941

The two policemen looked at the man, then over to the raging river and back to the man again. He didn't appear to be intoxicated, and had a sense of composure that caused the officers to pause. In his mid- to late-thirties, about five feet eight inches tall, well built at 175 pounds, and clean shaven, the man had clearly done nothing wrong. There was a bath tub-sized wooden box at his feet. It even said *Tub* on the side of the box. It was the spring of 1943, and the White River in downtown Muncie, Indiana, was at a near-record high level. He looked like he really was going to get in that little box and float the torrent. He was, after all, holding a canoe paddle.

Jacob Fulmer holds his granddaughter Thelma with his son Francis seated next to him. His daughter-in-law Emma stands behind her husband. Jennie Fulmer, Jacob's second wife, stands next to her son Winfield by a previous marriage, 1899. Courtesy Priss Becker

The policemen informed the man he was not going downstream any farther as there was "a bad spot" ahead. The man's response was cool and collected. He had done it before, and besides, rough water was just what he was looking for. The two officers "stood with mouths open for a moment and then suddenly jumped in the squad car to go down close to the main show. Hundreds of people were out looking at the river." It wasn't that he was an exhibitionist, far from it. He simply knew how important practice was, and he was just practicing on his local river. He happened to be wild about whitewater, and the whitewater of his dreams was on the Colorado River, well over a thousand miles to the west.

As he got in the *Tub* for yet another run down the turbulent river, he knew this wasn't the first time that people of authority had told him what to do. This had been happening to Stephen Moulton Babcock Fulmer since the day he was born.

It had started a few hours after his birth, back in Oshkosh, Wisconsin, on Monday, July 9, 1906. When his elder sister Thelma was introduced to her new baby brother, the seven-year-old put her foot down. Thelma didn't like a boy she knew in school named Stephen, and no little brother of hers would be called by that wicked name. And with that, the baby Mo would grow up as Moulton, or simply Moulty, to his family and friends.

Thelma, Moulty, and Roscoe Fulmer, about 1911.
Courtesy Priss Becker

Moulty's father, Francis Burton Fulmer, was raised on a dairy farm in upstate New York, where he learned the trade of cream and butter making from his father, Jacob. A Union soldier only twenty years old at the end of the Civil War, Jacob was following in the footsteps of his great grandfather Conrad Fulmer, who had served in the New York Militia in the Revolutionary War.

Francis graduated from the Wisconsin College of Agriculture in 1892. It was there he studied under the brilliant tutelage of Dr. Stephen Moulton Babcock, "the laughing saint of science." A selfless man credited with founding the science of modern nutrition, Babcock would claim no patents for his discoveries, and refused to profit from his research.

After graduation, Francis taught creamery techniques at the University of Wisconsin and the University of Saskatchewan. Francis met a stunning young woman, Emma Claire Greenwood, six years his junior, and the two were married in 1898.

The couple's first child, Thelma, was born in 1899. A son, Roscoe, was born in 1903. By the time Emma was pregnant with her third child, Francis had become so impressed with Professor Babcock that he named his next child after the laughing saint. The boy would follow his namesake not only with an overflowing sense of humor, but he would unassumingly add to the "science" of river running and would take no credit for his contributions.

The Fulmer family moved to the booming town of Muncie, Indiana, in 1910. In 1915, Moulty's parents divorced. Emma was only thirty-seven and Francis forty-three. Francis then moved to San Jose, California, to join his father Jacob who had moved west in the late 1800s to start a dairy business.

Divorce in the early 1900s was uncommon, and Emma, with three children, stayed in Muncie. It was a difficult time for the family. Thelma quit school when she was sixteen, taking menial jobs to help with the family finances. A year later, Emma enrolled Moulty, an energetic ten-year-old, in the Muncie Young Men's Christian Association (YMCA). The Y was good for young Moulty. It was there he learned how to swim, and more importantly, to play basketball.

Moulty Fulmer, Ball Teachers College (now Ball State University), 1928-1929.
Courtesy Vander Hill and Edmonds
Ball State Men's Basketball 1918-2003,
Arcadia Publishing, 2003

From left to right: Roscoe, Thelma, Francis, and Moulty Fulmer, Oakland, California, about 1921. Courtesy Priss Becker

Moulty was as crazed about basketball as the rest of the Hoosiers of his day. In his teens, he made up in speed and accuracy what he lacked in height. On enrollment at Central High School, he was deemed too short to play on the Muncie Central Bearcats team, so he joined the local YMCA basketball team. Coached by H.J. Pettijohn and called the Midgets, the YMCA team was a powerhouse in Indiana independent basketball, and was restricted to boys eighteen years old and younger weighing less than 125 pounds. Moulty captained the 1924-1925 team in his senior high school year, scoring 400 points. The Midgets went undefeated in twenty-nine straight games to capture the state tournament. Basketball aficionados will tell you that in the 1920s, the rules were written such that the score for most games didn't go higher than thirty points.

After graduating from Central High, Moulty enrolled in Ball Teachers College, now Ball State University. In his freshman year, Moulty was the third-highest basketball scorer in the entire state at 185 points. He scored twenty-nine points in a single game against Rose Poly in 1926, a record that would remain unbroken until 1940. In his sophomore year, Moulty was the second-highest point scorer for the team, and the following year as a junior he made the Collegiate All-State squad, leading all of the Indiana college and university basketball players with 226 points. As captain of the Cardinals that year, Moulty led his 1928 team to clinch the championship of the first-ever Indiana Intercollegiate Tournament which included all the state's colleges and universities.

Besides college basketball, Moulty joined Ball's track team the year it was formed, in 1926. In 1929 he was captain of the team, and pole vaulted eleven feet nine inches, a record that stood for nine years. He lettered all four years in both basketball and track, and was elected by his classmates as president of both his sophomore and senior classes. While in college, Moulty maintained a strong presence at the Muncie Y basketball court, while also serving as assistant to the physical director.

The Muncie Young Women's Christian Association (YWCA) building was right next door to the YMCA. Managers at the YWCA would occasionally come next door to the YMCA, or if speed dictated, make a phone call to young Moulty, asking him to help restore order when young men would harass the young women at the YWCA. A model of good behavior, Moulty was always straight and narrow and wouldn't put up with any nonsense. Though he was short and a bully might get the first punch in, it would be the last the bully would recall once Moulty was done with him. At the same time, Moulty took kids under his wing who didn't have a stable home and were almost living at the Y.

Moulty and Janice Fulmer, 1931.
Courtesy Priss Becker

In 1929 Moulty graduated from Ball Teachers College and continued to assist the YMCA physical director. While the pay was poor, the need was great. The Y was busy with both men and boys looking for inexpensive ways to pass the time. With only the bare bones of equipment, Moulty was able to offer a full program of activities.

As if college sports were not enough, after graduation Moulty played on the Senior YMCA team, going to the quarter-finals in the National YMCA tournament at Oak Park, Illinois. Moulty also played for an independent statewide traveling basketball team called the Russell-Ball All-Stars. While playing for the Stars, he played against another Hoosier named Johnny Wooden, four years his junior. The local paper put it this way:

> Moulton Fulmer, the bounding little feller who will be the starting floorguard with the Russell-Ball All-Stars, has yet to meet a man too good for him on the basketball floor, and he has played against the best of them. Twice he has been sicked on Johnny Wooden on local floors, and both times the esteemed Martinsville and Purdue alumnus has been hog tied and ham-strung by the fleet Muncie boy.

Wooden would go on to a sterling career as coach of the University of California Los Angeles (UCLA) men's basketball team, where his UCLA teams won ten national championships in the National Collegiate Athletic Association.

A young woman named Janice Zehring took notice of the fleet-footed Fulmer. She grew up on her family's farm near Galveston, Indiana, not far from Muncie, and often visited the Muncie YWCA. Janice liked to play the piano there and grew to count on Moulty to keep the peace. Though not athletic, Janice was an excellent cook and whistler. The two became friends, and then a couple.

Janice and Moulty were married on July 25, 1931. He was twenty-five, and Janice twenty-two. The future looked bright and promotion soon followed. Moulty took over as physical director at the Y in 1934. He would hold this job for the next thirty-two years. Janice started working as a receptionist at the Warner Gear automobile transmission and clutch factory in Muncie, a position she would hold until retiring in 1966. The couple attended the Muncie Quaker Friends Meeting Hall, where Janice put her piano skills to good use. While they never had children of their own, Moulty would work with children his entire career.

This typical story of how a boy meets a girl in Middle America and they live happily ever after would never have merited a place in a book on Grand Canyon river runners, had it not been for Francis Fulmer moving to California. Moulty's mother Emma remarried in 1917 to a very kind man named George Schmidt. About that time, Moulty's older brother, Roscoe, moved to Oakland to work in the dairy business with his father. Emma, George, Moulty, and his sister Thelma would occasionally visit Roscoe in California. It was during one of these visits, in the summer of 1928, that the family took the train on the spur line north out of Williams, Arizona, to see the Grand Canyon. Many years later,

Ever the explorers, Moulty's mother Emma and stepfather
George on Pikes Peak, 1939. Courtesy Debbie Woodroof

Moulty would speak of his first view of the Canyon, noting that besides wanting to give his right arm for a color camera, he couldn't believe what he was seeing.

Even after the tragic death of Roscoe in 1935 in a motorcycle accident in Oakland, Moulty and Janice kept going west for vacations. Eventually, their travel expanded to include northern Arizona and southern Utah's Monument Valley. During their trips, Moulty took photographs and then showed slides to friends, family, and social clubs back in Muncie.

In the summer of 1941, Janice and Moulty went to Monument Valley and on to spend a week at Bill Wilson's Rainbow Lodge on the south side of Navajo Mountain. The couple rode by mule to Rainbow Bridge, nestled in the slickrock sandstone country of remote Glen Canyon. Their mule guide told them of river parties who hiked up to the bridge from the Colorado River. While the guide said he'd never float the Colorado in a little boat, Moulty was curious.

At a showing of his Monument Valley slides in Muncie that winter, Moulty was given a few articles from the *Grand Junction (CO) Daily Sentinel* by someone in the audience. The newspaper had run two stories in October 1941 with full-page spreads about a fellow named Norm Nevills. Norm was taking paying passengers on small boats through Glen Canyon. Interestingly, Norm had signed the Rainbow Bridge register on the page just before Moulty and Janice's entry, saying he was making his twelfth trip by boat through Glen Canyon. Moulty decided to contact Nevills about a river run. As Moulty and Janice were falling in love with the American West, the United States officially entered World War II.

Rainbow Bridge in the 1940s. Note the rider on a horse under the right side of the bridge. Courtesy Dick Griffith

3

The River Bug Bites

1942

The flow of the Colorado River in the Grand Canyon is the result of many smaller tributaries combining to form the mighty Colorado. The San Juan River is one of those tributaries. Starting high in the San Juan Mountains of southwestern Colorado, the San Juan joins the Colorado deep in Glen Canyon, not far from Rainbow Bridge. Along the way, the San Juan passes the small windblown hamlet of Mexican Hat, Utah.

An oil boom in the early 1920s drew William "Billy" Eugene Nevills to Mexican Hat. In 1928, Billy was joined by his wife Mae "Mo" Davies Nevills and their only child, Norman. Born in Chico, California, in 1908, Norm had finished two years of college in Stockton, California, by 1928. In October of 1933, Norm married nineteen-year-old Doris Drown. The newlyweds floated the San Juan River from Mexican Hat twenty miles downriver to the Honaker Trail in December 1933. In the spring of 1934, they floated the San Juan from Mexican Hat roughly seventy miles downstream to Copper Canyon. Accompanied part way by Billy and Mo, the ever-thrifty Norm had built the two boats the group would travel in, using lumber salvaged from an old outhouse and a cattle trough.

Norm was hired as a river guide on the San Juan for a party from California in 1936, and in 1938 was paid to organize a river trip from Green River, Utah, through Cataract and Grand canyons, all the way to Lake Mead. The 1938 expedition was the outcome of a meeting the previous year between University of Michigan botanist Elzada Clover and Norm. The 1938 Grand Canyon journey included Dr. Clover and one of her students, Lois Jotter.

Clover and Jotter were the first women to travel all the way through the Grand Canyon by boat, although one other woman had preceded them part way through the Canyon. In 1928, the honeymooners Bessie and Glenn Hyde had made it over 226 miles through the Canyon before they went missing and were never seen again. In the fall of 1938, another honeymoon couple made the attempt. The French couple, Bernard and Genevieve DeColmont, with their friend Antoine DeSeyne, paddled wood and rubberized canvas kayaks to Phantom Ranch, where bitter cold forced them to hike out.

The success of the Clover expedition did much to develop Norm's fledgling river running business, and articles like the one Moulty saw in the *Grand Junction Daily Sentinel* only added fuel to his business fire. In April 1942, Moulty wrote to Norm inquiring about a river trip on the San Juan. Moulty, now thirty-seven, expected to be drafted and wanted to see if he could arrange a river trip with Norm after the war. Four days later, Moulty wrote Norm again, saying he could do the river trip before entering the military. Moulty sent Norm $100 as a fifty percent deposit for a June San Juan River trip, reserving two spaces for Janice and himself. In that letter he wrote "The Southwest is my favorite part of the country. I like the big open spaces where people are few and far between."

A month later he and Janice drove out through the sand traps and miles of choking dust to Mexican Hat, arriving on May 31, 1942. Janice was hesitant about the trip, but would laughingly recall years later that "if he was going to go along and get drowned, I would go too." Mexican Hat boasted a one-lane bridge across the San Juan. The town was named for a wonderful sombrero-shaped rock naturally balanced on a tower of sandstone just north of town. While there was plenty of year-round sunshine, the lack of nearby firewood for heat and cooking, high winds, and no electricity beyond the occasional stand-alone generator made the Hat a rough and lonely outpost. Moulty was "looking forward to being lost to civilization for seven days between the 'Hat' and the 'Ferry'."

The San Juan was in full spring runoff, 10,800 cubic feet per second (cfs) the day they arrived, down from 12,300 cfs three days earlier. The plan was to take two boats. The first boat, named the *Hidden Passage*, was one of Norm's wooden boats known as a San Juan punt. The second boat was a canvas-on-wood frame boat Moulty called the *Walker Special*. Norm would row the *Hidden Passage*, while Preston Walker, a boatman working for Norm at the time, would row the canvas boat.

In the 1940s, Norm used the punts to carry passengers on the San Juan. Moulty noted the punts were sixteen feet in length, with a narrow width at the oarlocks of between four and five feet. The sides were about fifteen inches high, and the boats sported large square ends bow and

Norm Nevills in his San Juan punt, with the canvas boat in the background, June 1, 1942. Courtesy Moulton Fulmer Photo, Marston Collection, reproduced by permission, the Huntington Library, San Marino, California

stern. Passengers sat on the flat bow and stern decks, and gear was placed under the decks. The boats had no watertight chambers and no bulkheads. Picture a floating cattle trough and you will get the basic idea. The punts were flat bottomed and ideal for the mostly calm water of the San Juan and Glen canyons.

The group of four, Moulty, Janice, Preston, and Norm, launched just before 9 a.m. on a clear, warm day. They floated through the meandering Goosenecks before lunch. Janice and Moulty rode with Norm, and Preston ran solo in the canvas boat. At one point that morning Norm gave Moulty the oars "for ten minutes."

After lunch, the group floated all the way past Government Rapid to camp at the mouth of Slickhorn Canyon, a journey of almost forty miles. The three men swam in the pools at the mouth of Slickhorn. With his antics about not liking cold water, Norm had the others laughing "so hard that tears came to our eyes."

The next morning, Moulty rowed the *Walker Special* for twenty miles. He noted in his log that it "was quite a thrill. In one rapid it spun half way around like a flash before I could get it under control." On pulling in for lunch, he stepped out of the craft with the bowline in hand and instantly sank past his knees in quicksand. Moulty, as if on cue, sat down to his waist and forlornly held the bowline. The other three river runners burst out laughing. Camp that night was fifty-one miles downriver from the previous night's camp.

On June 3, Norm and Preston ran Syncline and 13-Foot rapids, while Moulty and Janice walked around the rapids carrying some of the baggage. Moulty noted both boats took on a considerable amount of water. The boaters floated to the end of the San Juan River at its confluence with the Colorado River, deep in Glen Canyon. Camp for the night was on a sand bar near Hidden Passage Canyon. The next day, the party explored Mystery Canyon, also known as Anasazi Canyon, and camped at Forbidding Canyon.

Up early on June 5, the group headed up Forbidding Canyon for the six-mile trek to Rainbow Bridge. In less than three hours they reached the bridge, and the Fulmers signed the register as they had done the year before. Moulty, Preston, and Norm climbed to the top of the bridge, while the sensible Janice took photos from below. After hiking back to the Colorado, Moulty played in the knee-deep river mud, pretending it was quicksand. Everyone laughed so hard their ribs hurt. The next day the group floated to Outlaw Cave for camp.

On their last day on the river, Norm spotted a big cottonwood log on the river bank, and the three men worked it into the river. After riding the log for a while, Norm told Moulty to "have at it." Moulty estimated the log to be thirty feet in length and stable enough for a headstand. After Moulty did three headstands on the log, Norm shouted with glee saying "that's one record for the Colorado that I do not hold." Moulty rode the log backwards through a rapid, and was hoping to ride it all the way to Lee's Ferry, but the log encountered an eddy, where cross currents drove hard into shore and back upriver. The log followed the eddy current and plowed right into shore "with a thud and a terrific jolt." Regretfully, Moulty boarded the *Walker Special* and headed on to Lee's Ferry, where the Colorado was flowing about 79,000 cfs.

The *Walker Special* on top of Norm's punt, Lee's Ferry, June 7, 1942.
Courtesy Moulton Fulmer Photo, Marston Collection, reproduced by
permission, the Huntington Library, San Marino, California

Later that evening the remote Marble Canyon Lodge, at the base of the towering Vermilion Cliffs and roughly five miles from Lee's Ferry, rang out with music. The group danced while Janice got quite a workout playing the piano and whistling. The next day, they all traveled the 210 teeth-jarring and lung-choking dusty miles back to Mexican Hat through the stunning scenery of Monument Valley.

Since college, Moulty had been enamored with photography, both still images and 16mm movie film. In late June, he sent Norm some photos of their trip. Moulty had already been showing his film footage in Muncie, and within a few weeks of his return he had booked four showings of his film of the San Juan trip. Drawing large crowds, he charged 25¢ a person and had over 130 people pay for two of the shows. The audiences liked what they saw, especially Norm tap-dancing on the floating cottonwood tree trunk.

The river journey from Mexican Hat to Lee's Ferry had touched Moulty and Janice. Moulty wrote to Norm that the trip "makes my feet itchy to get back on the water. Never had so much fun in all my life as did Janice." He also asked Norm for "a list of places that I might write to get information about boats and what boats you would recommend." He also noted being "just whacky enough to try my hand at some of the tame rivers sometime before trying the tougher ones." Of course, he noted he would "probably hit every other rock and hole in them if I ever try it, but I am willing."

Being the practical joker that he was, Moulty also sent Norm a trick can opener to use with his passengers. Norm was tickled to get it, and wrote Moulty that the can opener would find its way onto his next Grand Canyon river trip only a week away. Norm promised to write later about boats, after his return from running the Canyon that July.

When Norm passed Phantom Ranch on his 1942 Grand Canyon trip, he mailed Moulty and Janice a postcard, which they were thrilled to get. Moulty wrote Norm again, sending a copy of his river log of the San Juan trip, and asked where he could get maps for the Green, Colorado, and San Juan rivers. Norm replied in September that maps could be obtained through the Superintendent of Documents in Washington, D.C.

For pleasure, Moulty pored over Frederick Dellenbaugh's *Romance of the Colorado River*, and Lewis Freeman's *National Geographic* article "Surveying the Grand Canyon of the Colorado" at the Muncie Library. These were the only two accounts of the Colorado River the library had. In September 1942, Moulty gave four more presentations of his San Juan film. More significant was the fact that without waiting for any plans from Norm, he built his first boat.

4

Indiana Boating in a *Tub*

1942-1943

It had been a wonderful run for the Fulmers, from Mexican Hat, through the lower San Juan River to Glen Canyon, then down the Glen to Lee's Ferry. Through the rest of the summer of 1942, both Janice and Moulty kept talking about the San Juan and wondering out loud how Norm had managed on his Grand Canyon run. Waiting for boat plans from Norm was too much for Moulty, and he began to take matters into his own hands.

Indiana's White River is a small waterway lined by large stately trees, running in a big "U" for eight miles through the manufacturing heart of Muncie. A few train trestles cross the river and the bridge supports offer some wave action, as do the three or four low-head rock dams that span the river. In the spring, the White has a good flow during runoff. Moulty figured these dams would add some excitement during high water. With a river in town and having not heard from Norm about where to get information on boats, in mid-September Moulty went ahead and built a boat. If anything, he wanted to know if he could build something that would actually float.

The first boat Moulty built was a small, five-foot-long by three-foot-wide, snub-ended tub built from ¼-inch plywood, with oak stays added for strength. The boat floated like a cork and weighed about fifty pounds. Moulty used no glue, just ordinary caulking compound for seam sealant. Moulty wrote Norm that he used "as few screws as possible, around 400, and it will hold one person with-

Moulty's first boat, the *Tub*, Muncie, Indiana, 1942-43. Courtesy Moulton Fulmer Photo, Norm Nevills Collection, The Marriott Library, University of Utah

out any leakage." If you picture your bathtub, you get the idea of the boat's size. Indeed, it resembled his bathtub so much so that Moulty called his boat the *Tub*. Operated with a canoe paddle, the *Tub* had a surprisingly large amount of rocker. Rocker is a term used to describe the shape of the bottom of a boat from front to back. In this case, the *Tub* had a continuous arc in the bottom of the boat, like a smile on a smiley face. Being only five feet long, the *Tub* was very responsive. Most of the boat fit in the trunk of his car, so no trailer was needed for transportation. The *Tub* cost Moulty all of four dollars to make and he was happy with the build. He wrote Norm he was "Just plain nuts – that's me. Tried to see if I could build a boat that wouldn't sink, and much to my surprise, it floats!" Moulty made his hometown boating debut in the *Tub* on the White River. While it's most likely no one noticed a grown man paddling a wooden bathtub through town, Moulty was thrilled that the *Tub* didn't sink. There was some leakage through the seams, but bailing was easy. Needless to say, Janice was not impressed.

Moulty requested a list of reading material on river running from Norm, and noted "hardly a day goes by that I don't dream about those rough rivers or reminisce of our own trip." In February, Norm sent Moulty a list of books. Norm's recommended reading included Powell's *Exploration of the Colorado River of the West and its Tributaries*, Stanton's *Colorado River Controversies*, Stone's *Canyon Country*, Kolb's *Through the Grand Canyon from Wyoming to Mexico*, and Eddy's *Down the World's Most Dangerous River*. Norm ended the letter with the note "Please write and keep us posted on everything, and when this war is over we'll get together and have a bang-up trip." Moulty went right out to the local bookstore to see if he could get Eddy's *Dangerous River*. The store was unable to get any of the books he requested, so instead Moulty reread the two the library had for the third time, finding "something new every time" in the reading.

Moulty and a neighbor on the White River in flood, May 18, 1943. Courtesy Moulton Fulmer Photo, Norm Nevills Collection, The Marriott Library, University of Utah

Across the seas, the war was escalating. Muncie factories operated around the clock. In the winter of 1942-1943, Moulty had his military physical and wrote Norm that he expected to be drafted by the first of March. Moulty had gone to Chicago in December for an interview with the Navy, seeking a position as a physical education instructor. He had been, after all, teaching swimming for the previous fifteen years. In February he received a deferment until May 20, as he was teaching 120 high school boys how to swim in daily classes.

In the spring of 1943, Moulty noticed that the water in the White was starting to pick up. Unfortunately, keeping the streets free of bullies wielding baseball bats twenty years earlier had broken cartilage in his nose. Corrective surgery to unblock a nasal passage had him sidelined from any boating most of early April. When Moulty found Eddy's book in the Ball State library, he read it three times over in six weeks. The Fort Wayne library had both the Stone book and Dellenbaugh's *A Canyon Voyage*. Moulty read each of these books, twice, during the same time period. At this time his employer, the YMCA general secretary, requested and received another deferment for Moulty, until July 21.

By mid-May Moulty was feeling as good as ever and the White was up after several days of heavy rain. Typical May flows in the White were around 100 to 200 cfs, but on May 11, 1943, Moulty made three runs of the White in the *Tub* at around 1,300 cfs. Then it really rained. The unusually heavy rains pushed the White to over 9,800 cfs on May 18. With the White running at its third highest flow in twenty years, Moulty made three more runs in the *Tub* that afternoon after work. The first run he made with a neighbor's teenage son.

Moulty in the *Tub*, White River, Muncie, Indiana 1943.
Courtesy Moulton Fulmer Photo, Norm Nevills Collection,
The Marriott Library, University of Utah

After that run, the neighbor kid decided quickly that he had had enough. After speaking with the two local police officers, Moulty went back for more, playing in the lateral waves coming off the railroad bridges. On the third run, he cut too close to a bridge pylon and a piece of driftwood knocked the *Tub* over. Moulty swam with a paddle in one hand and the swamped *Tub* in the other. He was under water a few times during the half mile before he reached shore. Moulty would write to Norm, "It is a good way to feel the power of a mad stream, but a little dangerous." While this was his first experience in big water in a little boat, it would not be his last.

Moulty was out in the *Tub* again the next day, but the White had dropped to 4,000 cfs. At least he could see the piece of driftwood lodged against the bridge abutment that had spilled him and the *Tub* the day before. Marking the anniversary of his and Janice's meeting with Norm, Moulty wrote Norm about the White runs and thanked him again for such a great river trip. After reading Moulty's letter of May 31, 1943, Norm, then working as a stream gauge operator for the United States Geological Survey (USGS) at Mexican Hat, wrote back, noting "Well I'll be damned! You really took on the local Old Man River with a vengeance!" Norm was impressed enough to add that there was no reason "why you shouldn't get polished up a bit and go as a boatman on one of my Canyon trips. Think it over."

On receiving another deferment, Moulty went to California by train to visit with his father. Francis was then in his seventies and in poor health. Moulty wanted to spend time with him knowing full well that once he was drafted he might not see him again.

The train from Muncie to California took Moulty past Williams, Arizona, gateway to the Grand Canyon. Moulty decided to make a side trip to the South Rim by bus, as he was curious to see if he could hike to Hermit Rapid from the South Rim. Arriving August 8, Moulty met with Grand Canyon National Park Superintendent Harold C. Bryant to inquire about the Hermit Trail conditions. Hermit Camp had been abandoned over ten years earlier, and Superintendent Bryant told him that only one person had attempted the hike to the old camp in the last two or three years. Moulty

Moulty in the *Domino*, Muncie, Indiana, November 1943. Courtesy Moulton Fulmer Photo, Norm Nevills Collection, The Marriott Library, University of Utah

then paid a visit to Emery Kolb, and watched the Kolb brothers' film about their 1911 river trip on the Colorado River. Moulty thought Emery "a not very friendly cuss" though he admitted he hadn't been overly friendly either. He took the opportunity to plug Norm Nevills during the question-and-answer period, but Emery "skillfully evaded the plug."

At first light the next morning, Moulty started down the Hermit Trail and made it to the abandoned Hermit Camp after a little over seven hours of hard hiking. What remained of the trail was often obscured in many places by rockslides. After resting and looking at the camp for an hour, he headed down Hermit Creek for the Colorado River. Moulty figured he was about two-thirds of the way from the camp to the river when a monsoon rainstorm engulfed him. Hermit Creek was soon in flood, and he had to quickly abandon the waterway for higher ground. Once out of the creek bed, he encountered thickets of skin-ripping catclaw acacia, which made further travel toward the Colorado slow and painful.

When the storm finally passed, Moulty realized he must turn back as the day was almost over. It was slow going as he tried to work his way along the side of the drainage. Besides, his feet were covered in blisters and he knew he needed to be out of the Canyon the following day. Reluctantly, he retraced his steps to the abandoned camp, arriving at his small backpack about dark. After a long and uncomfortable night, the next morning he was up and on his way to the rim, reaching the top at 2:50 p.m. exhausted and footsore. While he had been unable to reach Hermit Rapid, one of the river's major rapids, he had learned that hiking in the Grand Canyon was not to be taken lightly. With little time to clean up and catch the bus back to Williams, he promised Superintendent Bryant he would write up his experiences of the hike and mail him a report.

Back in Muncie that fall, Moulty built another boat, pulled together mostly from used odds and ends. The bits of scrounged wood included a ping-pong table the Y was discarding. This boat was a nine-footer. It had fore and aft decks and was big enough for real oars, even if they were only five-and-a-half feet long. The sides were ¼-inch plywood, with ⅜-inch plywood on the bottom. The width at the oarlocks, called the beam, was thirty-nine inches, and the boat weighed in at 130 pounds. He used the new boat, called the *Domino*, to make one run down the placid White River that November. Janice was still not impressed.

At more than twice the weight of the *Tub*, Moulty could not have helped noticing that increased weight, width and length meant increased boat stability. It didn't hurt that he was a great swimmer and unafraid of water. He was learning about boating and boat building in Indiana, far from the Colorado River way out west. Norm again wrote that he was "planning on your being a boatman on the next run we make, and that looks to be from Green River, Wyoming ----immediately after the war." Whatever plans Moulty or Norm had at the time, boat building and river running would have to wait for a while, as thirty-seven-year-old Stephen Moulton Babcock Fulmer entered active service with the U.S. Army January 4, 1944. As it turned out, the wait would be surprisingly short.

5

The Boating Soldier Meets a Boat Builder

1944-1945

Having failed to obtain a position with the Navy, Moulty was drafted into the Army and was sent to Fort McClellan, Alabama, for basic training. The daily routine from 5:30 a.m. until 9:00 p.m., or even later, kept him on the go. Though thirty-seven years old, he was in excellent physical shape on arrival and kept up with the fittest men in his unit.

While Moulty found bayonet training most difficult, he was very skillful at throwing hand grenades. He did, after all, have a history of quick and excellent aim with a basketball. The seventeen weeks of basic training were often conducted in a sea of mud, and included marching up to twenty-four miles a day with a pack weighing as much as 107 pounds.

During this time Moulty wrote to Norm that he was "intensely interested in your future canyon trips. It gave my spirits a big lift, and I've been looking forward to another river thrill for the past twenty months, and it's one of the things I'll be fighting for – next to only my loved ones and friends." While out on marches, Moulty would see a small stream and note every "little ripple suggests a rapid with all the accompanying thrills." He had hoped to be on the White River at high water, careening past bridge abutments and dropping over river-wide waterfalls in the *Domino* on a March furlough. But the furlough never materialized, and it didn't help when Janice wrote him that the White had spiked again in mid-April, almost as high as the year before. After basic training, Moulty was sent to Fort Meade, Maryland. Sadly, a furlough was unexpectedly authorized in late July, 1944, when he was informed that his father, Francis, had suffered a heart attack and had passed away.

Stationed at Fort Meade during the fall, winter, and spring of 1944-1945, Moulty served as an athletics instructor and edited the weekly newspaper. In January 1945, he wrote Norm asking if he had "any river trips planned for this year? It is a hundred to one shot but perhaps if you were making a short run of some kind I might be able to be with you."

Private Moulty Fulmer, January 1944.
Courtesy Priss Becker

On January 21, 1945, Moulty went to Carnegie Hall in New York City to see the Burton Holmes' *Travelogue on the Colorado River, Source to the Sea*, filmed in 1944. Footage included Norm doing a headstand on a floating log on the San Juan. Moulty wrote to Norm "Say, what do you mean stealing my stuff – standing on your head riding a log down the river – that was great!!!!!"

In the spring of 1945, Moulty was transferred to Special Services, 7th Regiment while still at Fort Meade. Meanwhile, Norm had been contacted by Twentieth Century Fox to film a travelogue about the San Juan River. Norm had run a late-season, low-water trip in 1944 with the studio's film crew in which a camera was lost and a large amount of film spoiled.

Norm assured the Fox crew that the river would rise during the runoff in June, so another filming trip was scheduled to catch the higher water. Norm wrote Moulty asking if he would like to row one of the San Juan punts for the trip. Moulty received Norm's invitation May 8, 1945, the same day German forces surrendered to the Allies in Europe. Within two hours of receiving the letter, he had contacted his section leader and company commander and obtained a furlough for the trip.

Getting from Maryland to Mexican Hat in remote southern Utah was more of a challenge than Moulty anticipated. He took the train to Chicago on May 30, and then caught the overnight train to Denver. From Denver, he headed on to the whistle-stop of windswept Thompson, Utah, arriving a little after midnight. Somewhere on the journey Moulty had come down with a flulike bug. Arriving at the bleak station, he had to hitch a ride the 163 lightly traveled miles from the railroad south to Mexican Hat. A passing mail truck gave Moulty a lift south, and he arrived at the Hat on the first of June.

Fox Film Crew, Moulty Fulmer is third from left, June 1945. Courtesy Hal Rumel, Fulmer Collection, reproduced by permission, Utah State Historical Society, all rights reserved

The flow on the San Juan was better than it had been the previous year. The filming party launched June 3, 1945, on 5,200 cfs and consisted of eight people in three San Juan punts. Norm rowed the *Music Temple* with his daughter Joan and Edmund Reek. The second boat, *Hidden Passage*, was run by Wayne McConkie with Chubby Lehman and the manager of the trading post at Mexican Hat. Moulty rowed the *San Juan* with Hall Rumel as his passenger.

Downriver, the first stop was the Honaker Trail, where the trip met Jack Kuhne and Ray Ziess. The two cameramen had driven out to the top of the Honaker, and hiked down the old mining trail to the river. As planned, Joan and the trading post man hiked out. Moulty was still running a fever with a sore throat, and ate very little. Fortunately, he felt better the next day. Unfortunately, since launching the trip, the weather had been mostly overcast, and the film crew was not happy with the light. They ran Government Rapid and camped at Slickhorn Canyon that night.

On the second day, Moulty was surprised when he barely "scraped an oar in some shallow water and it broke." On closer inspection, they found the oar had been broken for some time. By now the group had run about fifty-six miles, and Moulty's hands were blistered and sore. The next day, the group rowed out of the tight upper canyon of the San Juan and entered the wide open Paiute Farms area. The boats hung up on a few sandbars, but the river runners still covered thirty-six miles for the day, camping at the same camp Moulty, Janice, Norm, and Press had used three years earlier. On June 7, they arrived at 13-Foot Rapid. The rapid split the river into three channels, with the roughest water in the right-hand channel. Norm and Moulty ran their boats down the right side while the camera captured the run. For the first time in the trip, the cameraman was happy with the footage.

On June 8, the party waited for the right light to film the confluence of the San Juan and the Colorado rivers, and then ran to the mouth of Hidden Passage for camp. The next morning, much film was taken of camp life, including Moulty and Norm shaving. The party then headed to Forbidding Canyon for camp.

On June 10 they hiked to Rainbow Bridge. It was the third time Moulty had seen the bridge, but this time it was in the rain. Late in the day, Norm, Wayne, and Jack hiked back to the boats, while the other five men hiked about a mile to Wilson Camp where they sought shelter from the storm. There, they found three rat-infested comforters and two metal cots. Ed Reek used one comforter and tried to sleep on the ground, while the other four men squeezed in on the two cots with a comforter above and one below them. It rained during the night and became quite cold. In the morning, a new blanket arrived in the form of fresh snow on nearby Navajo Mountain. The five men had eaten the last of their food the night

Camp Adair from the air, 1940s. Courtesy Oregon State University Archives, image HC0816b, Corvallis, Oregon

before, and were very glad to see Norm, Wayne, and Jack arrive with some grub. The day was clear and bright, so with the camera rolling, Norm and Moulty climbed to the top of Rainbow Bridge.

The next day the river party rowed the punts out to Lee's Ferry on 51,900 cfs, landing at the sandy point just below the Paria Riffle. They were met by Doris Nevills and Hal's wife, and spent the night at the Marble Canyon Lodge. Norm asked Moulty if he wanted to work as a boatman for three months during the next summer season, and Moulty replied that he "would have to await developments." On the train trip home Moulty was able to visit with Janice for two days and after the trip, Moulty wrote Norm to thank him for the privilege of being allowed "to make the run."

Norm was pleased with Moulty's rowing and all-around good nature after that trip, and wrote to express his appreciation for "the swell job you did on the river – and that with a handicap of not feeling up to your normal self. How you could handle a boat with the big swelling in your throat is a mystery to me. Any time you want it there is a berth as a boatman with me." The filming went well, and resulted in the Fox Movietone picture *Along the Rainbow Trail* which Moulty watched three times during its run in Muncie in the winter of 1946-1947.

Moulty shipped out once again, all the way across the country to Camp Adair, Oregon. On the way he saw a number of rivers, including the Columbia. His thoughts often drifted to what boating runs he would make on the rivers he was seeing.

Camp Adair was situated in the rolling hills of the Willamette Valley, about ten miles north of Corvallis, Oregon. The Willamette River heads north toward the Columbia, and passes within two miles of the camp. Tributaries of the Willamette include the Santiam and Clackamas, Long Tom and McKenzie. What Moulty didn't know, and was about to find out, was that he had just been stationed in a part of the country where river running was a way of life.

The McKenzie River, especially, had a long history of boating, originating in the late 1800s and early 1900s as fisherman worked the clear cold river for rainbow trout. In the early twentieth century, McKenzie river runners began modifying the small dories they were using. The term dory, as defined by the Oxford Universal Dictionary, refers to "a small flat-bottomed boat." Many types and varieties of small flat-bottomed boats were being used in the Pacific Northwest, and names were given to the styles and designs of these boats. Sometimes names included the river where the boat was run *and* what the boat was used for, or the river name *and* how the boat looked. It would not be uncommon to hear terms like McKenzie riverboat, square-enders, or double-enders.

Construction of the Pacific Northwest boats changed as available materials changed. Plywood, thin veneers of wood glued together with the wood grain of each layer going in a different direction than adjacent layers, was first patented in 1865. It wasn't until the 1920s that demand for plywood began to accelerate, first in the automobile manufacturing market. Waterproof glue to bond the

Woodie Hindman circa 1935 before he started making steep-rocker boats. Courtesy Ruth Burleigh and Roger Fletcher

thin wooden sheets was developed in the 1930s. Until the late 1930s, Pacific Northwest dories were still made of wooden planks. Once introduced to this lightweight, flexible, and strong wood sheeting, plywood quickly became the material of choice for Oregon boat builders. As an aside, the first plywood boat to traverse through the Grand Canyon was used on a 1934 low-water run.

It wasn't long before the McKenzie River dories were being made with just a little more beam, the distance from one side of the boat to the other. The boats were also being built with just a little less length from end to end. This made the boats more stable in the McKenzie's rapids, and more responsive to turning.

At the southern end of the Willamette Valley, a boat builder and fishing guide by the name of Wood Knoble Hindman, "Woodie" to his friends, was guiding fishing trips in the summer and building McKenzie River dories in the winter. Woodie had learned to build McKenzie River boats from master boat-builder Torkel "Tom" Kaarhus in the mid 1930s. The early Kaarhus boats were typically made of fourteen-foot-long plywood sheets and

A typical McKenzie River dory circa 1950. Courtesy Marston Collection, reproduced by permission, the Huntington Library, San Marino, California

were about twelve feet from end to end, with one pointed end upriver behind the rower and one wide square end in front of the rower which went down the river first. This boat style had today's classic dory shape with a forty-eight-inch wide bottom that was flat side to side and a crescent-shaped profile that raised the ends of the boat twelve inches higher than the bottom at the middle of the boat. With skills learned from Kaarhus, Woodie Hindman soon struck out on his own, becoming a prolific boat builder. He constructed roughly ten to fifteen dories a year in the late 1930s through the 1940s.

Beginning in the winter of 1940 to 1941, Woodie started making a dory pointed at both ends. The classic Hindman McKenzie River dory was also called a double-ender, and would become Woodie's calling card. His typical double-ender was fourteen to fifteen feet long, although he would make these dories up to eighteen feet by special order. They were typically four feet wide at the widest point in the floor, and five to five-and-a-half feet wide at the oarlocks. Woodie would later make the double-ender with a transom. This dory had a pointed end and a small squared-off end. Both the double-ender and the double-ender with a transom had that unmistakable dory crescent shape in the floor from bow to stern.

Camp Adair happened to be in the heart of the Willamette Valley, so it was not surprising that early one Sunday in July 1945, Moulty bought a round-trip bus ticket from Camp Adair to Eugene, Oregon, fifty miles to the south. Arriving in Eugene, he hitched into Springfield, four miles east, and walked two miles to Woodie's house on the banks of the McKenzie. Arriving a little after lunch, Moulty found the fifty-year-old Hindman taking a nap on the front porch.

Woodie, as most Oregonians are, was obliging enough to rouse from his nap and show a stranger the boat he was building. The two talked rough-water boats as best as they could. The master boat-builder and clear-water trout fisherman boated rivers intending to fish every eddy possible along the way. Moulty, only a month back from the San Juan run, was an athletic director who happened to like river running and preferred to travel through remote country few had explored. In Moulty's river world, the river was liquid mud, and eddies were to be avoided at all costs as the boat rower tried hard to keep moving downriver. Fishing was optional. Woodie took Moulty to the boat shop to look at what he was building. The two men spent a few hours discussing "rough water boats." Moulty told Woodie he "was contemplating the construction of one" and that he thought "the rake of the McKenzie type had merit but did not have enough beam for heavy, rough water."

Moulty told Woodie he was "considering a double-ender." He liked the constant rocker of twelve to thirteen inches, and asked Woodie his thoughts about making the boat wider than four feet across the bottom for more stability. Woodie stated that "such a type could be the rough water boat of the future."

It was an amazing encounter between the student and a boat-building maestro. The exact boats Woodie had around the shop the afternoon of Moulty's visit are unknown, but most likely Moulty saw a simple fourteen- to fifteen-foot-long double-ender with a constant rocker bottom of about twelve inches, with a side flare of about six inches. Within a few weeks of visiting with Woodie, Moulty wrote Norm about what he had seen:

> Was in Eugene, Ore. and looked up a fellow who builds some of the so called McKenzie River boats. Made of ¼ inch ply and have a terrific rocker effect. Depth near the stern is over 30 inches. It would ride so high that one could not see where he was going. Would have to quarter it through rapids. Might be O.K. for whitewater here in the Northwest, but on silt-laden water I have my doubts. Said he had run the middle fork of the Salmon seven times, which he says is the roughest of all. It flows northward into the big Salmon.

With the McKenzie dory's ingenious hull design firmly planted in his brain, doubting-Moulty would soon build the first generation of Colorado River dories, and they wouldn't be anything like the *Tub*, the *Domino*, or the San Juan punts.

6

Eating Sand Waves with the *Moja*

1945-1947

In October 1945, Moulty was shipped to Camp Beale in California, where he was honorably discharged with a good conduct medal and the rank of sergeant. After a short vacation with Janice, Moulty, then thirty-nine years old, returned to work at the Muncie YMCA. In November, Norm wrote to offer him a job running boats in the 1946 season. Norm noted he would have Moulty as "second in command, and could pay you $300 per month and your expenses." Norm noted Janice could stay in Mexican Hat and "drive one of the cars to Lee's Ferry. Please let me know right back on this."

Moulty wrote right back that he had "given a lot of thought to what you mentioned in your letter, but as much as I would like to I don't see how I could do the river trips." Besides, he explained, he was "flirting with the idea of building a light weight fourteen or fifteen footer and doing a little river running in it. The boat probably would end up on the rocks and I would be in the 'drink', but I'd have fun doing it."

Moulty settled into life in Muncie as best he could, again showing his river film to a half dozen groups. After playing on organized basketball teams for twenty-five years, he finally hung up his hoop shoes. In the summer of 1946, Moulty and Janice took a road trip to Lewiston, Idaho. Before heading out on vacation he started that next boat. Moulty used drawings he had made after "seeing Nevills' boats and some of the rough water boats I had seen in Oregon." His build was based on two objections that he had to Nevills' San Juan boats. They were "(1) lack of space to keep duffle dry (2) boats needed more rake or rocker effect to avoid digging in and slapping hard at the trough of waves." The construction took place in a corner of the machine shop where his stepfather George was employed. Moulty started planning a San Juan run from Bluff, Utah, to Lee's Ferry in his new craft for the 1947 river season.

The new boat was fifteen feet long and was pointed at each end. It had a twelve-inch continuous rocker, which meant that when it sat on flat ground the bottom of the boat at the bow and stern points were each twelve inches off the ground. The widest width of the floor was four feet, and the typical McKenzie River dory small side flare had the beam measuring in at five feet across the oarlocks.

For flotation, the boat had sealed compartments at the bow and stern fifteen to eighteen inches back from the nose and tail of the boat. Inboard of these compartments were gear storage areas roughly thirty inches deep. Access to the gear areas was through a hinged door about 15 x 24 inches, positioned in the ¾-inch thick, vertical bulkheads. A small splash guard on the top of the bulkheads protected the six-foot-long cockpit somewhat, and passengers would sit on the four-foot-long front or back decks.

The ¼-inch plywood sides measured twenty inches from the chine to the gunwale at the oarlocks. The bottom was made of ⅜-inch plywood with ⁵⁄₁₆-inch thick by four-inch wide oak strips running full length bow to stern, placed an inch apart all the way across the bottom of the boat. There were two oak rub rails, each roughly two inches wide, along both the chine and gunwale of the boat to protect the corners of the hull from abrasion by rocks. A third rub rail, roughly four inches wide, was positioned along the lower third of the side panel. The boat weighed a little over 250 pounds and was a perfect rough-water craft for two people. Moulty noted the construction technique he employed was to build a while, stand back and ponder a while, then go back to sawing and fitting. He was an athletic director after all, not a carpenter. The boat was called the *Moja*, short for Moulty and Janice.

The *Moja* needed a good set of oars. Norm had suggested Moulty go to any sporting goods store for oars and recommended he also get a spare oar. Moulty purchased two sets of eight-foot-long solid ash oars. They happened to be a brand called Smoker, still considered premium oars by today's river runners.

The Smoker Lumber Company was formed in the late 1920s in New Paris, Indiana, and began manufacturing solid wood oars in the 1930s. In the 1940s the company was awarded a contract to provide oars for the war effort. At full production, they made a linear mile of oars every day. Made of solid ash, Smoker oars came in a variety of lengths, from eight to sixteen feet. They were so strong that three men could stand together mid-shaft on an oar that was supported on each end and the oar wouldn't break.

Moulty then asked Norm for information on the San Juan River from the town of Shiprock, New Mexico, to Bluff, Utah. He and Janice had seen the San Juan at Shiprock in 1942, and Moulty figured Shiprock was as good a place as any to put the *Moja* in the water. They would see some new river country and could visit Norm and Doris in Mexican Hat along the way. Most important, the shuttle would be easier. Someone would drive the car and trailer to the take-out, and then take the bus back from Marble Canyon Lodge near Lee's Ferry to Shiprock. In the winter of 1946-1947, Norm had built a small dirt airstrip at Mexican Hat, and purchased a Piper J3 Cub. Norm wrote back he had not run that section, but had flown over it. The open country and numerous sandbars had not attracted Norm to try that stretch of the San Juan. Moulty replied he figured Norm was "having a lot of fun with your plane. Must get some very majestic views of the canyon country."

Norm also warned Moulty about his new boat, writing that a "pointed boat at both ends isn't so hot for big sand waves, so watch out for them. Least bit of side whipping and you'll roll." The San Juan did indeed have sand waves, up to three feet high, formed as the river traveled over its sandy bed. Norm was concerned that if the waves weren't hit perfectly straight, Moulty might roll the *Moja*. Roll or not, Moulty had a new boat like he had never had before, and a river he longed to run. He thought he would be going alone, until Janice said she was going too. The boat was called the *Moja* after all, and this time Janice was impressed!

Before heading to Shiprock, the White River came up again in April, from its normal few hundred cubic feet a second to almost a thousand. Moulty got the *Moja* on the White and was very happy with its performance. He reported to Norm that it "handled quite well." With final details to be sorted out and an itinerary coming into place for the San Juan run, Moulty was thinking ahead. In the same letter, he wrote Norm that if he was "planning a trip through the Grand Canyon in 48 (next year) I would like to be included in the party if at all possible. Let me know how much it would cost me so I can start saving my pennies and dimes for it. Janice told me the other day she knew I'd never be satisfied until I made the trip – maybe she is right!"

The *Moja* just out of the shop, Muncie, Indiana, Fall 1946.
Courtesy Fulmer Collection, reproduced by permission,
Utah State Historical Society, all rights reserved

The couple arrived at Shiprock, New Mexico, June 3, 1947, after a four-day drive from Muncie, Indiana. Located in the northwest corner of New Mexico on the Navajo Nation, Shiprock is named for a butte dominating the skyline about ten miles southwest of the town that looks like a huge, black, tall-masted sailing ship in the middle of a desert ocean. Moulty and Janice found a location to put the *Moja* onto the San Juan, floated the boat to the shade under the highway bridge on the outskirts of town, and then Janice took off in the car with the empty boat trailer for Marble Canyon.

A month before Janice and Moulty headed to Shiprock, another couple had run the San Juan for the first time with Norm Nevills. That couple was Susie and Pat Reilly. Neither the Reillys nor the Fulmers knew at the time that they were destined to do large amounts of river running together.

Plez Talmadge Reilly, known as Pat to his friends, was born in Dallas, Texas, June 9, 1911, of good Northern Irish stock. Pat's father was a machinist and inventor of machine tools. Within three months of Pat's birth, his family moved to Los Angeles. As a teenager, Pat spent almost every weekend surfing, using a ninety-pound solid redwood surfboard. A strong swimmer, Pat was also keen on sports in high school, lettering in football, basketball, and track.

While attending Los Angeles High School in 1930, Pat met Mary Elizabeth "Bee" MacLean. On a trip to Death Valley in 1933, Pat nicknamed Bee "Stovepipe Susie" while at the small desert oasis of Stovepipe Wells. Bee was out and Susie stuck. After graduating from high school, Pat got a job with the United States General Land Office on a survey crew in 1936. The job provided board and $60 a month, which Pat saved carefully. In 1937 Pat purchased a plot of land in Studio City, California, and on December 31, 1937, he and Susie were married. The couple built a house on their lot in 1938, and Pat left the land office to take a machinist job with Lockheed's Burbank plant in 1940. Pat excelled at Lockheed and soon was a floor supervisor.

Janice Fulmer about 1947. Courtesy Marston Collection, reproduced by permission, the Huntington Library, San Marino, California

Through the war years, Pat worked for Lockheed seven days a week. The surfer-surveyor realized in 1947 that after seven years of nonstop work, he was "burned out." The thirty-six-year-old took a month-long leave of absence from work, and he and Susie drove all over the West, camping out along the road or staying in motels. Before they left home, Pat had seen a small advertisement in *Desert* magazine about a Nevills Expedition San Juan River trip. He showed the ad to Susie and they both agreed to give river running a try.

The couple stopped at the South Rim of the Grand Canyon on the long drive to Mexican Hat, Utah. They took the mule ride to Plateau Point, and Emery Kolb took their photo out the upstairs window of the Kolb Studio as the mule riders departed into the Canyon.

The drive from the Grand Canyon to Tuba City and on to Kayenta was over a rutted dirt road. From Kayenta north through Monument Valley toward Mexican Hat the road became nonexistent. Small boards laying on the ground with arrows drawn on them were the only road signs. Eventually the Reillys reached Mexican Hat late in the evening of April 30, and met Norm.

The river trip started the next day, with the San Juan running a little over 1,000 cfs. For the first three days, the river runners needed to get out of the punts to push the boats off the sand bars in the shallows. One of the boatmen was George Wing. Every time Pat asked if he could row, George eagerly obliged. Just above Johns Canyon, George grounded the punt on some rocks and Pat helped push the boat back into the water.

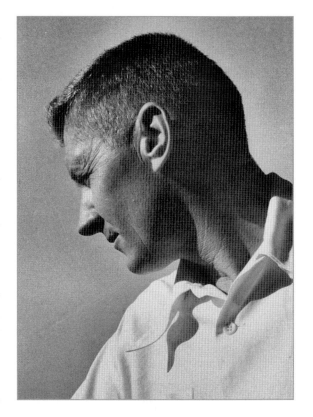

Susie Reilly, 1947. Courtesy Marston Collection, reproduced by permission, the Huntington Library, San Marino, California

Though George was not having a good time and Norm was clearly upset with him, Susie and Pat were having a blast. After a few days, the flow in the San Juan started to rise noticeably. By day five of the trip, the San Juan had risen to almost 5,000 cfs, and pushing the punts through the shallows was a thing of the past. On entering Glen Canyon, Pat and Susie were hooked, as was forty-four-year-old Ruth Pieroth, a fellow traveler on the trip. Ruth was also from southern California, where she lived alone and worked as an elementary school teacher. Ruth, Pat, and Susie would soon become good friends.

Pat Reilly, 1947. Courtesy Marston Collection, reproduced by permission, the Huntington Library, San Marino, California

Norm had been observing how well Pat took to the oars, and when they reached Lee's Ferry he offered him a job rowing on the San Juan for the 1948 river season. Thrilled at the offer, Pat quickly agreed. The couple headed back to California, unaware that a month later a lone man and boat would be patiently waiting under the highway bridge at Shiprock to trace the same route on the San Juan River.

A man doesn't just sit under a bridge with a boat for a few days without attracting the attention of the local townsfolk. The locals found the man was nice enough, and the boat had a distinctly Navajo-sounding name. Janice returned only two days after she had left Moulty and the *Moja*. After driving to Marble Canyon Lodge, she took the long bus journey to Flagstaff, over to Gallup on Route 66, and then north to Shiprock. Once reunited, she and Moulty made the boat ready. They pushed off on June 5, 1947, on 5,600 cfs. A Navajo on horseback rode along the river bank, pacing the couple for over eight miles to see the little boat run a riffle.

With two weeks of food, camping gear, and two adults, the *Moja* only sat four to five inches deep into the water. All went well for the first seventy-five miles or so, until they ran aground near Recapture Creek. Moulty estimated the river was over a half mile wide but only three inches deep in the main channel. The couple had no choice but to get out and push the boat along in ankle-deep water. San Juan river runners, even today, can appreciate this experience. Fortunately, the river narrowed and deepened below Recapture, and the couple did not run aground again.

The run from Recapture Creek, past Bluff, and on to Mexican Hat, passes through stunning canyon country, with multicolored sandstone and limestone cliffs towering behind large cottonwood trees along the river. A very short section of the river passes through tight narrows and there are some sporty rapids. Numerous Ancestral Puebloan dwellings are visible from the river. This was all an unexpected treat for Moulty and Janice, who were pleasantly surprised. They rated it "about as much fun as anything on the San Juan" except for "the Syncline and the 13-Foot Rapids."

They arrived at Mexican Hat most likely on June 9, having traveled about 110 river miles from New Mexico, through the southwest corner of Colorado, and on into Utah. Norm was away, but Doris greeted the two with her usual wonderful hospitality. With the flow in the river now at 8,000 cfs and going up, the couple said their goodbyes to Doris the next day.

The rest of the trip was fun and uneventful. Moulty ran 13-Foot Rapid on Friday the 13th, filling the boat half full of water. Janice, on shore, caught it all on 16mm color film. The weather was ideal except for one cool, cloudy morning after leaving Slickhorn Canyon. This was Moulty's third and Janice's second run through this section of the San Juan. Returning from a hike up Hidden Passage Canyon, Moulty and Janice ran into another couple who had also recently taken to river running.

Harry Aleson and Georgie White were making a motor boat up-run of Glen Canyon from Lee's Ferry. Harry was seven years older than Moulty, and had been exposed to the Colorado River first at Lake Mead in 1939. Georgie White was the same age as Janice, and had been introduced to the Colorado River by Harry just three years earlier. Later that same year, Harry and Georgie would row a twelve-foot inflatable raft from Green River, Utah, through Cataract Canyon to Hite, Utah, repeating part of Amos Berg's 1938 rubber raft run from Green River, Wyoming, to Lake Mead. In 1948, Harry would start leading guided float trips on the San Juan and on through Glen Canyon, and Georgie would start leading commercial Glen Canyon trips by 1954. The Fulmers, Harry and Georgie exchanged pleasantries and each went on their way, unaware of how or when the future would bring them all together again.

Janice and Moulty then made the six-mile hike up Forbidding Canyon to see Rainbow Bridge and signed the guest register, Janice for the third time, and Moulty for the fourth. Finally, they arrived at Lee's Ferry on June 17, 1947, having boated through a small part of four states. On their arrival at the Ferry, the mighty Colorado River was running 54,700 cfs.

Moulty was thrilled! The *Moja* had handled like a dream boat, with "no bruises or scratches on it." The decked McKenzie River dory had not rolled in the big sand waves as Norm had feared. In fact, it sliced its way with ease into the biggest waves the San Juan had to offer. The boat would ride high up on a wave, then drop forward and thunder down on the water below. It was a lot of fun! After a coat of white paint for the boat and linseed oil for the oars, Moulty was ready to go boating again. He had sold the *Tub* before the San Juan trip and, on arriving back in Muncie, he sold the *Domino*.

Sadly, Janice's father, having had heart troubles for some time, passed away in November. Janice took a job as a receptionist in Warner Gear's Muncie Plant #3, "to keep busy and not think of his passing." With the new job, Janice would not have time for a long vacation in the summer of 1948. That was not the case for Moulty, as his job with the YMCA allowed him time off in the summer. He wrote Norm the first of the year, again saying he wanted to run the Grand Canyon.

Norm wrote back that he would "really love" to have him on the 1948 Grand Canyon trip as a passenger. While Norm charged $1,100 for the whole trip, he would only charge Moulty $1,000 "in deference to your boating, etc." Norm pointed out that as a passenger, he could get a lot of great pictures. Besides, Norm already had boatmen for the 1948 run.

That kind of money, in 1948, was huge. The median yearly family income at the time was $3,200. By the end of January, Moulty had sent Norm $200 "as partial payment for the canyon trip." While a bitter cold winter had Muncie in its grips, Moulty was planning his itinerary for the summer trip, including a quick jaunt to the South Rim for a sunset and sunrise filming shoot.

In March, Moulty sent another down payment of $400 to Norm, jokingly writing "This should take me a stop or two west of Hermit Falls, which I tried in vain to see in 1943 when I hiked down the old Hermit Trail." It was shaping up to be a fun trip.

7

The Grand at Last

1948

San Juan punts at the Paria beach, Lee's Ferry, Arizona. From left to right: Norm Nevills, George Wing, Pat Reilly, and Frank Wright, June 21,1948. Courtesy Joe Szep

While Moulty was counting the weeks before his Grand Canyon trip, Pat and Susie Reilly were back at Mexican Hat in the late spring of 1948. Earning $10 a day as a paid boatman for Norm, Pat rowed two trips on the San Juan from Mexican Hat to Lee's Ferry. Susie traveled with Pat on the first trip, and then helped with land-based logistics for the second trip. As on today's commercial river trips, the passengers and boatmen all got to know each other as they journeyed down the river, without necessarily having any knowledge beforehand as to who would be on the journey.

One of the passengers Pat met was a brilliant engineer from the sprawling Lockheed Burbank facility, named Joe Szep. Soft-spoken and unassuming, the thirty-year-old was fun loving and ever willing to help with camp chores. Joe and Pat became fast friends, and when Joe met Susie at the end of the six-day trip, that cinched the friendship. In the years to come, Joe, his wife Winnie, Pat, and Susie would spend a considerable amount of time together. Norm once again encouraged Pat to return for the next season as a boatman, including a possible run through the Grand Canyon.

At the end of the San Juan season that spring, Pat and Susie Reilly returned home to Studio City. Back at Lockheed, Pat worked out a deal with the company to allow him to take unpaid leave on either side of his paid vacation. This would give him enough time in the summer to get away and go boating. Like Moulty, Pat read everything he could find about the Grand Canyon and the San Juan and Colorado rivers. Pat also took a lot of pictures, both still and 16mm movies, and showed them to large hometown audiences. This time, when Pat and Susie left Lee's Ferry, they missed meeting Moulty by three weeks.

Meanwhile, Norm Nevills was gearing up for the summer's Grand Canyon cruise. By 1948, twenty river trips had successfully completed the run from Lee's Ferry to the Grand Wash Cliffs through Marble and Grand canyons. Uniquely, Norm had participated in five of those twenty trips. Ten people from across the country arrived at Marble Canyon Lodge for the twenty-first run through the Grand Canyon on the 1948 Nevills Expedition. Besides Norm from Mexican Hat and Moulty from Muncie, the passenger list included a wide array of people. Wayne and Lucile Hiser were from Toledo, Ohio, where Wayne owned a small electric motor manufacturing plant. Florence and Bestor Robinson were from Oakland, California. Bestor was a fifty-year-old lawyer and an avid mountaineer. In 1931 he made the first ascent of Thunderbolt Peak, the last unclimbed fourteen-thousand-foot peak in California. He had joined the soon-to-be famous environmentalist David Brower in 1939 for the first successful ascent of Shiprock, the butte Moulty and Janice knew well from the previous year's San Juan run. In 1948, Bestor was also president of the Sierra Club.

Another passenger making his first trip through the Grand Canyon was Frank Masland, Jr. Hailing from Carlisle, Pennsylvania, Frank was president of the large carpet manufacturer, C. H. Masland and Sons. The fifty-three-year-old would later serve on the National Park Service Advisory Committee, and was instrumental in the formation of Canyonlands National Park.

As with many river trips today, an exchange of passengers was scheduled for Phantom Ranch roughly one-third of the way through the Canyon. The Robinsons would hike out, and hiking in would be John Doerr, National Park Service Chief of the Division of Naturalists, stationed in Washington, D.C. Doerr had just been transferred to his new job after serving at Rocky Mountain National Park from 1940 to early 1946 as assistant, and then acting superintendent. With a degree in geology from the University of Wisconsin, Doerr had previously been stationed at Hawaii Volcanoes and Crater Lake national parks.

Also joining the group at Phantom was eighteen-year-old Nancy Streator from Salt Lake City, in her freshman year at Scripps College. Her father had checked out Nevills Expedition, and had allowed his daughter to boat with Norm on the San Juan in 1946. Like Moulty, this was her first journey through the Grand Canyon. Rosalind "Ros" Johnson, a horse riding instructor from Pasadena, California, was joining the group as well. Rosalind had participated in Norm's 1947 Grand Canyon trip, but had hiked out at Phantom Ranch, and was now returning to run the lower Canyon. Another addition to the group at Phantom Ranch was Howard "Cowboy" Welty, a school teacher from Oakland, California, who had run the Salmon and Snake rivers with Norm in 1946.

The four boatmen were Norm, Frank Wright, and Otis and Garth Marston. Frank Wright had met Norm in Blanding, Utah, earlier in the year, at Lyman's Garage where Frank worked as a mechanic. A multi-talented man, the forty-five-year-old had worked as a coal miner, barber, music instructor, piano tuner, mechanic, welder, machinist, and mail carrier. With his wife Dora, the couple shared duties for the National Weather Service, reporting the Blanding weather every three hours, seven days a week, year round. Frank was also a licensed radio operator, had his own darkroom to develop photographs, and held a private pilot's license. Besides, Frank Wright could make the best Dutch oven biscuits around. Norm had invited him on a San Juan River trip in the spring of 1948 and was impressed with how quickly he took to the oars. Not only would this be Frank's first time rowing the Grand, but his first year rowing a boat. Whatever Frank may have lacked in rowing experience was offset by a keen understanding of individuals. Before the 1948 trip even started, he had sized up Norm's operation.

Frank understood that as Norm introduced him as "head boatman," he would be the one to do the cooking, supervise the loading and unloading of the boats, and do any chores that arose, in addition to rowing all day. Indeed, when Norm invited Frank to row as boatman for the 1948 Grand

Canyon run, Frank had at first answered with a resounding "No!" Norm wouldn't take no for an answer, and made Frank feel as though he was indispensable to the success of the trip. Frank reluctantly agreed to take the position.

Otis Marston and his son, Garth, had run with Norm on the 1942 Grand Canyon cruise as passengers. The elder Marston had been deeply bitten by the river running bug on that trip, and rowed from Mexican Hat to Lee's Ferry for Norm on a 1944 San Juan run. The father-and-son team next rowed for Norm on his Grand Canyon run in 1947. Garth, twenty years old at the time, was energetic, fit, and handsome.

Redwall Cavern, just over a mile downstream from Vasey's Paradise. From left to right: Florence Robinson, Bestor Robinson, Frank Masland, Lucile Hiser, Norm Nevills, Garth Marston, Frank Wright, Moulton Fulmer, and Dock Marston, July 14, 1948. Courtesy Frank E. Masland, Jr. Papers, Archives, and Special Collections, Dickinson College, Carlisle, Pennsylvania

Otis Reed Marston, nicknamed "Dock" by Norm, was born in 1894 in Berkeley, California. A strong swimmer, Dock swam across the Golden Gate from San Francisco to Marin County in 1915. He received his bachelors in electrical engineering from the University of California at Berkeley in 1916, then went on to receive his masters in industrial engineering at Cornell University in 1917. After that, Dock joined the United States Naval Academy where he graduated as an ensign in 1918. By the close of 1919, Dock Marston had completed his qualifications as a submarine commander with the United States Navy.

During his submarine training, it had been drilled into Dock to identify problems, look at the skills available to the team, and formulate a plan to deal with the problem at hand. He would apply those skills to his activities long after his naval career was over. Independently wealthy, Dock was also interested in psychology, and was curious about the psychological makeup of individual river runners. With his critical eye, he began to look at the history of river running on the Colorado River. He would eventually amass an unparalleled collection of interviews, trip logs, letters, film footage, and photos of anything and everything to do with people who boated the entire Colorado River watershed. In his river studies, Dock would compile a list of the first 200 individuals to travel through the Grand Canyon from Lee's Ferry to the end of the Canyon at the Grand Wash Cliffs.

Moulty easily fit into this menagerie of people. One can only surmise that in traveling together with such a crew for twenty days, Moulty may have come away from the trip with a little better understanding of environmental awareness, Dutch oven cooking, and a keen sense of what makes a good, or in this case, not so good, Grand Canyon boat.

There were four boats on the trip, named the *Wen*, *Mexican Hat II*, *Sandra*, and *Joan*. All four were of the cataract boat design, named by Norm and designed by Norm's father, for whom the *Wen* was named. As seen from above, cataract boats had the shape of an iron, with a pointed bow and very broad flat stern, with the stern end roughly the same width as the boat at the oarlocks. Also called "sadirons," they had only a few degrees of side flare at the chine. The width across the bottom of the boat at the widest was about sixty-one inches, and that flared out to sixty-four inches at the gunwales. The boats were just short of sixteen feet long, had roughly nine inches of rocker, with side panels measuring twenty inches at their widest. Passengers sat on the fore and aft decks, nervously aware of the hard, sharp edges of the pointed hatch lids where they were sitting. The boats were made with ½-inch marine plywood with oak chines and ribs.

Norm's boats sat low in the water, and the open and spacious footwell had no sidebox storage. When the rower's area was visited by a rogue wave, the footwell would hold over 100 gallons of water. They also had a tendency to plow into waves instead of riding up and over them, as the boat was rowed downriver with the boatman looking downstream facing the broad stern. The sadiron's advantages were that when repairs were needed, which was rare, the boat would easily rest on its side. Another advantage was that the wide beam made for a very stable boat.

Norm Nevills, Frank Masland, and Moulty Fulmer (toasting bread), Nankoweap, July 1948. Courtesy Marston Collection, reproduced by permission, the Huntington Library, San Marino, California

The group pushed off from Lee's Ferry July 12, 1948, on 17,600 cfs, well after the peak runoff for the year of 92,400 cfs in late May. The first rapid worth a scout was Badger, which all the passengers walked around on shore. Norm had a habit of using hand signals from shore to assist boatmen through the rapid. Dock and Bestor signaled Norm and Garth as they rowed through the rapid, and they shipped very little water. Badger Rapid has a large boulder in the middle of the channel with water pouring over the boulder. This rock is difficult to see from upstream, so having someone to signal from shore can help. The trouble is, if the person on shore wants the rower to, say, go left, the rower has no idea how far left to go. If the rower went too far left, the signal from shore would suddenly change to the right. Go too far right, and the signal would be reversed. Dock knew that the shore signaling had not gone so well in 1942, and was aware of the fact that shore signaling could be inaccurate. As Dock entered the rapid, Norm signaled him to go right. Dock, aware that the large boulder was just to his right, ignored the signal. After the run, Norm admitted he had misjudged the set of the current. River runners would soon learn how to "read water" as Dock had done, and reliance on shore signaling would become a thing of the past.

The group stopped to scout at Soap Creek, the next large rapid. After good runs in Soap, they went on to camp at a large beach right at the top of House Rock Rapid, having traveled seventeen miles for the day. With two Franks on the trip, Garth started calling Frank Masland a host of nicknames like Fish, Fish Eyes, or F.E., for the way he lay flat on his stomach over the stern deck of Frank Wright's boat with his head out the front, taking every wave straight in the face. The river water was a warm seventy-seven degrees, and Garth swam House Rock Rapid wearing his life jacket and using his air mattress for flotation.

Camping accommodations along the river in those days were simple. For the bathroom, females went upriver for privacy, and males downriver. Cooking was over an open fire right on the beach. Bedrolls were laid out on the sand, and dishes were done in the river.

The next day, the elder Marston noted in his log "the passengers were showing symptoms of the incurable rapid happiness." The group stopped at South Canyon for lunch and camp. A few of the more intrepid in the party made their way downriver along the large swath of shoreline boulders, sand, and solid bedrock to Vasey's Paradise, a large freshwater spring. From there, they retraced their steps back to the boats, and then hiked up to view a human skeleton on the Redwall bench a hundred feet above the river. This skeleton, first discovered by a river trip in 1934, was now missing its skull. Once back in camp, Dock noted in his journal that the group was short on juice and fruit.

A few large piles of driftwood attracted the attention of the river party the following day and were set on fire. Besides tons and tons of sand, the free-flowing Colorado River carried a lot of driftwood. River runners on Norm's trips were encouraged to burn the backyard-sized piles of flotsam they encountered all the way from Lee's Ferry to the headwaters of Lake Mead. If a river runner was able to start a driftwood pile on fire with one match, they were "in" the Royal Order of Drift Wood Burners, or DWB for short. Inducted into the DWB that day were Moulty, Lucille, Bestor, Fish Eyes, and Frank. At lunch, a few of the river runners explored a sheer-walled side canyon with a small trickle of water flowing along the drainage bottom, most probably Buck Farm Canyon.

Nankoweap Canyon has a very large delta where it reaches the Colorado River. Huge mesquite trees mark the high water line and provide some shade. Towering walls surround this location, making it a very attractive place for hikers and river runners alike to explore. The river party decided to camp here, and a small amount of shoveling diverted the clear flowing creek right into the camp's kitchen for drinking, cooking, and cleaning.

In the days before Glen Canyon Dam, finding clear drinking water was important to river runners. This made camps with a clear water supply highly sought-after. The Colorado River typically carried lots of suspended sediments. The river water often required overnight settling in buckets to be drinkable, with clear water poured off in the morning. Camping near springs or side streams eliminated the need to settle river water.

The party laid over for a day at Nankoweap, where they hiked high up a very steep hillside to the base of the towering cliffs. There, they visited some Ancestral Puebloan food storage rooms, called granaries. Thought to be roughly 1,000 years old, the granaries were clearly visible from camp far below on the Nankoweap delta.

On the fifth day, the group was back in the boats traveling downriver, with the Little Colorado River the next stop. Before Glen Canyon Dam, the Colorado would deposit silt quite a ways up into the Little Colorado River canyon. When they landed, the group saw the Little Colorado was running brown. Dock hiked up far enough to encounter blue water before it started to cut through the sediment that had been deposited during high water several weeks earlier. He called to the others, who all came up for a swim in the warm mineral-laden water. Back on the boats, they floated on to Lava Chuar Canyon.

After lunch, Dock headed up the side canyon looking for a miner's camp by a clear, freshwater spring only a mile or so from the Colorado River. After finding the spring, Dock kept on exploring the wide open Chuar Valley. Spotting Norm and Frank, Dock was surprised to find it was 6:00 p.m. and that the two men were out looking for him! The threesome hightailed it back to the Colorado, and after a quick dinner, the group headed to Tanner Rapid for camp. There was a reason it was important to camp at Tanner. Norm would light a signal fire on the beach there on the evening of the trip's fifth day, for Doris to spot from the Canyon's rim as an "all's well" signal.

On July 17, the group ran twenty miles from Tanner to Phantom Ranch. Garth went over a submerged boulder in 75 Mile Rapid, and the hydraulic hole on the downstream side of the rock threw Moulty onto one of the boat's hatch covers. The sharp edge of the hatch removed some skin from his chest. The group ran Hance down the left side on a little over 12,000 cfs. Norm and Garth both hit rocks in the rapid, but the boats suffered no harm. The group stopped for a late lunch after running Grapevine Rapid, then pushed on to Phantom Ranch, arriving at the boat beach just after 4:30 p.m.

The 1948 Nevills' party, at Phantom Ranch, Arizona. From left to right: Frank "Fish Eyes" Masland, Bestor Robinson, Wayne Hiser, Garth Marston, Lucile Hiser, Moulty Fulmer, Dock Marston, Frank Wright, Norm Nevills, and Florence Robinson, July 17, 1948. Courtesy Plez Talmadge Reilly Collection, Cline Library, Northern Arizona University

In August 1869, John Wesley Powell and his expedition members were the first boaters to document a stop at the mouth of Bright Angel Creek. Early river runners after Powell stopped too, for the creek's clear drinking water. Soon to follow was a camp started by David Rust in 1907 not far up Bright Angel Creek from the river. Rust built a cable tramway across the Colorado to allow access to the South Rim. Rust's Camp was further developed by the Fred Harvey Company in 1922, when architect Mary Jane Colter designed and oversaw the construction of a rock-walled cafeteria and cabins for overnight guests. That same year the United States Geological Survey started a gauging station just upriver from the mouth of the creek to take daily measurements of the flow of the Colorado River. Rust's Camp, renamed Phantom Ranch, offered shade, along with a trail to the South and North rims. This allowed for resupplying river trips with food and exchanging trip participants. It was not uncommon in the 1940s and 1950s for river trips to spend a few nights at the ranch. River runners would leave their boats tied up at the black Kaibab Suspension Bridge, built in 1928 to connect with the Kaibab Trail going to the South Rim.

As the river party arrived at Phantom Ranch, they were greeted by Doris Nevills, Nancy Streator, and Ros Johnson. The group swam in the swimming pool, had their meals at the canteen, and bunked for the next three nights at the ranch. During the first evening's meal, Moulty enjoyed seven glasses of ice water and three of iced tea!

While at the ranch, besides swimming, writing letters, taking short hikes, and lounging in the shade, Garth noted in his log that late afternoon entertainment included watching the "nightly arrival of the mule train bearing its load of tortured dudes." The river trip's supplies arrived by pack mule as well, and depending on the mule packer, were either deposited on the beach in a nice pile or spread out all over the nearby rocks in what Dock called an artistic style reminiscent of the "extreme modernistic." Either way, some of the supplies were crushed, a number of requested food items turned up short, while other items were oversupplied. What they received would have to do for the rest of the trip.

On Tuesday, July 20, 1948, the river party set off downstream from Phantom while Doris headed up the trail. They were now running on 11,400 cfs as they made their way through the rapids at Horn Creek, Granite, and after a stop for lunch, Hermit. All the passengers except Nancy walked around Horn Creek. Norm let her ride with him because she had such bad blisters on her feet from the hike into Phantom. At Hermit Rapid, Moulty took the opportunity to hike a mile up Hermit Creek to the location he had hiked down to in 1943. On his return, he and the rest of the passengers walked around Hermit while the boatmen ran the rapid on the left to avoid the large waves in the middle. A large sandy beach at Boucher Rapid was camp for the night where a strong wind blew sand over the river runners as they tried to sleep.

There was a reason the river party camped at Boucher, and it had to do with three men jumping out of an airplane. Four years and one month earlier to the day, a B-24 Liberator bomber had lumbered over the desert Southwest in the middle of the night. The four-engine bomber, based out of the bomber training airfield at Tonopah, Nevada, was conducting high-altitude celestial navigation exercises at 23,000 feet. It was a perfect night for the training, without a moon. Suddenly, the number three engine began spitting flames and then all four engines gave out. Without the usual roar of the engines, the resulting silence was thunderously frightening to the crew. A B-24 cannot glide well without power, and the pilot ordered the crew to bail out. Exiting the bomb bay door into the night went the navigator, flight engineer, and bombardier. As the pilot was getting ready to jump, a motor coughed back to life, and he scrambled back to his seat, restarting three of the four engines. The crippled plane flew on to Kingman, Arizona, where it made a safe landing. Unfortunately, it was too late for three of the six-man crew. They were parachuting in pitch darkness into the Grand Canyon, to a location only a few miles west of Boucher Rapid.

The Tonto Platform as the airmen might have seen it above Tuna Creek. Tom Martin photo

47

For all practical purposes, the three parachutists had disappeared. Captain Fred Milam was the 466th Bomb Group's commanding officer. When he heard he had three men missing, he flew the almost 300 miles from the Tonopah base to Kingman to assist in the search. At Kingman, Milam became concerned that not enough was being done to find his men. He was given permission to assist in the search by his Tonopah base commander, with the condition that he returned to Tonopah nightly. Through Milam's direct efforts, three B-24s began flying daily twelve-hour search-and-rescue missions looking for the lost airmen. In three days and thousands of miles of flying over rugged desert terrain covered by steep-walled canyons and jagged mountains, he was becoming seriously worried about his crew. It was late in the afternoon of the third day when he finally spotted a parachute and swung the lumbering bomber around for another pass to mark the location.

Milam's men had jumped out of their plane in the middle of the night three days earlier. In an amazing stroke of luck, Lieutenant Charles "Goldie" Goldblum's parachute caught in the Tapeats cliffs high above Tuna Rapid. Goldblum came to an abrupt stop as he bounced sideways into something very hard, and his feet did not touch the ground. The airman had his wits about him and stayed in his harness the rest of the night, climbing up the rock wall onto a small ledge. It was a decision that may have saved his life; at first light, Goldblum could appreciate his precarious perch on the side of a cliff a few hundred feet high. Goldie climbed up his parachute lines to the flat Tonto Platform above and looked around. He was deep in the Grand Canyon.

Later that morning Goldblum found Flight Officer Maurice "Moe" Cruickshank, who had landed hard and broken his foot. The two airmen slowly worked their way off the Tonto and down into the steep-sided schist of the Tuna Creek drainage. Goldie was able to hike down the drainage to the Colorado River and drink some water. He then hiked back to Moe and was able to help him get to the river for a drink the following morning.

That year, runoff in the Colorado was long and sustained. The river had peaked at 94,400 cfs on May 19, and all of June, water levels varied between a high of 85,000 cfs and a low of 59,000 cfs. The river water needed to be settled for good drinking, but the two airmen didn't worry about a little silt. This was the first water Moe had had in over thirty hours.

The two men began to work their way downstream along the river's edge. A short distance below the mouth of Tuna Creek the duo thought they were rescued when they saw a man walking along in a green sweater. The man thought he was rescued too on seeing the two airmen. Only on reaching each other did Goldie and Moe recognize flight instructor Engineer Corporal Royce "Roy" Embanks, the third

The Tonto Platform near where the three airmen returned to find Roy Embank's burned parachute. Tom Martin photo

48

man to exit the crippled bomber.

Embanks had landed on a steep slope just below the relatively flat Tonto Platform and scrambled up to the Tonto where he laid out his chute and pinned it down with stones. If there was a search, maybe his chute would be spotted. Seeking water, he had then cut the cords off his chute thinking they might come in handy and then worked his way down to the river where he met Goldie and Moe. This was the men's second day in the Canyon.

The three decided to keep working their way downriver. The terrain consisted of steep slopes and sheer granite cliffs with occasional small sand banks right at the water's edge. The trio made their way along the river bank and, where they had to, Roy swam downstream around cliff edges with Goldie paying out the parachute cord. Roy would find the next place he could get out of the river, and then he would reel in Goldie and Moe as they swam down after him. They worked a driftwood log into the river thinking maybe they could build a raft, and then watched it spin in lazy circles in an eddy. So much for that idea.

The sun beat down on the men with a vengeance and they made little progress. Late in the day they heard the heavy roar of a B-24 flying close overhead. At this point they realized it would be better to be up on the Tonto where rescue planes had a chance of spotting them.

On the third day, the men worked their way up a small side canyon back onto the Tonto Platform. Moe's broken foot was stable as long as he kept his rubber-soled flight boot on, but hiking in the Canyon in June with no way to carry water made the trio's progress very slow. This was also the third day the men labored without food. Still, their hopes were lifted when another B-24 roared by and dropped a smoke bomb where Embanks had spread out his parachute. The airmen slowly worked their way back to the east toward Tuna Creek and late in the day, dehydrated and exhausted, they returned to where Roy's chute had been, only to find it burned to a crisp by the smoke bomb.

It was a long night with no water. Dawn greeted the three men on the fourth day of their ordeal in silence, punctuated only by Moe's occasional humming. The flat, waterless Tonto Plateau stretched out around them covered with small spiky black brush, Mormon tea, and acres of beavertail cactus. There really was nothing left to do but sit in the ever hotter sun and wait.

Fortunately, the trio didn't have to wait long. At 9:30 a.m., another B-24 came rumbling along the Tonto, just over the deck, and they were seen. The plane came in low and slow again, and this time dropped K-rations and canteens wrapped in blankets, along with a handwritten note which read "Greetings! You are in the Grand Canyon. Do not leave your position until notified by message dropped from an Army airplane." The note was signed by Captain Fred Milam.

The next message dropped was more detailed. The men were advised to stay at the parachute until "a lot of equipment" was dropped just east of them. The rest of the day was spent dropping supplies onto the Tonto near the trio whose luck had turned from bad to best. Goldie, Moe, and Roy set up a small camp and outfitted themselves happily with all the airdropped gear that arrived over the next few days. Raining out of the sky came canteens of water, sleeping bags and blankets, two flare guns with lots of ammunition, a large two-way radio, ten pounds of steak, K-rations, a hatchet, clothing, shoes, food, medical supplies, cans of sterno to cook with, and two bottles of whiskey.

Rescue parties were sent in from both the South and North rims. The North Rim team consisted of National Park Service Ranger Ed Laws and Canyon hiker Alan MacRae. The two made their way off the North Rim east of Point Sublime on the morning of June 28, and reached the airmen the next day. Led by MacRae and Laws, Moe, Goldie, and Roy reached the North Rim and a waiting crowd a little after midday on June 30. All told, they had spent ten days in the Canyon. When the five headed for the rim, they left behind a well-stocked camp.

It was the equipment from this incident that the Nevills party hoped to recover. Leaving Boucher, the group ran the riffle at Crystal without a thought. It would be just short of twenty years before Crystal Creek would flash flood, making a major rapid, where in 1948 none existed. The party ran the rapid at Tuna Creek, and pulled ashore on the right bank below what is today called Nixon Rock. While Moulty, Doerr, Garth, Fish Eyes,

Remains from the airmen's 1944 camp. Such artifacts are protected by law and need to be left undisturbed by today's Canyon visitors. Tom Martin photo

the Hisers, Cowboy and Frank stayed with the boats, Dock, Nancy with her blistered feet, Ros, and Norm began the difficult trek up to the Tonto Platform. After attempting to head up a small side tributary, the hikers climbed east up to the base of the Tapeats cliff where Goldie's parachute had caught four years prior. Here they found a rolled-up mattress with a quart canteen full of water. Having not brought any food or water themselves, they made short work of drinking the canteen dry. Ros and Nancy found some shade in the Tapeats cliffs while Norm and Dock began exploring the Tonto. After some searching, they found the flyers' base camp, complete with radio, medical kits, food, blankets, rotting sleeping bags, two flare guns, much flare ammunition, and a lot of empty canteens.

Norm and Dock loaded up as much gear as they could carry and started heading back toward the river. Though only a mile away, the route was anything but easy. To attract the attention of Nancy and Ros, Norm fired off a signal flare. About half-way back to the boats, Dock found a small bundle tied up with string. Inside it was a pair of pants, Air Force tee shirts, and a pair of shoes. As a joke on the party waiting by the river, Dock put on the white pants. Slowed by the heavy radio, and with Nancy making poor time on her blistered feet, Norm told Dock to take the three boats downriver to find camp while Norm, Nancy, Doerr, and Fish Eyes would all stay with Norm's boat, the *Wen*, for the night. Norm and Nancy made the *Wen* at dusk and, as Dock put it, "Nancy's rear end indicates the rocks were not soft to slide on." The four had little to eat that night while the downstream party camped at a small sandy beach a few miles further down. Wind in the night blew so much sand over Moulty he moved his bedding down to the *Sandra* and attempted to sleep on the boat deck. The upstream party was on the water early and arrived in time to have breakfast with their fellow travelers.

The next stop was to investigate the all-metal boat, the *Ross Wheeler*, near the foot of the South Bass Trail. The *Ross* was designed by Bert Loper in 1914 and was modeled after the Galloway-Stone expedition wooden boats used in 1909. The boat was used in late 1914 into 1915 by Charles Russell, August Tadje, and Goddard Quist, in a failed attempt to travel through the Grand Canyon. Abandoned in 1915, the boat was then used by

William Bass where his trail met the river. Eventually, the boat was pulled up on the rocks above high water. When the 1948 river trip stopped to look at it, the *Ross* still had oars with oarlocks and two cork life jackets in the front hatch.

After inspecting the boat, the group headed to the mouth of Shinumo Creek for lunch, and then Dock, Moulty, and Cowboy went in search of Bass's camp up Shinumo Creek. They used a hole in the rocks behind the main waterfall to gain access to upper Shinumo Creek, just as river runners do today. Besides seeing a few wild burros, the hikers returned to the river without reaching Bass's camp. They rowed against upcanyon winds the rest of the day, before reaching Elves Chasm for camp.

The river runners awoke in the morning to see a red Colorado River. Rains in the night upstream had washed red mud into the river. The group hiked up to look at the Elves Chasm waterfall, then headed on downriver. Large driftwood piles were used to see if Nancy and "Little John," as Doerr was now called, would enter the DWB order. Little John was inducted, but Dock noted "Nancy remained in the second grade." Lunch was at Specter Rapid with the burning remains of driftwood piles left miles upstream. Garth swam Specter, and Moulty took Garth's boat, the *Sandra*, through the rapid. Moulty was thrilled to have oars in his hands once again. This trip would be his only opportunity to row Norm's cataract-style boat. All too soon he had to relinquish the oars to Garth.

They reached Bedrock Rapid just as a rain storm swept in. The river was running around 11,000 cfs, and a hard pull to the right was required to miss hitting a large granite outcrop in the middle of the river. Sheets of rain pelted the boats and gale force downstream winds pushed them straight toward the infamous bedrock. Frank was thrown from his seat in the *Mexican Hat II* as he didn't quite make the required move and slammed into the rock island. Dock hit the giant rock as well, a glancing blow that put a small hole in the *Joan* just above the waterline.

The rain stopped in about fifteen minutes, just in time for the group to scout Deubendorff Rapid and run the right channel. The party pulled in for camp at the foot of Tapeats Rapid. Little John and Dock went to fish the creek, and caught a number of rainbow trout before dinner. Signal flares lit up the late evening sky. The following morning there was an "unexplained" rearranging of passengers on the boats. Moulty found himself now riding with Frank Wright, and Fish Eyes was transferred to the *Sandra*.

They spent the rest of the day and camped that night at Deer Creek Falls. Norm, Nancy, still with badly blistered feet, and Dock worked their way up a broken hillside away from the river. Once they had hiked up the steep slope high enough, they contoured around into a tight narrows of Tapeats sandstone. The three worked their way through the narrows on a series of ledges along a sheer cliff face. While Nancy and Norm stayed at the end of the narrows by the clear flowing waters of Deer Creek for the rest of the day, Dock continued exploring up the drainage, reaching Deer Spring and hiking up behind the waterfall where it exited the solid rock. Moulty hiked up the hillside from camp to the top of the falls, enjoyed the view, and then hiked back to the river. That evening, another flare lit up the night sky.

July 25, 1948, was Moulty's seventeenth wedding anniversary and he noted in his journal that his "thoughts drift back to Indiana and home each evening. I think of Janice and how I miss her. My family is in my prayer each night." The Colorado River had turned red again overnight, and Moulty shot some 16mm film footage riding on the boat through a few small rapids. Upset Rapid was next. This rapid has a large hole that the river runners tried to avoid with all passengers walking around the rapid. Camp was on the baking-hot rock ledges at Havasu Canyon, and a number of the travelers had trouble sleeping in the heat. After the remaining canned goods were inventoried, Dock noted he was carrying ninety-four more cans of food than anyone else, almost twice as many cans as Norm or Garth.

The next day the river runners dealt with the heat by hurling buckets of water at each other as they floated to Stairway Canyon for lunch. Wayne's spectacles were one casualty of the morning's water fight. During the customary siesta in which most of the party dozed, Dock explored up Stairway over a mile.

It was on to Lava Falls, also known as Vulcan Rapid, in the afternoon. Landing on the left above the falls, the passengers and crew immediately began portaging all the river gear down the left shore to the foot of the rapid. Then the boatmen all rowed across to scout the right side. Dock thought he saw a possible run on the right but was outvoted by the others, and they rowed back to the left shore where they stayed the night.

Early the next morning the boatmen lined the boats along the left shore of Lava Falls. Lining a boat past a major rapid was, at that time, considered safer than attempting a run of the rapid. If a boat flipped and was lost downstream, it would mean serious hardship to the remaining crew. The safer option of lining a heavy boat along a rocky shore in fast-moving water also had its risks, including injury or drowning.

Lining required letting the boat float downriver along the shore with ropes tied to it, with a number of people on shore holding the ropes to slow the boat's descent. One person, or sometimes two or three, usually pushed or pulled the boat off the rocks right next to shore. These people were often in the swift river water, hanging onto the boat. A small hand line ran all the way around the boat and allowed the people in the water something to hold on to.

For the mostly seasoned Nevills crew, it took thirty-five minutes each to line the *Mexican Hat II* and the *Wen*. But practice was leading to proficiency, and it took only twenty minutes for the *Joan*, and fifteen for the *Sandra*. One of the passengers noted to Dock that they were concerned about Norm's lack of care of the river equipment during the lining job.

With Lava Falls behind them, the river party rowed to Whitmore Wash for lunch. Dock set off for a hike up the Whitmore drainage during the after-lunch siesta. Fortunately an afternoon thunderstorm cooled things off as they floated to Parashant Canyon for camp. Six burros greeted the party as they pulled in to shore, and they noted that one burro was wearing a bell. Moulty had been feeling the effects of the heat and took it easy.

The next day Norm decided that the river party could save a day if they rowed the twenty-eight miles to Diamond Creek, and spent a layover day at Diamond. They covered sixteen miles in the morning, with two boats having a big ride in 205 Mile Rapid. Moulty ended up with another stomach abrasion as a result of contacting sharp hatch edges in the rapid. At 217 Mile Rapid, the group pulled to shore on the left. There they found a red flag and a cache of six five-gallon fuel cans that Dock had left there five weeks earlier. The down-running, oar-powered river runners were looking at a cache from one of the first motor-powered river up-runs. And Dock knew all about it.

Six years earlier, the same year Norm had taken Moulty and Janice down the San Juan, Norm had led a party through the Grand Canyon. One of the passengers on that 1942 traverse was a thirty-four-year-old pharmacist named Ed Hudson from Paso Robles, California. Dock had been on that trip as well, and the two had become friends. Hudson had an interest in motor boats, and had down-run the Colorado River from Hoover Dam to Needles in 1941 in a fourteen-foot skiff with a 1½ horsepower (HP) outboard motor. Also on Norm's 1942 trip, and hiking out at Hermit, was Harry Aleson, the same Aleson that Moulty and Janice later met in 1947 in Glen Canyon.

Aleson had started up-running the west end of the Grand Canyon from Lake Mead in a motor boat in 1938. In the spring of 1944, Harry and Ed Hudson teamed up and attempted an up-run of the Grand Canyon in the boat *Up Lake*. The party reached Granite Springs Rapid at 221 Mile where they hit a rock and destroyed the propeller shaft of their 22-HP four-cylinder Evinrude Sportfour outboard motor.

Hudson then went to work building his own boat, which he completed in the spring of 1948. Called the *Esmeralda II*, the boat was named after the ninety-three-foot stern-wheeler that came up the lower Colorado from the Sea of Cortez to Callville in October 1866. The *Esmeralda II* was nineteen feet long and had a 75-HP inboard motor. In June 1948, Hudson, Dock, Wilson "Willie" Taylor, and Hudson's son, Edward, attempted an up-run from Pearce Ferry with the river running over 60,000 cfs. The boat ran into one of two rock outcrops in mid river adjacent to today's Upper 220 Mile Camp, damaging the rudder. After repairs, the up-runners made it to the foot of 217 Mile Rapid, but the *Esmeralda II* lacked enough horsepower to climb the rapid. The group stashed some gear at the rapid and returned to Pearce Ferry.

It was this same gear that Moulty, Dock, Norm, and the others were now looking at five weeks later. By the time Dock had rowed all the way downstream from Lee's Ferry and reached his cache at 217 Mile, he was certain a motor boat could make a down-run of the river.

After looking at the up-run cache, the "dudes" got to pilot the oar boats through 217 Mile Rapid, with Moulty running the *Joan* right down the middle of the rapid for a "nice ride." There had been an upstream wind blowing all day, and everyone was glad to finally make Diamond Creek and camp. That night, and for the first time in a while, Moulty slept well and was even cool enough to burrow into his sleeping bag.

The next day was a go-nowhere-do-nothing layover day. Diamond Creek was where Norm would hold a ceremony to initiate his passengers who had made it this far into the Royal Order of Colorado River Rats. This initiation would include being blindfolded, then walked to Diamond Creek, a small clear stream. Here, the hapless river runners were told to wade into the creek, get on their knees and forearms with their rear ends in the air, and answer questions about the river's rapid names and geology. The questions came in quick order, and any wrong answers were rewarded with a whack to the rear from a paddle. There were six initiates that day, including Fish Eyes, the Hisers, Frank Wright, Ros, and Moulty.

On Friday, July 30, the group left Diamond Creek on just under 10,000 cfs. They had good runs of Diamond, 232 and 234 Mile rapids, though all boats took on a lot of water. After a stop to look at Travertine Falls, the group passed the location for the proposed Bridge Canyon Dam and reached Bridge Canyon City for lunch. The "city" was a camp used by Bureau of Reclamation workers doing location and survey work at the proposed dam site. The camp was deserted, and after lunch Norm and Frank took a siesta in the shade of one of the wooden cabins, which Dock then set on fire. The sleeping duo awoke, dashed out and put the fire out to much laughter from the rest of the party.

The next stop was Separation Canyon where a group photo was taken at the plaque honoring the brothers O.G. and Seneca Howland and William Dunn who had left the 1869 John Wesley Powell river trip and were never seen again. By this time, the group was rowing on the still headwaters of the reservoir called Lake Mead. The mighty Colorado River was now silenced in the impoundment caused by Hoover Dam, 112 miles downstream. The river runners took turns rowing on the lake to Spencer Canyon for camp. Wind blew fine sand over everyone in the night, so much so that Norm and Frank rowed their boats across the lake to tie up on the basalt cliffs opposite the mouth of Spencer Canyon.

Away early on the morning of July 31, they planned to row twenty-nine miles that day to Columbine Falls, a wonderful waterfall in Cave Canyon. The party reached the falls just at dusk. Unfortunately, to find anything resembling a decent camp, they had to scramble up a ten-foot bank. Dinner was in the dark, and Dock noted while he still had over twenty cans of food in his boat, Norm had none. It would be the last night the two would spend on the river together. Dock would leave oar-powered boats for the wheel and throttle of motorized down-runs the following year.

Early the next morning, two large cabin cruisers appeared with Garth's wife Shirley among the passengers. The tow-out boats had camped just a mile down lake, and arrived with ice cream, cold beer, and ice-water. A food fight eventually erupted between the two motor launches, with tomatoes, "oranges, eggs and other missiles." Moulty's wicked throwing arm made his boat the one to be on.

The oar boats were all tied to one of the motor launches and the happy party headed out across the lake. Moulty Fulmer became the ninety-eighth person to travel through the Grand Canyon all the way from Lee's Ferry to the Grand Wash Cliffs, according to Dock's records. Moulty had finally run the "Big Boy," as Norm liked to call the Colorado River in the Grand Canyon, and had seen firsthand how the cataract boats handled. He had also made some new river running friends. Indeed, Moulty's friendship with Dock Marston would strengthen and remain untarnished until Dock's death some thirty years later.

Group photo near Columbine Falls at trip's end. From left to right: Moulty Fulmer, Frank Wright, Rosalind Johnson, Howard "Cowboy" Welty, Nancy Streator, Norm Nevills, Frank "Fish Eyes" Masland, Wayne Hiser, Garth and Dock Marston, Lucile Hiser and "Little John" Doerr, August 1, 1948.
Courtesy Norm Nevills Collection, Marriott Library, University of Utah

8

Tragedy and Gasoline

1949-1950

Moulty was buried in work and family duties when he got home to Muncie after the 1948 Grand Canyon journey. Still, within five weeks he had all his 16mm movie film developed and had organized several bookings to show his films, including a short thirty-minute version and a longer, hour-long production, both titled *Grand Canyon Adventure*.

There was a lot of demand for Moulty's films. It was fun for him to talk about the river, and he was a good presenter. Besides his work at the Muncie YMCA, showing the films kept him busy and helped with the cash flow. In the late spring of 1949, Moulty wrote Norm that he had eight presentations booked "with no end in sight. Have a big show booked for early part of June at the College to be given before 2,000 or more people. They are making it well worth my time and effort." At least Moulty could cover his camera and film costs.

Travel plans for the summer of 1949 were settled as soon as Janice's vacation was approved. And travel they did. The couple drove from Muncie in early July 1949, to Glacier National Park, then north to visit the Canadian Rocky Mountains, and on west to the Pacific Coast. Their route then went south through Washington, Oregon, and California to land at Dock Marston's, where they spent an enjoyable afternoon. Next stop was Lake Mead, then on to the South Rim and back to Indiana. All told, the Fulmers drove just over 9,000 miles in twenty-nine days.

By summer's end, Moulty was getting the River Bug itch, and he wrote to Norm that he was playing with the idea of running the Yampa or Green rivers, and maybe even the San Juan in the summer of 1950. He did some work on the *Moja*, including adding a permanent compartment for gear storage under the boatman's seat. Another change to the *Moja* was the addition of a removable covering for "a good portion of the front part of the cockpit."

While the Fulmers were enjoying their travels during the summer of 1949, Pat Reilly headed back to Mexican Hat. It was his time to run the Grand with Norm. A new boatman working for Norm that year was a young man named Jim Rigg. A pilot also, the twenty-four-year-old Rigg had served in World War II in the Philippines and now worked as a flight instructor, aircraft mechanic, and operator of a charter airplane service out of Grand Junction, Colorado.

Pat rowed on two San Juan River trips with Norm, Jim, and Frank in late May and early June. As the river runners approached Lee's Ferry at the end of their second trip on June 12, Ed Hudson and Dock Marston were getting ready to depart from the Ferry in the *Esmeralda II* for what would be the first successful motorized down-run of the Grand Canyon. The two groups hailed each other, and Norm's group rowed over to inspect the motor boat.

The previous winter, Hudson had swapped out the *Esmeralda II* motor. Gone was the 75-HP unit, and in its place was a 125-HP Gray Marine Phantom Flathead Six. With Dock, Ed Hudson, his son Edward, Willie Taylor, and the same Bestor Robinson who had traveled with Moulty in 1948, the *Esmeralda II* was ready to attempt the down-run.

The *Esmeralda II* crew ready to launch at Lee's Ferry, June 12, 1949, on 57,900 cfs. From left to right: Dock Marston, Willie Taylor, Edward Hudson, his father Ed, and Bestor Robinson. Courtesy Edward Hudson

In the 1940s through the 1950s, the boat put-in at Lee's Ferry was roughly fifty yards upstream from where the present boat ramp is. River travelers arriving at Lee's Ferry from upriver would pass this put-in and run another mile downstream, through the Paria Riffle, taking out at a large beach on the right side of the river.

As the two river parties conversed, Norm graciously invited Dock to row Pat's San Juan punt through the Paria Riffle, then running at 57,900 cfs. Pat obliged, and rode on the punt's deck as Dock rowed the last mile to the take-out at the Paria beach. This brief first encounter between Pat Reilly and Dock Marston would be the start of an early friendship that would, unfortunately, fall apart later and descend into animosity.

Hudson picked up Dock and they were off downriver in the *Esmeralda II*. Only four days after leaving the Ferry, the Hudson crew pulled into the mouth of Havasu Canyon on a little over 70,000 cfs, with water backed all the way past the first waterfall.

The *Esmeralda II* cruise set a speed record at the time, with the party leaving Lee's Ferry June 12 and arriving at Pearce Ferry on June 17. The Colorado River peaked for the year June 22 at 119,000 cfs. This river trip was Dock's first do-it-yourself river trip in the Canyon. Dock and Willie would run the Canyon again in 1950 and 1951, and the two would be the first to boat the river for three consecutive years in a row without commercially guided motives in mind.

While Dock and Hudson motored off downriver to Pearce Ferry and the history books, Norm didn't miss a beat. He took Pat, Frank, and Jim to Green River, Wyoming, for a run through the Gates of Lodore and Split Mountain to Jensen, Utah, in his cataract boats. On completing that run on the Green River, the crew headed back to Lee's Ferry for a run through the Grand Canyon, launching July 12, 1949.

The July 1949 Nevills Expedition Grand Canyon river trip included four people from the 1948 trip. Norm, Frank Wright, and Frank "Fish Eyes" Masland would make the complete trip, while young Nancy Streator would start at Lee's Ferry and hike out at Phantom Ranch. The river flows at the start of the trip were roughly 43,000 cfs and at the end of this nineteen-day trip were close to 17,000 cfs. Everyone seemed to have fun on the Canyon cruise, which included the usual burning of driftwood.

Just a few days ahead of the Nevills trip, another oar-powered trip was underway. The party included Bert Loper, Harry Aleson, Howard "Cowboy" Welty who had run with Moulty in 1948, and five other men. Loper was a few weeks shy of his eightieth birthday, and had lived most of his life

The NPS congratulates the crew of the first motor boat to travel through the Grand Canyon. Top row left to right: Bestor Robinson, Willie Taylor, Edward Hudson; bottom row left to right: Otis Marston, unknown NPS official, Ed Hudson, Lake Mead, June 17, 1949. Courtesy Edward Hudson

Ed Hudson, Willie Taylor, and Bestor Robinson (standing), in Havasu Canyon, June 16, 1949. Courtesy Edward Hudson

along the rivers of the Southwest. He had worked as a miner and prospector along the banks of much of the Colorado River, and had run through the Grand Canyon just ten years earlier. He also had a serious heart condition. When Loper rowed his boat *Grand Canyon* into 24½ Mile Rapid, his passenger noticed Loper became unresponsive. The boat flipped and was later found by his trip mates and pulled high up away from the river to rest under a mesquite tree below the mouth of Buck Farm Canyon. The Nevills Expedition trip saw Loper's abandoned boat just days after Bert had died, and they pulled over to investigate the craft. From there, Norm, Pat, and the others went on to President Harding Rapid for camp.

That night, Norm mentioned to the group at dinner that they were going to "have a driftwood fire to end them all." Later, while the other boatmen were doing the dishes, Norm torched a gasoline cache Dock and Hudson had placed under some driftwood only four weeks earlier. Not knowing that Norm was burning Dock's fuel, Pat underlined in his log "Norm lit big driftwood fire." Hearing about the destruction of the fuel a year later, Dock speculated that Norm knew this "would mean the destruction of his security in his boats." Dock assumed the inferno was Norm's way of getting even with him "and his new boats which were destroying his cataract boats." If Dock's speculation was correct, it was the first spark of the decades-long and still ongoing controversy over the place of motorized watercraft in the Grand Canyon.

The group spent two days at Phantom Ranch, and exchanged passengers. Susie Reilly and Doris Nevills hiked in to spend the two days with their men at Phantom, and were dropped off at Pipe Creek for the hike up the Bright Angel Trail. The group ran Granite and Hermit rapids, and below Tuna Creek they waited while a few of the party hiked up to the B-24 crew's camp. Many of the river camps, such as Boucher and Havasu, were used as in previous years. The Havasu ledges were as miserably hot to camp on in 1949 as they had been the year before. The river party lined Lava Falls on the left, and camped for two nights at Diamond Creek where Pat and Jim Rigg were initiated into Norm's Royal Order of River Rats.

The term "river rat" as applied to fast-water participants didn't sit well with Dock, especially given that Dock thought river rats typically liked slow moving rivers. Dock noted "Canyoneer would be a good term to apply to those who have run in the Grand Canyon" and that the term "Grand Canyoneer would apply to those who have completed a traverse." Dock noted that Frederick Dellenbaugh had first used the term long before Dock showed up. Whether they were Grand Canyoneers or river rats, Dock counted Pat as the 109th and Jim the 110th to run the full length of the Grand Canyon.

It had "seemed" like a wonderful trip, but all was not quite right. Pat learned a few things that summer. One was not to upstage your boss. Pat's rowing style was a little more aggressive than Norm's. While the passengers may have enjoyed the runs Pat was taking, Norm was not pleased. Pat also knew the geology and history of the region better than Norm, and shared that with his fellow river travelers.

These differences between Norm and his boat crew, including Dock and Pat, meant that boatmen often changed favor with the boss. One season's golden boy would not be invited back the next year. Had Norm run in 1950 through the Grand Canyon, Pat would most likely not have been on the team. Dock had moved on to powerboats, jumping before he was shoved, and Pat was about to move in a completely different direction as well. Even Frank Wright had made up his mind that he would not be back for the 1950 Grand Canyon river trip.

After the 1949 summer river running season, Norm gave away three of his four cataract boats, and by September 14 had ordered sheets of plywood and new oars and oarlocks, intending to build all new oar boats. He wasn't the only one to start a build. In the fall of 1949, Moulty Fulmer, the quiet Hoosier, was thinking he would like to try his hand at rowing his own boat through the Grand Canyon. The 1947 San Juan trip had him convinced that the McKenzie hull design was the best style for a two- or three-person big-water boat. The 1948 Grand Canyon river trip had shown him that a wide beam added considerable stability to a boat in the Canyon's big water. The *Moja* was just not wide enough. He would build another boat.

Dock, on hearing that Moulty was considering building again with a wider beam, was encouraging. He wrote to Moulty that one of the good things Norm contributed to boat design was "the wide beam to his boats," and he encouraged Moulty to consider a "compartment amidships." The seed was planted, and while it grew, there were rivers to run.

Moulty added another boat to his collection in 1949: a military surplus, five-man, inflatable rubber raft ten feet long and five feet wide with five-foot oars. It would be good for "fun and thrills at opportune moments." Rubber boats first made their appearance in the Grand Canyon in 1938, when thirty-seven-year-old Amos Burg rowed the *Charlie* through the Grand Canyon on a two-boat trip with Haldane "Buzz" Holmstrom and Willis Johnson. Burg's inflatable boat *Charlie*, made by the Goodyear Tire and Rubber Company, was sixteen feet long and five-and-a-half feet wide.

Moulty wasn't the only one starting a new build. Soon after the 1949 Grand Canyon river trip, Pat started working on a boat design as well. One thing that had troubled Pat was the huge amount of water the Nevills Expedition boats held in the footwell. In a letter to Dock in January 1950, Pat noted "my basic design for my new type cataract boat is set and my expectations are high. I have borrowed features from several sources, some quite removed, and combined them as efficiently as I know how." A month later, Pat wrote to Dock with more specifics, noting his boat would be seventeen feet long and sixty-six inches wide. His design would move the gear from fore and aft compartments closer to the boat's middle with seats for two passengers as well as the boatman.

Sadly, Norm Nevills never got to build his boats. In a terrible twist of fate, he and his wife Doris were killed instantly on September 19, 1949. Only moments after takeoff from the dirt strip at Mexican Hat, his new Piper PA-12 Super Cruiser's engine quit and the plane crashed into a cliff-lined ravine. Of Doris and Norm's passing, Dock wrote to Moulty October 17, 1949, noting the "Nevills' death was tragic but it was sure to happen. Reliable sources report he neglected his plane as badly as he did his boat." Reliable sources or not, Dock had it right that Norm's death was indeed tragic.

The tradition of running cataract boats would continue for another two decades after Norm's death. However, by 1970 no more cataract-style boats were carrying passengers in the Grand Canyon. In 2006, a Grand Canyon river concessionaire began taking one along on a few commercial trips each year, otherwise very few if any cataract boats ply the waters of the Grand Canyon today.

After Norm's death, Frank Wright served as caretaker of the Nevills' estate, assisting Norm's mother as best he could. Jim Rigg was a frequent visitor, and with encouragement from Norm's mother, Frank and Jim submitted a bid for the estate. The bid was accepted and they formed Mexican Hat Expeditions. The material Norm had purchased in 1949 to build new cataract boats now belonged to Frank and Jim, and the Wright and Rigg families all pitched in to build three new cataract boats in the spring of 1950, just like the ones Norm had used. Frank and Jim sent out a mailing to all of Norm's river contacts, looking for passengers for a Grand Canyon run in 1950. Pat and Susie responded that they would like to join the trip from Phantom Ranch, downriver to Lake Mead.

Amos Burg in the rubber inflatable boat, *Charlie*.
Courtesy Oregon Historical Society, image bb008476

Moulty was making plans to go boating in 1950 as well. His plans included a possible run of the Yampa River in northwestern Colorado, a wonderful river winding through high sandstone-walled canyons that ends where it joins the Green River at Echo Park. The Green, a major tributary of the Colorado River, begins high in the Wind River Range of west central Wyoming. From there it runs south through the town of Green River, Wyoming, and then on through Lodore Canyon to Echo Park where it picks up the Yampa. The Green then flows west into Utah just before turning south again and carving its way through the aptly named Split Mountain. The Split Mountain portion of the Green is fast moving with a number of mid-sized rapids.

Moulty wrote to Dock, asking for information on the Yampa, which at the time had been run by less than a hundred river runners. Dock suggested he contact Dr. Russell Frazier, a physician working at the copper mining town of Copperton, Utah. Frazier had been on a low-water Grand Canyon river trip in 1934, and according to Dock was "very enthusiastic about the Yampa." Moulty wrote Frazier who replied in February, noting the Yampa "is one of the most beautiful river canyons in our west." Frazier also suggested "your boat should be decked over fore and aft" and have "watertight compartments."

With a tentative launch date of June 5 or 6, Moulty wanted to know if Dock was interested in coming along. The day after Moulty wrote Dock, Janice had her vacation request denied. Warner Gear had just received a contract to provide automatic transmissions to Ford Motor Company, and Warner was planning for a very busy summer. Janice told Moulty he should spend his vacation the way he wanted. What Moulty wanted was "to be on some river – being a river mouse!" Moulty now had extra room, so invited Dock again to join him, boat or no boat. "We can go down the river as long as the *Moja* lasts, then ride the rubber boat, then the air-mattresses, and if necessary finish the rest of the trip by swimming or walking."

While the *Moja* would work perfectly for the Yampa, Moulty still had his eye on rowing the Grand. In March 1950 he placed an order for plywood for his next boat, and by April he had started construction.

Dock wrote back he couldn't make the run with Moulty as a motor trip in the Grand Canyon was forming for a June 12 launch. Indeed, Ed Hudson wanted to attempt down-running the Canyon again. This time, there would be two boats, and Dock would drive a 158-HP Chris Craft Speedster named *Hudson*. Dock asked if Moulty fancied joining the Grand Canyon motor down-run. Moulty responded that he was not interested "in the motor run – but thanks for the information relative to it."

On May 16, twenty-seven-year-old John Lyons wrote to Dock asking if he could join in the Grand Canyon run. A herpetologist and school teacher from Las Vegas, New Mexico, Lyons was a combat swimming instructor in the military and had good outdoor field experience. Dock suggested Lyons might want to join Moulty for a run on the Yampa as Dock's Grand Canyon trip was full. Dock noted he would be joining Moulty after the Grand Canyon run. Lyons and Moulty made contact and the two launched at Lily Park on June 12. With the trusty *Moja*, the pair made a five-day run to Jensen, Utah, on a dropping water flow of around 6,700 cfs.

While Moulty and Lyons launched the *Moja* on the Yampa in Colorado, far downstream in Arizona Ed Hudson and Dock were launching the *Esmeralda II* and *Hudson* at Lee's Ferry the same day.

The trip would prove to be a most eventful one. The *Hudson*'s small "unbreakable" glass windshield shattered in the pounding it took in Badger Rapid on the first day. Marston was able to replace the windshield with a piece of 1 x 12-inch board from the Redwall Cavern Dam site construction crew's supply of scrap wood.

On the second night the river party stopped just above Palisades Canyon for the night, across from the mouth of Lava Chuar Canyon. Dock wanted to hike in Lava Chuar the next day, and chose the night's camp as it was in full view of the Desert Watchtower. The trip's rim party, including Dock's wife, Margaret, were supposed to be watching for an "all's ok" signal fire. The camp was a long bar of sand flanked on one side by the river and the other side by a thick stand of green looking catclaw, arrow-weed, and willow.

Ed and Dock lit a pile of driftwood on fire and shouted to the others that they had seen an acknowledgement of their signal fire from the Rim some seven miles distant and 4,000 feet above them. Unfortunately, all was NOT ok. A sudden wind picked up, fanning the fire to the vegetation beyond and sending a heavy shower of sparks onto the boats with their precious cargo of gasoline.

The crew scrambled to heave all their gear onto the boats and cast off, spending the next half hour standing by their boats, engines idling, ready to shove off into the river as the fire blazed bright. The fire seemed to die down, so the boats were tied back to shore, only to have the wind pick up yet again. The blaze sent the men retreating back to the water's edge for another thirty minutes, bowlines untied and boats ready to go out into the river. After repeating this fire drill yet a third time, the fire finally died down enough for the boats to be secured to shore and the exhausted crew to attempt some sleep.

The 1950 down-run crew stopped at the foot of Kwagunt Rapid in Grand Canyon. From left to right: Joe Desloge, Willie Taylor, Guy Forcier, and standing on the *Esmeralda II* is Ed Hudson, June 13, 1950. Courtesy Edward Hudson

Only, the typically cheerful Willie Taylor was having none of it, and it was his turn to blow up. He dressed Dock and Ed up one side and down the other, saying that he didn't care about himself or his gear that was now scattered in a mess, but he couldn't "stand to think of all the little animals being burned out of their homes." Both Dock and Ed handled the situation as best as they could, but Willie, like the fire, "didn't cool off until the next day."

Shortly after departure from Lee's Ferry, the *Esmeralda II* had begun to experience motor and clutch troubles, and eventually Ed Hudson abandoned the boat to the river on June 17, 1950, just below Tuna Creek near river mile 100. It was there that Dock nearly killed Willie.

Just below Hermit Rapid, the *Esmeralda II*'s motor gave out, with the engine misfiring and running very rough. One of Hudson's passengers suggested removing the cylinder head because it looked like the head gasket had blown. Hudson would not allow it, saying "it would ruin the machine." The *Esmeralda II* was fitted with oars and oarlocks for just such an event, but the heavy boat required one person on each oar to maneuver it. Hudson turned off the struggling engine, and the crew started to row the *Esmeralda II* downriver. The party soon stopped to camp for the night.

After much discussion, the next day they decided to again attempt to row the *Esmeralda II* on the river. Dock motored nearby in the *Hudson*.

Just below Tuna Rapid, the river makes a bend to the left. As the crippled boat ran through the bend, it was captured by a powerful eddy along the right shore. At one point, the craft heeled way over on its side, pitching Willie Taylor into the river. As Willie was washed downriver, the rest of the crew worked frantically to get the *Esmeralda II* tied to shore.

Dock, seeing Willie in the water, gave chase in his Chris Craft. A passenger threw Willie a rope, and it looked like Willie had caught it. Dock swung his boat around and began powering back upriver. This sent Willie right under the water's surface. One of Dock's passengers now tapped him on the shoulder, pointing out the rope going into the water with no sign of Willie. Dock throttled back and Willie surfaced with the rope wrapped around his neck. Willie eventually made it to the deck of the *Hudson*, but had black and blue marks around his neck for days afterwards. Still, he made light of his near drowning for the rest of the trip. Willie's good-natured humor and appreciation of the Canyon were a few of the reasons Dock invited him back to run the Grand Canyon year after year.

Meanwhile, Hudson was convinced the *Esmeralda II* was sinking with a crippled engine, burnt out clutch, destroyed propeller and bashed rudder. On hearing of this, Dock assumed the repair of the boat was too much to consider. Removing some personal gear, Hudson and his passengers abandoned the boat to float away and sink. Coincidentally, Hudson set the *Esmeralda II* adrift at about the same spot the two B-24 airmen, Goldblum and Cruickshank, had met up with Embanks on their ill-fated attempt to hike along the bank of the Colorado six years earlier. The bend in the river at Lower Tuna Rapid is still known as Willie's Necktie today, though Dock also humorously called it Esmeralda Elbow.

Dock took the *Esmeralda II* passengers straight across the river in his now-overloaded Chris Craft, to a large beach known today as Lower Tuna Camp. After much discussion, it was decided to leave Ed and Edward Hudson where they were, with some food and water. Their plan was to take the *Hudson* to Havasu Canyon where one member of the party would hike out and arrange a helicopter rescue for the Hudsons. After saying their goodbyes, Dock and his four passengers motored thirty-four miles downriver to the mouth of Tapeats Creek. While cooking dinner, the river runners were surprised to hear the *whop whop whop* of a helicopter, which came out of nowhere and landed on the beach. The group was joined by Dock's wife, Margaret, who had chartered a small helicopter and flown in to check on everyone. Marston immediately notified the pilot that Hudson and his son were back upriver in need of rescue.

Later the next day, two helicopters flew in to rescue the father and son, the first helicopter rescue of a river party ever attempted. Unfortunately, the helicopter carrying the elder Hudson malfunctioned and made a hard landing on the Tonto Plateau. Hudson had to stay overnight with the wreck, and was helicoptered out the next day, as Dock and his crew went on to complete the second successful motor run of the Canyon in his Chris Craft. The abandoned *Esmeralda II* did anything but sink. It floated empty down the river on 54,000 cfs for twenty-three miles and went aground in a shallow eddy.

Immediately after completing the Grand Canyon run, Dock and Margaret drove to Lily Park, Colorado, to join Moulty for his second run on the Yampa in as many weeks. The trio launched there on June 26, 1950, on about 3,900 cfs. They made the run in four days while the river dropped about 1,000 cfs. Dock rowed the *Moja* through a number of rapids, including Big Joe and Moonshine, while Moulty filmed from shore. The group stopped at Signature Cave near Harding Hole, visited the Mantle Ranch and explored a nearby cave, and then stopped at Echo Park. By all accounts the Yampa runs went very well, and the Marstons and Moulty, now among the first 100 people to travel the Yampa, greatly enjoyed each other's company.

Almost a month later during this busy summer of river running, Susie and Pat Reilly hiked into Phantom Ranch on July 17, 1950, where they joined the Wright-Rigg river party for the run to Pearce Ferry. Jim's little brother, Bob, was on this trip, making his first transit through the Grand Canyon rowing a boat. Bob was nineteen, and just starting college. When Pat came in at Phantom, Jim and Frank gave Pat a boat to row. It was Bob's boat! Having an extra boatman along just increased the trip's safety factor. If Bob was upset about turning his boat over to Pat, he didn't show it. None of them knew that in just a few short days, Bob would take over his brother's boat, and Jim would be running a very different craft.

Boating on about 19,000 cfs, the Wright-Rigg party was three days below Phantom Ranch when they came upon an unusual sight just above Forster Rapid. It was the *Esmeralda II*. She was sitting in a pile of small boulders, right side up, as if dry-docked for the season. The group salvaged several packets of cigarettes, chewing gum, and tennis shoes from the beached boat. Both Jim and Frank had substantial mechanical skills, and just for fun started messing around with the engine. To their surprise, with a cough and a cloud of smoke, it started. While the motor sounded rough, it would run.

The 1950 Wright-Riggs river party inspects the *Esmeralda II* above Forster Rapid, July 21, 1950. Courtesy Edward Hudson. This image also found in the Plez Talmadge Reilly Collection, Cline Library, Northern Arizona University

While Hudson had assumed the rudder and propeller were damaged, the Wright-Rigg crew could easily see there was no problem with the prop or steering mechanism. The river runners used driftwood logs as rollers under the boat and rolled her seventy feet down the beach and back into the Colorado. It was hot, hard work in the noon-day sun, but the job was done in two hours.

A little caulking and a patch on the boat's side were applied after the boat was in the water. Once afloat, the boat was limped to camp below the mouth of Tapeats Creek.

The Wright-Rigg party pulls the *Esmeralda II* back to the river, above Forster Rapid, July 21, 1950. Courtesy Edward Hudson. This image also found in the Plez Talmadge Reilly Collection, Cline Library, Northern Arizona University

The *Esmeralda II* had a few more items on board, including a good set of tools and a map of where fuel was stashed along the river. Frank made it clear to Jim and Bob at camp that either the motor boat would run well or they would leave it right where it was. The *Esmeralda II* then received some much-needed mechanical repairs. Using his expert mechanical skills, Frank made a small insert to the cylinder head gasket between the fifth and sixth cylinders. Other repairs included unclogging the fuel line and adjusting the clutch. With the boat and motor now in much better working order, the next day a number of the Wright-Rigg party rode in the *Esmeralda II*, leaving only two people in each oar boat. Pat took the opportunity to have Susie row while he coached her.

The first time a motor boat is parked next to oar boats in the Grand Canyon, above Forster Rapid, July 21, 1950. Courtesy Edward Hudson. This image also found in the Plez Talmadge Reilly Collection, Cline Library, Northern Arizona University

After a day of traveling on the *Esmeralda II*, the river runners all abandoned Jim Rigg to run the motor boat by himself and went back to their oar boats. Susie noted in her journal "they prefer the cataract boats for their thrills, so they are coming back to their regular places." It was a good thing Hudson had rigged the *Esmeralda II* to be operated with oars in the event of mechanical failure. The boat ran out of gas and the group ended up rowing it below Havasu Canyon until they reached a fuel cache above Tuckup Canyon.

At Lava Falls, the river party got into a heated argument over whether to line or run the rapid. In the 1950s, Lava had two large holes on the right side, one at the top of the rapid and one at its foot. A center left run could bypass both holes. Pat Reilly and Jim Rigg argued for a run, while Frank Wright and Bob Rigg spoke in favor of lining. In the end, the oar boats were lined down the left shore, and then Jim drove the *Esmeralda II* through the rapid.

When the party arrived at 217 Mile Rapid they found Hudson's next stash of fuel, and rightly figured they had enough fuel to motor the "Esmeraldy" all the way to Boulder Landing on Lake Mead. The party used the motor boat to tow their cataract boats across the slack water of Mead.

A tussle over who now owned the *Esmeralda II* ensued between Hudson and the elder Rigg. Hudson had given the park the boat trailer and the possessory rights should the motor boat ever make it out of the Canyon. Since the boat had indeed made it out it was neither man's boat anymore. The *Esmeralda II* is now in the fleet of historic watercraft at the South Rim, Grand Canyon National Park. In late May 1955, Hudson would motor

Susie Reilly on the oars in the Grand Canyon, 1950. Courtesy Marston Collection, reproduced by permission, the Huntington Library, San Marino, California. This image also found in the Plez Talmadge Reilly Collection, Cline Library, Northern Arizona University

another boat from Glenwood Springs, Colorado, through Westwater and Cataract canyons, and on to Lee's Ferry. Hudson piloted the sixteen-foot-long 65-HP inboard named *Finally* for the run, and became the first person to travel the entire Colorado River from Glenwood Springs to the Sea of Cortez under motor power.

At the end of such a busy boating season, Moulty returned to working on his next boat. The beam would be just over six feet at the oarlocks with a little more rocker than the *Moja*. The cockpit was two feet wide, with storage either side of that. This configuration had "practically all storage in the mid section." Dock was encouraging, writing to Moulty, "In my opinion you are building the best of the Colorado River boats at this time."

The river called sooner than anyone might have thought, interrupting Moulty's boat building yet again. Turkey Run State Park near Marshall, Indiana, is a steep-walled sandstone canyon cradling the clear waters of Sugar Creek. Lush emerald vegetation and large maple trees cover the canyon's steep walls. In mid-October, Moulty happened to be at the park standing by a steep bank above the creek. Suddenly, twelve-year-old Larry Curtis tumbled down a rocky slope and into a deep pool of cold river water. Moulty had no way of knowing Curtis couldn't swim. He instinctively dove right into the river, grabbed the boy, and swam him back to shore. Moulty later wrote to Dock that the water felt as cold as Tapeats Creek and that the old woolen army clothes he was wearing at the time kept him wet for many hours afterwards.

On hearing the news, the townsfolk in Muncie were not that impressed. After all, having taught 12,000 kids how to swim during his career, Moulty was always pulling their spluttering kids out of the pool at the Muncie Y. Still, in mid-November Moulty received a special certificate of honor from the National YMCA Aquatic Committee for rescuing Curtis. Throughout the winter Moulty continued to slowly work on his next build, and would soon finish his gem.

9

More Practice and the *Gem*

1951-1952

In the spring of 1951, Moulty and Dock communicated about a possible run on the Green River, traveling from Split Mountain as far south as Green River, Utah. The trip planning included fifty-one-year-old Adrian Reynolds, who Dock had first met on a Nevills Expedition trip at Green River, Wyoming, in 1947. Reynolds in turn, had met Norm in Green River, Wyoming, in 1940 while serving as a writer for the local newspaper. Reynolds, with his son Adrian Kenneth, or "A.K." for short, had built two cataract-style boats after seeing Norm's craft at Green River on the 1940 trip. Dock wrote to Adrian and Moulty that before he would join the river party for the Green River run, he was going to try another motorboat run through the Grand Canyon.

Dock called this trip the Marston Grand Canyon Motorcade. The trip launched from Lee's Ferry, Arizona, on June 8, 1951, and consisted of five motorboats. Three of the boats were inboard Chris Crafts, including the *Boo*, the same boat Dock had taken through the Canyon the year before when it was named the *Hudson*. Two of the five motorboats were each powered by an Evinrude outboard motor, the first such mode of transport to travel through the Canyon. Willie Taylor, Joe Desloge, and Guy Forcier accompanied Dock on this trip as they had the year before. At the end of the trip, Dock counted Lake Mead powerboat captain Jimmy Jordan as the 122nd person to traverse the Canyon and the first to pilot an outboard motorboat, the *June Bug*, through Grand Canyon. The second of the two outboards, named the *Twin*, was piloted by Bureau of Reclamation employee Rod Sanderson, the 124th person to traverse the Canyon.

After the successful completion of the motorcade trip, Dock, his wife, Margaret, and one of the Marston's twin daughters, twenty-three-year-old Maradel, headed to Utah for the Green River trip. Also joining the trip was Adrian Reynolds' wife, Helen, and twenty-two-year-old A.K. The group met at Ouray, Utah, in the middle of the hot barren Uinta Basin, and launched on June 28 on about 16,000 cfs. Moulty brought the *Moja* and the Reynolds brought their two cataract boats, the *Lodore* and the *Galloway*.

Maradel Marston stands on Moulty Fulmer's shoulders at Three Fords camp on the Green River, July 1951. Courtesy Marston Collection, reproduced by permission, the Huntington Library, San Marino, California

In 1951, this stretch of the Green had copious quantities of mosquitoes, as it still does today. At camp the first night, A.K., Dock, and Moulty imagined they could beat the mosquitoes by sleeping on a ridge about 100 feet above camp. The trio figured "any slight wind would blow the creatures away." As it turned out, the mosquitoes blew the river runners away, and after a sleepless night they named their ridge camp "Purgatory Hill." A high wind buffeted the river runners the afternoon of the second day, whipping spray up off the river and driving it up the river bank for sixty to seventy feet. After the wind died down, the ever-present mosquitoes were back and enjoyed having the river runners for dinner that night.

On day three, the party entered Desolation Canyon proper, leaving the open Uinta Basin behind. The fast-moving water of the tight canyon greatly decreased the mosquito population, and Moulty enjoyed his first good night's sleep. The rest of the run through Desolation and Gray canyons was uneventful, except for the good humor provided by A.K., Maradel, and Moulty.

The group ignited some firecrackers during breakfast on July 4, and later that day ran the low-head Tusher Wash Diversion Dam before traveling downriver to the take-out at the highway bridge at Green River, Utah. Even the mosquitoes did not keep the congenial party from making new friends all around.

Moulty then headed straight back to Muncie, driving through the great 1951 Kansas and Missouri floods. At one point he had to divert 100 miles around a flooded bridge in Missouri. Fellow highway travelers noted Moulty was smart to trailer his own boat.

As Moulty arrived back home in Indiana, Pat and Susie Reilly were just leaving their house in California for another commercial trip with Frank and the Rigg brothers. They drove to Lee's Ferry and launched on the traditional Nevills Expedition put-in day of July 12. Jim and Bob Rigg were making their second run through the Grand Canyon by boat for the year, the first time anyone would ever complete two runs in the same year. This happened to be the second record the two brothers had broken that summer.

A month earlier, Jim and Bob had rowed the sadiron boat *Norm* through the Canyon in a record-breaking three days. They launched on Saturday, June 9, rowed right past Dock's motorcade, and 52 hours and 41 minutes later arrived at Pearce Ferry. Boating on 43,100 cfs, the pair broke the speed record set only two years earlier in the *Esmeralda II*. The Riggs'

Moulty Fulmer shaves sitting on the *Moja* while Maradel Marston adds humorous commentary, Desolation and Gray canyons, 1951.
Courtesy Fulmer Collection, reproduced by permission,
Utah State Historical Society, all rights reserved

record time still stands for two men in a wooden oar-boat. For sheer speed, their record remained unbroken for thirty-two years. Finally, in 1983, Kenton Grua, Rudi Petschek, and Steve Reynolds broke the Riggs' record. The trio rowed a dory through the Canyon on 72,000 cfs in just under 37 hours, a speed record that still stands today.

After breaking the speed record in June, Jim and Bob were back in July for a more relaxed cruise. Also on the trip was the school teacher, Ruth Pieroth, whom Pat and Susie had met on the 1947 San Juan trip, and forty-one-year-old Tad Nichols, who had been on a Mexican Hat Expeditions San Juan trip with Jim and Frank the year before. Edward Tatnall "Tad" Nichols was a photographer who had studied with world-renowned Ansel Adams and Brett Weston. The 1950 San Juan run through Glen Canyon to Lee's Ferry would be the first of more than thirty runs through Glen Canyon Tad would take before this magical place was inundated with water behind the cold concrete of Glen Canyon Dam. Tad's *Glen Canyon, Images of a Lost World*, published in 1999, haunts river runners to this day with stunning photographs of what is buried under the waters of the reservoir called Lake Powell. Nichols would run from Lee's Ferry to Phantom Ranch on this 1951 river trip, as would Ruth, Susie, and Pat. The river, unusually free of silt and with a faint greenish tinge, would slowly drop during their run from about 21,000 to 17,000 cfs.

In those days, boaters wore life jackets when running rapids, but typically, not on smooth-water sections of the river. On the morning of July 13 when pulling out of camp at 12.5 Mile, Jean Wyckoff fell over the side of the cataract boat *Sandra*. Frank was at the oars, and it happened fast. The boat hit the eddy fence where the upstream eddy current joins the main downstream river flow. The sadiron momentarily rocked up on its side. Caught off balance Jean plunged into the river. Fortunately, she remained calm while being rolled over and over in the turbulent waters. When she finally surfaced and inhaled a much-needed breath of air, the rest of the river party heaved a collective sigh of relief and pulled Jean from the water, wet, but otherwise, unhurt.

Maradel Marston and Moulty Fulmer run the Tusher Wash Diversion Dam on the Green River in the *Moja* on about 14,600 cfs, July 4, 1951. Courtesy Marston Collection, reproduced by permission, the Huntington Library, San Marino, California

Ready to depart from the Paria beach, July 12, 1951. Back row left to right: Pat Reilly, Bob Rigg, Tad Nichols, Jim Rigg. Front row left to right: Paul Wright, Esther Renthrop, Helen Wright, Susie Reilly, Naomi Heale, Ruth Pieroth, and Jean Wyckoff. Courtesy Bevan and Elaine Wright

This group, like others before them, would continue the tradition of trying to ignite large piles of driftwood on fire with only one match. Susie and Ruth joined the DWB club as blazing piles of wood were left behind to burn themselves out. The group camped at President Harding Rapid, where they discovered the freshly dug grave of fifteen-year-old David Quigley who had drowned in Glen Canyon that June. Another river party only days ahead of the Wright-Rigg trip, led by Don Harris and Jack Brennan, had found the body in the drift at Harding and had buried the boy.

The river runners camped at Tanner their last night above Phantom Ranch. Susie was inducted into the Royal Order of Colorado River Rats, with congratulations from Frank Wright, the Riggs, and a long kiss from Pat. She was thrilled to finally be a Colorado River Rat, or as Dock would say, a Grand Canyoneer. Dock would count Susie as the 126rd person to travel all the way through the Grand Canyon. Susie, Pat, and four others rode mules up the Kaibab Trail on Wednesday, July 18, 1951.

The *Sandra* at Cliff Dwellers, Arizona, 1951. Courtesy Dick Griffith

The party had no way of knowing that on July 1, 1951, a do-it-yourself party of three people in two, ten-man rubber rafts had departed Green River, Wyoming, and were just now entering Desolation Canyon. The three river runners were newlyweds Dick and Isabelle Griffith, along with Johnny Schlump. They were headed to Lake Mead.

In 1948, Dick Griffith, like Moulty and Janice the year before, had run from Shiprock, New Mexico, to Lee's Ferry. The twenty-one-year-old had built a small San Juan punt called the *Padre* for his 1948 run. In 1949, he met the striking Isabelle Galo. Joined by another friend, the three attempted a run through Lodore Canyon. The *Padre* was lost in Disaster Falls, but Dick took their remaining rubber raft on to Lee's Ferry. At Aztec Creek, Dick met Norm, who on looking at the ten-man rubber boat Dick was rowing, pronounced there was no future in river running for inflatable rubber boats. That didn't stop Dick from trying.

Dick Griffith's boat *Padre* on the banks of the San Juan River at Shiprock, New Mexico, 1948. Shiprock dominates the center of the photo. Courtesy Dick Griffith

Dick Griffith in his rubber raft, *Queen*, running Lava Falls on approximately 10,000 cfs, August 31, 1951. Courtesy Dick Griffith

From left to right: Johnny Schlump, Isabelle and Dick Griffith
at Lake Mead, September 7, 1951. Courtesy Dick Griffith

Dick and Isabelle, ten years his senior, were married in 1950. Joined by thirty-four-year-old Johnny Schlump the next year, the threesome launched in rubber rafts from Green River, Wyoming. This time, they ran Lodore Canyon, past Echo Park, on through Split Mountain, and kept right on going. They had to race clouds of mosquitoes through the Uinta Basin, and then headed on through Desolation and Gray canyons. After resupplying in Green River, Utah, they ran the canyons of Labyrinth, Stillwater, and Cataract.

Resupplying at Hite and Lee's Ferry, they continued through the Grand Canyon. The trio were holed up just above Upset Rapid for a few days as a large monsoon storm rolled in. When Dick, Isabelle, and Johnny arrived at Lava Falls on August 31, 1951, they intended to line their rafts along the left shore. After lining Johnny's raft down to the foot of the rapid, Dick got in his ten-man rubber raft called *Queen* and ran the rapid.

Dick is credited with rowing the first rubber raft through Lava Falls. The trio successfully completed their run to Hemenway Harbor on Lake Mead, arriving September 6, 1951, in all travelling 1,200 river miles that summer.

After the end of the 1951 river season, Moulty went to work boatbuilding in a big way. The design of his new boat was finally settled as he attempted to make a simple double-ender, like the *Moja*. What he had not figured in his planning was that plywood does have a breaking point. By increasing the floor width to sixty-four inches with a rocker of thirteen and a half inches and a bow-to-stern length of fifteen feet, the plywood side panels would not bend from one end of the boat to the other.

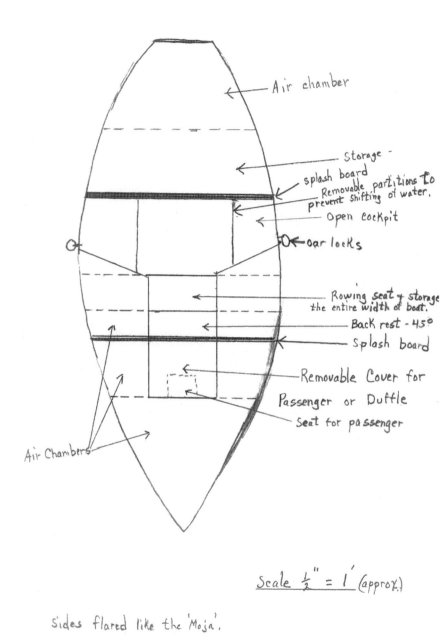

Air chamber

Storage

splash board
Removable partitions to
prevent shifting of water.

Open cockpit

oar locks

Rowing seat + storage
the entire width of boat.

Back rest - 45°

Splash board

Removable Cover for
Passenger or Duffle

Seat for passenger

Air Chambers

Scale ½" = 1′ (approx.)

Sides flared like the 'Moja'.

Drawing of the new boat Moulty sent to Dock March 10, 1952, Marston collection

As he attempted to bend them around, the sound of splintering plywood became alarming. Moulty held the plywood in as much of a curve as he dared and made a small transom, sixteen inches high by twenty inches at the bottom and twenty-one inches at the top. The McKenzie River double-ender he was trying to make suddenly became a double-ender with a transom. While Moulty's transom was a simple way to finish off the end of the boat, the Pacific boat designers and builders like Kaarhus and Hindman had already worked out various transom designs, either to hang a motor to or allow two passengers to sit comfortably side by side.

The sides and bottom of Moulty's new boat were made of ⅜-inch marine plywood. The floor was made by attaching two 4 x 16-foot sheets of plywood together along their long edge with a sixteen-foot-long 1 x 6 oak board. The bottom of this floor was then covered with full-length bow-to-stern strips of four-inch by ⅜-inch oak striping, set ¾-inch apart. This essentially made a ¾-inch-thick floor. It was the strength of this floor that would save the boat through the long test of time it would eventually endure. The boat would be heavy, but rocks would present little trouble to a floor like this.

Holding all this plywood together was a series of five ¾-inch-thick bulkheads, plus the ¾-inch-thick transom. The main dry storage area was accessed from the boatman's footwell area through a vertical hatch in the stern bulkhead. The chine was strengthened with pieces of 1¼-inch-thick square oak stock running from bulkhead to bulkhead. This same oak stock ran the width of the boat next to one side of every bulkhead. Moulty used cadmium-plated wood screws he obtained from his nephew Burton. After experimenting with various wood glues, Moulty decided to forgo glue entirely, and he troweled caulking compound onto all the joints with a putty knife and screwed the pieces together.

With the basic shell of a McKenzie River double-ender with a transom complete, the next thing to do was to deck the boat and finish off the footwell. Moulty thought he would deck over the entire boat except for a small area where the boatman could sit, and incorporate a transverse splash board across the stern like he had done with the *Moja*. He also thought that some sort of baffles in the large footwell should be incorporated to help stabilize it when swamped. Behind the rower Moulty added a footwell and seat for a passenger. This area also had a lid, so if additional storage was needed, the passenger could sit on top of the cover with gear stowed in the seating area below.

Dock was pleased with the overall design but suggested Moulty give consideration to a self-bailing cockpit and include a V-shaped splash board across the deck. Dock was also concerned that all the decking might impede the swing of the oars. Moulty knew things weren't quite right, and wrote to Dock that there were still "a lot of problems dealing with oarlocks, compartments, etc. that require a lot of thought from me. Slow work!!"

Dock wrote back in late November 1951, explaining how the self-bailing, hard-hulled motor boats had a floor just higher than the water line. The boatman sat higher in the air, thus raising the boat's center of gravity, but the craft's cockpit shed water without the need to bail. Most critically, Dock proposed sloping "the entire seat…so it would drain out either side of the boat." He also suggested that both "the seat and any other space in the center of the boat should be used for the stowage of heavy material which would give much better action of the boat." Finally, Dock suggested that water draining out of the footwell through the side of the boat could be controlled by a small hood over the opening. This would prove to be a pivotal letter. Dock wrote again in December, continuing to champion the merits of a V-shaped splash guard.

In February, Moulty almost died from a severe case of hepatitis. By March, he had recovered enough to send a rough plan view of the boat to Dock. Eight days later, Dock replied "you are pushing toward a marked improvement over that in common use." Dock also noted that keeping the flare of the *Moja* was a good idea in that the "boats used on the Rogue use this as do many of those on the Salmon."

Meanwhile Moulty was impatiently waiting for oarlocks to be made at a local machine shop. He purchased a new twelve-foot-long rubber boat he and Janice named the *Sausage*, pronounced 'Saw-sage', and the plan was to take both the *Moja* and the *Sausage* to the San Juan that summer, around June 5.

By mid-April, the new boat had oar blocks in place, with oarlocks and oars. While not completely finished and missing final painting, the hull was ready to be launched. It wouldn't be on the White in Muncie, which was running very low. Moulty ended up trailering the boat over to his sister Thelma's in Fort Wayne, Indiana. The St. Joseph and St. Mary's rivers joined in downtown Fort Wayne to form the Maumee River, and there would be plenty of water in the Maumee. Moulty wrote Dock, "Hope it will float!!!"

On May 11, 1952, Moulty put his new boat on the water for the first time in downtown Fort Wayne. Passengers along for the ride were Moulty's niece and nephew, Priscilla and Burton. Moulty was very happy to see how easily the boat pivoted. The new boat had a name, too. It would be named for Moulty's step-father, George, and mother, Emma, and simply be called the *Gem*.

Moulty sent a few photos of the *Gem* in the water to Dock, who was impressed enough to write straight back. Dock noted "I think you have worked out some of the factors for a much better heavy water design. I believe your new lines will give much better action."

Dock had also been corresponding with Pat Reilly for over a year. Their correspondence, usually two to three single-spaced typed pages per letter, covered a wide array of river running activities. In May 1952, besides writing to Moulty, Dock wrote to Pat about a fellow named Moulty Fulmer, "who says he is putting his new boat into the water this week." Dock went on to note one of the features of Moulty's boat "is to have his openings into his compartments by way of the bulkheads." While Pat's hatch openings would all be horizontal, Dock had introduced Pat to the fact that Moulty was building a new boat for the Grand, and "Since you are interested in boat design, Moulty is a good one to follow."

The summer of 1952 saw Moulty headed out for the San Juan in late May with Louis Nelson, a sixty-four-year-old friend of the Fulmers who also lived in Muncie. The two brought the *Moja* for the run as the *Gem* was not yet finished. They launched at Bluff, Utah, on June 4, 1952, with the San Juan running 11,700 cfs. The next day, they could not have helped but notice the rise in the river's flow to 20,400 cfs, the river's peak flow

The *Gem* on the Maumee River in Fort Wayne, Indiana. Moulty
Fulmer at the oars with niece Priss Ratican and nephew Burton
Woodroof, May 11, 1952. Courtesy Fulmer Collection, reproduced
by permission,

for the year. The rapids between Bluff and Mexican Hat were all washed out by the high water. What Moulty and Louis did encounter were some large sand waves. Fortunately, the *Moja* handled them with ease. The two men stopped at River House Ruin and explored a few other ruins before reaching Mexican Hat. Once past the Hat, the rapids at Johns Canyon, Government, Slickhorn, Syncline and 13-Foot were all rough and powerful as the flow held fairly constant at around 18,000 cfs.

One lesson river runners may learn early in their river education is that when floating sideways to the current, they shouldn't dip the downstream oar too deep into the water. The reason is simple. The downstream oar blade may hit something. It could be the bed of the river or a submerged boulder. When this happens, the oar comes to an abrupt stop, while the boat keeps moving downstream. The now stationary oar either slides through the oarlock at an alarmingly high rate of speed, or is drawn rapidly under the boat.

Louis was rowing the first day just below Bluff, floating sideways in the current and sure enough, the downstream oar caught on something underwater. In the 1940s and 1950s, oarlocks were not open like those used on western rivers today. The *Moja*'s oarlocks were solid circular cast iron rings with a metal stem going down into the oar block. As the oar shot out of Louis's hand, the oar became trapped and bound hard in the oarlock ring. There was a quick snap of splintering wood as the oar block tore off the side of the *Moja*. After all, Moulty was running Smoker oars. The oar, with oarlock and oar block still attached, was fished out of the river and the *Moja* limped to shore. In less than an hour the oar block was reattached to the boat using a piece of dimensional driftwood that just happened to be at hand.

13-Foot Rapid, now submerged under the waters of Lake Powell, was where the next boat damage happened. Moulty was at the oars at the top of the rapid, making a left to right move away from shore, when the downstream chine of the *Moja* struck a submerged rock and put a hole in the chine. The footwell began to fill with water as Moulty ran the rapid, and on reaching a sandy beach at the foot of the rapid, eight inches of water was sloshing around in the bottom of the boat. A five-hour stop ensued while watertight repairs were made to the *Moja*'s side, bottom, and chine.

Moulty and Louis arrived at the confluence of the San Juan and the Colorado in Glen Canyon on the year's peak runoff of 123,000 cfs. It was a quick trip to Lee's Ferry, where the pair arrived on June 13, 1952. It had been another great trip and the *Moja* had again proved its merits.

While Moulty was on the San Juan, he just missed Pat by a few weeks. A boatman for the Wright-Riggs team on one San Juan run in 1952, Pat was on the last run he would make for Mexican Hat Expeditions. Pat was not invited on the 1952 run of the Grand Canyon, which staged at Lee's Ferry on July 11, for a departure the next day. The Rigg brothers had taken two Chris Crafts through the Canyon in May of that year, and Jim brought one of the motor boats along for the July cruise.

As the party put their trip together at Lee's Ferry, another one-boat two-person party was doing the same. It was Georgie White and Elgin Pierce on a do-it-yourself trip. This would be Georgie's first complete run through the Canyon, and the first time a woman would row a boat through Grand Canyon. While the two trips would mostly run separately, Georgie and Elgin waited at Lava Falls in their oar-powered ten-man neoprene raft for the other party to arrive. The two groups lined the rapid together, sharing the work. Hiking in to join the Mexican Hat Expeditions trip at Lava Falls was a young reporter named Martin Litton. Litton hitched a ride with the Mexican Hat trip the eight miles downstream to Whitmore Wash and hiked back out of the Canyon.

While Martin Litton and Pat Reilly would become friends in the years to come, not being invited to row a boat on the Mexican Hat Expeditions Grand Canyon run may have forced Pat to consider why he wanted to be in the Canyon. It could be that he realized he wanted to explore and share the Canyon with friends. There was a big difference between a river trip of shared camaraderie and exploration by companions, and being a boatman working for someone else. Pat was about to learn the hard way that even on trips where there *is* shared camaraderie and exploration, key components needed to be sorted out ahead of time to make such a journey successful.

Meanwhile, Moulty was putting finishing touches on his new boat. In the winter of 1952-1953, Moulty put a V-shaped splash board on the stern deck of the *Gem*. Moulty wrote Dock he would like to run the Grand "if I can get lined up with a party going through." He was also flirting "with the idea of running it solo." Moulty was sure the river fever would get the best of him and he would be on a river somewhere even "if I have only lizards and mosquitoes for company."

10

A Hell of a Good Time

1953

1953 was not a good river year for Moulty Fulmer. In late March, Moulty's mother had a stroke, then a second one in the latter part of May. Emma passed away three days later. Then quite unexpectedly, Janice's brother had a heart attack and died in early July. Moulty wrote to Dock that "Perhaps I can tie up with someone for a run through the Grand Canyon in 1954."

For Pat and Susie Reilly, it was a different story. In the spring of 1953, Pat corresponded with A.K. Reynolds, and the two agreed to try their hands at rowing the Grand Canyon just for fun. Pat thought he would be the trip leader and take care of the food pack, while A.K. thought he would be the trip leader as the group would use the three cataract boats named *Galloway*, *Lodore* and *Ashley* that Reynolds and his friend Lug Larsen owned. By this time A.K. was leading river trips through Lodore Canyon on the Green River downstream of Green River, Wyoming, where the food was good and the trips easy paced. Pat Reilly wasn't known for his fine cooking or his late starts out of camp.

Making up the river party on the Grand would be Pat and Susie, A.K. and his twenty-seven-year-old bride Ellen, and Willis "Cappy" Rowe, who was seventy-six years old. Cappy had just had intestinal surgery a few weeks prior to the trip's launch. An amazing individual in his own right, Cappy had served in the Spanish American War in the Philippines, and as a young lad of only eleven had sailed alone at night from the Los Angeles coast to Santa Catalina Island in a small canvas boat. He had served as president of the Los Angeles Adventurers Club, of which Pat was a member. Besides all that, Cappy had visited the inner gorge of Grand Canyon, hiking in from the rim in 1896.

Gerald "Lug" Larsen would be rowing one of the boats. Lug had met A.K. in Green River, Wyoming, when the two were children. In World War II, Lug had served in the South Pacific on a mine sweeper, and in 1950, he started rowing as a guide for A.K.'s river guiding company, Reynolds Canyon Expeditions. The trip's "photographer" was A.K.'s brother, George Reynolds, recently returned from the Korean War. Also on the trip were Pasadena school teacher, Ruth Pieroth, and Paul Terry.

Pat had become friends with Paul Terry at Lockheed when they were both jig builders in the early 1940s. Paul and his wife, Helen, had joined Pat on his last run of the San Juan working for Frank Wright and Jim Rigg in 1952. When Helen died unexpectedly of lung cancer shortly after that river trip, Pat invited Paul to accompany him through the Grand Canyon in 1953. Paul began developing film as a hobby in the 1940s, and after he retired from Lockheed he operated a film developing studio in Sun City, Arizona. Paul would do almost all of Pat's dark room work in later years. Of the nine people on this river trip, the only members with prior Grand Canyon experience were Pat, Susie, and Ruth.

Pat and Susie did the food shopping from a menu of Pat's creation. Breakfasts always consisted of grapefruit with either pancakes with syrup, sausage, and coffee, or Spam, milk with cereal, and coffee. River lunch consisted of Kool Aid, peanut butter and jelly with bread and pickles, sometimes with canned tuna, corned beef, Vienna sausages, and possibly some cheese. Dinners always had hot soup with crackers for starters; canned meat of some sort like ham, sausages, beef stew, corned or chipped beef, or tuna; canned vegetables like yams, creamed corn, mushrooms or peas; and a dessert of canned pineapples, pears, peaches or fruit cocktail. Most everything except the packets of soup and crackers were in cans or jars.

A.K. and Ellen completed a commercial river trip through Lodore Canyon and Split Mountain, then drove through the night to get to Lee's Ferry to meet up with the other river runners on July 8, 1953. Ellen suffered from the heat on the searing drive to Marble Canyon. Besides Ellen's illness, two of the three boats, the *Galloway* and *Lodore*, had to be patched from damage sustained in the Lodore Canyon run prior to launch. Then, there was the river flow to contend with. The Colorado was running at 17,400 cfs and falling, well below the summer high of 69,600 cfs just three weeks earlier. The group finally left Lee's Ferry after lunch, and scouted both Badger and Soap Creek rapids, camping at the big sand dune at 12.5 Mile. Pat was too tired to eat, and Susie and Ruth did the dishes in the dark.

The next morning, Lug flipped his boat in a lateral wave in an unnamed riffle below North Canyon. The boat and swimmers were recovered with minimal loss of gear and supplies. Lug had a good attitude about the flip, realizing a little too late that he needed to turn his boat head-on into large waves approaching from the sides. As the river continued to drop, Pat recognized the river was flowing slower between the rapids, and where there had been riffles at higher water, there were real rapids at this lower level.

Trouble between A.K. and Pat started within forty-eight hours of the trip's launch. Pat refused to share his maps and notes with A.K., even though A.K. had asked him to mail him the maps in May. A.K. eventually refused to continue downriver without seeing them, and Pat grudgingly agreed. The river runners stopped at Vasey's Paradise for drinking water, and then rowed on to Redwall Cavern, a large overhang right at water's edge with deep sandy shade in the hot summer. While Pat and Lug pulled in to Redwall, A.K. with Ellen and Cappy floated on by. According to Pat, Cappy told A.K. to pull in as he'd like to see the cavern, and A.K. replied "You can see it next trip, Cap." At his age, Cap knew there wouldn't be another trip. "I'm seventy-six years old and there probably won't be a next trip for me," he said as A.K. silently floated past the cavern. A.K. was, in fact, trying to avoid Pat. Both Ellen and A.K. found Pat's early morning starts, late arrivals at camp near dark, poor food and long hours on the river an unwelcome change to their way of river running. The group landed not far below Mile 38 for camp after a twenty-six-mile day. George was feeling sick. Things clearly weren't going all that well.

With the river dropping past 15,400 cfs, the group ran the next day to the Little Colorado for camp, twenty-four miles downriver. The following day they stopped at Lava Chuar Canyon for a hike, found ancient pottery on Unkar Delta, and ran 75 Mile Rapid late in the day to camp at the top of Hance Rapid, a run of fifteen miles.

On Saturday, July 11, the river was holding at 15,000 cfs and the group ran Hance on the left, hitting a few rocks without serious damage. The boatmen ran without passengers to lighten the boats, pulling to shore at the bottom of the rapid where a large sandy beach made for an easy pull-in. The rest of the group walked the left shoreline past the rapid. Lunch was in the shade at an overhang across from the mouth of Vishnu Creek, known today as Grapevine Camp. The river party then ran to Phantom Ranch and camped at the boat beach just downstream of the Kaibab Suspension Bridge. At this point, George seemed to be improving, but now Lug had the flu. The river runners purchased some cold beers from the Phantom Ranch canteen, but ate and slept by their boats at the boat beach.

The river dropped to 14,300 cfs overnight, and on Sunday, July 12, the party made a late start from Phantom and headed off downriver to Horn Creek. Pat had never seen Horn look this bad, rating it a 10 on a 1 to 10 scale. After lunch and scouting on both sides of the river, the group decided to line the boats down along the rocky right-hand edge of the rapid. The *Lodore* was first, with three men holding the boat from upstream, and two men operating a side line to shore. At one point, the cockpit of the boat filled with water. Pat climbed into the swamped boat and started to bail, leaving Paul as the sole person on the side line. Once the boat was bailed, Pat looked up. To his surprise, he saw that A.K. and George had left the upstream rope to Lug. Unable to hold the boat alone, Lug lost control of the upstream line. Paul was now the sole person connecting the boat to shore. The force on the line pulled him right off his feet and he let go of the rope. Pat was left standing alone in a boat whose oars were tightly strapped to the gunwales, in the middle of the right side of Horn Creek Rapid.

A.K. Reynolds at the foot of Kwagunt Rapid, July 9, 1953.
Courtesy Marston Collection, reproduced by permission, the Huntington Library, San Marino, California.
This image also found in the Plez Talmadge Reilly Collection, Cline Library, Northern Arizona University

It was a quick flip. Pat eventually surfaced after an uncomfortably long time under water. Luckily, he was wearing his Mae West life jacket. Unfortunately, he was unable to swim to the boat on surfacing, and kicked to shore on the right side of the river as the upside-down *Lodore* floated away out of sight. The boat took with it the trip's kitchen utensils, three of the party's sleep gear kits stowed in a hatch, and their best lining ropes. Pat walked back to the group at the rapid and there was a long discussion on the dangers of lining.

The *Galloway* was then lined down the right side of the rapid and pulled up on a small ledge with assistance from Susie and Cappy. After a very long afternoon, Pat hurt his back as the party pulled the *Galloway* out of the water at twilight. A small sandbar made do for camp. The group whittled spoons from driftwood and ate dinner straight out of cans. Pat gave Cappy his sleeping bag, air mattress, and ground cloth. Life jackets served as sleeping mattresses. A ringtail cat, a relative of the raccoon common along the shores of desert rivers, visited the camp in the night. The cat woke the river runners as it tried to get food scraps from the tin cans lying about.

Ellen and A.K. Reynolds with their dog Hideout, 1953. Courtesy Ellen Reynolds

First thing on arising the morning of the 13th, the group decided Pat would row Susie, Ellen, and George in the *Ashley* across the river and attempt a climb out Horn Creek to the Tonto Plateau. Pat figured they could walk the few miles to Indian Gardens on the Tonto, and then hike the Bright Angel Trail up to the South Rim. The hikers quickly learned they could not hike up to the flat Tonto Plateau just 1,300 feet above them because the creek bed was blocked by sheer cliffs. The boaters-turned-climbers tried to scale the steep schist walls. Susie soon found the attempt beyond her abilities. The party rowed back across the river above Horn Creek Rapid, and Pat decided to run it right down the middle in the *Ashley*. Before the attempt was made, the *Galloway* was put back in the river, ready to rescue Pat if need be.

The river was holding at 14,300 cfs, and Pat had a good center run of Horn Creek. After everyone was on board, the two overloaded boats were run to Monument Creek at the head of Granite Rapid. While scouting Granite, A.K. spied the *Lodore* along the far right-hand shore below the rapid. Pat ran Granite Rapid first without passengers and landed at the foot of the rapid, followed by A.K. who landed much farther down. It took quite a while for A.K.'s passengers to reach his boat, but eventually all hands and two boats arrived on the right shore to retrieve the *Lodore*. Once flipped right side up, the river runners took stock of the craft. The boat had its splash boards ripped off, and most of the trip's bread, cereals, and crackers were ruined by water in the forward hatch. Nevertheless, the oars were still fastened tight to the boat, and the group was happy to retrieve their lost craft. A little after 3:00 in the afternoon, the party arrived at Hermit Rapid for a very late lunch and camp. Pat and A.K. went to work fixing the battered hatch and replacing the *Lodore*'s missing splash boards.

It was a struggle for Pat to get Ellen, George, and A.K. out of their sacks the next morning, a recurrent theme on the trip which exasperated Pat to no end. A.K. had learned that late starts irritated Pat, and worked it for all he could get.

Once finally up, fed, and with gear loaded, Lug, A.K., and Pat ran Hermit without passengers. Hermit at about 13,000 cfs has a series of large crashing waves, with the biggest in the lower part of the rapid. Pat tried to miss this line of waves on the left, but he lost his angle and headed into the big wave train backward. The pointed end of the cataract boat sliced right through the series of large waves, even the biggest one. To say a light bulb went off in Pat's mind may be too dramatic, but in both his river log and in subsequent writing to Dock, it is clear Pat was impressed with how well the boat sliced through the waves pointed end first. This concept would fit nicely into Pat's boat designs and actual boat construction the next year.

The party finally left the tail waves of Hermit about 10:30 that morning. The rapids below Hermit, including Boucher and a series of rapids known as the Gems, including Crystal, Sapphire, Emerald, Ruby, and Serpentine, were all run without scouting. Lug and George were washed out of their boat in Serpentine. As they were floundering in the water by their boat, Paul Terry sat firmly affixed to the bow deck. With hands gripping tightly onto the boat, Paul watched the two swimmers and sternly ordered them to "get back in this boat" as if his voice alone would haul them up out of the river. The group stopped at the mouth of Shinumo Creek for a late lunch and to replenish their drinking water. Late that afternoon they ran all the way to Elves Chasm for camp, a twenty-two-mile day.

The party arrived the next day about midafternoon at Bedrock Rapid. This rapid was, and still is, notorious for the large rock island the size of a semi-truck in the middle of the river. The run in the 1950s was as it is today, with river runners trying to pass the rock island on the right. The left run went into a tight eddy with a fast-water exit chute. Flipping or damaging a boat either by hitting the mid-river island or inadvertently heading left of the island was a real possibility.

The group scouted, and Pat ran first. With his boat pointed toward the right shore and rowing hard, the others watched as he cleared the bedrock island with twelve to fifteen feet to spare. A.K. ran next and didn't pull as hard on his oars. He slammed into the bedrock and then was washed down the right channel, but still in his boat and still upright. Then it was Lug's turn. Completely missing the idea of rowing toward the right shore, Lug rowed straight into the rapid with his stern facing downstream and his bow upstream.

There was a sickening crunch as the boat rolled onto its side and was held fast against the mid-river rock by the river current. Paul fell out of the boat and was flushed out the left channel where A.K. picked him up below. Meanwhile, Lug and George climbed out of the boat and up on top of the bedrock. The two men then worked their way down to the bow of the boat and using their legs, were able to push the *Ashley* loose. The boat careened down the left chute and out the rapid, full of water but still right side up! Lug and George

Ruth Pieroth, 1953. Courtesy Marston Collection, reproduced by permission, the Huntington Library, San Marino, California

Paul Terry, about 1953. Courtesy Marston Collection, reproduced by permission, the Huntington Library, San Marino, California

George Reynolds, 1955. Courtesy Marston Collection, reproduced by permission, the Huntington Library, San Marino, California

walked to the far downstream end of the island, then jumped into the river and swam to the boats waiting below. It had been another close call.

The party scouted Deubendorff Rapid and camped at the foot of Tapeats Rapid. A heavy monsoon downpour pounded the river runners as they arrived at camp about 7:30 in the evening. Dinner that night was soup, tea, canned ham, canned yams with cranberry sauce, with canned pineapple for dessert, plus light rain and thunder for ambiance.

George was very ill the next day and stayed with the boats while the rest of the party hiked up into the cottonwood-lined creek in Surprise Valley above the Deer Creek Narrows. Later in the day the group moved downriver to camp on a large sandy beach about a half mile above Olo Canyon. George was given some soup and hot compresses. A heavy rainstorm moved in at dawn the next day and they watched in awe as multiple waterfalls poured off the top of the Redwall Limestone some 2,000 feet overhead and cascaded down to the river below. Water courses cut down through the sandy beach where the river runners were camped, making ten-foot-wide by five-foot-deep channels through the fine river sand. After breakfast, the group headed downriver through the rain as waterfalls still poured off the cliffs all around them.

Upset Rapid was the next major rapid they stopped above to scout. This rapid has a large hole and an enormous crashing wave right in the middle of a tight channel. Pat ran first, and tried to make a left to right run, attempting to miss the Upset hole. Realizing he was not going to clear the hole, Pat swung the boat around, stern first, and dropped deep into the bottom of the hole. Pat looked up to see a tower of water crashing over him. It was the last thing he saw for a while, as the boat flipped and Pat went for a long swim.

Eventually, his trusty Mae West life jacket brought him back to the surface where he found himself under the overturned boat. Pat pushed himself out from under the boat, grabbed the bowline, and frog-kicked the boat to the right-hand shore. A.K. and Lug walked down to where Pat had made it to shore, and the three righted the *Galloway* with no loss of gear or damage to the boat. The two other boats were then run through safely.

The group stopped at a small spring, called Ledges by today's river runners, for lunch and fresh water. The afternoon included a short stop at Havasu Canyon, then an afternoon float to around 161.5 Mile for camp. The good news was the river was coming back up with a lot of driftwood and cans floating past. The bad news started about 10:00 p.m. that night. It had been a rainy day on and off, as the summer monsoon season was in full swing. The group was sound asleep when a *boom* was heard directly overhead. Then another *boom*, only louder. A.K. grabbed Ellen in her sleeping bag and threw her up the beach as a huge torrent of water landed right next to the couple. Sand flew everywhere in a thick mist. The river runners gathered their wits and sleep gear, realizing a flash flood was pounding the lower end of their camp with a thunderous roar. When all heads were accounted for, the group tried to go back to sleep farther up the beach.

In the morning, they saw a huge fourteen-foot deep by twenty-foot wide gash carved in their sandy beach. Some of the sand had been blown into the *Galloway's* cockpit, and Lug and Pat scooped it out in big handfuls. The day was spent rowing to Lava Falls, where another boat-lining was undertaken, this time without incident. While some of the group walked supplies to the foot of the rapid over the uneven cobbles and small boulders, others lined the boats down the left-hand shore to the foot of the rapid around car-sized boulders. The job went smoothly, with two ropes to upstream anchors and one downstream while two people worked the boat away from the large boulders along the shore. It was backbreaking work,

Pat Reilly upsetting in Upset Rapid, July 17, 1953. Courtesy Marston Collection, reproduced by permission, the Huntington Library, San Marino, California

Willis "Cappy" Rowe, early 1950s. Courtesy the Los Angeles Adventurers Club

but the job was done in two and a half hours. Once the boats were reloaded, the party ran downstream in the last light of the day to a large sandy beach on the right for camp. Today this camp is known as Lower Lava or Tequila Beach. It was another long day, but the skies had cleared and it was a restful night. The group awoke sore and stiff the next morning. The late risers had by now realized that if they got up earlier, the trip would cover more river miles each day, and so end earlier. They had breakfast and were on the river by 7:35 a.m.

George Reynolds was washed off the deck of the *Ashley* in a riffle below Parashant Canyon. He wasn't wearing a life jacket, and tried to protect his Rolleiflex camera as he went overboard. Into the river he went, holding the camera high overhead. A small whirlpool sucked him and his camera underwater. He eventually waded ashore with his now-ruined camera. Fall Canyon was the group's camp for the night, and the rising river floated away an unsecured life jacket. The river spiked at over 19,000 cfs, and then dropped over 5,000 cfs the next day.

By noon on Monday, July 20, the river runners had arrived at Diamond Creek where clear water for bathing and drinking was available. As Norm had done before, Pat, Susie, and Ruth initiated A.K., Lug, Ellen, Cappy, Paul, and George into the Royal Order of Colorado River Rats. Up to 1953, Cappy Rowe was the oldest person to travel through the entire Grand Canyon by boat. The river travelers stopped at Travertine Falls, and camped for the night at Spencer Canyon. Pat discovered he had put a hole in his boat while parked at Travertine Falls. It was patched with thick resin and the group rowed out across the headwaters of Lake Mead all the next day. The last boat pulled into Pearce Ferry a little after 6:00 p.m. It was A.K. and Ellen, the honeymooners.

By trip's end, Pat had learned a valuable lesson about defining pre-trip expectations. He had a clear vision of how he wanted to run a river trip, including what to eat, when to arrive at camp, when to get up in the morning, and when to load the boats and head downriver. Pat's vision may have been clear to him, but it was clearly out of focus with the Reynolds. Ellen would never eat another slice of grapefruit in her life, nor would A.K. ever run with Pat again. This lesson in establishing trip style ahead of time is one contemporary river runners would do well to discuss and finalize before showing up at Lee's Ferry.

After the trip, Pat wrote Dock that while this was the hardest trip he had been on, it was also the most interesting. He found the Canyon much more photogenic at low water and wanted to do another trip on similar water. He recounted the highlights, including Lug's flip below North Canyon; Pat's flip, swim and loss of boat while lining Horn Creek; and Lug and George washing out in Serpentine. Then there was the pin at Bedrock with Paul's swim, Pat's flip in Upset a flash flood booming into their camp one night, and George's swim and loss of his camera. Pat noted low water appealed to him "as I never thought it would. The old timers who ran on low water were really running on the roughest water, if they had only known." All in all, Pat wrote it was "a hell of a good time, everything considered, and are still steamed up about it." Indeed, in comparison to the Nevills Expedition and Wright-Rigg trips, this one had been a humdinger.

Pat also commented on the boats, noting they handled "with no appreciable difference from those of Nevills and Mexican Hat Expeditions." Dock wrote back, discussing among other things, boat design. In Dock's opinion, the cataract boat layout was "some kind of cruel joke played on Colorado River boatmen." He also opined that an eighteen-foot-long boat with a six-foot beam would prove to be ideal. Dock thought the blunt stern was "all wrong (period) for the Colorado." Dock understood that Norm's boat design could use improvement and "always believed it, but when I handled Moulty Fulmer's boat, the *Moja*, I knew it."

Five weeks later, Dock received a letter from Moulty, with a new photo of the *Gem*. Moulty was clearly excited and mentioned he might take two to three months off during the summer of 1954 for some river running, traveling, and loafing.

Moulty did a little more work on the *Gem*, including stopping by the Smoker Lumber Company to purchase four custom-made, ten-foot-long oars. He had the oar handles shortened eight inches and would cut an additional three inches off the blade end before running Grand Canyon. Dock encouraged Moulty to keep working on the design for the footwell of his boat, writing in October 1953, "When do you add a self-bailing cockpit?"

While Dock had helped Moulty with some of the design aspects of the *Gem*, he now began assisting in the design of Moulty's future river trips in the Grand Canyon.

Lug Larsen, George, and A.K. Reynolds loading a cataract boat onto a two-boat trailer. Courtesy Marston Collection, reproduced by permission, the Huntington Library, San Marino, California

Dock met up with Pat in early 1954, and mentioned to Pat that Moulty was looking to do some "fancy work this year." In February, Pat wrote to Dock asking if he knew of any boatmen available for the summer. Dock did, and had already mentioned Moulty Fulmer. So once again in a March 1, 1954, letter to Pat, Dock mentioned Moulty was looking to join up with someone to row the Grand Canyon. Dock had made three river trips with Moulty and had found him to be "able and good company."

Dock then wrote to Moulty about Pat, noting that "Pat is very capable but may run his risks a little high. I believe you would find him a good river companion." Dock also mentioned that Pat's record would "throw him a little onto the reckless side" not unlike Moulty's reckless river float on the flooding White in the *Tub*. He noted that Pat was "rather widely condemned by the followers of Nevills and Wright because he thinks that the equipment they use isn't the final word." Moulty could relate, remembering when Norm had told him the *Moja* would flounder on the San Juan's sand waves.

Dock went on to note Pat's impressive three runs through the Grand Canyon. By the end of 1953, less than a dozen people could claim a record of three full runs through the Canyon to the Grand Wash Cliffs. Dock also mentioned that Pat was "young enough and tough enough to take any of the problems involving physical strength for a canyon trip." Of Susie, Dock wrote that she was Pat's chief asset, and "quite capable of handling a trip through the canyon and has now made two." Dock enclosed Pat's address. On March 16, 1954, Moulty sent Pat Reilly a letter of introduction, expressing his interest in a Grand Canyon run. With Dock as the matchmaker, the two river runners, one from Indiana and the other from California, were about to meet each other, each with a new boat in tow.

Moulty Fulmer in the *Gem* with V-shaped splash boards and strengthened oar blocks, fall 1953. Courtesy Fulmer Collection, reproduced by permission, Utah State Historical Society, all rights reserved

11

The Trip That Never Left Lee's Ferry

1954

While Pat may have been all steamed up about low water in the Grand Canyon after his 1953 trip, he had his limits. By early March, the snow-pack was not looking good for 1954. Indeed, the peak runoff for the year would be a meager 34,300 cfs on May 26 and May 27. Four weeks later, the Colorado's flow had dropped to 9,220 cfs.

Without knowing how low the flow would be, that March Pat and Moulty were still making plans for a summer Grand Canyon cruise. After Moulty's outreach to Pat, on March 24 Pat replied that he was optimistic that he could launch in the last ten days of June on 50,000 cfs. He mentioned he had taken out on 17,500 cfs the year before, noting "It was the lowest I have ever run in the Grand Canyon."

Pat described his 1953 Grand Canyon river trip, including flipping in Upset, as if it was no big deal:

> I am inclined to think that capsizes have not been regarded too objectively. Panic is the big danger in such a case, aside from being slammed against an underwater boulder. You should know about this Reilly guy before you travel with him, as there are those who do not commend his judgment, though they may secretly envy the rides he gets. He figures that if he isn't after rough water he should stay out of Grand Canyon.

Pat asked about life jackets and the food pack, noting he would do the food if Moulty wanted. There was also a query about Moulty's ability to bring a passenger for his boat. Pat noted he had "latched onto a chap" with crew experience in college and who is "wild to go" but did not name the individual. Pat also mentioned that three boats would be superior to a two-boat party, and also noted he did not run a commercial endeavor but hoped to make the trip pay for itself.

It was clear Pat planned to build two boats in the spring of 1954 for the Grand Canyon run. Since he worked for Lockheed, he had been exposed early on to a new material called fiberglass. Gathering up large scrap pieces of the stuff at work, he figured the material would be lighter and tougher than plywood and the perfect building material for his boats.

Moulty described his boats to Pat, and Pat wrote back that Moulty seemed "to be one of the few original and objective thinkers regarding cataract boat design, which is in sharp contrast to the square stern – open and wasted cockpit – brigade." Pat then went on to describe what he was building out of fiberglass, plywood, and stainless steel. Pat's cataract boats would be seventeen-foot-long double-enders with a sixty-five-inch beam, including a "self bailing passenger compartment, small boatman cockpit, weight concentration in center, and a few other features. I think they will be the most efficient cataract boat to have hit the river unless your new job proves to be better."

While Pat was busy modifying the cataract boats he had learned to row on, and indeed would be improving the cataract hull design by eliminating the huge square stern and centralizing storage, Moulty would show up with a completely different hull design. The boat Moulty would show up with would not only last the test of time, but also the Grand Canyon's rapids as well.

Moulty wrote back to Pat within the week expressing his interest in accompanying Pat on a Canyon run. Moulty noted that "50,000 cfs sounds good to me. I like high water and dislike low stuff. Not enough action and too many rocks." Moulty added that he was still putting the finishing touches on his boat, including a V-shaped splash board and self-bailing side hatches in the footwell.

The self-bailing side hatches on the *Gem* were the one detail Moulty took the longest to finally sort out. This detail had been bugging him for two years since Dock had suggested a self-bailing footwell back in November 1951. In a March 29, 1954, letter to Dock, Moulty noted he had "just about figured out how to have a practical self-bailer for the *Gem*." All he needed to do was to get the *Gem* in the water to establish the water line. The concept was simple. Moulty built side storage boxes in the footwell that had tops sloping down and away from the center of the boat, to a low corner at the side of the boat, where a 2¼-inch diameter hole was drilled clear through the side of the boat. The hole, called a scupper, was just above the normal water line.

What Moulty had done was to create a space where gear could be stored on either side of the boatman's footwell in water resistant compartments. The scuppers would drain away any water in the footwell above the scupper line, leaving only a small area of the footwell for the boatman to bail. It was an efficient system that allowed for a spacious footwell, with easily accessible gear storage on either side of the center of the boat, while self-bailing three-quarters of the cockpit. At about this time, Moulty painted the footwell and splash boards of the boat blue, oarlock boards red, and the rest of the boat white. Moulty would change the areas of the boat that received red or blue paint, but the simple red, white, and blue theme would be used throughout the *Gem*'s boating days in one form or another.

By mid-March, forecasts for the summer's runoff were beginning to drop steeply, and Moulty wrote Dock that he was hoping there would be some late season snow. It was not to pass. Dock wrote back he would most likely be running another motor-powered down-run in June, but the water flow was uncertain. Toward the end of April, Pat was still looking hopefully at the snowmelt runoff reports, but things were not looking good and he had yet to set a firm launch date. Besides, he had just made the mold for his fiberglass boat on April 22 and planned to lay up his new boat over the next few days. At this point he had less than two months to build two boats and he was working full-time at Lockheed.

Using ⅛-inch mahogany plywood supported by external braces, Pat made a mold in which to lay the fiberglass he used to form the hull of his new boat. Wood pieces and metal bracing were used where needed. Five friends had shown up at the Reilly home to help the day the glass was laid into the mold, and all five struggled to clean their epoxy-coated hands when the job was done.

For the first eleven days of April, Moulty was in the hospital with pustular folliculitis and food allergies, developed after the bout of hepatitis in 1952. Eliminating wheat from his diet made Moulty a new man, and by the end of the summer he could eat anything at any time without trouble. On April 24, Pat wrote Moulty that June 21 looked like the best date to launch. Pat also had a few side hikes

Pat Reilly's first boat taking shape just two months before anticipated departure from Lee's Ferry, April 24, 1954. Courtesy Plez Talmadge Reilly Collection, Cline Library, Northern Arizona University

he wanted to do on the trip, including a hike up Tapeats Creek to Thunder Spring.

On that same day in April, a small group of men struggled in the hot sun at Lee's Ferry, pushing a large pontoon boat into the river. The black neoprene, oval-shaped, World War II army surplus bridge pontoon was the largest piece of rubber yet to attempt the cruise through the Canyon. The boat was set up to be operated by two rowers sitting roughly ten feet apart, one in front of the other. Called the *Millipede*, it was the first of a wave of this type of craft that would soon be used to traverse the Canyon.

That trip was the idea of Tyson "Ty" Dines, a brilliant and wealthy man with multiple degrees including one in law, from Oxford, Cambridge, and Yale. An accomplished world traveler, the thirty-six-year-old was a very athletic man who enjoyed the out-of-doors like few others. Tyson had fastened a cable across a canyon in the Rocky Mountain foothills outside his home near Denver, Colorado, and would cross the cable hand over hand, challenging his friends to do the same.

Bus Hatch, far right, with Smuss Allen, as the *Millipede* is pushed into the river, April 24, 1954. Courtesy Chuck Warren

Ty talked a number of family and friends into joining him on this trip, including his cousin Bruce Dines, Jim Nelson, Chuck Warren, Walt Emery, surgeon Matt Pfeiffenberger, and Smokey Stover. The *Millipede* was purchased, outfitted, named, and rowed by Ty's crew, none of whom had been through the Canyon before.

Ty had rafted the Yampa in 1952 with long-time river runner Robert Rafael "Bus" Hatch, and in 1953 had run with the fifty-two-year-old Bus through Lodore Canyon all the way to Green River, Utah. The elder Hatch, from Vernal, Utah, was impressed when Ty did a handstand while piloting his eighteen-foot canoe through some of the rapids.

Bus was coming back to the Grand Canyon after a twenty-year absence, having boated through in 1934. When Ty invited Bus to return, Bus agreed, bringing two Grand Canyon neophytes, his son, Frank, and fellow river runner, Smuss Allen. The voyage of the *Millipede* was accompanied by Bus's ten-man rubber raft, also operated with oars, but with a 5-HP Johnson outboard motor hanging out the back.

The trip left Lee's Ferry on just over 11,000 cfs, and emerged at the Grand Wash Cliffs, eight days later on roughly 14,000 cfs. It was an exciting cruise, with one major accident. At Bedrock Rapid, the *Millipede*'s run was "miscalculated" and the boat ran into the bedrock, sideways. Gear that had simply been placed in the bottom of the boat soon began to wash out. Then the bottom of the boat tore open, and much more gear abandoned the boat, including a banjo, most of the trip's cooking supplies and foodstuffs, along with six bottles of Scotch. Luckily, once the floor failed, the raft floated off the rock, as the *Millipede*'s air flotation chambers had not been ruptured.

Fortunately, there was a 300-foot-long sandy beach right below the rapid. Steering his ten-man rubber raft with its tiny motor, Bus gathered in many floating items, including the *Millipede*. Surgeon Pfeiffenberger's skills were put to use the rest of the day lacing up the bottom of the boat. Wet loaves of bread were laid, slice by slice, on the beach to dry. By chance, the small raft had a case of Skippy peanut butter on board. Food was in short rations for the rest of the trip, but the river runners had an incredible journey.

While Ty's *Millipede* was making history, Pat was feverishly trying to complete his build. In letters to Dock and Moulty on May 13, he was still looking to launch from Lee's Ferry on June 21. Even with Paul Terry helping with the boat building, Pat admitted to Dock he was abandoning an attempt to complete his second boat and was now committed to running with Moulty on a two-boat trip. It didn't help that the person Pat had talked into rowing his second boat had backed out of the trip. The "chap" had just landed an editorial job "he could not afford to turn down." Paul Terry backed out of the trip as well, and suddenly the planned Canyon run, if it launched at all, would be seriously short of manpower.

On May 17, 1954, Dock received the latest runoff reports which predicted a peak flow of 25,000 - 35,000 cfs. Dock noted the same prediction had been made the year before when the river runners actually got between 50,000 and 65,000 cfs. Regardless of the flow, Dock was gearing up for a Canyon cruise himself, with three eighteen-foot-long aluminum boats, each with twin 15-HP Evinrude outboard motors. Dock set his start date from Lee's Ferry for June 4, and with him would be someone Moulty knew well, Frank "Fish Eyes" Masland. Other than a few holes in the boats,

Pat Reilly's first of two fiberglass boats, only four months out of the mold, Studio City, California, August 28, 1954. Courtesy Plez Talmadge Reilly Collection, Cline Library, Northern Arizona University

Dock's trip was uneventful. Meanwhile, in California, Pat was working "like hell" to finish his boat with the assistance of Paul. When he received the runoff report from Dock, Pat realized his estimate for a flow of 50,000 cfs was "probably too high."

On June 19, 1954, Moulty Fulmer and Pat Reilly actually met for the first time at Marble Canyon. Pat was towing his new fiberglass boat, as yet unnamed and unpainted. Still, he thought it was completed enough to make the trip. The hoped-for flow of 50,000 cfs was way too optimistic, as the Colorado was now running at a mere 9,640 cfs at Lee's Ferry that day.

The two river runners must have had a good time looking over each other's boats. What Pat had done was to take the cataract sadiron hull design and point the boat at both ends. A cataract double-ender, if you will. Gone was the wide rectangle-shaped stern. Retained from the Nevills Expedition boat design was the wide beam at the oarlocks, roughly nine-inch rocker, and almost ninety-degree corners along the chine where the bottom and the side of the boat met. Where the Nevills' boats had an open cockpit, Pat's was very narrow, with waterproof storage compartments on each side of the boatman's seat. Gone was storage in the bow and stern areas. Like Moulty, Pat made a seat for a passenger just behind him. Pat's third passenger seat was forward of his splash guard, on the front deck in a self-bailing contoured seat. This was definitely a plus for the third passenger over Moulty's flat stern deck.

The boat that emerged from Pat's mold was seventeen feet long and five-and-a-half feet wide at the oarlocks. Spare oars were located in scabbards on either side of the boatman's legs, and provided handy arm rests for the rear passenger. The flat-topped storage compartments were accessed through flat flush-mounted hatches placed along the deck. The hatches were inboard of low splash boards that ran along the side of the boat to the oarlock area. A large splash board was attached to the stern deck, just in front of the rower. While Pat's double-ender cataract boat made a step forward in design, it would be a short step in a dance that only Pat would fox-trot to. Future river dancers would embrace the *Gem*'s McKenzie design Moulty had just captured for Grand Canyon cruising.

One thing was certain, both Pat and Moulty agreed there was not enough water in the river to attempt a traverse of the Canyon. While today's river runners happily launch on 9,000 cfs, in 1954 the two boat builders decided the Grand Canyon run was over right from the start.

Moulty was undaunted. He had a boat, and by golly, he was going to go boating. His next stop was the Rogue River in southern Oregon where he put his oars in the water but did not run the river. In a late June letter to Pat, Dock noted he couldn't get away to join Moulty for the trip on the Rogue.

By the end of July, Moulty and the *Gem* joined A.K. Reynolds, Lug Larsen, and Walter "Wally" Furen for a four-boat low-water Green River run through Lodore Canyon. There were eight people on this trip, including the above-mentioned boatmen and Ellen Reynolds, Wally's mother, Mildred, and a couple from New York, Rosalie and Milo Waldes. Moulty rowed the *Gem* and took along a passenger in his jump seat, A.K. rowed his *Lodore*, Wally rowed the *Galloway*, and Lug paddled a canvas-and-wood-strip Folbot, the precursor of today's kayak. The Green River, Wyoming, flow gauge registered 3,250 cfs at the trip's start, and four days later came in at 2,310 cfs. The group launched at Brown's Park July 24, on what would be a fun but rocky run.

From Moulty's log of this low-water trip, it is clear Pat should have let the Reynolds do the food pack for the previous year's Grand Canyon river trip. The chow included fresh vegetables like tomatoes, corn on the cob, potatoes and lettuce, along with hamburgers, pancakes, strawberry shortcake, bacon and eggs.

On the second day, while the boats were floating in an eddy, the *Galloway* rammed into the *Gem*, putting a small hole through her side just below the gunwale rub rail. Moulty was not worried about it as the hole was well above the water line. They ran Upper and Lower Disaster Falls without incident, though Moulty gave the bottom of the *Gem* a workout on a number of rocks. At noon and forty-eight hours into the trip, the group had lunch at the top of Triplett Falls. The river runners had covered twelve miles in two days, what the 1953 Grand Canyon river trip under Pat Reilly's schedule would do in a morning.

The *Gem* in Lodore Canyon. From left to right: A.K. Reynolds, Wally Furen, Mildred Furen, Milo Waldes, Lug Larsen, Ellen Reynolds and Rosalie Waldes, July 1954. Courtesy Moulton Fulmer, Plez Talmadge Reilly Collection, Cline Library, Northern Arizona University

The group camped below Triplett Falls. On July 27, and just thirty minutes out of camp, they approached Hell's Half Mile, a long and difficult rapid that at low water demanded some fancy boat maneuvering. After a thorough scout, Lug's Folbot was portaged 200 feet past the worst spot, but the wooden boats were run through. A.K. and Wally ran together in the *Lodore* and spent almost ten minutes pinned on a rock in the lower end of the rapid. Moulty ran next, wearing a leather football helmet, and without the extra weight of a passenger did just fine. Moulty then hiked back up and ran the rapid again as a passenger with Wally at the oars of the *Galloway*, and the two had a good run as well. Lug came down in the Folbot, and the group ran past the confluence of the Yampa and Green rivers, through Echo Park to just above Jones Hole for camp.

On their last day, they boated through Split Mountain. Moulty ran the *Gem* up on a few rocks as they made their way, and he was happy not to hang up on any of them. They arrived at the take-out that afternoon, hot and tired. Moulty's car and trailer were there, as was the Reynolds' crumpled Pontiac which had been rolled earlier in the day by Ellen's brother. While the car still ran, it was soon retired out of shuttle service. The happy river party went to Vernal for a post-trip dinner, and then Moulty said his goodbyes and climbed behind the wheel of his Mercury. Forty-four hours after leaving Vernal, he stepped out of the Merc back in Muncie, Indiana.

With a little vacation time still remaining, Moulty and Janice headed back west to New Mexico and Arizona. Things went awry when Janice drove the Mercury off the road, overcorrected, and rolled the car. This was in the days before seatbelts, and Janice was knocked unconscious and spent the next five days in a hospital in El Dorado, Kansas. The Merc was a total loss.

While the road trip was considered a disaster, Moulty had just run the first decked McKenzie River dory through Lodore Canyon. The *Gem* had handled very well and exceeded his expectations. In August, Moulty made the *Gem*'s splash boards permanent, and added gaskets to his hatches. In a letter to Pat in late August, Moulty mentioned that a sloped footboard in the cockpit of the *Gem* really "helped me to no end." Moulty encouraged Pat to add one to his boat. Moulty began seeking out passengers for a 1955 run of Grand Canyon. As the last of 1954 turned into the start of 1955, Pat noted in a letter to Dock, "Have silently thanked you several times for bringing Moulty and me together. He's a swell egg."

There was one other river running event in 1954 that was to have a huge impact on the future of river running. Throughout the 1950s, as river running was slowly beginning to grow as a recreational activity, Grand Canyon National Park had, at the most, nine permanent and a handful of seasonal field rangers. Their priority was the rims, where visitation topped a half million in 1950 alone. A new hire was brought on board late in 1953, Ranger Dan Davis. Interested in the backcountry, and being a new ranger, Davis was assigned to Phantom Ranch. With ten river trips making the attempt in 1954, he was immediately introduced to river runners.

In that first year stationed at Phantom Ranch, Davis was exposed to a river trip led by Elmer Purtymun of Sedona, Arizona, that had not gone as planned. Just a week before Moulty and Pat met for the first time at Lee's Ferry, the fifty-year-old Purtymun was at the Ferry, along with his seventeen-year-old nephew Don Van Deren, and friends Bill Towne, J. E. "Ed" I'Anson, Dale Slocum, and John Pederson. Purtymun's group, all seasoned Glen Canyon river runners, launched two ten-man life rafts on Sunday, June 13. The men had decided they

Rigging rubber rafts at Lee's Ferry. Left to right: Elmer Purtymun, Dale Slocum, Bill Towne, Don Van Deren, John Pederson, and Ed I'Anson, June 12, 1954. Courtesy Dale Slocum

Elmer Purtymun rows Don Van Deren past a hole in
Marble Canyon, June 15, 1954. Courtesy Dale Slocum

would attempt a record-breaking speed-run through the Canyon.

The river was only flowing at 12,400 cfs when they launched, and any thoughts of a speed-run evaporated the first day as the men camped below Navajo Bridge, only four miles from the put-in. In the next forty-eight hours, the men made it to the Little Colorado River, having traveled a little over sixty miles in two and a half days. They made only fifteen miles in the next two days, with one entire day spent getting their rubber rafts through Hance Rapid, on around 10,000 cfs.

Despite making poor time, the men's spirits were high, and they jokingly ranked the rapids they ran as riffles or raffles. In recounting the trip events a month afterwards, Dale Slocum noted "Riffles were tame, but we gambled our lives on the raffles."

On the day the men were working their rafts through Hance, Elmer told them he had promised his nephew's parents that the young man would not have to run the more dangerous rapids. The map the men were using showed there were two dangerous rapids between their location and Phantom Ranch, only eleven miles downstream. Purtymun said he was going to walk overland to Phantom with his nephew Don. On the morning of Friday, June 18, the group split up. By noon, the river party arrived at Phantom Ranch, having had no troubles. They waited out the hot afternoon at the ranch, with no sign of Purtymun or Van Deren.

What the overland party had not anticipated was that hiking from Hance to Phantom is not a straight shot. The route wound its way in and out of a number of deep drainages, increasing the overland distance to about thirty-three miles. While today there is a well-worn trail in this area, in 1954 there was none. The two men spent considerable time working their way over the rough terrain, and quickly ran out of food and water hiking in the 111 degree summer heat. That afternoon the exhausted Purtymun told his nephew he could go no further.

That night, the river party at Phantom became concerned. On Saturday morning they hired mules and a guide to head out and search for Elmer and Don. Just before their departure from Phantom Ranch, Don stumbled into their camp, desperate for a drink of water, his feet raw and bleeding. I'Anson and a mule guide immediately departed with three mules to retrieve Purtymun. They returned nine hours later with the exhausted hiker. The party spent the next day at Phantom Ranch waiting for the two hikers to recover from their overland march.

On Monday, June 21, Purtymun and his nephew reluctantly decided to ride out of the Canyon. The remaining four men in two boats agreed to continue the trip. The river was now running 9,340 cfs and the foursome did not get far. One of the rafts was pinned against a rock at Horn Creek Rapid, and after freeing the boat, the river runners arrived at Granite Rapid late in the day. At this point, the party noticed I'Anson had a badly infected and swollen leg, from a foot injury a few days earlier. He had not mentioned the fact to the other men, as he had wanted to continue with the river trip. Faced with a medical emergency, Towne and Slocum hiked out the Hermit Trail to the South Rim while Pederson stayed with the injured I'Anson. Towne and Slocum returned with hired mules, and after stashing their river gear, all four men reached the South Rim Friday morning, June 25, to be greeted at the top by Purtymun and Van Deren. Purtymun returned to the Canyon later that year with pack stock and recovered the stashed boats and river gear.

With the misfortunes of the Purtymun trip in mind, late in 1954, Ranger Davis attempted to put together the first permit for river running in Grand Canyon. Davis wanted some way of knowing when a river trip was supposed to show up at Phantom Ranch and who was supposed to be on the trip. The Park Service was also fairly sure that wearing life jackets was important, as was having enough boats so that if one was lost, the rest of the trip could be completed by all hands in the remaining watercraft. Finally, the park required there be at least one person on the trip with prior Grand Canyon river running experience.

While requiring prior river running experience in the Grand Canyon made sense to the Park Service, it made no sense to others, including Dock Marston. He wrote then Superintendent Preston Patraw the following:

> In 1953 there was a narrow escape from death in the party under guidance of experienced riverman Wright. In 1952 experienced riverman Rigg put his passengers to extreme hazard. In 1954 experienced rivermen Bus Hatch and Don Hatch got into one of the wildest wrangle-tangles with great hazard to their passengers. Experienced riverman Reilly critically exposed his party in 1953. Experienced riverwoman White had several tizzies in 1954 which involved serious risk to life. Under the laws of chance and the increase in difficulties in handling a larger party, the odds are against her this year. The talk of experience on the river borders on hokum and tends to create a false sense of security. I will take a good lifejacket over an experienced riverman any day. Some rivermen just don't learn anything by experience.

Marston's thoughts on experience versus a good life jacket still ring true decades later. There are many river runners today who have no experience running the Canyon, and yet have wonderful and safe river trips. Indeed, the park would later change their policy to require permit holders to have either prior Grand Canyon river running experience or "other comparable whitewater" experience. Until the park relaxed that requirement, only those with one or more Grand Canyon river trips would receive a permit. This led a number of Grand Canyon river runners not only to think of themselves as experts, but also to market themselves as "authorities." This simple requirement of needing prior experience set the stage for the rapid commercialization of the river that was soon to follow. With or without prior experience, the need to apply for a permit was ignored by a number of river trips in 1955, but that, like many other aspects of river running in the Grand Canyon, would soon change as well. Meanwhile, Moulty Fulmer and Pat Reilly were already starting to organize their next Grand Canyon adventure.

12

Only One Flip

1955

Talking river at a Lockheed coffee break. Left to right: Carl Pederson, Paul Terry, Brick Mortenson, and Pat Reilly, Spring 1955. Courtesy Carl and Earline Pederson collection

The snowflakes were slowly piling up across the Colorado River high country, and a handful of dedicated river runners were watching every storm. After the previous year's bust, Pat Reilly was one of the few paying very close attention. The snowpack was certainly looking better in January 1955, but it was still very early in the season. All Pat and Moulty could do was watch and wait as it was way too early to settle on a launch date. Dock was watching too. The reports up to early February had him predicting a summer flow of around 30,000 cfs. Dock was close, as the peak flow at Lee's Ferry would only be 35,600 cfs on June 13, with only fifty-one days in May and June for the entire year having flows at or above 20,000 cfs.

Pat spent the winter deciding who would go on his trip. Along with Susie and Moulty, there was Pat's fellow Lockheed employee, thirty-eight-year-old Vernon "Brick" Mortenson. Brick had spent some time as a lifeguard and water polo player and had considerable canoe experience, so was comfortable around boats and water. When Pat approached him asking if he would like to come on the trip, Brick had replied he would first need to check with his wife. With permission obtained, Brick was thrilled to participate. Paul Terry, having canceled on the 1954 trip, said he would like to go and would bring his 16mm camera and try to shoot some good film.

Two other Lockheed employees Pat knew, Tommy Cox and Carl Pederson, were also photographers and interested in going on the trip. Carl was scheduled by Lockheed to move to Japan in August, but was determined to float the Canyon. While he was eager to go on what was considered at the time to be a very dangerous adventure, he would be leaving his young wife to sort out the details of the move with two small children in tow. Carl's wife, Earline, was not enthusiastic about his participation and let him know it. Carl was committed to go however, and would prove to be a strong asset to the success of the trip.

In February, Pat wrote Lug Larsen, who had been on the 1953 Grand Canyon trip, asking if he wanted to bring his cataract boat to Lee's Ferry and join the group for a three-boat trip. Pat noted that there would be "no old men or scared photographers" on the trip. Lug wrote back he was not too interested in the deal.

Then there was a fellow Pat had recently met named Martin Litton. A UCLA graduate in English, Martin was the same age as Brick and had served in World War II as a transport and glider pilot. Martin had been writing for the *Los Angeles Times* and had met Pat at a Colorado River film showing in Los Angeles. He then left the *Times* and started working for *Sunset* magazine in 1954 as travel editor, and was working on writing a story about the Grand Canyon in 1955. He was interested in the trip, and wanted to bring his wife, Esther. It was Martin who Pat had lined up to row Pat's unbuilt second boat in 1954. In the early spring of 1955 Pat asked Martin if he would row the second boat.

Paul Terry sits in the *Flavell* while Pat Reilly attaches stern decking, Spring 1955. Courtesy Carl and Earline Pederson collection

Pat began giving much more attention to building his second boat, and in March laid up a second fiberglass hull with help from Carl Pederson. Interestingly, it would have the exact same beam as his first boat, except it would be a foot shorter in length. In researching the difference in boat lengths, replica boat builder Ian Elliot thinks he may have stumbled on the reason. Elliot conjectures that Pat would have needed to cut his mold for the first boat in half to get the boat hull out of the mold. He would then have shortened the mold by a foot and reattached the halves.

By early May, Pat's second boat was in the home stretch. Besides the length, there were a few other notable differences between the two boats. While both had a comfortable passenger seat behind the rower, Pat added another seat just in front of the rower to his second boat. The person who sat there faced directly at the rower, and shared the same small leg space. There was another design flaw that came with the shortened overall length. The spare oars now got in the way of the hatch lids and the oars would have to be removed from their scabbards to access the rear side compartments. While both boats had cockpits and hatch covers that did not self-bail, Pat figured he had reduced the huge Nevills-style footwells by almost seventy percent, so he really didn't care about having to bucket out the rest. Another difference was the color scheme.

Pat had seen Moulty's red, white, and blue boat the year before, and while that was all well and good, Pat had a neighbor named Ralph. It just so happened that Ralph was rather good with color and design schemes. The year before, this neighbor had been the design inspiration behind his boss, a fellow named Walt Disney, winning two Academy Awards for a film called *20,000 Leagues Under the Sea*. His full name was Ralph Harper

With the addition of a second boat, Pat took his one-boat trailer back to the shop and had the trailer modified to hold two boats, one on top of the other. Pat Reilly's new boats at Marble Canyon, 1955. Courtesy Plez Talmadge Reilly Collection, Cline Library, Northern Arizona University

Goff, and when Goff suggested a color scheme for the two boats, Pat not only listened but took notes and then got to work. The colors Goff worked out for Pat's boats included Aztec Red, Beryl Green, and Refrigerator White. While Moulty's *Gem* was nicely done, Pat's boats on the 1955 trip were stunning, assisted as they were with a little rocket power thrown into the mix by Goff. Dories today in the Grand Canyon continue the tradition of bringing color and flair to the river, started by Moulty and Pat.

Before the 1955 cruise, Pat named his two boats. The longer one with the built-in reclining front passenger seat he named the *Susie R*. In April, Dock had sent Pat a copy of a river trip log from 1896. In that year two men, George Flavell and Ramon Montez, ran the Colorado in a flat-bottomed boat about the size of Pat's second boat. Flavell had considerable boat-building skills before he and Montez built their boat, named the *Panthon*, at Green River, Wyoming. Flavell and Montez are recognized as being the first to utilize the "stern first" rowing technique. This simple rowing style, used today by countless river runners, entails the oarsman facing downstream while rowing. Pat was so impressed with the story after reading the log he named his second boat *Flavell*, and wrote to Dock that Flavell was one of "the first to make noteworthy contributions to the art of running big water." Besides, Pat thought *Flavell* a better name than *Sunset*, a name he had at first considered.

There were still innumerable details to sort out. Pat was thinking of charging each passenger $250 to help offset costs. He also wanted to know if Moulty would be interested in helping with shuttle costs and a tow out across Lake Mead by Bill Belknap. And there was the park permit to obtain.

Pat filled out the two-page application and sent it back to the Park Service. Pat's approved permit was returned to him May 5, 1955. The application required the trip leader's name, launch date, boat description, and list of trip participants. Also requested was who would be financially responsible for rescue should that be necessary. This person could not participate on the trip, and the NPS wanted to know if this person would be following the trip's progress from the rim overlooks during the trip, or waiting, no doubt anxiously, at home. The NPS then wanted answers to a series of questions. Would the boatmen and passengers be equipped with "life preservers plus extras?" Would the river runners have maps, signal mirrors, and extra oars? Would the oars be made of ash? Would the trip be signaling the tower at Desert View, and if so, how and when? Today, the noncommercial regulations handbook is twenty-nine pages long.

All the myriad details seemed to be coming together in early June. Susie was working on the food purchases; the team was set; boats built, named, and painted; shuttles and lodging arranged. Then Pat received a telegram on June 11. Martin Litton was in the high Sierra on a horse-packing trip for *Sunset*. The horse Martin was riding had stumbled down a ravine, and he had dislocated his shoulder during the quick and unanticipated dismount. The doctor who looked at his shoulder told him to forget about participating on the river trip. Martin asked for an alternative, and the doctor said if he could strap his upper arm to his side for twenty-one days and not move it, then the river trip could work.

Pat strode over to where Brick was working at Lockheed the next day, and while Brick was happy to see him, the look on Pat's face told Brick something was up. In his typical matter-of-fact way, Pat asked Brick if he wanted to row the second boat. Brick was quiet for all of a few seconds, and then burst out, "Just don't tell my wife!"

Moulty Fulmer approaches Flagstaff, AZ, on Route 66, the *Gem* in tow, June 1955. Courtesy Fulmer Collection, reproduced by permission, Utah State Historical Society, all rights reserved

The drive to Lee's Ferry, as it often is today for river runners, meant people were traveling in from all over the country. With the *Gem* towed behind his new Mercury, Moulty could not see out his rear-view mirrors. Unable to tell if he was being overtaken on a two-lane road, he could not pass slower vehicles, or drive across the center line to pull off at roadside services not located on his side of the road.

With the constraints imposed by towing a boat, he drove from Indiana on Route 66 to Flagstaff, then headed north on Highway 89 to Cliff Dwellers Lodge, driving right past Marble Canyon Lodge. Art Greene had managed the Marble Canyon Lodge in the 1940s, and Norm had taken his business there. Art was well liked, and ran a great kitchen. When the opportunity arose in 1949, Art purchased Cliff Dwellers Lodge, ten miles farther up the road. River runners, including Frank Wright and Pat Reilly, followed Art's good cooking and wonderful hospitality there.

Meanwhile, Brick, Pat, and Susie did a seventeen-hour drive from the San Fernando Valley to find Moulty already at Cliff Dwellers. Frank Wright was at the lodge having just

Susie Reilly, Brick Mortenson, and Paul Terry at the foot of Soap
Creek Rapid, June 20, 1955. Courtesy Carl and Earline Pederson

completed a San Juan run, and Pat also ran into Harry
Aleson and, later the same day, Georgie White. Paul,
Tommy, and Carl arrived at Art's midday on June 19.
In the afternoon, the boats were taken to the river, after
a drive to the Badger Rapid overlook on the rim. The
Littons arrived in the afternoon, and Moulty spent the
night sleeping by the boats while the rest of the crew
stayed at Art's for the night.

Moulty, Pat, and Brick were giddy with excitement on the morning of June 20, 1955. After final gear
loading was done, Pat pushed off from shore first in
the *Susie R*, with Susie and Paul as passengers. Brick
launched second rowing the *Flavell*, with Esther and
Martin. A little after 9:30 that morning, Moulty left
the beach with Tom and Carl in the *Gem*. This would
be the group's running order, with Pat in the lead, Brick
in the middle, and Moulty last as sweep. The Colorado
River sleepily carried them along on 28,800 cfs. After
thirteen years of boat designing and building, Moulty
was rowing the first McKenzie River dory, designed
with decks and waterproof hatches for the rough waters
of the Grand Canyon. It was the debut of the first dory
on the Colorado in Grand Canyon.

The group stopped to scout Badger Rapid. Pat had
Brick ride with him through the rapid before Brick ran
the *Flavell* through on his own. Moulty came through
last and all had good runs. Lunch was at the foot of
the rapid. Next it was on downriver to Soap Creek. As
Moulty made his entrance and began to pull hard on
his oars to land at the foot of the rapid, the film crew
on shore heard a loud *crack*, like a rifle shot. It was the
sound of the *Gem*'s left oarlock snapping in two. Between the Smoker oar and the oak oar block, the cast
iron oarlock didn't have a chance.

Moulty was using ring oarlocks, and each oar had
an oarlock attached to it. He did the best he could to
steer the *Gem* with the right oar while he grabbed his
spare oar. As he tried to put the new oarlock into the

Ring oarlock design like that used on the *Gem*, 2011. Tom Martin photo

Drawing from Fulmer Journal of his broken oarlock in Soap Creek Rapid, 1955

Soap Creek

oar block, he discovered the broken cast iron pin had jammed in the block. Moulty landed the boat on the right shore, where a hammer was needed to drive the broken oarlock stem out of the oar block. The group camped on a long sandy beach below Sheer Wall Rapid on the right where Pat saw a muskrat run to the river from about ten feet away. Dinner was soup, salad, steak, and fried potatoes. Moulty had a restless night dreaming of breaking more oarlocks.

The next morning, in typical Pat Reilly early-bird style, the river runners were ready to depart before 8:00 a.m. As Pat was about to pull away from shore, he called out "Is everybody about ready?" It was a call the crew would come to know well for the rest of the trip.

Scouting North Canyon Rapid, the group was overtaken by a motor boat party being run by Jim and & Bob Rigg. Moulty hung back so that the Rigg party could walk down and watch his run of the rapid. On passing him later they all congratulated Moulty on a good run.

While Moulty had solved the oar problem and was now breaking oarlocks instead, Pat had not. In 21 Mile Rapid just below North Canyon, Pat snapped one of his Pelican Brand oars in half. Then it was Brick's turn to experience a few mechanical failures. Before scouting 24½ Mile Rapid, Brick broke the weld in one of the *Flavell*'s oarlocks. Unbeknownst to Brick, somewhere during the day's run he had hit a rock and had put a twenty-inch crack in the chine of the *Flavell*. Brick was also trapped by a number of eddies the other two boats had avoided.

The river runners stopped at the lower end of the South Canyon eddy where a large sandy

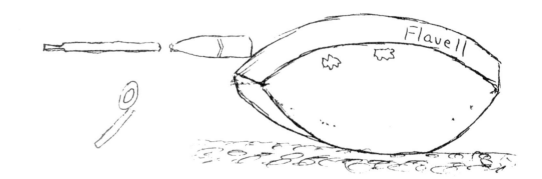

beach allowed for ample camping. Brick almost missed the pull-in, but was able to get the *Flavell* to the right bank just above Vasey's Paradise. With help from Martin, Tommy, and Moulty, Brick was able to line the boat back upriver to camp. When Brick went to unload the *Flavell*, he discovered a lot of water in the aft port hatch. The *Flavell* was completely unloaded, pulled from the water, and rolled onto its side to dry prior to patching.

Moulty wrote in his trip log that the "party is not too gay this evening as we are having our share of hard luck. At the present rate there is a little doubt in my mind if we will be lucky enough to last out the trip. I have my fingers crossed!!" Pat spent most of the night "sick at both ends."

With the *Flavell* patched, put back in the water and all gear reloaded, the group headed on downriver, departing around 10:00 a.m. on June 22. After stopping at Redwall Cavern for lunch, the river runners floated to President Harding Rapid for camp. Moulty was happy as there had been "no mishaps today!!!" Pat was feeling much better as well. The next morning the group was on the

Patching the *Flavell* at South Canyon, June 21, 1955. Courtesy Fulmer Collection, reproduced by permission, Utah State Historical Society, all rights reserved

water by 7:00 a.m. They stopped to hike up to the Nankoweap granaries, a popular hike for today's river runners as well.

Moulty was now sick with what Pat had, and was unable to keep his lunch down. After the rest of the group ate, the party headed downriver, stopping to scout Kwagunt Rapid. Once they got below the rapid, Pat started looking for a man who had recently drowned in the river. Less than a month earlier, forty-eight-year-old Grand Canyon hiker Dr. Harvey Butchart, a math professor at Arizona State College in Flagstaff, Arizona, had tried to cross the river about four miles below Kwagunt Rapid with fellow hiking partner, twenty-two-year-old Boyd Moore. The two had attempted to use their air mattresses for flotation to cross the river wearing their heavy backpacks. Neither man wore a life jacket. Moore was deathly afraid of water and became paralyzed with fear while attempting the crossing. Harvey had tried heroically to assist Moore, including getting Moore to shed his backpack about a half mile below the Little Colorado confluence. It was to no avail, as Moore eventually became separated from Harvey and drowned. Pat had been contacted both by the Park Service and the Moore family to please keep a keen eye out for the lost hiker's body.

After an eleven-hour day, Moulty was still not feeling up to par. As he swung his boat by the pull-in at the mouth of the Little Colorado River for camp, the river current started drawing him away from shore at an alarming rate. It was all Moulty could do to get the *Gem* and the two other men on

Moulty Fulmer, Susie Reilly, Tommy Cox, Esther Litton, and Paul Terry at Nankoweap granaries, June 23, 1955. Courtesy Carl and Earline Pederson

it back to shore. The Little Colorado River, if not in flood, is fed by large springs of light blue water and makes for enjoyable swimming. This was not the case that day, as it was in flood and running a deep muddy red. The group had rowed sixty-two miles in four days, and Brick's hands were badly blistered. Wind whipped sand into the group's dinner and across their beds during the night.

The next day, Moulty was feeling better and was looking forward to eating breakfast. This would be the fourth day in a row the group would have eggs for breakfast, and the last. From here on out the breakfast would consist of grapefruit (of course), pancakes, and sausage. Occasionally, the pancakes were replaced with cold cereal.

The river runners scouted Lava Canyon, Tanner, and Unkar rapids. Brick continued to be trapped by a number of eddies the other two boaters missed. While scouting Unkar, Pat spotted a two-foot-long, ⅝-inch metal rod that he recalled seeing on the 1953 trip among the copious quantities of driftwood. It was just the thing to build new oarlocks with. Sadly, Pat also found a partially decomposed rucksack, empty of all contents except for two one-inch safety pins attached to the canvas. Pat left the rucksack, but Georgie picked it up on her next trip and took it on to Phantom Ranch. The pack was later identified as belonging to the drowned man. Boyd Moore's body was recovered below Hermit Rapid in early July by another river trip.

Pat and Susie Reilly watch while Paul Terry and Moulty Fulmer rig a temporary oarlock at the foot of 75 Mile Rapid, June 24, 1955. Courtesy Carl and Earline Pederson

After lunch, they scouted 75 Mile Rapid. Moulty was in the middle of the rapid pulling sideways to avoid a large pour-over when there was another sickening *crack*. He had broken another oarlock. Moulty went right into the hole he was trying to avoid, but he kept the boat straight with the remaining oar and eventually made it to shore. It was hard to remove the broken pin from the oar block, but once this was done Moulty and Paul made a rope oarlock, and the party continued on to the top of Hance Rapid for camp.

Once the boats were unloaded, Pat and Moulty took turns slowly filing the ⅝-inch steel rod in half. Using a claw hammer, Pat was able to bend the rod somewhat, but it was not enough. Then Carl had a brilliant idea. Why not build a fire and heat the rod. Pat knew that mesquite wood burned very hot, so he collected some for fuel while Carl found a windy spot for a fire next to a large boulder. Carl figured the breeze would make good coals and he was right. The half-rounded rod was placed into the fire, and after forty minutes Pat pulled the red-hot steel from the fire with a wet wash-

Drawing from Fulmer Journal of the second oar lock break, 1955

cloth for a glove. Using the hammer and Brick's small hatchet, the men were able to bend the rod into a ring and pin. It took them until after dark to finish fitting Moulty's oar with the new oarlock. Dinner was soup, creamed corn, hot dogs, and green beans, with fresh catfish caught by Brick.

The roar of Hance Rapid greeted the river runners the next morning. After breakfast, they scouted the rapid one last time. Pat told Brick and Moulty he was going to run the rapid, and that if he flipped, they were to line the remaining two boats. Pat ran the left side of Hance on about 26,000 cfs and had a great run, pulling into the surging eddy along the left shore to wait for the other boats. Brick ran second, and had a great run as well. While Moulty recognized that lining the rapid looked mighty attractive, his run was easier than he had expected it to be, although it required a lot of maneuvering of the *Gem* in the rapid. While Pat waited for the other boats, the surging eddy took its toll on the *Susie R*, putting two small holes in the boat. Brick and Moulty were elated at their runs. Things were looking up. Sockdolager Rapid was next, then Grapevine. Both rapids were scouted and while the waves were big and the rides exciting, the runs were otherwise uneventful.

While Moulty was running Clear Creek Rapid, the third of his original cast iron oarlocks failed. Moulty ran the rest of the rapid and Zoroaster Rapid with one oar more or less, then made a rope oarlock to get to Phantom, another three miles downriver. The party arrived at the large beach at the mouth of Bright Angel Creek just before 2:00 p.m. Moulty and Pat spent the afternoon using the ranch's hammers and anvil to make some new oarlocks, one out of the ⅝-inch remaining steel rod Pat had found at Unkar, and two more out of ½-inch rod that the ranch shop had on hand. All this playing with steel only happened after Moulty made a phone call to Janice and took a quick swim in the pool while Pat had a beer. The river runners spent the night at Phantom Ranch, and both Moulty and Brick declared dinner that night "was delicious!!" Pat noted in his log the good Phantom Ranch food may have the crew throwing rocks at his cooking. The river runners had a brief visit with Jim Layton, operator of the USGS Phantom Ranch river flow gauge. Layton told them the river temperature was a very pleasant seventy-four degrees.

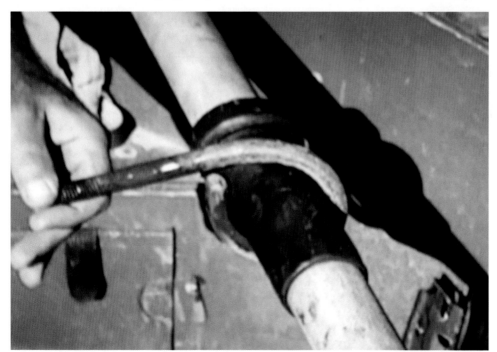

Homemade oarlock for the *Gem*, June 25, 1955. Courtesy Barbara Crookston

They were off downstream the next day, with the river still running about 26,000 cfs. Moulty bent one of his new ½-inch oarlocks after only a mile on the water. Their next stop was to scout Horn Creek Rapid. Horn Creek is a short, but sharp drop, and to Moulty looked "very mean." Pat once again instructed the crew to be ready to line the rapid should he flip, which he didn't. Neither did Brick. The two pulled in at the bottom of the rapid to pick up their passengers. Moulty changed out oars to replace the bent oarlock for the 'P'-shaped oarlock Carl and Pat had made at Hance, then untied his boat and pushed off into the river. The *Gem* entered Horn Creek on the left, and Moulty did not straighten the *Gem* around in time. It was an easy enough entrance, but Moulty had the *Gem* sideways to the current and when he started to pull on his left oar to swing the boat around, the oarlock jammed. He floated right into a strong lateral sideways and the *Gem* rolled right over.

The *Gem* had a safety line all around the side of the boat, and on surfacing Moulty luckily found himself right next to the boat. He grabbed the safety line and started swimming the boat to shore. Roughly a half mile downriver, he was able to get the boat to a rocky cove on the right. Moulty rested with the boat until the others came along. In the resulting confusion, the *Gem* floated out into fast water and he once again had to swim the boat to shore. It took some doing, but the *Gem* was righted at last. Missing were the two main oars. A gasket had given way on the large stern com-

The *Gem* flips in Horn Creek Rapid, June 26, 1955. Courtesy Carl and Earline Pederson

Drawing from Fulmer Journal of Moulty's flip, 1955

Esther Litton sits on the *Flavell* while Martin Litton checks
a light meter, June 25, 1955. Courtesy Carl and Earline Pederson

partment hatch, and after ninety minutes of being upside down, most of the compartment was flooded. Tommy and Carl's gear was wet, as were Moulty's two cameras and equipment. Esther helped spread out the wet gear to dry. Luckily, the *Gem*'s two spare oars were still lashed to the deck, and after drying the gear out, eating lunch and repacking the boat, the group moved on to Granite Rapid.

Pat asked Moulty if he was up to rowing the *Gem* through Granite, encouraging him to show the river who was boss. Moulty knew who the boss was, but rowed the *Gem* anyway. Pat gave him signals from shore, and even with the late afternoon sun in his eyes, he had a good run. This helped stoke the sputtering fires of his confidence and the group rowed to Hermit Creek for camp, arriving a bit before 7:00 p.m. As they were about to pull into shore, Martin called out that an oar was floating in the river. Moulty spun the *Gem* around and raced out to retrieve it, rowing like a demon to get the oar and then back to shore without running the big rapid just below. Writing in his log that night, Moulty noted the recovery of the oar was like "finding another arm, even if it was the 'P'-shaped one."

On June 27, the river runners packed up and scouted Hermit. It was big, looking even bigger in a little boat than it had when scouting from the shore. Pat and Brick both ran right through the big hole at the foot of the rapid for a thrilling ride. Moulty was able to miss the hole by staying along the left shore. The group ran Boucher and the Gems and stopped at Shinumo Creek for lunch. The afternoon was spent rowing to Elves Chasm. At one point Pat was jotting in his notes and didn't realize where he was. The roar of a rapid took him away from his journal scribbling, and

Lunch stop near Bedrock Rapid, June 28, 1955.
Courtesy Carl and Earline Pederson

111

he suddenly realized he was floating into Walthenberg Rapid. The *Flavell* crew, just a few hundred feet upstream, was surprised to see Pat jump up and frantically put on his life jacket, shouting "My God, it's Walthenberg!" The rapid nearly swamped all the boats, and tore the spare oar off the *Gem*, but Moulty and his crew recovered the wayward oar a few seconds later. There were some tired but happy folks in camp that night, as the river runners had covered twenty-two miles for the day. Once again, camp was chosen close to a side stream providing clear, fresh water for drinking and camp cooking. Now it was Susie's turn to feel sick.

With the Phantom gauge now reading 25,000 cfs, they ran to Tapeats Creek, seeing ten bighorn sheep within a mile of leaving Elves Chasm. At Bedrock, the canyoneers ran all hands in the boats, and all ran down the right-hand side of the rapid with no trouble. Brick took a while getting out of the eddy at the foot of the rapid, but otherwise everyone did well. Deubendorff Rapid was run without incident. The camp for the night was at the foot of Tapeats Creek. The *Flavell* and *Susie R* had to be moved upriver to a calmer location along the shore, as the camp was at a surging eddy, much as it is today. The only difference was the 1955 trip found copious amounts of sand all along the right shoreline where today a boulder field exists.

Tommy Cox, Moulty Fulmer at the oars, and Carl Pederson seated behind Moulty on the *Gem* near Kanab Creek, 1955. Courtesy Fulmer Collection, reproduced by permission, Utah State Historical Society, all rights reserved

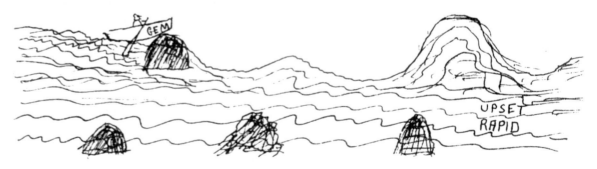

Drawing from Fulmer Journal of his run through Upset Rapid, 1955

In the morning, Pat decided that it was time to patch the ever-growing number of small leaks in the *Susie R*. The boat was unloaded, pulled out of the water, rocked up on her side, and left to dry out. While the *Susie R* dried, the river runners hiked up Tapeats Creek to Thunder River and on to Thunder Spring, crossing the creek nearly a dozen times along the way. Today's river runners make the walk from the river to the spring along a well-maintained trail that was barely visible in 1955. The hikers returned to camp late in the day tired but happy. Brick had enough energy to try some fishing, and very quickly had a string of nine rainbow trout for dinner.

First thing on June 30 was the patching of the *Susie R*. This required sanding off the paint to about three inches around the location of the puncture, and then a piece of fiberglass cloth was cut to cover the hole with about an inch or two of overlap. Two-part, fast-setting epoxy was then mixed, consisting of measured amounts of a resin and a hardener. The liquid epoxy was applied by hand to the repair location then the cloth was laid over the wet epoxy and dabbed into place. Following this, another layer of epoxy was hand-daubed over the cloth. Nobody wore gloves during this work, and a solvent was used to clean up sticky hands once the patch was applied. In a half hour or so, the patch was cured enough to put the boat back in the water.

With the *Susie R* back in the water and loaded with gear, the next stop was Deer Creek for a bath, hike, and camp. After lunch and some swimming in a large pool of clear water at the base of the Deer Creek waterfall, a number of the party hiked up to Surprise Valley, hidden from view of the river behind a short passage of sheer Tapeats sandstone cliffs. To get to the valley, one had to negotiate the Tapeats cliffs along a series of narrow ledges. Moulty noted in his journal it was a beautiful hike. It still is.

On Friday, July 1, with the river flowing 20,000 cfs, the river runners stopped below Matkatamiba Canyon for lunch in some shade where the river makes a sweep to the north. Carl headed up a small side canyon while others took a siesta after lunch. Late in the afternoon the group floated on to Upset Rapid for a quick scout. The afternoon sun shone right in their eyes as they made their entrances. Pat ran the Upset hole for fun, with Martin sitting behind him filming. Brick had a good run solo, and like Pat, pulled into the right-hand eddy at the foot of the rapid to pick up passengers. Moulty tried the right-hand run, but miscalculated his entrance and ended up too far to the right at the top. The *Gem* hit a submerged rock hard and then went sideways through a small hole below the rock. Once clear of the small hole, he passed the main Upset hole on the right. In the eddy below, Moulty inspected his boat for leaks, and could only find a little dent in one of the bottom oak strips. Camp that night was at Ledges, where a trickling stream from a nearby spring provided good clear drinking water.

On the way to Havasu, a small side stream cascaded over a cliff maybe forty feet above the river. For fun and to cool off a little, Pat rowed Susie and the *Susie R* right into the cascading water. Havasu Canyon is a large tributary entering the Colorado River deep in the heart of the Grand Canyon. Like the Little Colorado River, the mineral content in large springs found up Havasu Canyon makes for gorgeous light blue water when the creek is not in flood. The group worked their boats up Havasu Creek's turquoise waters right to the base of the first waterfalls for swimming, photographs, and lunch.

In the afternoon they ran to Fern Glen for camp. Even today's river runners can usually find some large driftwood along the shoreline in the big eddy below Fern Glen Rapid. In 1955, before the construction of Glen Canyon Dam, the driftwood quantities here were epic. So were the fires the group built that night. Before he fell asleep, Pat could clearly make out details of the Canyon walls on the other side of the river from the light cast by the huge bonfire.

After breakfast on July 3, the group hiked Fern Glen Canyon and then floated on to lunch just upriver from Toroweap Point. Through his field glasses, Pat spotted some people high up on the rim of the Canyon at Toroweap Point. He flashed his signal mirror and the people flashed back with their own signal mirror. One of the rim-side observers was John Riffey, Grand Canyon National Monument's Tuweep Ranger. Riffey lived at this remote location with his wife, and was very well liked by the local ranchers and the occasional tourist who managed to work their way out to the remote Toroweap Overlook.

Carl Pederson shepherds the *Flavell* in the water of Lava Falls while Brick Mortenson sits on shore and slowly releases one of the three side lines holding the boat, July 3, 1955. Courtesy Fulmer Collection, reproduced by permission, Utah State Historical Society, all rights reserved

114

LAVA FALLS

GEM

The river runners tried eating some barrel cactus for fun, and Moulty found it palatable. Once lunch and the cactus snacks were completed, the party continued their downriver slide ever closer to Lava Falls, passing a thumb of black lava rising right out of the water called Vulcan's Anvil. Lava Falls, also called Vulcan Rapid at the time, looked as wicked as ever. After a scout on the left, Pat decided to line the *Flavell* while he pondered a run on the left in the *Susie R*.

After unloading all the *Flavell*'s gear, the boat was lined along the left shore. Carl was nearly swept under the boat at one point, and only quick action by the rest of the lining crew protected him from injury or drowning. The *Flavell* chine sustained damage during the lining, and once at the bottom of the falls, it was pulled out of the river as the fiberglass would not stand the eddy's heavy surge.

Meanwhile, Martin, Esther, and Susie worked like Trojans moving the entire outfit's gear along the rocky riverside. Esther found lining rather enjoyable. She delighted in the chance to walk and enjoy the view. She had been worried before the trip that she would find the Grand Canyon oppressive and had been pleasantly surprised at how much she enjoyed walking around rapids. In later years, she would rate this as the best Grand Canyon trip she would ever have.

After the *Flavell* was down and out of the water, the *Gem* was lined next. It suffered a little worse handling but sustained no leaks. During the process, Pat couldn't help but notice how well built the *Gem* was, sustaining no damage in the lining. With dusk fast approaching, Pat decided to line the *Susie R*. It was a good decision as had anything adverse happened during the run, he would have floated off into darkness at the end of an already very long day. Lining the *Susie R* was finally completed at 6:40 p.m. The *Flavell* was moved back into the river and quickly loaded up, then Pat sent Brick, Esther, and Martin down to camp below Lower Lava Rapid to start a fire for dinner. It was an exciting ride for the trio, and Brick noted he was so close to the left wall in Lower Lava he could have written his name on it as they went zipping past.

Pat and Moulty hastily loaded up all remaining gear and hands, then ran Lower Lava down to where a fire awaited them on the beach. The weary crew pulled in and unloaded the boats, then started to work on dinner. The *Flavell* was removed from the river and turned on its side to dry out overnight. It was bedtime right after dinner for the tired, but happy, crew.

Brick and Pat were up early to patch the *Flavell* and get the boat back in the water by 7:30 a.m. While the two men were patching the boat, most of the rest of the party hiked back upriver for a few more photos of Vulcan Rapid.

Lunch was under the ample shade of a large willow tree at the foot of Parashant Rapid, twenty miles downstream from Lava. On the way down to Spring Canyon, they passed a few beavers along the way. At camp, Martin did his best to be patriotic by lighting several driftwood piles on fire to celebrate the 4th of July, and managed to accidentally set much of the Spring Canyon vegetation on fire.

The *Susie R* and *Flavell* arriving at Whitmore Wash,
July 4, 1955. Courtesy Carl and Earline Pederson

On the 5th, the group ran 205 Mile Rapid with Brick and Moulty going solo, after watching the exciting ride Pat had with Tommy and Paul. Lunch was at the foot of 217 Mile Rapid. As Pat was exiting the tailwaves of 224 Mile Rapid, a whirlpool about twelve feet across and four feet deep formed out of the last big wave and pulled him to the right-hand cliff, then as quickly as it formed, it was gone. Camp for the night was at Diamond Creek, and as Norm had done to Moulty seven years earlier, Moulty, Pat, Susie, and Paul initiated the others into the "Royal Order of Colorado River Rats." Moulty took the opportunity to have a bath in the warm, clear, flowing waters of Diamond Creek.

They were away from Diamond by 8:10 the morning of Wednesday, July 6, on about 16,000 cfs. Carl had been expressing interest in rowing a boat, so Moulty graciously let him row the *Gem* out of camp and on to Travertine Canyon. Lunch was at Bridge City, after good runs of the last of the rapids before the impact of Lake Mead began silting in the river channel. The group stopped at Separation Canyon, and then went on to Spencer Canyon for the night's camp. It was a festive evening, and the party composed a number of limericks, such as:

"If you don't pull to the right at Unkar, you are sure to dunker"

"When you cast a glance at Hance, you are almost sure to change your pants"

"When you first lay eyes on Horn, you curse the day you wuz born"

River runners to this day compose lyrics on river trips. Dock had it right when he noted it was called "the incurable rapid happiness."

A riot of bird songs awoke the river party at 4:40 a.m. on their last day on the river. After breakfast, the boats pushed off by 6:45 a.m. In just under three hours, the group was at the guano mine at Bat Cave. An Australian named Buck Moore was the caretaker at the mine, and he happily showed the river runners his live scorpion collection. Disentangling themselves from Buck's hospitality, the group was back on the water by 11:00 a.m.

Happy river runners at trip's end. Left to right, top row: Tommy Cox, Brick Mortenson, Pat Reilly, Martin Litton, Moulton Fulmer; bottom row: Carl Pederson, Susie Reilly, Esther Litton, Paul Terry, July 7, 1955. Courtesy Plez Talmadge Reilly Collection, Cline Library, Northern Arizona University

Drawing from Fulmer Journal showing the three boats being towed across Lake Mead, 1955

In 1955, the water level of Lake Mead was very low. Lake Mead would almost go this low again in 1964, and then not again until 2010. As the river runners worked their way downriver, silt banks slowly rose above them. From Bat Cave to below Columbine Falls, they encountered almost continuous sand waves up to four feet in height. The group passed the Pearce Ferry area early that afternoon, with the river well-defined between thirty-foot-high silt banks that would occasionally collapse into the river with a *whoosh* and raise a large cloud of dust. Suddenly, the high silt banks were gone and the river became very shallow and very wide as it twisted its way back and forth across a growing delta of sediment. The water was shallow enough to ground the boats and the rowers had to choose their channels with care.

With little fanfare, on July 8, 1955, the first Grand Canyon dory reached the end of the current in the headwaters of Lake Mead. While Moulty Fulmer was the builder of the boat, Woodie Hindman was the hull designer, with splash guard, self-bailing, and footwell side compartment design assistance from Dock Marston. The McKenzie River dory had been transformed into a Grand Canyon dory.

At Grand Wash Bay, roughly river mile 286, the group saw Bill Belknap in his motor boat. Bill had cold drinks for those so inclined. Pat's weary crew had covered forty miles that day to reach Belknap and were in need of a cold one. Or two. The three oar boats were tied in a line behind Bill's small outboard boat for the long six-miles-per-hour tow down-lake to Temple Bar, arriving dockside about 10:00 that night. Waiting at the water's edge were Ruth Pieroth, Jean Wyckoff, and Janice Fulmer. The group cooked a quick dinner then bedded down by their boats engulfed by "the aroma of dead fish."

At trip's end, both Moulty and Pat had a chance to size up their watercraft in correspondence with Dock. Moulty wrote that his boat had handled beautifully, but noted multiple failures with gear, in particular the three oarlocks breaking and one gasket leaking. Then there was the loss of his main oars in the Horn Creek flip. All the gear problems were nothing compared with how well the *Gem* managed the daily pounding from in-river and shoreline rocks. Pat was very pleased with his boats as well, finding them easier to maneuver when compared to the Nevills sadiron. Both Pat and Moulty agreed that fiberglass as a building material was vastly overrated. Pat at least took comfort in learning that the field patching was relatively easy and quick to do.

In writing about the other guy's boats to Dock, Moulty wrote that Pat's boats "had good rough water control" and performed well, but noted the fiberglass boats could not stand the rocks and would need additional rub rails "as they are too fragile at the present." Pat noted Moulty's *Gem* "to be the best built wooden boat I have yet seen on the river."

Moulty blamed himself for poor boatmanship when he flipped at Horn Creek, and at Upset for hitting a rock, but both experiences only added to his skill level. Brick Mortenson had done exceptionally well, and Pat commented to Dock on just how fine Brick had done. Like Moulty at the Little Colorado, Brick had almost missed a critical pull-in at South Canyon, and he had gone around in a few eddies the others missed. That said,

118

he had not flipped or sunk the *Flavell*, and he had handled the Canyon's rapids like a pro. The group had gotten along well, not run out of food, or had any major injuries. Besides, the weather had been great. Pat noted this trip had been his best yet.

Within five weeks of finishing the trip, Moulty was contemplating changes to the *Gem* for the next run through the Canyon. On his list of things-to-do were improving the water seal on the stern hatch, having four forged oarlocks made, changing the angle of the oar block so the oar sleeve was parallel to the side of the boat, and being able to wire his oarlocks into the oar block. Before the trip, Pat had written to Moulty that the oars would not fall out in case of an upset, but in field testing they had indeed done just that.

Pat was considering another Canyon run about the same time as Moulty. In an August 14 letter to Dock, Pat noted that a run in 1956 was in his calculations. There were changes to the *Susie R* and *Flavell* that he was thinking about. These included tilting his hatch decks toward drain holes on the outside of the boat, but Pat admitted this major change was one he most likely would not make. Another problem worthy of correction was that Pat had built his oar blocks into his aft compartments, and when the oarlock was submerged by a wave, water would flow past it into the storage space below. He was also thinking about loosening the tolerance for his hatch clasps, as the river silt had made them very difficult to open. Another improvement that Pat recognized he needed, but would not make, was the addition of a stainless steel chine guard. In hindsight, this was one of those additions Pat most certainly should have made, as this oversight would cost him his boats in the end.

The 1955 river running season was also notable for Georgie White's first trip through the Canyon with a large raft made up of three big pontoon ovals tied side to side and powered by an outboard motor in the back. While Frank Wright was lining his cataract boats down the left side of Hance, Georgie motored her big black rubber rig right on through the rapid. Her party waved at Frank's lining crew as they sped past. At the time, Georgie's trips were also inexpensive. Marketed as "Share the Expense Plan River Trips," Georgie asked her passengers to purchase their own waterproof gear bags, and she tried her best to limit passenger gear to thirty pounds each. For an eleven-night trip through the Grand Canyon, she charged her passengers $300 each.

Also of note was the sheer number of river trips making the journey through the Grand Canyon in 1955. Two young men from California, Bill Beer and John Daggett, swam the river wearing life jackets and holding two river bags, one under each arm with a small piece of rope between each bag acting as a "seat." Jim Rigg motored the river in hard-hulled craft, Frank Wright took a rowing trip through as did Malcolm "Moki Mac" Ellingson. There was Moulty's and Pat's oar-powered trip, Don Harris leading a commercial group, another self-guided group led by Dale Atkinson and Reed Jensen, and two trips that went from Lee's Ferry to Phantom Ranch. River runners who started in the 1940s, like Dock, Pat, and Moulty, were beginning to comment on the crowds and ever increasing size of the large rubber pontoon boats. Pat asked Dock in a late July letter if he couldn't use his research talents "toward finding us a river that doesn't need traffic signals?" In a mid-August letter to Dock, Pat wondered at the incompatibility of seeking out the most turbulent water in America but doing so in a rubber pontoon boat so big it was capable of neutralizing the turbulence.

Another portent of things to come was the formation of the Western River Guides Association in Salt Lake City. The association was organized "to develop an appreciation for the natural resources of the west and assist in their preservation and development." It wouldn't be long before the few doing a business of getting "dudes" through the Grand Canyon on rubber boats would start looking out for the development of their bottom lines, often at cross purposes with self-guided river runners like Moulty and Pat, and eventually, with the very resource itself.

13

The Perfect Run, Almost

1956

There was a two-month period over the winter of 1955-1956 when Moulty didn't hear back from Pat, and Moulty's plans for another cruise of the Grand Canyon came to an abrupt stop. During the cold Indiana winter, Janice would find Moulty out in the garage making the needed changes to the *Gem* he had identified after the 1955 trip. While Moulty was certainly looking forward to running with Pat again in 1956, Pat, it seems, may have had other intentions.

Working closely with Martin as the author, Pat had been providing editorial review for an article on the Grand Canyon for *Sunset* magazine. Pat wrote Martin on February 19 that a two-boat, six-person trip was in order for 1956, and that Brick would be devoting his vacation to his family that year. Pat wanted to know if Martin would be interested in coming along. Martin replied that he would "move heaven and earth to try to scrounge the extra week beyond my vacation."

Moulty and Janice on Kauai, Hawaii, 1956. Courtesy Fulmer Collection, reproduced by permission, Utah State Historical Society, all rights reserved

On March 5, the Littons and Marstons attended a film showing that Georgie White had organized in San Francisco. Attended by about a thousand people, each paying 90¢ for the two-hour show, Martin found the film "hi-larious" with lots of footage of water fights, horseplay, and shots of people stuck in the wonderful mud found in many locations along the water's edge of the Colorado River.

At one point during the evening, Dock mentioned Moulty had not heard from Pat and would like to run the Canyon again. Martin said he was under the impression Pat had not heard from Moulty. The two agreed it sounded like a misunderstanding, so Martin and Dock began to work on reconnecting Moulty and Pat.

Two days later, Dock, the matchmaker, sent Pat, Moulty, and Martin the same letter. Dock pointed out that while it was none of his business, he had noted that the 1955 crew had been well balanced and was trying to solve some vexing problems of watercraft design which "certainly needed more study." Dock noted that both Pat and Moulty seemed set on going again in 1956, and given the good combination of the previous year's crew, the question unanswered was "Why didn't they get together for another cruise?" Dock noted that if the two were not going to run together again, they had some explaining to do, to him anyway.

Meanwhile, in the spring of 1956, Hawaii called Moulty and Janice. They were not only canyoneers, but were interested in travels to other far-away places beyond the Grand Canyon. Still, the Canyon call was loud enough that the couple traveled to Chicago, then took the non-stop flight to San Francisco where they broke their journey to spend a night with Dock and Margaret. Then it was on to the islands on an overnight flight.

Pat responded only to Dock, thanking him for taking the trouble to attempt a reconnection, and for handling the "problem." Pat also explained that while he did owe Moulty a letter, Moulty had not responded to his pointed inquiries about the dates of the trip to Hawaii, whether Moulty contemplated a river trip, and if so, which river. He noted he preferred to wait for Moulty to answer the questions he had asked rather than to respond to Moulty's letter that didn't have the answers he was looking for. Letter etiquette in the days before cheap phone calls and email meant that when you received a letter, it was your "turn" to reply. Pat had not replied and Moulty had written to Dock to figure out what was up.

In his response to Dock, Pat expressed concern about Moulty's upset in Horn Creek the year before. He was also worried about Moulty's run of Upset, stating Moulty's "judgments and reactions are not as good as they probably were formerly." Pat noted Moulty "seems to desire excessive clearance of the hazards, and gets in trouble by so doing and freezes in indecision." No mention is made of Moulty's oarlock trouble at Horn Creek or the sun in his eyes at the top of the Upset run. He went on to note that Moulty "is a fine companion and a definite asset to a party."

Dock didn't see things quite as black and white as Pat had described them, and while he clearly enjoyed trying to get to the root of a problem, he lamented that he and Pat couldn't drop the "identity of the individual and merely discuss the situation as pertaining to boatman x." What surprised Dock on looking at Carl's film footage of Moulty's flip was how little "violence" the river used to roll the *Gem* over. Dock discounted the boat's design as the cause of the flip, and could only conclude it was boatman error. That said, he wrote Pat he doubted Moulty's skills with fast water had lessened any.

On returning from Hawaii, Moulty began to seek out two passengers from the Eastern states. He welcomed some driving assistance on the long two-lane drive from Muncie to Lee's Ferry and Temple Bar. Early contacts with Wayne and Lucile Hiser, Moulty's 1948 Grand Canyon companions, were initially positive, but the Hisers had to back out when another commitment arose. Pat wrote Martin that the trip might just be two boats after all, given that he doubted Moulty could "afford to run without at least one passenger." In a letter to Dock at the same time, Pat noted the events with the Hisers dropping out, and how Moulty had asked if Pat knew of anyone who could fill their places. Pat's response to Dock was that he had "too good a party of six to have it spoiled by indecision and poor planning."

Dock was not pleased with Pat's response. While he admitted there was a time when he had not practiced what he preached, Dock was convinced a two-boat trip that could not carry all the trip's participants on any one of the two boats was a bad idea from the point of safety. Dock also wanted Pat to make a little more effort "to assure participation by Moulty." Dock even offered a suggested passenger should Pat need someone.

Though Pat may have had no qualms if Moulty dropped out, even with Dock's concerns about the safety of a two-boat trip, he had no idea how much the trip meant to Moulty. When the Hisers backed out, Moulty approached "Big" Guy Taylor. The thirty-five-year-old had served in the Army in New Guinea during World War II, and his sewer and drain cleaning services were used at the Muncie YMCA on a number of occasions. Moulty had learned that Guy liked to travel, and when he asked Guy if he wanted to cruise through the Grand Canyon, Guy had jumped at the chance.

In early March, besides trying to reconnect Pat with Moulty, Martin also began to lobby Pat for another passenger to accompany the trip. According to Martin, Esther did not want to leave their two small children for such a long time, and besides, the 1955 trip had been perfect for her and any other trip would be anticlimactic. The passenger Martin proposed bringing was a female co-worker at *Sunset*, all of eighteen years old, five feet eight inches tall and weighing 130 pounds. Martin noted he would have no trouble sitting face to face with her for eighteen days, as she had won a number of beauty contests. Martin also said he spoke at length with Esther about this and "all is harmonious, if not quite exactly hi-larious." Pat wrote back in jest that he had divorced Susie and was in training to wrestle Martin for the privilege of being boatman for Martin's "Venus."

Amrette Ott, also known as Martin's "Venus," was the daughter of an insurance salesman. She started working at *Sunset* during her last year in high school. Eventually she began assisting Martin with articles for the magazine. One such story was titled "Learning to Fly in a Day." Sitting in the pilot's seat with Martin doing the actual flying, and with a photography plane just off her wingtip, Amrette appeared to be flying the plane while Martin hunched out of sight. After seeing Martin's films of the 1955 river trip, Amrette dropped out of her summer session at Stamford University so she could make the trip.

By mid-March, Dock noted the runoff prospects were looking good, and he worked on plans for another three-boat motor run through the Canyon. Pat was watching the water as well, and by the middle of April had chosen June 18 as his launch date. It was a good choice, if not a tad late. The Colorado River slowly rose from a low of 3,570 cfs on February 7 and passed the 20,000 cfs mark April 26. The river would stay above 20,000 cfs through June 26, with the peak flow of the year occurring at Lee's Ferry on June 6 at an impressive 69,600 cfs.

Martin rented a Cessna 180 and piloted an April 16 flight with Dock, Pat, and Brick around the Grand Canyon on a picture-taking tour. It was the second flight of the year Pat had made over the Canyon with Martin. The foursome landed at the small dirt strip at Tuweep. Ranger Riffey drove his pick-up out to the airstrip to take the city-slickers over to the Toroweap Overlook, and then to "Park Headquarters" where John's wife, Laura, had lunch waiting. It was not until later that spring while using a magnifying glass to look at the photos he had shot that Pat discovered he had taken photos of a previously unknown arch up a side canyon called 140 Mile. Pat added a stop at that remote canyon onto the trip's itinerary.

As for the rest of the 1956 trip crew, Pat made it clear in an April 19 letter to Martin the type of passenger he was looking for. "To have the intense desire is the first requisite for any passenger or boatman." These words of advice to Martin were as true in 1956 as they are fifty-five years after he penned them. Desire and motivation are the key to success in a lot of life, as they are for a successful cruise through the Grand Canyon where the social and physical environment can be a challenge. The crew for the 1956 cruise would be as diverse a bunch of folks as were on the previous year's trip.

Besides Pat, Susie, Martin, Guy, Moulty, and Amrette, the trip roster would include an artist named Bob Watson. Pat had purchased a large painting by Watson called "The Bridge" that moved him like "a thunderbolt when I first saw it and the feeling has intensified with time." Bob was internationally known for his paintings of vast barren landscapes with a small person or two for scale. Pat thought Bob would enjoy living the painting as a small person in a big landscape. Bob, who lived in Hollywood at the time, was excited to participate. William "Bill" McGill would also join the team. A young outspoken ex-Marine working at Lockheed, Pat noted of McGill that he had lived Hemingway's *From Here to Eternity*. The last addition to the crew would be Dr. Norman Day, whom Pat had known for fifteen years. Norm was in his early to mid-fifties, an enthusiastic sportsman, and active in many service clubs.

Willie Taylor grave marker in the heart of Grand Canyon, 2008. Tom Martin photo

While the Reilly-Fulmer expedition was still weeks away from launching, Dock launched on his Grand Canyon cruise with three motor boats. On the trip were his son Garth and, of course, the ever good-natured Willie Taylor, now fifty-nine. When the group stopped at the top of 24½ Mile Rapid for lunch, Willie began having chest pain. Dr. Josh Eisaman was on the trip, and administered some sedatives to Willie at Redwall Cavern. At the camp at President Harding that night, Doctor Eisaman gave Willie some opium to help him rest. Willie woke once in the night in pain, but otherwise slept well. The group pulled out of camp about 11:00 a.m., June 6, but Dock quickly noticed the other boats were not following him. Willie was unable to climb into the boat by himself and the others had a difficult time getting him into his seat. When the two boats caught Dock only a mile below Harding, Willie was moved from the boat to the shade of a large mesquite tree. In another fifteen minutes, the ever amiable and fun loving man had run his last rapid. He was buried that afternoon up against a low cliff. The river crested for the year at Lee's Ferry the day Willie died, at 69,600 cfs. Dock had listed Willie as the 100th person to travel through the Grand Canyon, on the 1949 *Esmeralda II* run.

Nine days after Willie ran his last rapid, the Reilly-Fulmer river party coalesced from the west and the east at Art Greene's Cliff Dwellers Lodge. Moulty and Guy arrived first, unloaded the *Gem* at Lee's Ferry, then Moulty left Guy at Art's and drove to Boulder City, Nevada, to meeet Pat, Susie, and Bill. After shuttling Moulty's car and trailer out to Temple Bar, the foursome headed off to Art's, arriving about 8:00 p.m. that night.

The next day the party of five drove to the Badger Rapid overlook, then to the Ferry where they put all three boats in the water and loaded most of the gear into the boats. Moulty stayed with the boats that night while the rest of the group returned to Art's. Martin, Norm, Amrette, and Bob arrived in Martin's car after dark.

On the third Monday in June the group was ready to depart. It was the same third Monday that Moulty, Martin, Susie, and Pat had launched on the year before. Like then, the water was falling off the spring's peak. The group launched on about 37,900 cfs, but the river was dropping quickly. Pat lead the way in the *Susie R* with Bill McGill and Susie, then came Martin in the *Flavell* with Amrette and Bob, and Moulty once again brought up the rear, with the "Big Boys" Norm and Guy riding in the *Gem*. The team ran Badger and stopped at the foot of the rapid for lunch in the shade of a hackberry tree.

Camp that night was at House Rock Wash. It was steak-to-order night, with Pat and Susie doing all the cooking duties for the trip, as was done the year before. The river fell a good foot during the night, and on Tuesday, June 19, was at 35,200 cfs. The group was up early and on the water by 7:15 a.m. for the run to North Canyon. The party stopped to scout North Canyon Rapid, and then ran it with all passengers on the boats. At the foot of the rapid, Martin got an oar tangled with a rock under the boat and snapped an oarlock. The group set a driftwood pile on fire below 22 Mile, then rowed to South Canyon for camp. Once there, they hiked up to the ruins on the limestone bench above the river, looked at the headless skeleton there, and camped at the lower end of the South Canyon eddy, just above Vasey's Paradise.

Susie Reilly and Amrette Ott at Redwall Cavern, June 20, 1956. Courtesy Amrette Butler

Bob Watson, Martin Litton, and Amrette Ott, June 20, 1956. Courtesy Amrette Butler

By June 20, the river had dropped a little over 5,000 cfs in forty-eight hours. The party broke camp early and stopped at Redwall Cavern. The boatman shared their oars with the passengers, and Bill got to row the *Susie R*, Bob the *Flavell*, and Guy the *Gem*. Lunch was in the shade at about 40 Mile.

In the afternoon, the party traveled past the Marble Canyon Dam site and stopped to look at Bert Loper's boat, the *Grand Canyon*, then went on to the big eddy at the foot of President Harding Rapid for camp.

Bill, Guy, Norm, Amrette, and Martin all caught catfish which Pat cooked up after dinner for a late snack. Bill lit a big driftwood pile on fire, and he, Pat, and Bob sat around a small fire chatting late into the night. It was a very pleasant evening with no wind to move the ever-present sand.

The river continued to drop slowly overnight and throughout the next day. The party left camp and headed to the big eddy below the mouth of Nankoweap Creek. Pat walked the half mile over to the clear flowing water in Nankoweap Creek to fill canteens. On his return, they headed on to

Pat Reilly and Amrette Ott at Bert Loper's boat,
June 20, 1956. Courtesy Amrette Butler

Upstream view from camp at the
mouth of the Little Colorado River,
June 21, 1956.Courtesy Amrette Butler

the mouth of the Little Colorado River for camp. On arrival, the party was pleasantly surprised to see the Little Colorado River running its heavenly blue color.

In the morning, some of the river runners sacked in as the photographers waited for the sun to light up the blue Little Colorado River waters. The boaters were underway at 9:30 a.m., stopping to explore and have lunch at the mouth of Lava Chuar Canyon. A short way below Lava Chuar Rapid, the *Susie R* was harassed by a whirlpool. Pat estimated the funnel was the length of his boat, and the force of the four-foot-deep liquid cyclone drew the top of the *Susie R* right down underwater. The footwell began to fill at an alarming rate as the boat was spun around like a top. Terrified, there was nothing Pat or his crew could do. Suddenly, the whirlpool disappeared, leaving the boat to be bailed. This was the biggest whirlpool Pat had seen on the river, which was now running just over 29,000 cfs.

At Unkar Rapid, the group didn't even stop to scout, and all had good runs. They scouted 75 Mile Rapid, and the run was made with all hands in the boats, with camp at the top of Hance Rapid. It was here that a few of the crew took a piece of burned wood that looked like an oar blade and carved "JW POWELL 1869" in the charred wood. They left the fake oar on the beach. Someone on Georgie White's trip later in the year found the oar, and Georgie dutifully delivered the "artifact" to the South Rim.

Amrette Ott with fake oar at the top of Hance, June 23, 1956, Bob Watson in background. Courtesy Amrette Butler

By the morning of June 23, the river was a perfect stage for running Hance, allowing for an easy left run. The boatman all took their boats through without passengers. As had happened a year earlier, the fiberglass boats suffered from contact with rocks in the eddy surge at the rapid's foot. The *Flavell* sustained a four-inch crack on the chine that Pat had to temporarily patch with caulk before the run to Phantom. A small hole was knocked in the *Susie R*, but it was hardly worth patching.

The group headed into the Granite Gorge and did quick scouts of Sockdolager and Grapevine rapids. Grapevine had what Pat guessed to be a twelve- to fifteen-foot high lateral wave on the left side near the top that he and Martin cleared by going right. Moulty took it straight on in the *Gem*, and had a wild but dry run, the same as Pat had done the year before. A deserted beach at Phantom Ranch greeted the river crew a little after noon. While Susie and Amrette made lunch at the Bright Angel campground, the rest of the crew unloaded all the gear out of the *Flavell* and *Susie R*, pulled the empty boats out of the river, and pushed them up on their sides to dry out prior to patching. The group swam in the Phantom pool and enjoyed a cool beer after Martin and Pat patched the boats. Everything seemed to be going fine according to Pat's log, except that Bob Watson was contemplating leaving the trip "to get his next show together." At least that was what Pat's log said.

The show that Bob was worried about was more of a "showdown." According to Bob, he was working overtime on the trip as a psychologist way over his head. Bob became the confidant at first for Bill, and then for Martin, as each confessed their hatred for the other. Bob noted he "was a sounding board for a pair of egos far more monumental than my own even." Bob had expected Bill and Martin to tangle by the time the trip arrived at Phantom, and while that had not happened, Bob still wanted none of it. The mule train that departed from Phantom for the South Rim on Sunday, June 24, carried ex-river runner Bob Watson, who noted that being cooped up on the boat "with that unpleasantness was not good for already shaky nerves."

To their credit, this would be the only trip Pat and Moulty would run where any member of the party would depart early due to disharmony among the group. If Pat was concerned for what would come later in the trip, he made no mention of it in his log.

By the time the canyoneers arrived at Horn Creek Rapid on June 24, the river had dropped over 12,000 cfs, a third of the flow the group had launched on just seven days earlier. Still, Horn Creek was running at about 26,400 cfs when the party stopped to scout the rapid. All passengers were walked to the foot of the raging torrent, and then Pat, Martin, and Moulty had good runs down the far left side of the rapid.

Lunch, with a siesta afterwards, was in the shade at the top of Granite Rapid. Then it was time to run Granite. The three boatmen all ran solo. Moulty gave signals from shore to Pat, who then gave signals to Martin and Moulty. At Hermit, the rowers ran solo again. The mouth of Boucher Canyon, with its clear-running stream of good tasting water, was camp for the night. While it was ninety degrees in camp just after sundown, there was no wind to blow sand in the dinner or to chase Moulty out to sleep on his boat. Besides, the river water was seventy degrees, making for enjoyable swimming.

On June 25, the group boated from Boucher Canyon to Elves Chasm on about 25,000 cfs. There was no Crystal Rapid to worry about in those years, and the rest of the Gems were wet and fun. The group pulled into the mouth of Shinumo Creek for a quick walk up to the nearby waterfall. The wind had picked up and was blowing so much sand about that lunch would really have been "sand-witched." In-

Stopping for a candy break above Specter Chasm, June 26, 1956. Courtesy Amrette Butler

Bill McGill and Moulty Fulmer take a dip at the mouth of
Stone Creek, June 26, 1956. Courtesy Amrette Butler

stead, they had some candy and floated on down-river, passing under the Hakatai Canyon cable car. A small wooden and metal basket still clung to the cable midspan. Bill Bass had set up this cross-river tramway to move several tons of high grade asbestos ore from his mine on the north side of the river to the railroad south of the Grand Canyon in 1917.

As the river runners approached Elves Chasm for lunch and camp, a black-chinned hummingbird flew in to check out the brightly colored boats. Once onshore, Pat and Susie sought the shade of a large overhang where they could see out across the river to Redwall Limestone cliffs towering high overhead. Meanwhile, the others explored Royal Arch Canyon. It was here that the showdown Bob Watson skillfully avoided finally happened. Pat would recount many years later that at one point Martin "let loose a 50 pound rock at Bill McGill's head" but fortunately "missed him by three feet." Bill was just a bit more careful after that but "threatened to kill Martin."

Pat realized he needed to do something to restore trip harmony, but was not sure what exactly to do. The next day, figuring a change in who-would-ride-where might help, Amrette rode with Norm and Moulty in the *Gem* while Guy rode with Martin and Bill rode with Pat and Susie.

With passengers rearranged, on they went, running Specter without scouting. Bedrock Rapid was scouted, and the run down the right side was made easily with everyone in the boats. The group also scouted Deubendorff Rapid, where a large eagle watched Pat, then Martin, then Moulty, run their boats solo through the rapid.

With boats tied up at the sandy mouth of Stone Creek, the river runners hiked the short distance to the first waterfall in the creek, enjoying a cool shower in the falls. Pat decided to camp at the mouth of Tapeats Creek instead of pulling in at the base of the rapid, where the shoreline was hammered by a surging eddy.

The river dropped enough in the night that the three boats were high and dry on a bed of sand in the morning, with the river now running at about 22,000 cfs. The next day was a layover day for those who wanted to stay in camp or go hiking. Moulty, Martin, and Guy went up the steep talus slope from camp and spent the day hiking to Thunder River while the rest of the party fished, washed, rested, and looked for fossils. Dragonflies darted through the horsetail and willows, while collared lizards hunted for flies. Clear and cold Tapeats Creek was flowing about a foot deep, and about fifteen feet wide. The channel cut through steep-banked river sand on either side of the creek, and on occasion a large chunk of sand bank would drop away into the creek to be swept back out to the muddy river whence it had come.

The hikers returned late in the day. Moulty had spoken with three backpackers at the confluence of Thunder River and Tapeats Creek, while Guy, on reaching level terrain at the bottom of the talus slope, kneeled down and kissed the ground after the ten-mile hike.

Amrette Ott at Deer Creek Falls, June 28, 1956. Courtesy Amrette Butler

On the 28th, the group ran Tapeats Rapid first thing, with the next stop a large cave on the right. In the back of the cave, Pat noted a small stalagmite that looked like a "spruce tree." It is known as Christmas Tree Cave today.

From here, they rowed on to Deer Creek Falls for an early lunch. After taking photos of the falls in sunlight, all but Moulty hiked up through the Tapeats Narrows into Surprise Valley. Martin and Pat worked their way up the valley toward the upper spring. Martin found a nice spot on the way to take a nap, and Pat pushed on to the mouth of the spring, where a ten-inch-diameter water spout gushed from a crack in the sheer cliff and arced down to land on a series of rocky blocks cascading into a pool below. The water course was lined with catclaw acacia, willows, redbuds, maidenhair ferns, and moss. This was the second time Pat had worked his way up to this spring, and he enjoyed this visit as much as he had the first time.

On the return journey, Susie and Amrette accompanied Pat back down to the boats. Camp for the night was at the base of the falls. A strong wind whipped up the riverside sand, and fine grit seasoned their dinner.

The group was on the water the next morning a little after 7:40 a.m. for the easy float to 140 Mile Canyon. Pat's goal for the day was to hike up this side canyon to see if he could locate the natural bridge he had seen in his aerial photos. Moulty, Bill, Martin, and Guy went with him. What the photos didn't show was that 140 Mile is a very rugged side canyon. The hikers immediately faced a series of pour-overs and large boulders within the first half mile up from the river. The men toiled up the dry canyon floor in full sun, through thick catclaw acacia. With a sturdy trunk, this truck-sized tree has strong, thin branches coated by small but very sharp thorns that shred anything they touch, including clothing and skin.

On reaching a fork in the canyon, the party took the side canyon heading to the southwest. More dense thickets of catclaw and a jumble of boulders choked the canyon floor. The going was very rough. Pat stashed his 4x5 camera, tripod, and his Rolleiflex camera, continuing on with two Leicas in a small metal ammunition can. After another half mile of treacherous bushwhacking, Moulty and Guy turned back.

Pat continued on another quarter mile or so to where he could get a photo of the bridge, then he too turned back. Bill and Martin got close enough to see light through the roughly fifty-foot-wide by two-hundred-foot-high bridge. Martin found some Ancestral Puebloan pottery and corn cobs near the base of the arch. The hikers returned to the river exhausted, and all took a swim. Pat would later submit the name "Keyhole Natural Bridge" to the United States Geological Survey Board of Geographical Names, while the rest of the crew submitted the name "Reilly's Folly" which made the *Los Angeles Times*.

Thick cumulus clouds were building to the east, south, and north as the river runners had a late lunch and headed west toward Kanab Canyon. Given the lateness of the day, Pat elected to camp at a large sandy beach by a spring just upstream of Matkatamiba Canyon. As Pat worked on dinner, enough of a rain shower swept in from the east to send the campers scattering for rain gear. The quick shower only dampened the sand as Pat pondered the weather. Typically, rain showers moved upcanyon from the west. This storm was from the east heading downcanyon. Scattered showers, sheet lightning, and thunder kept the travelers entertained until well after dark.

About the time everyone was sound asleep, the boats started crashing into each other. Through the beam of his flashlight, Pat was surprised to see the river had risen a good three to four feet. The rising water had carved away the sand at the camp to such an extent that Bill was about to be dropped into the river, his feet dangling in the air off the leading edge of the beach. As the storm headed off to the west, the boats were retied, and those who had been sleeping near the river found new spots higher up the beach.

Dawn on Saturday, June 30, arrived with light rain and intermittent thunder. Surprisingly, the river had receded a foot overnight. The dropping water had left the *Susie R* high and dry. The party had a tough job on their hands to refloat the boat. The rain stopped, and breakfast consisted of grapefruit, melba toast and jam, oatmeal and coffee. The river was now running about 17,000 cfs, less than half the flow at the trip's start. The group launched just before 7:30 a.m., and was quickly at the top of Upset Rapid for a scout. The three boats were run through without passengers, in the standard running order of Pat, Martin, and Moulty. Pat and Martin both made it just to the right of the big hole, but Moulty plowed right on through it.

As the boatmen picked up their crew members at the foot of the rapid and headed on downriver, Trans World Airlines (TWA) Captain Jack S. Gandy throttled up the Lockheed Super Constellation "Star of the Seine" and took off from Los Angeles International Airport with seventy passengers on board. Gandy was heading east for Kansas City, Missouri, and minor mechanical difficulty had kept his plane on the ground for an extra thirty minutes. Three minutes later, United Airlines Captain Robert F. Shirley powered the Douglas DC-7 "Mainliner Vancouver" under his command down an adjacent runway at the same airport, also headed east. The fifty-eight travelers on board were headed for Chicago. Both pilots typically made a detour over the Grand Canyon for sightseeing on their flights, and June 30 was no exception.

Big Guy Taylor puts yet more wood on the fire on a hot summer evening at Fern Glen, June 30, 1956. Courtesy Amrette Butler

The top of this photo shows the lining route past Lava Falls on river-left, as seen from river-right where Amrette Ott is standing, July 1, 1956. Courtesy Amrette Butler

The river runners rowed past Reilly's Roost, known as Ledges Camp today, and spotted a golden eagle perched about 150 feet above the river. The eagle flew downstream ahead of them, then landed on a cliff edge only 100 feet above the river and watched the canyoneers row by. The group arrived at the mouth of Havasu Canyon mid-morning. The normally blue water in the creek was red with silt and mud washed down by the recent rains. Still, the party worked their boats up through the tight narrows at the mouth of Havasu to the first falls. About the time the river party was tying up their boats next to a loud waterfall, ninety-five miles back upriver, the DC-7 sliced into the Super Constellation, incapacitating both aircraft. The planes were off-course when the accident happened, sightseeing over the confluence of the Little Colorado River and the Colorado. Unfortunately, visibility was limited by scattered clouds and the occasional thunderstorm. All 128 passengers and flight crew were killed in the midair collision, the worst airline disaster the country had yet experienced. The river runners could not have heard the impact. Had the roar of the distant tragedy actually made it to them, the noise would have been indistinguishable from the low growl of distant thunder.

Unaware of the disaster that had just occurred upriver, the boaters pulled back out of Havasu about 11:00 a.m. on a red river heavy with debris, including many "slabs of cactus, from the flash flood of last night." A few hummingbirds continued their investigations of the boats throughout the day, and after lunch the crew rowed on under towering cumulus clouds to the big eddy at Fern Glen for camp. Copious quantities of driftwood made

for a large fire after dinner. While there were still tensions among the crew, they were only slowly boiling.

Dawn on the first of July came all too soon. Cumulus clouds were already forming, and the river was still blood red from upriver rains. The group was out of camp and on the river early as usual. As they passed an area known as the "Red Slide," Martin and Guy spotted a mountain lion near the water's edge. They pulled to shore and hiked up to where they had last seen the cat while Pat looked on with his field glasses. Unable to flush the cat out, the two returned to the boats and the crew carried on to Lava Falls for a scout, first on the right, then on the left. It was agreed that the rapid could not be run, and after lunch a lining operation commenced down the left shore.

Prospect Canyon, on the south side of the river, contributes the debris responsible for making Lava Falls. It had flashed since the previous year, and the receding high water of the Colorado had exposed a fairly level walking path along the shore which made carrying the gear easier. The *Gem* was let down first, then the *Flavell*, and last the *Susie R.* Once at the foot of the rapid, the boats were reloaded, and they were underway just after 6:00 p.m. Camp for the night was just below Lower Lava. During the lining along Lava, the two fiberglass boats had been punctured by rocks. Once at camp, the boats were unloaded of their gear, pulled from the river and set up on their sides to dry. Pat made dinner that night with his standard soup and crackers, followed by canned chipped beef, rice and beans, with canned pears for dessert. Everyone retired to bed soon after dinner.

A large gust of wind boomed up the Canyon and awoke the sleeping canyoneers at dawn on July 2. The sky was hazy as if high winds were stirring up dust on the plateaus above. Bill made breakfast while Pat patched the boats, and then the photographers went back up to Lava for more pictures. The bowlines were finally untied just before 10:00 a.m., and upstream winds in the afternoon made rowing a challenge, especially on the slow-moving sections of river above Parashant and Spring canyons. The boaters saw a few burros and beaver, and pulled into Spring Canyon for camp about 5:30 p.m. The water in Spring Canyon tasted good, but the creek bed had a strong smell of burro.

The next day, Amrette ran 205 Mile Rapid as a passenger in the *Flavell*, and then walked back up to the top of the rapid to run it again 'fisheying' on the stern deck of the *Gem* with Moulty at the oars. The group stopped at what is today known as Pumpkin Spring, just below 213 Mile, and then rowed on to Three Springs Canyon for lunch.

Pat had seen fresh water while rowing past the mouth of Three Springs Canyon the previous year, and so a stop to explore was in order. The group camped at Diamond Creek for the night, and as was the custom, inducted Norm, Guy, Amrette, and Bill into the Royal Order.

On the morning of July 4, with the river running around 15,000 cfs, the canyoneers left Diamond Creek and stopped at Travertine Grotto. A previous river party had left a lot of trash here, including exposed 16mm film, tin cans, papers, and other odds and ends. Pat's party cleaned up the mess, and Pat wondered in his log how "the average man seems to be such a despoiler." The rest of the runs that morning were uneventful. The group stopped at Bridge City for lunch, then took photos at the Separation Canyon cenotaph. Camp for the night was at a small sandbar at around 257 Mile after a thirty-mile day on the oars.

Following a quick breakfast, the group was once again on the move through the west end of the Grand Canyon, passing Bat Cave about 7:30 a.m. The caretaker at the guano mine waved as his dog barked at the boats. The group passed the Pearce Ferry area about 9:30 a.m., and stopped in the shade at current's end at the mouth of Grand Wash Bay. About 2:00 that afternoon, Fred Clayton of Temple Bar arrived with his motor boat and some cold beer. The tow-out was slow because floating driftwood kept fouling the motor boat's propeller.

The river runners reached Temple Bar that evening. Ruth Pieroth and Jean Wyckoff met them, having driven Pat's truck and trailer along with Martin's car around from Marble Canyon. The boats were loaded on their trailers, and the group split up. Moulty and Guy departed for Kingman, while Jean, Ruth, Pat, and Susie stayed at Temple Bar, and everyone else went west.

The letters reveal there were some rough words spoken between some of the river runners at the Temple Bar ramp, but they don't say who was doing the talking or what the trouble was about. Pat noted in his log that from the standpoint of running rapids, it had been a "wonderful trip." Besides, Pat found "the human element secondary." Secondary or not, whatever the "situation" had been, Pat would write seven years later that at the end of the 1956 trip, Moulty and Martin hated each other's guts.

The drive back to Indiana was a challenge for Guy and Moulty. As they were driving on Route 66 just east of Flagstaff, a car approaching from the opposite direction sideswiped them and kept right on going. The two men were unable to get a vehicle description. Then, while at one stop somewhere along the way, an idling vehicle's exhaust burned a perfectly round hole clear through the chine of the *Gem*. It was a miracle the boat didn't catch on fire. Moulty didn't even notice the *Gem*'s damage until he was back in Muncie.

Susie, Jean, Ruth, and Pat towed the *Susie R* and *Flavell* to the South Rim on Friday, July 6. Pat met with Lynn Coffin, Grand Canyon National Park Chief Ranger, to inform the NPS about the discovery of the natural bridge. Coffin had other things on his mind, and asked Pat if he would be available for a boat run to the TWA-United crash area should he be needed. Pat stated he would be glad to cooperate, and he would want Brick Mortenson to run his second boat. From the South Rim, the foursome drove on to Art's where Pat left his boats, thinking they might be used sooner than he had originally anticipated. By July 12, Pat and Susie were back home in Studio City.

Within a week, Pat was planning another Grand Canyon river run, to depart three weeks later. Everett Chapman, an aeronautical consulting engineer, had been hired by the legal firm representing TWA. Chapman and his wife, Hildegarde, were good friends with Pat and Susie and knew of their river running capabilities. While Chapman had taken telephoto pictures of the TWA wreckage from the rim near Cape Solitude, he wanted a piece of the Super Constellation tail section showing signs of blue paint from the wing of the United plane.

Pat wanted Brick and fellow Lockheed employee, Bill McGill, to accompany him as boat crew, while Chapman would be providing two "investigators." Pat's itinerary included four nights camping at the crash location. The trip would only have enough food to get to Phantom, and Pat arranged to have additional food packed into the ranch. Since the investigators would be leaving at Phantom, hopefully with recovered pieces of the Constellation's tail, Chapman arranged for two of his nephews to fill the vacancies. Pat had worked on Super Constellation tooling for Lockheed since 1941, and wrote to Chapman he never dreamed he would be "sweating over an empennage in Grand Canyon."

With funding for the trip secured from TWA, Chapman directed TWA's legal team to contact Lockheed to get Pat and his crew freed up to go on the trip. There would be three investigators, as Chapman was now on the trip roster as well. Pat applied for a permit from the park, including his itinerary for a four-day stay at the crash site. As he was now back at work, Susie was handling much of the correspondence and trip logistics.

By the second of August, Pat's bosses had not heard from TWA requesting leave for their employees, and Pat was getting nervous about the need to book lodging at Art Greene's, Phantom Ranch, and the South Rim, plus arrange a tow out, not to mention do the food pack and coordinate with the NPS to pick up the permit.

Within forty-eight hours, Chapman telegraphed Pat from Washington, D.C., where hearings were underway about the events surrounding the tragic accident. The trip would have to be postponed by a few weeks. Susie wrote the Greenes and the NPS about the delay on August 6. Pat had no way of knowing that his application for a permit, with a four-day layover at the crash location, had been sent to Washington, where it was quickly denied. Low water was cited as the reason for the permit denial, but it is just possible the National Park Service was not concerned about low water. It's true that Pat's overloaded fiberglass boats would have certainly suffered considerably on the Colorado at the 5,000 to 6,000 cfs water level the river maintained for most of August. More likely, the investigation of the air tragedy demanded a level of sophistication just a bit more thorough than sending a handful of river runners out to the crash site with hacksaws. Chapman eventually cancelled the trip. Pat figured he could use the supplies he had purchased for an upcoming 1957 river trip, and left his boats at Art's for the winter. One outcome of the Washington hearings would be the formation of the Federal Aviation Administration in 1958.

While Pat was storing his river gear for another year, and Chapman had missed out on a chance to float the Colorado, two young men waded into the Colorado River at the Paria beach. The two men each had a one-man life raft. The small rafts could barely hold all their gear. It was August 16 and the muddy Colorado River was running at 5,010 cfs. With food for twenty days, the two friends had never done anything like this before and had only been planning to do this trip since the winter of 1955.

Neal Newby was studying nuclear physics, and Frank Moltzen was painting houses. The two New Jersey fellows, then in their early thir-

Neal Newby (foreground) and Frank Moltzen arrive at Phantom Ranch, September 1, 1956. Courtesy Neal Newby

ties, had been friends since the third grade. While they had life jackets, Newby couldn't swim. Neither of the men had applied for the necessary permit. As a courtesy, Newby had sent a postcard to park officials at the South Rim two days before the pair paddled away from the Paria beach.

Newby and Moltzen portaged around Badger and lined their tiny boats around the upper part of Soap Creek. Newby was flipped out of his boat in Sheer Wall Rapid, and his legs were badly bruised on boulders as he made shore. The two ran their bathtub-sized boats through House Rock and portaged North Canyon. In a small rapid below North Canyon, both Newby and Moltzen were washed out of their rafts. When Moltzen made shore, he took stock of the situation. He had lost his paddle and raft, and could see Newby on the shore across the river, also without his boat. Luckily, Moltzen's raft was doing lazy circles in an eddy below. He swam out to retrieve it, along with his paddle, and then crossed the river to join Newby. While Moltzen waited, Newby took off downstream, hiking along the shore. After two or three miles, he spotted his boat on the opposite side of the river. He hiked back to Moltzen and left him with a few supplies, then paddled alone down to his boat where he set everything out to dry, including the men's now ruined cameras. At midnight, by the light of a bright moon, Newby paddled back across the river and hiked back to rejoin his very concerned friend.

Over the next few days, the two slowly improved their water skills. Still, at the top of every rapid as he slid down the tongue, Moltzen would drop his paddle in his lap, cross himself, then snatch up his paddle before disappearing from view into the rapid's foam.

On the seventh day of their journey, the duo arrived at Nankoweap, and decided to cache their gear and hike up Nankoweap Canyon to the North Rim. Once into the large Nankoweap basin, the two men could see no route through the towering cliffs overhead. They retraced their steps to the river, recovered their gear, and continued on by raft. Their next attempt to hike out was at Hance, following what they thought was a trail. The trail turned out to be a burro track leading no place in particular. The two once again returned to the river. Moltzen was flipped out of his life raft in Sockdolager, and Newby was jettisoned from his in Grapevine, knocking his elbow and legs on rocks. Sixteen days after they started their adventure, they paddled to shore at Phantom Ranch, happy to be alive and ready to hike out.

Chief Ranger Coffin interviewed the two at the South Rim, informing them that they had no permit but needed one. Coffin also wanted to know if the two had been to the wreckage of the TWA or United planes. The last thing the National Park Service wanted was river runners looking to plunder the wreckages of the planes. Searchers had only spent two weeks at the wreckage sites, looking for mail and human remains. It was hard to recognize either among the blackened debris and boulders at the TWA crash site, and the United plane had plowed into a vertical crack in a sheer precipice. The remoteness of these locations was one reason the recovery effort was conducted in such haste. The heat and stench were another. The air wreckages were grisly attractions that would indeed be alluring to river runners.

In the end, especially after looking at Newby's healing leg and arm wounds, Coffin let them go. Four months later, both men were interviewed by agents from the Federal Bureau of Investigation. The two were prime suspects in a failed attempt to retrieve $5,000,000 in negotiable securities one of the planes was purportedly carrying. Newby told the FBI agents he wouldn't know what to do with a negotiable security if he were hit over the head with one. The two men had proved the merits of life jackets, and the fact that with a good amount of freeze-dried food the river could be traveled by people with next to no river skills, minimal equipment, no prior Grand Canyon river running experience, or ability to swim. When Newby visited with him in 1960, Dock remarked that Newby and Moltzen managed to make their Canyon traverse with less equipment than the swimmers Beer and Daggett had taken in 1955.

Two other events in 1956 are worthy of note. The first was Dock's inventing the term "baloney boat" to describe the giant rubber pontoon boats that were now taking dudes through the Canyon. The second and much more momentous, was the first dynamite blast in the otherwise quiet Glen Canyon, fifteen miles upstream of Lee's Ferry on October 15, 1956, marking the start of construction of Glen Canyon Dam.

14

To Phantom on 126,000 cfs and We're Hiking Out, 1957

Over the winter of 1956-1957, Moulty and Pat kept up better correspondence about a 1957 Grand Canyon cruise. Moulty had two passengers from Indiana, so he was all set. The passengers he had in mind would be his wife Janice, who would join the trip at Phantom Ranch, and his sister's fifteen-year-old daughter, Priscilla. called Priss for short. Moulty saw the 1957 river season as his chance to introduce her to the Grand Canyon by boat. Yes, he would have to do all the driving on the way out, but Janice could help with that on the way back. The 1,900-mile drive, one way, took Moulty almost four full days.

Pat was looking at his passenger list as well. He had told Brick back in the spring of 1956 that he could row the *Flavell* in 1957. Brick continually reminded Pat about his promise, so he was set to take the oars of the *Flavell*. Pat was also reviewing Moulty's choices. In a December 23 letter to Dock, Pat was unhappy with Moulty's choice of passengers, and wrote Dock that one of his main unsolved problems "is a graceful backoff from having an excessive number of women." Pat noted that he preferred "no more than two of the nine be of that sex."

As in previous years, Pat held off pinpointing a launch date as long as he could, waiting till he received Georgie's 1957 schedule, which included a June 17 launch. He didn't want to compete with the "Queen," as he called her, for camps. If he wanted a Monday launch to fit his vacation schedule, that would be the 3rd, 10th or 24th. Moulty had suggested the 10th. The 1956 launch date had been just a little too late in the river runoff for Pat's liking. While he liked to be on the falling side of the runoff, he didn't like being too far along in the down-drop.

By mid-February, Pat had written to Moulty that an early June launch looked good, as Pat's "seventh river sense" was telling him there wouldn't be much water in the river for this year's run. Dock was also looking at his sources, who by mid-February led him to predict a peak flow of about 80,000 cfs. It would turn out they were both wrong. Very wrong. Moulty's sources for forecasting the water year were telling him something very different, as a friend in Winter Park, Colorado, was struggling to shovel out from one heavy snowfall after another.

In early April, Pat had decided on a tentative launch date of June 11. Things were looking good for Moulty, as that date allowed him a few extra days for the drive out. He also was looking forward to seeing Dock, even for a few hours, as Dock was making plans for a motor run with a launch date of June 10.

On April 17, Dock sent a letter to both Moulty and Pat. The snow reports were in. There was a lot of snow in the high country, and a cool spring had held it there. Runoff estimates were now as high as 100,000 cfs. Dock mentioned a few rapids might look different at such high water, and both Moulty and Pat were taking notes. One was right above Phantom, where a rapid would develop due to cross currents in the river; Dock rated it a five out of ten. There would be a rapid at Boulder Narrows and no beach at Vasey's. Sockdolager might be washed out, along with the rapids at Horn, Granite, and Hermit. Bedrock would be easy on the right, as would Deubendorff. Upset would be washed out, and Lava Falls would be easier as well.

Moulty replied to Dock on the 23rd, noting that Pat had changed the trip start to the 10th. Janice was barely able to change her vacation schedule at Warner Gear, as the date she had planned to hike in was now a day too late at Phantom. Moulty planned to be at Marble Canyon with Priss on the 5th or 6th to unload the *Gem*, then take Priss to Bryce and Zion before meeting up with Pat at Temple Bar to ride with him back to Lee's Ferry.

Moulty worked on repainting his boat over the winter, while Pat's boats overwintered at Cliff Dwellers. A large gust of wind during one of the area's many windstorms blew the *Flavell* right off the top of the trailer, but the boat sustained only minor damage.

While Moulty had been set with his passengers for some time, Pat was having trouble with trip participants backing out at the last minute. Brick was still a go, as was Susie, but beyond that, Pat was still looking for participants. The final crew roster would include Ruth Pieroth, back for her third Canyon run, and two Grand Canyon greenhorns. Making his first foray below Lee's Ferry would be the Lockheed engineer Joe Szep, whom Pat had met in 1948 on the San Juan River. The other rookie, another Lockheed Burbank Facility employee, was Duane "Nort" Norton.

The drive out to Lee's Ferry from Muncie was torturous for Moulty, if uneventful. Priss was not looking forward to wistfully watching restaurants, bathrooms, and other wonderful stops along the way pass her by on the "wrong" side of the road as she sat with a swollen bladder waiting for the next stop on the "right" side of the road. She avoided the drive out all together, and flew to Las Vegas. Between Janice and Priss, and behind his back of course, her fun-loving uncle was called "The Wagon Master." Moulty would have already worked out a schedule on three by five index cards, and the Wagon Master kept everyone on schedule. In that way, he and Pat were very much alike.

Plans changed somewhat as the launch day approached. Moulty drove directly from Muncie to the South Rim towing the *Gem*, where he was to meet up with Pat and Susie on June 4. The trio wanted to take a quick hike out to see the Keyhole Bridge from an area of the Grand Canyon called the Great Thumb. On arriving at the South Rim on the 3rd, the Reillys met with Chief Ranger Coffin who informed them that reports from the Thumb area indicated a lack of water in the region. The couple then met Moulty as planned early on the 4th, and they decided to take a day hike on the Hermit Trail out to Dripping Springs instead. Pat struggled on the hike, becoming sick on the way back to the rim. On June 5, the trio drove to Lee's Ferry, stopping along the East Rim Drive to look at the flooding river below.

On arrival at the Ferry, Pat and Moulty unloaded the *Gem* from its trailer. Meanwhile, Susie stayed back at Art's and bailed a large amount of rainwater out of the *Flavell* and *Susie R*, the water having accumulated in the boats over the winter. The river was running around 80,000 cfs. It was clear this trip would be on higher water than either river runner had ever experienced in the Canyon.

As they were unloading the *Gem*, the assistant Lee's Ferry USGS stream gauger Sam May stopped by. May offhandedly mentioned his boss, Dean Tidball, was away getting a month's worth of groceries. The gaugers anticipated the river was going to continue to rise enough to strand them at their residence at Lee's Ferry. May stated they wanted enough supplies on hand to continue with the water level recording work. He casually told Pat and Moulty his boss was expecting a peak flow of 125,000 to 150,000 cfs, and then walked away. One can only wonder if Pat and Moulty exchanged uneasy glances.

Moulty headed out that afternoon for Las Vegas via Kanab to pick up Priss. The next day, Don Harris and Jack Brennan departed the Ferry in powerboats. Pat observed that they would have a hard time competing with the baloney boats as the Harris-Brennan motor boats only took two paying passengers each. It suddenly occurred to Pat that he needed to get his boats down to the Ferry, as the rising water would soon cut off all vehicle access to the launch ramp. The road to the Ferry crossed the Paria River at a low ford. As Pat and Susie drove the *Susie R* to the Ferry, Pat noticed the Colorado River already had backed up the Paria to within fifty feet of the ford. The couple went back to pick up the *Flavell*, and on their next pass, the water was within thirty feet of the ford.

At this point, Pat began to worry. There was a lot of water in the river, with whole trees floating by. Camps would be underwater, rapids would be washed out. And how was Moulty going to make it to shore without a man to help handle the boat? With three days remaining until the launch,

Pat and Susie drove up to the North Rim and all the way out to Cape Royal. From there, the couple had a good look at the river upstream of Unkar Rapid. What Pat saw through his field glasses, even from five miles distant, did nothing to soothe his already troubled nerves. The river surface was "nearly covered with drift."

The next day Pat was still able to ford the Paria, but at a crossing farther up than the normal one. Once at the Ferry, he found Dock supervising the rigging of his three motor boats. Joe and Ruth arrived about noon, and late in the day Brick, his wife Bonnie, Marian Swanson, Nort, Priss, and Moulty all arrived in Brick's truck with camper. The river continued to rise, passing the 100,000 cfs mark. Since Moulty's arrival on the 5th, the river had risen over 30,000 cfs.

One of the many things Pat worried about was Boulder Narrows. Sometime within the last 50,000 years, a huge landslide had slid into the river channel. The rockslide most likely dammed it completely, but the river quickly flushed out most of the debris, leaving a huge house-sized boulder right in the middle of the watercourse. The river in 1957, as it still does today, split in two with a channel around either side of the boulder, unless the river was flowing with enough volume to completely overtop it. Pat had never seen Boulder Narrows at water levels above 43,000 cfs, and he was worried. At present flows, there might be a rapid at the narrows that would not allow for any kind of run, neither lining along the river bank, nor portaging.

The narrows were visible from the canyon rim, only about nineteen miles downriver from Lee's Ferry in Marble Canyon. Pat thought he knew how to get there overland for a look-see, and talked the manager at Cliff Dwellers into driving the lodge's four-wheel-drive Dodge Power Wagon Carryall out to the rim. Most of the river crew went along, and the view from the rim was stunning. With the Colorado now at 113,000 cfs, the boulder was still collecting driftwood along its upstream-sloping top. The right-hand channel around the boulder had formed a large hole at the foot

141

Duane Norton next to the *Flavell*, Susie and Pat Reilly in the *Susie R*, and Moulty Fulmer in the *Gem* loading gear
at Lee's Ferry, with Dock Marston's boats *Rattlesnake* and *Cactus* in the background, June 9, 1957. Courtesy Joe Szep

of the boulder, and did not look runnable in an oar boat. The left-hand channel looked clear, with a large eddy formed on the left side of the channel, choked with drift including the occasional tree and telephone pole.

After taking many photos and some film footage of the narrows, the party headed back to Cliff Dwellers and then went down to Lee's Ferry. Dock had his three power boats, The *Boo Too*, *Cactus*, and *Rattlesnake* in the water at the launch ramp. Dock retied his boats so that the *Susie R* and the *Gem* could be moved into the water, with the *Flavell* still on land but close to the river. Food for twenty-two days was distributed into three equal piles, and along with most of the necessary gear, was loaded into the boats with room to spare. While the rest of the party went back to Art's for the night, Moulty and Priss spent the night by the boats.

Finally, launch day had arrived. On June 10, the river was putting on quite a show, at 118,000 cfs, having spread to about a thousand feet wide and flooding across the entire Paria delta. Not to be outdone, the heavens opened with an unusual series of rainstorms well in advance of the normal monsoon season. The launch ramp and gauger's home were now cut off by road from points west, and Pat, Brick, Nort, and Joe walked the water's edge to get upstream to the Ferry. Priss and Moulty were glad to see them, having had a wet night sleeping out in the rain under a tarp.

Brick Mortenson rows the *Flavell* out the flooded
Paria River channel, June 10, 1957. Courtesy Joe Szep

They manhandled the *Flavell* into the river, and rowed all the boats over to where the dirt road from Highway 89 disappeared into the flooding Colorado. Remaining gear was loaded up, and farewells were said to Bonnie and Marian. The two women drove away in Brick and Pat's trucks headed for Temple Bar. Lunch was served up, then, departing in a light rain, the group was on their way a little after 1:00 that afternoon.

Once out in mid-river, the boats were swept along downstream at about eight miles an hour. In twenty minutes they passed under Navajo Bridge, where a stinging rain pelted them. Nearly blue with cold, Pat signaled to land at the mouth of Jackass Creek for camp. The sun came out enough to warm the freezing travelers a little. Dock's outboard motor boats went by in a flash about 5:30 that afternoon, and all wished them well.

Moulty was surprised when Pat said in all seriousness that he wanted everyone to know they could hike out from their camp. Yes, they were cold, but Moulty found it uncharacteristic of Pat to speak of quitting the river. A light shower dampened the party's spirits during the night, and rain showers continued on and off during the morning of June 11. The river was now at about 121,000 cfs, a liquid freight train rumbling along. Bright sun finally warmed things up considerably by late morning, so the canyoneers loaded up and were back in the thick of it about 11:30. Badger Rapid was completely washed out, as was Soap Creek. About thirty minutes after taking off, the river runners pulled in at 12.5 Mile for lunch. It

was warm enough that the group sought the shade of a Supai ledge to eat. Pat noted Dock had camped there the night before.

After lunch, there was nothing to do but keep on heading downriver. Sheer Wall and House Rock rapids were washed out. The party was now bearing down quickly on Boulder Narrows. Pat rowed the *Susie R* along the left side of the river with Brick and Moulty following suit. As Pat came around the last corner above the narrows a roar was heard from downriver, and everyone could see water was shooting up in the air. Pat found a small eddy just above Boulder Narrows and pulled in. The two other boats did the same.

The view downstream was unbelievable. A mid-river prow of water made a waterfall on the left, and a jet of crashing water shot into the air on its right. Brick called it a "gruesome twosome."

The group tied up the boats and scouted the run. It didn't look good. Pat, Joe, Ruth, Brick, and Moulty hiked up to where they could get a better view of the rapid. It didn't look any better from above. The right channel went into some large waves but the large hole seen two days before from the rim was gone, as was the driftwood pile that had been perched on the top of the boulder. Water now flowed right over the entire boulder. The left channel went into a strong eddy still clogged with trees and the occasional phone pole. Worst of all, where the upstream eddy current met the downstream flow of the river, there was a three-foot-high wall of water. Called an eddy fence, this turbulence alone would be enough to flip a boat. The right run was clearly the better route, but the river runners had landed on the left side of the river too close to the boulder to cross back to the other side of the river.

View downstream at Boulder Narrows,
June 11, 1957. Courtesy Joe Szep

144

Moulty Fulmer films Boulder Narrows, June 11, 1957. Courtesy Joe Szep

Pat said he would run first, Brick would follow, and then Moulty would bring up the rear. Everyone would run with all hands on deck. Brick watched and Moulty filmed as Pat made his run. Moving past the boulder on the left was the easy part. It was the eddy fence below that was the problem. The cross-current spun the *Susie R* end for end, but Pat's run went well otherwise. Brick was up next. As he floated past the waterfall, Ruth let out a whoop for the sheer joy of it. Brick hit the eddy fence square on, and though the boat was tossed, it was not spun around. Moulty turned his 16mm camera off, climbed back down to the *Gem*, packed away his gear, then he and Priss made their run. They did fine, and found the others pulled to shore waiting for them two miles downstream, below North Canyon. Camp for the night was on a sandy dune at 22 Mile. Brick had a hard time making the backbreaking pull-in, but once he was in the eddy, all was well.

When their party pulled in to camp at 22 Mile, there was a lot of sand at the camp, and dry driftwood well above the water line. The river came up a little more that night, and on Wednesday, June 12, the Lee's Ferry gauge was now at 126,000 cfs, almost four times the highest flow Moulty and Pat had run the year before. The river runners had no way of knowing it, but the river would go no higher to the day of this writing, fifty-four years later.

Since flow records at Lee's Ferry began to be recorded in 1921, and then at Phantom Ranch beginning in 1922, only two years had flows higher than the 1957 flood. The flow in 1927 peaked at 127,000 cfs, and the 1921 peak was approximately 170,000 cfs. The 1921 flood could have been as high as 190,000 cfs, but the flood took out the brand new gauge at Lee's Ferry, so the flow had to be approximated. The 1957, 1927, and 1921 floods were small in comparison to the flood of 1884, estimated to be between 180,000 and 240,000 cfs, with some estimates as high as 300,000 cfs.

Susie Reilly cooking eggs over an open fire built on the ground at 22 Mile Camp, June 12, 1957. Courtesy Joe Szep

In the years from January 1, 1921, through December 31, 1957, there were thirteen years with flows at or above 100,000 cfs as measured at Lee's Ferry. Two of those years, 1927 and 1923, are of note. In 1927, runoff peaked July 2 at 127,000 cfs, but by September 5, the river was only running 11,800 cfs, normal for that time of year. Ten days later, the river would be at 114,000 cfs, and ten days after that the river dropped back to 21,200 cfs. But 1923 gets the prize for speed of low-to-high-to-low movement at the Phantom Ranch gauge. After the spring peak flow of 97,300 cfs on May 31, the river was a mild 9,380 cfs by September 17. On September 19, the river had risen to 98,500 cfs, and by September 24 the river was back down to 14,200 cfs. Almost half of this high flow came from the Little Colorado River.

Unfortunately, the USGS Birdseye Expedition was right in the middle of lining Lava Falls when the 1923 flood came on them. What's worse, they had all just turned in for the night when the water started to rise. The group, including Emery Kolb, spent a sleepless night and all the next day moving their boats ever farther up the bank at the foot of the rapid. They were ten days late into Diamond Creek, but were otherwise fine.

Another flood was man-made. In 1983, poor reservoir management resulted in Lake Powell filling to the point that water began to be released through the spillways of Glen Canyon Dam. At Phantom Ranch, the 1983 flood reached 97,300 cfs on June 29. Flows exceeded 70,000 cfs for ten days, from June 28 to July 7. Clear water coursing through the spillways at Glen Canyon Dam stripped the concrete lining right out of the spillways. Engineers used sheets of plywood placed on top of the spillway gates to raise the level of the reservoir behind the dam, and the dam was saved. Needless to say, a huge volume of riverside sand was also stripped from the banks of the Colorado River in the Grand Canyon. The river has yet to recover from the 1983 sand-removing flood, and it remains to be seen if Glen Canyon Dam will be able to withstand another flood event like 1983.

Even with the river flow moving at twice the speed of the 1956 run, Pat had the camp up early for breakfast (yes, grapefruit again!) and the boaters were on the water by 7:15. Wherever they were headed, they were going to get there fast! Both Pat and Brick had to work their oars excessively once on the water. Pat stopped above 24 Mile Rapid to rest his forearms, and then pulled in above 24½ Mile Rapid. It was Brick's turn to have wrist cramps, and he missed the pull-in above the rapid and was swept downstream. The laterals were big and knocked the *Flavell* way up on its side at one point. Nort, Brick, and Ruth were all able to keep their seats and stay in the boat. While Brick looked to his oars, Ruth and Nort madly kept the bail buckets flying.

Eddies were few and far between at this high water level, but Brick spied a small eddy on the left at about 25½ Mile. He pulled in next to the shore to wait for Pat and Moulty, who were upriver scouting 24½ Mile Rapid. The rapid had some large waves in the middle, with strong eddy fences on either side of the main waves. Pat ran first, and broke an oar trying to keep the boat straight into the left eddy fence. He quickly changed out his oar and headed into 25 Mile, followed by Moulty. Seeing Brick pulled in on the left, the two boats pulled in beside him. While Pat was worried about Moulty not having an extra man on his boat, it was becoming clear that two of the three boatmen were having trouble, while Moulty and Priss were doing fine.

What happened next was totally unexpected. Pat had pulled the fully loaded *Susie R* close to shore in some relatively quiet water, and the three boatmen rested in the eddy for about five minutes. Suddenly the water in the eddy dropped eighteen inches. There was a snapping sound and Pat looked down to

Dave Mortenson with Reilly Canteen at 25.5 Mile, February 4, 2011. Tom Martin photo

147

see the sharp edge of a boulder working its way through the footwell of his boat right between his feet, followed by an inrush of water.

There was nothing to do but patch the boat. This would, of course, require getting the boat out of the river. The group pulled to shore and moved a few rocks from the only flat spot around. The *Susie R* was completely unloaded and pulled out of the water for repair. Pat and Duane applied a patch to the boat, both outside and in, while the rest of the party had lunch and watched the river boil on by.

Once the glass patch had hardened, the *Susie R* was put back in the river and reloaded. One of Pat's canteens fell into the water at the river's edge and was overlooked by the river runners as they untied bowlines and headed on downriver. Dave Mortenson, Brick's son, would find that same canteen some fifty years later.

As Priss and Moulty followed Brick and Pat downriver once more, Priss heard the Wagon Master mutter a four-letter word under his breath. Repeated again and again, slowly like a mantra, expressing Moulty's sentiments about fiberglass as a boat building material…over and over, like it would change the world. The word was "wood."

A flooded Redwall Cavern near 126,000 cfs, June 12, 1957.Courtesy Joe Szep

Bert Loper's boat *Grand Canyon* at a river flow of 126,000 cfs, June 12, 1957. Courtesy Joe Szep

It was a fast run down to South Canyon. The entire beach along the right shore was well and truly under water, as Dock had said it would be. The river runners managed a pull-in at Vasey's Paradise for drinking water, taking care to stay out of the poison ivy right at the water's edge. There was no stop at Redwall Cavern, as the river had completely flooded all the way to the back of the cave and was now climbing up the ceiling.

The river was fairly calm below Redwall, with 36 Mile Rapid completely buried. The boatmen finally had a chance to relax and look at the stunning scenery. Limestone cliffs towered overhead, with the east and west rims of Marble Canyon still visible. An amazing sight, almost as spectacular as the scenery, was Bert Loper's boat. The Colorado had risen so much it had flooded the stern compartment of Loper's *Grand Canyon*.

Susie Reilly and Priss Ratican at Little Nankoweap, June 13, 1957. Courtesy Joe Szep

While the river was fairly smooth below Vasey's, it contained a lot of fast-moving drift, including tree trunks, and sometimes the entire tree, root to branch. Occasionally it was dimensional lumber that torpedoed by and needed a wide berth. Often, when needing to dig an oar in to turn the boat, a *clunk* would alert the rower that the oar blade had just made contact with a log instead of water. The boaters would occasionally run over slower drift which would sound its passage under the boat with a "bump-bump-bump."

Pat pulled to shore just above President Harding Rapid, with Brick and Moulty following his line. While it had only taken an hour and a half to run the twelve miles from Vasey's to President Harding, Pat was tired. At 3:30 that afternoon he decided to call it a twenty-two mile day. Some clearing of brush was required to make this spot a camp, but the location would work. A few of the group made the short walk from where they had landed over to David Quigley's grave. Buried there in 1951, the fifteen-year-old's grave was now only a few feet above the river's surface. It had not only been an exciting day on the water, but a day spent on the highest water ever run in Grand Canyon.

On Thursday, June 13, the river was "officially" down 1,000 cfs, but it made no difference on the water. The party broke camp and shot on down to Nankoweap. Pat was a good distance ahead of the others as he approached Little Nankoweap. The water was at a stage where a large eddy on the right side of the river plowed into returning water from a somewhat smaller eddy on the left. Suddenly, a large whirlpool formed about thirty feet in front of Pat, Susie, and Joe. Pat figured it was thirty feet wide, ringed into the middle, and about ten feet deep. A nine-inch-diameter log Pat estimated at twenty feet in length stood up on end and rotated about the center of the whirlpool like a swizzle stick in a drink. Frightened by the sight, Pat rowed like the dickens to shore. Landing just below the mouth of Little Nankoweap Creek, he waved the two other boats in to join him.

The *Gem* in the Little Colorado River lagoon, June 14, 1957. Courtesy Joe Szep

In order to get the boats closer to the good water supply in Nankoweap Creek, Pat proposed lining the boats downriver a few hundred yards against the upstream eddy current, along the shore and past the place where the whirlpool would form every few minutes. There was one small problem. The high water meant the "shore" was a steeply sloping hillside covered with thick mesquite trees. The *Susie R* was lined down before lunch, and the other boats pulled down in the afternoon through the thorny brush. A storm blew through camp just after dinner, with gusty winds blowing sand and rain. This kind of storm was what Ranger John Riffey would call "a six-inch rain" … the raindrops being about six inches apart. Fortunately, almost all gear was already put away for the night, and the storm moved through quickly.

Another storm was brewing though, one Pat did not include in his log. He spoke openly to the group about stopping the trip. One option was to hike out the Nankoweap Trail from where they were camped. Other possible exit routes were at the Little Colorado River, where it was possible that a helicopter was still removing pieces of the airplane wreckage from the year before, or to hike out the Tanner Trail. After that, an easy exit at Bright Angel might also work. Another idea Pat offered was to stay at Nankoweap and see if the river dropped.

Susie spoke alone with Moulty about what he thought the trip should do, and he said he had no problems going on downriver, with a possible termination of the trip at Phantom "in view of how some of the party felt." Susie mentioned that Pat was worried Moulty would not be able to make the pull-in at the boat beach at Bright Angel. Moulty assured Susie he was not worried about that in the slightest.

After a good night's rest, the group took their time getting out of camp in the morning. Moulty took the opportunity to hike back up to Little Nankoweap and look at the whirlpool again, but it was no longer there. The river runners could now clearly see the river had dropped during the night. Indeed, the Lee's Ferry gauge was now reading 114,000 cfs. The canyoneers loaded up the boats and were back on the river by 10:00 that morning. Kwagunt Rapid was scouted but was washed out, as was 60 Mile Rapid. The island at the confluence of the Little Colorado River and the main stem was completely under water, and a large lagoon went for over a half mile up the Little Colorado River drainage. At the top of the lagoon was a very muddy Little Colorado River, turned from blue to red by the storm of the night before. The group had lunch in shade afforded by some small cliffs on the south side of the Little Colorado. While they could see pieces of the United and TWA wreckage on the slopes of Chuar and Temple buttes, there was no helicopter removing debris.

After lunch, the boaters left the Little Colorado River and headed toward Tanner. Moulty had asked Pat what he thought Lava Chuar Rapid would be like, and Pat replied that it "should be" all washed out. That was not the case. Laterals in a herringbone pattern off either shore collided in the middle of the channel to make the biggest waves the river runners had seen so far. Moulty had an exhilarating ride, getting the *Gem* well up in the air. The same was true for the normally small riffles at Espejo and Comanche creeks. A lateral wave came in on the *Gem* from the side and Moulty noted he took on six inches of water, while Brick caught some good air in the same rapid. Pat was ahead of him and got a good view of the underside of the *Flavell*. The *Susie R* received a boatload of water as well, and lost a bailing bucket.

Priss Ratican photographs her uncle Moulty Fulmer, and Susie Reilly, while
Pat Reilly repairs the fiberglass boat *Flavell*, June 15, 1957. Courtesy Joe Szep

Three boats at the top of Hance, June 15, 1957. Courtesy Joe Szep

The group was tired that evening, but in good spirits. They camped at a beach covered in driftwood across from Basalt Creek. While unloading his boat, Brick found he had cracked the aft port chine of the *Flavell*. The boat was completely unloaded, pulled up on the shore, and turned on its side to dry. While unloading the gear and piling equipment on some boulders, a California kingsnake was flushed out of the rocks. Ruth caught it and carried it off to safety. Priss was very impressed with the school teacher, and would later follow in her career footsteps, but not in her snake handling habits. There was no talk of abandoning the trip here as the last rays of the sun lit up the distant cliffs to the east in a fiery glow under darkening skies.

On Saturday, June 15, with a seven-mile run planned for the day, the group slept in till 6:00, and took their time in patching the *Flavell* after breakfast. The river was clearly dropping and was now around 110,000 cfs.

From left to right: Ruth Pieroth, Moulty Fulmer, Duane Norton, Pat Reilly, Brick Mortenson, and Priss Ratican patching fiberglass boats at foot of Hance Rapid, June 16, 1957. Courtesy Joe Szep

With the *Flavell* patched, the group left camp for the quick run to Unkar Rapid where they stopped to scout. Unkar was mostly washed out and was an easy run. Lunch was at the top of 75 Mile Rapid, where Joe and Pat discovered a small rattlesnake while scouting the rapid. The group pulled in at the top of Hance in midafternoon. Hance was rough but had a good run down the middle of the rapid, but Pat was sure such a run would not allow the boat rowers to get to shore at the lower end of the rapid. That was frustrating because they could see a good camp at the foot of the rapid. Pat knew he had no reservations at Phantom for the night, and there would be no place to camp between Hance and Phantom at this water level.

Pat was still worried about how Moulty was going to make the pull-in at Phantom, and decided to line the boats down the left side to the waiting camp below. Moulty wondered why they didn't camp right where they were at the top of the rapid and just run Hance in the morning, but he kept his thoughts to himself.

The boats were left loaded as they were lined around to the mouth of Red Canyon. Once in the Red Canyon wash, everything was unloaded. At this point, Pat tried to portage the *Susie R* up the sandy hill that made up the west side of Red Canyon wash. The men got the *Susie R* about fifteen feet overland before Pat changed his mind. The *Susie R* was then lined another 200 feet down along the shore, and the boat was rowed the rest of the way to the beach just below. They handled the *Flavell* the same way, without the attempt at portaging.

The *Gem* was the last boat to line, and Pat ended up rowing it down the last stretch to the camp below. This was the first time Pat had rowed the *Gem* in three years of running with Moulty. He had previously never cared to see what the *Gem* handled like. Now, at the end of the lining of Hance, Pat was well and truly surprised at how well it handled. Pat also liked the weight and feel of the Smoker oars. Pat typically broke one of his Pelican Brand oars every year, while Moulty had yet to break even one of the Smokers. The fiberglass boats were both damaged during the lining. Just before dark the group pulled both of them out of the water at camp and set them up on their sides to dry prior to being patched yet again.

The river continued its fall, and on June 16 was at 105,000 cfs on the Phantom gauge. The *Susie R* and *Flavell* were patched, moved back into the river, and reloaded with gear. The river runners pushed away from shore about 10:30 for the hour-and-eighteen-minute run to Phantom. It was a cold run in a stiff breeze, with the river still so high that Sockdolager was completely washed out, with only a few two-foot-high waves. On downriver in quick succession, Grapevine, 83 Mile, Clear Creek, and Zoroaster rapids were all washed out as well. Brick ended up in an eddy at Clear Creek and took on a boatload of water before getting back into the current.

Suddenly, there was just one last riffle, the unnamed one at the last bend in the river above the black bridge, the one Dock had warned them to be on the lookout for. Formed by cross currents with eddies colliding into each other, the already freezing party was soaked by the waves in this riffle. Just below was the black Kaibab Suspension Bridge and Phantom Ranch. Moulty easily made the pull-in, as did Pat and Brick. The chilled crew all lay down in the warm sand where Pat immediately fell asleep. Moulty spotted Janice hiking down the trail, and he and Priss went up the trail to meet her. After lunch, the group took some of their gear up to Phantom Ranch, where they planned to stay one night.

After dinner, Moulty had a chat with Pat. Since speaking with Susie at Nankoweap, he knew that Pat was worrying too much for his own good and would continue to do so all the way to Lake Mead. Moulty pointed out that Pat had repeatedly reminded him that he needed a strong male on board for safety. It was clear that Moulty and Priss were having no troubles safety-wise. That said, Moulty suggested to Pat that maybe just the men should continue down from Phantom. Pat was opposed to this idea. Moulty then told Pat he didn't think it would be wise for him "to continue the

Gem, Flavell, and *Susie R* left to overwinter at Phantom boat beach, June 17, 1957. Courtesy Joe Szep

trip with two women aboard the *Gem*." Moulty didn't mind being the excuse Pat could use to call off the trip. A short while later, Ruth told Pat she would leave the river trip at Phantom as well. Not sure what to do, Pat's quandary was quickly worked out in an entirely unexpected turn of events.

While Pat was chatting with Ruth, Brick was able to connect through to Bonnie on the phone. Bonnie was trying to call Phantom Ranch, as she had an important message to relay from the Temple Bar manager, Mr. Satran. Pat had arranged with Satran to tow the party from the end of current to Temple Bar across upper Lake Mead. According to Bonnie, Satran now refused to up-run to meet the trip through what would be a huge drift-wood mat extending for miles. The river runners would have to abandon their boats and walk along the lake shore to the other side of the drift dam to catch their shuttle. On hearing the news, Pat informed everyone that the trip had just come to an end, and all would exit the river at Phantom.

Brick had noted that while he had been exhausted at the end of every day, the higher water actually gave him less eddy trouble. He thought terminating the trip was most likely the wisest thing to do, but he nevertheless was disappointed. Both Moulty and Pat agreed they had nothing to prove, and that while running on huge water had been interesting, they had more fun on lower water. What none of them knew was that the worst of the river was behind them. The rapids below Phantom were mostly washed out, and many large sandy camps were now emerging from the receding floodwaters.

On hearing about the trouble with the drift, Joe Szep wondered how Dock Marston would get his motor boats through. Indeed, Dock had a handful of his own adventures. At Lava Chuar Rapid, where Moulty had such a wonderful run, two of Dock's boats suffered steering troubles simultaneously. While in a turn, the *Cactus'* steering wheel came clear off in Ballard Atherton's hands. The boat went hard up on its side and kicked her crew overboard. The boat and crew were picked up without difficulty, while at the exact same time the *Rattlesnake* had a turnbuckle come loose from the steering cables, and oars had to be deployed to get the boat to shore.

That wasn't all the excitement Dock's trip would see. At Lava Falls, while the entire crew was up on a bench high above the river scouting the rapid, the bowline holding the *Boo Too* to shore came undone. The helpless river runners stood on the scout rock and watched in disbelief as the crewless boat went through Lava without them, capsized, and headed downriver upside down. Dock and his crew caught the errant boat six miles below, losing two cameras and much film footage. In Iceberg Canyon on Lake Mead, the motor boats were bothered by wood in the props, but Dock noted "even there it wasn't too tough."

Back at Phantom Ranch, Pat made arrangements for the river runners to spend the night in the Bright Angel Campground. Pack mules were arranged for hauling out personal gear on the 18th. The three boats were pulled out of the water, flipped upside down, and their bowlines were then all tied to a large rock. The Phantom Ranch stream flow gauge attendant allowed the river runners to store their oars, non-perishable food, and camp gear in a locked shed. While Pat was accustomed to leaving his boats unattended over the winter, Moulty realized he would not be able to do any repairs or repaint his boat back in Muncie. He found himself suddenly saddened at the thought of having to leave the *Gem* for the winter.

On the 18th, Joe Szep was headed up the South Kaibab Trail at first light with a thirty-five-pound pack, after eating a grapefruit for breakfast. On reaching the trailhead at the rim, he began hitchhiking to Cliff Dweller's to pick up Ruth's car. Brick and Nort headed after Joe about fifteen minutes later, taking turns carrying a heavier pack between them. Priss and Moulty started hiking up the trail a little later. Pat received a lock and chain from one of the wranglers, given to him by NPS Ranger Dan Davis. Pat chained the boats together, lest someone attempt a cruise without the boat owners' permission. Susie, Ruth, Janice, and Pat rode the mules up, and were the last ones out of the Canyon. Everyone congregated at Mather Campground, and Joe turned up about 6:00 that evening in Ruth's car.

On the 19th, six adults packed into Ruth's car for the drive to Temple Bar. Only Susie, Priss, and Janice stayed at the South Rim. At Temple Bar, Brick, Ruth, Joe, and Nort headed west to California, while Moulty and Pat drove their respective vehicles back to the South Rim. The Fulmers and Reillys camped together that night, and had breakfast together the following morning. Pat failed to mention in his log where during the day on the 20th they said their goodbyes. While Pat and Susie headed for Mesa Verde, the Fulmers headed back to Muncie towing an empty boat trailer. It might have been just as well that the group pulled out at Phantom. Janice noted Pat "acts like a spoiled brat," and she made it clear to Moulty she would not be accompanying the river runners for the 1958 river season. Priss told her mom, on returning to Fort Wayne, Indiana, that she wanted to run the river again, only at a little lower water. To this day, Priss Becker, née Ratican, still has the distinction of being the youngest woman to run the highest water in the Grand Canyon.

In August, Moulty wrote Pat that his barber had just returned from a visit to the South Rim. Using field glasses, the man caught sight of their boats from Yavapai Point. Moulty was trying to keep track of his boat, and that was about to get much easier. In a reshuffling of the USGS gauge operators in the state, Dean Tidball, the Lee's Ferry gauger, wrote to Harry Aleson to see if Harry wanted the Grand Canyon gauge position. Harry's response to the offer was akin to Brer Rabbit asking to not be thrown into the briar patch. Harry officially took over the Phantom gauge on November 1, 1957.

Harry was in correspondence with a lot of river runners and old-timers throughout the West. One of Harry's pen pals was David Rust. It was Rust who had built a stock trail down Bright Angel Creek from the North Rim and started a camp a little way up Bright Angel Creek in 1907. Rust had also strung the first cables for a tramway across the Colorado River at Bright Angel Creek. Harry wrote Rust about his new job in late October before hiking in to start his duties. Rust wrote right back, overwhelmed at the thought that Harry was about to overwinter where Rust had done the same fifty years earlier. Rust recounted to Harry digging irrigation ditches, planting cottonwood saplings, and hiking to the South Rim once a week for mail and supplies. One visitor to Rust's camp was Emery Kolb. Rust had a small boat, and he rowed Emery quite a way up the Colorado. Rust noted in his letter that he was the one to show Emery the stern-first method of rowing rapids before Emery made his run through the Grand Canyon. Other details included catching ninety mice in three days and "fishing" the Colorado River with dynamite. A few days after receiving Rust's letter, Harry read it to the after-dinner party at the Phantom Ranch dining hall.

Harry also corresponded with Dock, who wrote Moulty that Harry was now stationed at Bright Angel, and included an address. Dock also noted Harry was willing to paint the *Gem* if sent supplies, and would "give it a few kicks" as well. Moulty wrote Harry direct in late November, sending a tarp and rope to cover the boat. Moulty asked Harry to either kick or pat the *Gem*, but either way, what was important was to block the boat a few inches up off the ground. In reality, Moulty was concerned that the decks would weather poorly resting right on the ground. He had good reason to be worried, as after five years the plywood holding the deck boards to the boat was showing signs of wear.

While Moulty thought Pat worried too much for his own good, on the whole the two were congenial, respected each other's boating skills, and worried, just about different things. One thing was certain, they both were looking forward to the 1958 river season. Moulty just wanted to be sure his boat was in good shape for the run out to the lake. Somewhere amidst the entire river running and planning of 1957, Moulty received his Director of Physical Education certificate, which corresponded to an advanced college degree. Moulty was only one of two men from Indiana to receive the degree that year.

Another river trip of note in 1957 was George Beck's two-boat run. Beck, a canyon explorer and spelunker, along with eight friends from the Pittsburgh area, launched from Lee's Ferry on June 22, 1957, with the river rising at 91,800 cfs. The team used canoe paddles to steer their two ten-man neoprene boats. On the first day, the two boats were tied together, but after almost flipping one raft over onto the other, they were separated. Once disconnected, it wasn't long before the two boats lost sight of each other as they zipped down the river.

The raft in the lead stopped well after sunset at South Canyon, thirty-two miles downriver from their launching point at Lee's Ferry. In the gloom of twilight, the river runners unloaded their boat, spread their wet gear out to dry, and made camp. Once it was completely dark, the river runners heard the second boat calling out to follow them downriver. The river runners on shore peered into the darkness and could just make out the raft with its passengers paddling along. What they could not see was that the raft was upside down and the paddlers were sitting on the overturned raft. Not appreciating the second raft's difficulty, Beck and his group stayed put.

In the morning, Beck's team headed downriver only to find their friends at Redwall Cavern. Regrouping, the river runners were able to travel together to the Little Colorado River for their second night's camp. The Colorado River was now reading 95,800 cfs at the Lee's Ferry gauge. On the third day, while scouting Hance Rapid, they watched a large tree float into a huge hole in the center of the river. The tree emerged in two pieces. Luckily, Beck's group ran the right side of Hance without mishap, and reached Phantom Ranch for camp.

While at Phantom, on June 25, four men decided to hike out, two from each raft. One raft was emptied of all gear and pushed into the raging river. Five men, including Beck, then continued their journey in the other boat. The river was dropping now, and the gauge at Phantom read 92,700 cfs. The crew became very good at paddling the small raft, and in two more days they were at the mouth of Havasu Canyon. The raft was slightly deflated to allow passage through the tight narrows at the mouth of Havasu into a clear water lagoon where the party camped for the night.

With the river running 84,900 cfs, near dusk on the evening of June 27, Beck's crew ran their paddleboat through Lava Falls, possibly the first paddleboat to do so. On June 28, the five men paddled forty-five miles to Diamond Creek, where they arrived late in the day. Fearing entrapment in the drift of upper Lake Mead, the crew pushed their empty raft into the river and began an all-night walk to the town of Peach Springs, twenty miles away. They arrived at Peach Springs about 8:00 a.m. the next morning, and eventually recovered their two rafts in the drift mat of upper Lake Mead. Both boats were found right side up.

15

A Race to Temple Bar Without Boats

1958

The snow fell deep once again in the headwaters of the Colorado River during the winter of 1957-1958. The heavy snowpack would eventually result in a runoff cresting at 105,600 cfs past Lee's Ferry at the start of June. Dock had already made a rough guess between 75,000 cfs and 150,000 cfs on March 4, 1958. He also admitted to Moulty it was way too early in the season to make a better guess, but a week later he had it nailed with "a peak of around 100,000 or better."

As the snow storms hammered the Wind River Range in Wyoming, Moulty and Pat corresponded about a 1958 run. Pat wanted to retrieve their boats and launch from Phantom early on the river's seasonal rise. That would be in May, and May was hard for Moulty to commit to. Moulty also needed a paying passenger to help with the driving and trip's expenses. Pat wanted to know if Moulty was interested in a quick run through the Canyon from Phantom. Following that, Pat's idea was to then put in at Lee's Ferry for a more leisurely cruise. Moulty replied he would rather do the leisurely exit option and call it good for the year.

On March 10, Pat wrote Carl Pederson, asking if he wanted to make the run from Phantom to Lake Mead. Pat wrote that they would take-off on May 20. He also noted that it didn't sound like Moulty could make the launch date, and asked Carl if he would mind rowing the *Gem* out. Carl wrote back saying he had the enthusiasm to go, but his new boss at Lockheed's Sunnyvale Plant would look askance at any absence.

A few days later, Moulty heard from the YMCA that he could have vacation in May, and he wrote to Pat with the news. In late March, Moulty wrote Harry Aleson to expect him at Phantom Ranch on May 17 or 18. Moulty's plan was to spend a few days working on the *Gem* prior to the departure of the three boats. Arrangements included writing Pat to get the key for the boat chain. Moulty wrote to Harry to do his "durndest[sic] to keep the ole river under control until we get our boats."

In the end, a crew of six people came together for the 1958 trip. The three boatmen would be the same ones who brought the boats to Phantom the year before, Pat, Brick, and Moulty. The three passengers would be Nort and Joe, also from the 1957 trip. Big Guy Taylor, from the Grand Canyon traverse in 1956 would round out the crew.

Moulty and Guy left Muncie on Sunday, May 11. In the trunk of the Mercury was Moulty's rubber raft. On the following Wednesday, the two Hoosiers did a day run on the San Juan from Bluff to Mexican Hat on almost 13,000 cfs. Guy dropped Moulty off at the South Rim, and Moulty headed down the Kaibab Trail packing in a bunch of boat repair supplies along with his sleeping and camera gear. Harry was glad to meet Moulty again, and let him camp at his quarters.

Meanwhile, from the west came Pat, Susie, and Joe in Pat's truck towing an empty boat trailer. The trio rode out from Studio City, California, departing at 1:30 in the morning, Saturday, May 17, 1958. They took turns driving through the remainder of the night, arriving at Temple Bar on the Arizona shore of Lake Mead after breakfast. At Temple Bar, besides finding a newly paved road all the way out to the marina, they found Brick

Georgie White's oar-powered "thrill" craft on the left, and her giant motorized elephant rig on the right, with Moulty Fulmer's *Gem* on the far upper right. The river flow is at 63,700 cfs, Phantom Ranch, May 18, 1958. Courtesy Joe Szep

Harry Aleson, USGS Gauge Operator, Phantom Ranch, May 20, 1958. Courtesy Joe Szep

and Nort chatting with Guy. The group carpooled back to the South Rim, and in the afternoon, arranged to have their provisions packed down to Phantom Ranch by mule.

Early on Sunday, May 18, they took their gear over to the mule barn at the top of the Kaibab Trail where packer Jack Bertram was outfitting the day's mule string. From there, they headed back to the village and managed a quick hello-goodbye with Emery Kolb. Emery wished them well, and the group headed back to the Kaibab Trail yet again for the seven-mile hike down to the river. Descending the last switchbacks on the trail, they spotted their boats.

Moulty already had the *Gem* in the water, having done considerable work on it. He had turned the *Gem* right side up, unscrewed and removed the top decks for inspection, then rolled the *Gem* to the river on driftwood logs. Once in the water, he checked for leaks, and seeing none he reattached the top decks. As Moulty was working on the *Gem* on May 17, Georgie White pulled in.

Georgie was motoring her "elephant rig." The elephant consisted of three bridge pontoons lashed together with an outboard motor in the back of the thirty-three-foot-long middle pontoon. The black pontoons were hotter than heck in the summer sun. Three hours after Georgie pulled in, her "thrill craft" arrived. The thrill boat consisted of three, fifteen-foot-long rubber rafts lashed together. This craft was powered by two rowers, each with a single oar on opposite sides of the rig. While Georgie was piloting a faster craft, she was limited in her daily mileage by the speed of the slower oar rig. Restricted by her oar-powered craft, her party of eighteen people would remain just a day ahead of Pat and his crew after their launch.

Arriving at the boat beach at noon, Pat and his group were greeted with a warm hello from Moulty. Pat had corresponded with Harry to pack in some provisions for the group, and Pat sought him out to pick up the supplies. The two men spent some time chatting about the river, which according to Harry's measurements, was at 64,000 cfs and rising. Just two weeks earlier the river had been at half that flow. The group hiked up to Phantom Ranch to swim in the swimming pool and rest in the shade during the heat of the early afternoon. Pat also spent some time talking with Chet Bundy, who was rowing one end of Georgie's oar rig. The two river runners had a lot of respect and mutual admiration for each other, but Pat didn't extend that respect and admiration to Chet's boss, Georgie White.

The next morning while Pat was oiling some hatch clasps on his boat, he had a visit from Georgie. In his log he noted:

> The Queen of the River slithers on to the deck with a cheery greeting and tells me all about herself and the river. Says she isn't exclusive like some river people and hopes to bump into us downstream. When I see I can't converse with this friendly woman, I give myself over as a captive audience to her monologue. I manage a couple of remarks but she doesn't hear them. She finally returns to her breakfast campfire, talking all the time. I can't hear what she is saying to me thirty feet away due to the roar of the river, but I nod and smile and all is well.

Georgie's group departed a few hours later, while Pat's group refitted and resupplied their boats. This included replacing the rubber gaskets on the hatches, reattaching ropes, stowing provisions and gear, oiling oarlocks, and making repeated trips back to the relatively cool shade and swimming pool at Phantom for lunch and snacks.

Early on the morning of Tuesday, May 20, 1958, Pat said goodbye to Susie and saw her to the mule train heading for the rim. Harry Aleson came down to the water's edge and told Pat the river was now at 64,200 cfs. With last-minute items stowed, the six people took their places in the three boats. The running order would be the same as the year before. Pat would run first with Joe, followed by Brick with Nort in the middle boat, and in sweep position would be Moulty with Guy.

The run downriver was uneventful that morning. The boaters stopped to scout Horn Creek and Granite Rapids. Brick attached a movie camera to the *Flavell* splash board to film his runs. Reaching Hermit Rapid by noon and with heavy clouds building, the group decided to camp there. It was a good decision. A strong afternoon thunderstorm moved in and pounded them for hours. At one point, a small funnel cloud twisted water 200 feet up into the sky right out of the rapid. By late afternoon all was pleasant once again, and Guy noted a large beaver swimming near the boats at dusk.

The first thing next morning was Hermit Rapid. At flows of 63,000 cfs, Hermit had an impressive wave train, as large as the waves today's river runners know well at lower water. In addition,

Guy Taylor on the *Gem* with Moulty Fulmer at the oars departing boat beach at Phantom Ranch, May 20, 1958. Courtesy Barbara Crookston

the higher flow made some wicked holes along the left side of the rapid. These holes were formed by water cascading over the large boulders modern river runners stand on when scouting the rapid. The run was down the tongue past the large holes on the left, then a move back to the left to avoid the big waves below. Pat went first and did fine through most of the rapid. At the very last moment, a large breaking wave landed right in Pat's lap, and the *Susie R* was suddenly full of water. Pat had to pull extra hard on his oars to get the swamped boat into the eddy below.

Brick had a wild ride right down the middle, sometimes bow first, sometimes stern first. While certainly getting style points, he missed the eddy at the bottom of the rapid. Moulty made the cut and pulled in below with little water in the *Gem*.

From here, the group moved on to Elves Chasm, nearly twenty-two miles downstream. The large overhang on the downstream side of the clear creek was a favorite camp of Pat's. Unfortunately, when the group arrived, the place was a mess. In his log, Pat wrote:

> Find a very dirty camp which is unusual for a Georgie White party. There is rubbish in the pools, tin cans, can lids, Kleenex, paper, cigar bands, partly burned papers, etc. all over the area. Some of the toilet area is poorly covered. There is a stack of cans filled with grease amounting to approx. a half gallon. At least another quart had been poured over a rock ledge. A large amount of bacon and rice had been thrown away. Tea bags are discarded promiscuously. The class of people who run this river today has certainly gone to hell.

Duane Norton in the *Flavell*,
Elves Chasm, May 21, 1958.
Courtesy Joe Szep

Before Glen Canyon Dam stopped the seasonal high flows, human waste and garbage would be flushed out of the Canyon every few years, if not yearly. It was not uncommon for river runners to leave messy camps, expecting the river to wash their garbage on downstream. Fortunately, today's river parties work hard at leaving clean camps, and they even pack out all solid human waste.

Despite the trash, the group made a good choice for camp, as rain and hail chased them to the nearby overhang. While sorting out some gear, Pat noticed there were letters drawn on some of the eggs. Closer inspection revealed there were messages to the group written on each egg of the two cartons that read "I smell-u smell-we all smell-oh phew –stinko-oh pshaw-we-all-love-you-youse-bums" and "In Calif-they-advertise-all kinds-of eggs-for sale-along the highways-but-never-a hen's-egg-why is this?" The group had a good laugh at Harry Aleson's jokes, as he had supplied the eggs for the group.

The water rose again overnight, and the river was running 70,000 cfs the next morning. Large logs and the occasional oil drum passed camp, and as the group loaded the boats Pat swore he heard the rumble of large rocks being rolled along the bottom of the river.

Just above Specter Chasm the current grabbed one of Brick's oars and turned it sideways under the boat. There was a loud *crack* as the oarlock ring sheared off its stem. While acting as a safety valve and protecting the oar block, the loss of an oarlock meant the group was down one spare oar until a new oarlock could be fitted to the oar. Specter and Bedrock rapids were washed out at this flow. Below Bedrock Rapid, the *Susie R* was surged into a large eddy full of driftwood. Pat circled through the eddy twice, hemmed in by large tree trunks and "a mass of small stuff" on each side of the boat.

Moulty Fulmer in the *Gem*, at Stone Creek mouth, May 23, 1958. Courtesy Joe Szep

The group scouted Deubendorff Rapid accompanied by a dull rumble and the occasional *whump* of boulders rearranging themselves on the river bottom. Pat decided to line the boats down the right side of the rapid, starting with the wooden *Gem*. The boat took a beating in the process, and Pat realized his fiberglass boats could not withstand what the *Gem* had just gone through. With no other option but to run the rapid or portage the boats, Pat decided to run. It was a big ride, and in the end Pat still damaged his boat. When he landed the *Susie R* on the rocky shore well below Stone Creek, he put a small hole in the floor of the boat. Brick had an equally big ride, but a more successful run, being able to reach the sandy beach at the foot of Stone Creek.

Pat called it camp and the next morning he, Joe, Brick, and Moulty hiked up Stone Creek a few miles to a large waterfall in a tight narrows. Not far from this waterfall the

Brick Mortenson and Moulty Fulmer return from a Stone Creek hike, May 23, 1958. Courtesy Joe Szep

Mouth of Tapeats Creek at about 75,000 cfs, May 24, 1958. Courtesy Joe Szep

group discovered a hummingbird's nest and a small granary on creek right, close enough to the creek bottom that previous flash floods had deposited driftwood next to the ruin. It was a gorgeous walk up a wonderful creek with yellow brittlebush flowers blanketing the hillsides.

Back in the boats and on an ever-rising river late that afternoon, the group made the quick ride downriver to Tapeats Creek for camp and a layover. Pat chose the lower camp in an eddy at the foot of Tapeats Rapid. On arrival, the canyoneers again found trash from the trip just ahead of them, with unburned refuse in a campfire and empty cereal boxes, cigarette packages, and "wieners" scattered about the camp. During the next day, Pat replaced the broken oarlock and patched the leaking fiberglass boats, while Nort and Brick tried their luck fishing for the trout stocked in Tapeats Creek. Dinner that night was soup, crackers, canned ham, canned yams, canned cranberry sauce, and canned pineapple.

On Sunday, May 25, the river rose to 83,500 cfs at the Phantom Ranch gauge. Pat's plan for the day was to scout Granite Narrows, hike at Deer Creek, and then proceed to 140 Mile Canyon for camp. One of Pat's goals on this trip was to repeat the 1956 hike up 140 Mile to the Keyhole Natural Bridge. The group packed up their camp at the foot of Tapeats, then headed downriver only a mile and a half to just above Granite Narrows, the narrowest point on the Colorado River in all of the Grand Canyon. Pat had heard from Dock that there were tricky currents here at high water. Indeed, with sheer granite walls dropping right into the river, the constricted channel had some very wicked cross currents going from a left eddy, right across the river and directly into the right cliff, where a small amount of driftwood was pinned against the wall. The six men stood on the cliff top and looked at the currents below. The trick to a safe passage was how well the boatman kept the angle of his boat to the wall. If the rower could hold

a cross river ferry and row away from the wall, the boat would avoid becoming entangled with the driftwood against the wall. A boat could pin there, and if the side against the wall rose up and the river side went down, the boat would stick to the wall. In river running terms, this is known as a "postage stamp." The running order was Pat first, then Brick, then Moulty, with all passengers on deck. Brick and Moulty would watch and film Pat, and then Moulty would film Brick and come on through with Guy.

Pat headed into the Narrows with Joe in his boat, entering mid-river and skirting the left eddy. A surge turned the *Susie R* completely around. Unable to control his boat, Pat ran sideways into the driftwood along the impingement wall. Trapped against the right wall for a horrifying three to four minutes, Pat and Joe moved to the pinned side of the *Susie R* to keep the boat from flipping. Suddenly the surge subsided for a moment. Pat quickly got in a few oar strokes and pivoted out of the trap.

Having watched all this from the scout, Brick and Nort headed back to the *Flavell* in total concentration. Brick worked his oars well, kept his angle to the swirling current, and avoided being trapped against the right wall. Just as he was about to clear the wall, an oar twisted under his boat. There was another sickening *crack* as the oar block pulled away from the side of the boat. The boat immediately swung sideways and slammed into the wall, but was flushed out. Meanwhile, just below the impingement wall, a large eddy was flipping giant logs around end on end. Brick quickly changed out his oars, thinking he had broken one. Moulty filmed Brick's run, then started his own. Having watched the previous two runs, he rowed like mad and managed to stay six feet away from the wall.

The group moved down to Deer Creek where the powerful waterfall was plunging directly into the river. The three boats pulled into a small cove on the other side of the river and tied up. Brick inspected his oar and realized he had broken the block, not the oar. As the block was not totally pulled off, this was something they could fix at camp. Pat wanted to wait until the waterfall was in full sun for pictures, so the group rested, and then had lunch and a siesta. They also watched masses of driftwood cruising past.

The three boatmen then rowed across the flooded river into the mouth of Deer Creek. Without a sand bank to pull up to, the group tied the boats to the cliffs on the downstream side of the waterfall at the start of the trail heading to Surprise Valley. While Joe, Brick, Nort, and Guy hiked up to Surprise Valley, Pat and Moulty stayed with the boats enjoying the cool spray coming off the waterfall. The hikers returned hot and tired just before 5:00 p.m. Up to this point, the trip had been going very well and spirits were high. However, the hikers' late arrival would mean boating at the end of the day on very high water, which almost cost Brick and Nort their lives.

Deer Creek Falls at around 81,000 cfs, May 25, 1958. Courtesy Joe Szep

Last photo of the three boats together, Deer Creek Falls on about 81,000 cfs, May 25, 1958. Courtesy Joe Szep

They loaded up and headed out, intending to spend about fifteen to twenty minutes on the water floating the three and a half miles to camp at 140 Mile Canyon. As they moved out into the river channel, Brick's boat ran aground on a submerged sandbar. He waved Moulty on to move out into the main current. By the time Brick and Nort worked the *Flavell* off the sand and gained the main channel, Pat and Moulty were way downriver. As he looked for their boats, Brick had the low sun directly in his face, with reflections sparkling off the river's muddy surface just down canyon.

The roar of a rapid got Brick up on his feet, squinting downstream into sunlight so bright it hurt to look at. It was 138 Mile Rapid, later renamed Doris in honor of Doris Nevills, and it had a large pour-over on the right side. Uncertain of what to do, Brick began to cheat the rapid in what he thought would be a safe move to the right. He did not see the hole until it was too late. From the *Gem*, Guy saw the *Flavell* capsize and immediately told Moulty who yelled the news downstream to Pat.

Moulty and Pat intercepted the swimmers hanging onto the upside-down *Flavell*. Joe got a line onto the *Flavell* and helped Nort into the *Susie R*, while Pat strained at the oars attempting to pull the *Flavell* to shore. Guy grabbed the upriver end of the *Susie R*. Both Pat and Moulty put their backs into rowing the overturned boat to shore. Their aim was a small eddy just above Fishtail Rapid. If they could make the quiet water in the eddy, they could get Brick out of the water and flip the *Flavell* right side up. The swift current proved too strong, and the rowers just missed making the eddy by a few feet. The mass of boats and men were swept into Fishtail Rapid. The *Susie R* headed sideways into heavy waves and swamped badly, almost capsizing. At the same time, Brick shouted he was cramping and let go of the *Flavell*. Joe had to let go of the *Flavell* too, and bailed as fast as he could while Pat headed after Brick.

From left to right: Brick Mortenson, Pat Reilly, and Duane Norton at Fern Glen, May 26, 1958. Courtesy Joe Szep

It was sickening for Brick to be washed mid-river past the mouth of 140 Mile Canyon, knowing this was where the group had intended to camp. Now he was heading on downriver leading a parade of rescuers in his wake. Pat was near exhaustion as he tried to gain on Brick, who remained out in front of the *Susie R.* Meanwhile Moulty had caught up to the *Flavell,* and Guy grabbed the boat's bowline. Moulty searched in vain for a location to land the upside-down *Flavell.* High water had its disadvantages, one of which was a lack of places where a boat could pull to shore.

Two miles past 140 Mile and totally exhausted, Brick realized that with his feet below him in deeper water, he was traveling downriver faster than Pat could row. Brick then began kicking his legs on the water's surface with his head upstream. This small decrease in his downstream speed allowed Pat to catch up to him after a five-mile swim in sixty-eight-degree water. Joe hauled Brick on board the overloaded *Susie R,* and Pat made for shore.

Meanwhile, Moulty and Guy were still trying to wrangle the overturned *Flavell* into an eddy. Any eddy would do. At the top of Kanab Rapid and still unable to gain shore, Moulty told Guy to let the *Flavell* go. Guy refused. Moulty told him again to let the boat go, under threat of an oar across the forehead. Guy did as he was told. At the bottom of the rapid the *Flavell* was 300 feet ahead of the *Gem.* With no sign of Pat upstream, Moulty finally got the *Gem* to shore.

Pat arrived about five minutes later and the group stopped at a small beach at 144.3 Mile. Pat called it camp, and wrote in his log "The drift has been very heavy, our luck bad and we are tired." As the *Flavell* had the group's pots and pans, the river runners cooked dinner in their bailing cans. The runaway boat also had Brick and Nort's sleep kits, cameras, and all their spare clothes.

Just after 7:00 the next morning, and on 85,000 cfs, the group was back on the water, covering the twenty-three miles to National Canyon in about two hours. They stopped at National to look for drinking water but found none. While hiking back to the boats, Moulty fell and severely lacerated his left knee down to his patellar tendon. He wrapped his lacerated knee in a bandana, and struggled back to the boats. The river runners then continued on downriver to Fern Glen Canyon where pools up the side canyon held clear water.

By mid-afternoon the group arrived at Lava Falls. At 85,000 cfs, Pat wrote Lava looked like "the most terrific rapids I have ever seen." The beach the group used to line the boats down the left shore in 1956 was completely under water, and the rapid itself was one big hole with huge laterals. After scouting the group held a consultation. Pat was worried. Georgie, only a day ahead, would most likely find the *Flavell.* She would know that Pat was in trouble, and might contact the Mohave County Sheriff when she got to Temple Bar. A search for the disabled river runners would ensue. That was something Pat did not want to have happen.

Pat presented three options to the men. They could run Lava with all hands on the two boats down the left side of the rapid. They could line the boats down the left shore, then run the remainder of the rapid with all hands on the two boats, or turn the boats loose and hike out the Lava Falls Trail to the Tuweep Ranger Station. It was seven miles north of the rim to Park Ranger John Riffey's ranger station. If they could borrow Riffey's car, they could drive to Temple Bar before Georgie got there.

The group took a vote. Only Moulty voted to attempt the run after a layover day. He thought there was a runnable line through Lava, and besides, his knee was a mess from the fall the day before. He was outvoted five to one and the third option won. The group worked their boats back upstream over a quarter mile and set up camp well above Lava, just across from the Lava Falls Trail. A sandstorm buffeted the crew most of the night making sleep difficult.

On the morning of Tuesday, May 27, the river was running about 88,000 cfs. The group shook off their covering of sand, broke camp, and rowed hard across the river to the north bank. Here they unloaded personal gear out of their boats, and cached oars, sleeping bags, and other gear under a mesquite tree.

Finally, it was time to let the boats go. Moulty and Pat snuck glances at each other. They were both kneeling by their boats, boats they had built by hand, run on 126,000 cubic feet a second, lined past Lava Falls, towed across the country, and here they were, pushing them into the river at the

top of Lava Falls. Both whispered a final instruction to their boats, "Go to Lake Mead, baby" and pushed them onto the fast-moving liquid conveyor belt.

The two boats knew what to do. Heck, they had been schlepping these guys around and knew who the boss was. The river took them around the corner and out of sight to run Lava Falls together. The first McKenzie River decked dory to run Lava Falls did it with no one at the oars. While both boats would follow orders to go to Lake Mead, the *Gem* was starting a game of hide and seek that Moulty would have to play for the next seven years.

At 7:00 in the morning, the group began the difficult hike up the Lava Falls Trail. The trail is only a mile long but almost straight up and is in full sun. There is also the annoying fact that the trail ascends through loose black volcanic cinders and boulders. People climbing the trail can't help sending cinders

and rocks sliding down toward anyone below them. Joe Szep carried all his personal gear in a backpack, while Brick, whose personal gear was down-river somewhere in the *Flavell*, carried very little. Most of the group stayed with the slower Szep and Moulty, whose knee was clearly bothering him. They were accompanied by a large fly that paid close attention to Szep. Here he was, out in the middle of nowhere, and this fly was driving him nuts!

Brick reached the top before anyone else, and headed off at a fast walk to Riffey's place. Arriving at the ranger's headquarters, Brick knocked on the front door. John Riffey was surprised to see Brick, but immediately sprang into action. It was not long after the group reached the trailhead that Riffey arrived in his pickup with Brick and fresh water for the party. Riffey gave the group a much appreciated ride back to Grand Canyon National Monument headquarters for lunch. He then loaned them his Chevy sedan and the group drove straight off for St. George, Utah, a steak dinner and a motel. Along the way they took a few breaks to wire the muffler back onto the car.

On Wednesday morning, at first light, they were on the road to Temple Bar, stopping at Boulder City for breakfast and a quick telegram to Susie in Hollywood, advising:

ALL OKAY LOST FLAVELL CUT SUSIE GEM LOOSE LAVA WALKED OUT MEET US IN PICKUP

TEMPLE BAR THURSDAY AFTERNOON BRING ALL JEEP CANS AND BOTH BAGS =PAT=

At Temple Bar, there was no sign of Georgie White. Guy and Nort dropped off Moulty, Joe, Pat, and Brick, and headed on to the South Rim for Moulty's car. The only boat available for rent was a sixteen-foot open boat with a small 10-HP outboard engine. The four climbed in and headed uplake. Midway through Virgin Canyon they encountered Georgie's group taking out a day early. Using his binoculars to look at the approaching group, Pat saw Georgie looking at him through her own binocs. Pat waved, and she waved back. As the two groups came within hailing distance, Brick could see the *Flavell* being towed behind Georgie's flotilla!

A happy Brick Mortenson retrieves the *Flavell* from Georgie's group, Lake Mead, May 28, 1958.
Courtesy Joe Szep

As the two groups met, so many questions were asked all at once that it was hard for Pat's group to answer. Georgie's party had found the *Flavell* floating upside down off Pearce Ferry. Chet Bundy had turned it over and bailed it out. On righting the *Flavell*, one hatch was open and empty, the one where Brick's camera and film had been stored. Julian Gromer, a well-known travelogue producer, happened to be on Georgie's trip. Gromer filmed the discovery of the *Flavell* and righting of the craft, clearly showing the open hatch.

By right, Georgie had found an abandoned watercraft and could have claimed it for herself. But much to her credit, she offered to tow the *Flavell* on to Temple Bar so the search for the two other boats could continue. The four men retrieved sleeping bags and some cooking equipment from the recovered boat, and then continued on their way uplake while Georgie towed the *Flavell* into Temple Bar.

The men continued north past Sandy Point and into miles of scattered driftwood. On they went, through Iceberg Canyon, past God's Pocket, then east and south to the Pearce Ferry area. Using their binoculars, they kept searching for the two remaining boats. Above Pearce Ferry, they spotted an orange object that turned out to be a basketball. Brick retrieved the ball for his youngest child, David. The group continued uplake, encountering strong current above Pearce. At Columbine Falls, they stopped for the night.

The next morning before sunrise, the ever-rising river, now at 98,000 cfs, caused Lake Mead to rise enough to flood out their camp. Joe Szep was startled out of a sound sleep to find he was being submerged by water in his sleeping bag. The group moved up to the remaining dry ground at the base of the falls. For weeks after the trip, Joe would have nightmares, awakening his wife as he took the bedding off their bed telling her they needed to move to higher ground.

After breakfast, the foursome filled their canteens with the clear water at the falls and resumed the search. A dejected Brick tossed the basketball back into the water saying "It's not much good" and the basketball floated on downstream out of sight ahead of the searchers. About an hour later, the group once again came across the basketball. Trying to keep their spirits up, and as if seeing it the first time, the three men gave the basketball to Brick, saying "Here's another ball for David. Now he's got two. Maybe the guy lost a gross and we can go into the ball business."

The group spent the morning zigzagging through the massive drift mats, searching without success. In the early afternoon, they gave up the search and began the downlake run to Temple Bar. Just as they were leaving Gregg Basin and rounding Sandy Point, they spotted the red bottom of a boat! It was in mid-lake in scattered drift. As they got closer, they could tell it was the *Susie R*. The group towed the boat to shallow water on the Nevada shore and flipped her over.

With several breaks in the floor and listing to one side, it was clear that the boat's 114-mile solo run had been an eventful one. While all four hatch covers were still closed, the gunwale was cracked open, the stern deck bashed through in two places, the rear splash board was broken, and some of the *Susie R*'s "watertight" compartments were no longer watertight. The men bailed her out, moved gear to the rental boat, and began towing her into Temple Bar. An uplake wind picked up, slowing them to a crawl. The group reached Temple Bar a little before 8:00 that night to find Susie Reilly waiting for them. After dinner, Moulty and Guy headed back toward Muncie. The next day Pat sought out Georgie in Boulder City, Nevada, and thanked her again for towing the *Flavell* to Temple Bar. Then he and Susie headed to St. George and on to Riffey's to return the Chevy.

On the long drive back to Muncie, Guy called Muncie reporter Bob Barnet. Moulty, clearly upset at the loss of the *Gem*, returned to town to a phone call from the reporter wanting a story. The next day, all of Muncie read about how he had lost his boat. Barnet noted that Moulty didn't say if he planned to run the river again. The reporter, knowing Moulty well, wrote that he probably would return to the river, because he was not the kind of guy to "quit when he's behind." No, Moulty wouldn't quit, but he was now in his fifties and his game was changing. Moulty had the foresight to insure the *Gem* and settled with his adjuster.

Given the troubles Pat had endured with his fiberglass boats, he looked into a way to get rid of them. In June, Pat wrote to Grand Canyon National Park to see if they were interested in taking the *Susie R*. Park Naturalist Paul Schulz replied that the park already had five boats in their historic collection. The boats ranged from the *Stone*, used during the 1909 Julius Stone expedition, to Norm Nevills' *Wen*, used from 1938 to 1949. Schulz expressed the park's appreciation of Pat's generous offer, but declined. Instead, he asked for a copy of Pat's trip log.

Georgie made another run that summer and looked for the *Gem* as she headed across the lake. Dock took a motor cruise through the Canyon in June and he searched too. On June 18 and 19, Pat and Susie rented a motor boat at Temple Bar and ran uplake into the drift to look for the *Gem*. They returned empty handed, as did Martin Litton, who did an aerial search. In early winter, Chet Bundy reported to Pat that part of a boat was seen below Whitmore Wash. Then there was a "hot flash" from Pat to Moulty just after the first of the year that the *Gem* was spotted in a mass of drift in upper Grand Wash Bay. It was not the last time someone would see what they thought was the *Gem*, but none were the real thing. Moulty's hopes would rise, and then fall, like the flow of the river. On receiving the insurance money for the loss, Moulty figured it best to let sleeping boats continue to slumber.

While we don't know for certain, it's highly possible the run from Lava Falls to Lake Mead took a high toll on the *Gem*. The oars and splash guards were most likely ripped off. The splash guards were attached to the decks, and the decks were attached to the gunwales with caulk and wood screws. After six years of being unscrewed, recaulked, and rescrewed, the deck screws had no doubt wallowed out their plywood attachments. Whatever sheared off the splash guards most likely took the decks with it. Only the stem deck board, free of any splash guards, remained attached. Alone and driven into God's Pocket by the upcanyon winds, the *Gem* would have only been floating a few inches above the water line and easily out of sight of a search party. Without being discovered, the *Gem* slowly sank into the deep waters of Lake Mead.

In the winter of 1958-1959, Colorado River boaters through Glen and Grand canyons knew the river and canyons were about to be radically altered by the construction of massive dams. River flows would soon be a trickle of their former levels downstream of the new dams, and upstream of the plugs, the rivers would be drowned under reservoir water. Boaters had a choice. One was to run the Grand Canyon before the construction of Glen Canyon Dam. The other was to run the San Juan and Glen Canyon before Navajo Dam was finished. That new dam had just been constructed on the San Juan upstream of Shiprock. These two new dams would change everything. Time was running out for the Grand Canyoneers and their little boats on the last of the wild Colorado's big water.

Pat Reilly (left) and Moulty Fulmer bailing out the *Susie R*, Lake Mead, May 28, 1958. Courtesy Joe Szep

16

The Sinking of the Reilly Fleet

1959

In mid-December, after five months of silence, Pat wrote Moulty. Pat was indefinite about a Canyon run, but wanted to know if Moulty was willing to try the Grand again, with just the two glass boats and four people. Moulty was as indefinite about a Grand run as Pat. He wanted to get one last run of the *Moja* through Glen Canyon down the San Juan, but the snowfall in the San Juan Mountains had been poor up to early March 1959. Another option Moulty was considering would be a Yampa run if the San Juan proved a bust. There was something else he was doing to occupy his time. Guy Taylor had asked Moulty to build another boat, just like the *Gem*.

The new boat, called the *Eva L* for Guy's wife, had a width of five feet across the bottom. Moulty used a five-foot-wide sheet of plywood for the floor, which eliminated the need for the two-piece plywood floor Moulty had used in the *Gem*. The stern bulkhead was tilted toward the stern, serving as a built-in foot rest for the boatman. The outside of the boat was fiberglassed for additional strength.

In the latter half of March, Pat wrote Moulty once again about a summer Grand Canyon river trip. Pat had discussed the Grand trip possibility with Carl Pederson, and also had sent a letter off to Joe Szep. It was a hard decision for Carl, as he and his wife Earline had a new baby at home. Pat noted that Dock was going to run the Grand again under motor power, launching June 8. That was the same day Georgie was to depart Lee's Ferry as well. Pat suggested a launch date of June 22, the third Monday in June. Moulty was uncertain and wouldn't know if he could commit until early in May. While monumental changes were about to happen to the river, little things like Pat's launch date choice of the third Monday in June and Moulty's inability to commit earlier in the year, remained the same.

Moulty Fulmer in his fifth boat, the *Eva L*, Muncie, Indiana, 1959. Courtesy Marston Collection, reproduced by permission, the Huntington Library, San Marino, California

Like Moulty, Pat had considered a San Juan run through Glen Canyon, but he too was looking at the very low water forecast for the San Juan. As it would turn out, the highest June flow for 1959 on the San Juan would be 3,810 cfs. While today's river runners would jump at the chance to launch on that flow, for the pre-dam river runners it was low water indeed. Given the prospects of low water on the San Juan, and hearing in mid-May that he was ok'd for time off in June and July, Moulty threw in his lot with Pat. Carl had decided to make the trip, and asked Pat if he could try his hand at rowing the *Flavell*. Pat wrote to Moulty about Carl's request, and the easygoing Hoosier had no problem with that, being happy to go as a passenger.

Coordinating his schedule with Dock's, Moulty arrived at the South Rim via train and bus on June 16. The next day he hiked from the South Rim down to Plateau Point, which offers a commanding view 1,300 feet down to the Colorado River and Horn Creek Rapid. Moulty's timing was good. He saw Dock's party motor by below him, and the sixteen-foot power boats of the Harris-Brennan trip.

Moulty was back at Williams, Arizona, on June 19, where he met up with Pat, Carl, and Joe about noon. The trio had started driving at midnight from Pat's home in California, towing the *Flavell* and *Susie R*. With Moulty aboard, the party arrived at Art Greene's Cliff Dwellers Lodge late in the afternoon. The next day, the four river runners drove to the rim overlooking the Glen Canyon Dam construction site. At the time of their visit, work was focusing on building the dam's foundations. The Colorado River had already been rerouted around the construction site through one of

Foundation work at Glen
Canyon Dam site, June 21
1959. Courtesy Joe Szep

two forty-one-foot diameter, concrete-lined bypass tunnels drilled in the Navajo Sandstone on each side of the canyon. The game changer was well underway.

River runners who had seen either Glen Canyon, or Grand Canyon, or both, knew the dam would transform the two canyons. They had seen a wild and free river, winding its way through a paradise that the river had carved over millennia. While they certainly knew there would be changes, it is unclear if the river travelers understood the full ramifications of those changes. Even fewer Americans, outside the small handful of river runners who had traveled through the canyons, could fathom the huge transformations that would happen to both the Colorado River in the Grand Canyon below the dam, and Glen Canyon above.

After looking at the dam, the four men returned to Lee's Ferry. On the drive to the Ferry, the canyoneers passed a new sign erected by the National Park Service, stating that river running without a permit

New sign on the road to Lee's Ferry, June 21, 1959. Courtesy Joe Szep

Rigging the *Susie R* and *Flavell* at Lee's Ferry, June 21, 1959.
Moulty Fulmer is on far right. Courtesy Joe Szep

through the Grand Canyon was not allowed. Pat had heard from Paul Terry, recently returned from a visit to the South Rim in the fall of 1958, that "the rangers really recommend Georgie's trips through the Canyon. He wondered if they were working under commission." The pieces of the puzzle that would usher in commercialization of the Colorado River in the Grand Canyon were falling into place.

Arriving at Lee's Ferry, the four men wrestled the heavy fiberglass boats into the river and loaded the *Susie R* and *Flavell* with supplies. Moulty stayed with the boats as he had in years past, while Pat, Carl, and Joe headed back to Art's for the night. The next day the two-boat four-person trip launched without fanfare from Lee's Ferry. The date was Monday, June 22, 1959, well after the peak runoff. The Colorado River was running 33,000 cfs at Lee's Ferry for the start of their trip, and by the time they reached Phantom Ranch seven days later, the river had dropped to 30,000 cfs.

The weather on the first day was wonderful. Unlike the freezing first day on the river in 1957, it was

Moulty Fulmer looks up at driftwood with Brown's Riffle in the background, June 22, 1959. Courtesy Joe Szep

a pleasant ninety degrees. They ran Badger Rapid wide open without scouting, and Badger was the first major rapid Carl rowed himself. The group stopped and scouted Soap Creek. Moulty shot 16mm film footage of Pat's run with Joe, and of Carl, who ran solo. The two boats had good runs, but Carl missed the pull-in at the bottom of the rapid. Pat gave Moulty a ride downriver to where Carl was waiting below. The river runners then ran to 12½ Mile on the left for lunch. Pat decided to call it camp, even though it was still early in the afternoon. The four men walked back upstream along the river to see if they could find the Frank Brown cenotaph Jimmy Jordan had discovered on the 1951 Marston motorcade trip. Moulty stopped to examine a huge driftwood log lodged on a boulder well above his head, most likely from the flood two years previous.

It was a very pleasant afternoon and evening. Dinner that night was out of cans. On Tuesday, the group was away from camp about 7:00 a.m., ready for the run through Sheer Wall and House Rock rapids. At over 30,000 cfs, both rapids were completely washed out.

The group stopped for an hour at Boulder Narrows, to take comparison photos of the Narrows at low flows compared to the 1957 flood flow. Early that afternoon, the group headed to 24½ Mile Rapid for a scout. A trip ahead of the river runners had left a messy camp there, with cans and papers scattered about.

The rapid looked simple enough. The main center hole was washed out for a fun ride right down the middle through big waves. There was a series of large laterals on the left, but they didn't look too troublesome. Pat and Joe ran first in the *Susie R*, while Moulty and Carl filmed from the shore. As the two men watched from the boulders, the *Susie R* was hit by a pile-driving lateral on its left side, and rolled right on over.

Pat and Joe swam out from under the overturned craft in the tailwaves of the rapid. In a short but quiet stretch of the river just above 25 Mile Rapid, Pat shouted to Joe to leave the boat and try to swim to the right shore. Joe followed Pat's com-

Moulty Fulmer and Carl Pederson below Boulder Narrows, June 23, 1959. Courtesy Joe Szep

Pat Reilly flips the *Susie R* in 24½ Mile Rapid, June 23, 1959. Courtesy Carl and Earline Pederson

mand and left the boat. Even though the water was a warm seventy degrees, Joe struggled in his Mae West life jacket. The bulky jacket, with its large flotation bags in the front, prevented any meaningful attempt at swimming. He was only a few feet from the right shore when he was swept into the tongue of 25 Mile Rapid and the crashing waves below.

Still hanging onto the boat's side line as the upside-down *Susie R* bobbed through 25 Mile, Pat was now well ahead of Joe. Suddenly, Pat realized he was getting sucked by a strong undertow to the left as he entered the rapid's tailwaves and he knew this was the same location where two men had already drowned. On July 25, 1889, two members of the Stanton expedition, Peter Hansbrough and Henry Richards, had been thrown into the river after flipping their boat in 25 Mile Rapid. Neither had a life jacket. Pat later wrote that as he clung to the *Susie R* and floated along in the tailwaves of the rapid, the undertow caught his body and his legs "were pulled out straight and my tight fitting shorts were nearly lost."

Fortunately, Joe was pushed by the river current to the right side of the river as he swam through 25 Mile. Joe had remembered to float feet first through the rapid and had no problems. Both men swam Cave Springs Rapid at 25.7 Mile, with Pat still hanging on to the *Susie R*, followed a bit later by Joe. Once below Cave Springs, Joe was able to swim to the left shore and get out of the water in a little alcove while Pat floated on downstream with the boat. The side line rope Pat was hanging onto broke below Cave Springs, but he kept his grip on the free end of the rope, wrapping the line around his hand. At this point, Pat couldn't see or hear Joe, and was "sick with dread." With the help of a friendly surge of current, Pat eventually swam the upside-down craft into a quiet eddy and to shore at 28.2 Mile, having traveled in the river with the boat almost four miles.

View downriver from the top of the South Canyon eddy, June 23, 1959. Courtesy Joe Szep

Unbeknownst to Pat and Joe, Carl Pederson had run down the boulder-strewn left side of the river far enough that Carl was able to see Joe reach shore. Carl turned around, hiked back, and rejoined Moulty. Carl was learning to row on this trip and had gotten the *Flavell* from Lee's Ferry to this point. But, given the situation, he turned the craft over to Moulty, who had run 24½ Mile Rapid three times before and was the more experienced oarsman. Now was not the time to risk flipping the only other boat the trip had.

Joe Szep was worried. The river was fairly loud below Cave Springs Rapid, and he couldn't see any sign of Pat downstream. Joe did not want to be left stranded on the shore if the crew of the *Flavell* did not see him in the small alcove or hear his shouts for help. To maximize his visibility, Joe took off his yellow swimming trunks, and as soon as the *Flavell* came into view, he began to wave his bright trunks on a piece of driftwood in a large arc over his head and shout as loud as he could. He was not overlooked by the amused Moulty and Carl.

After picking up Joe, the three rowed on downriver looking for Pat. It had seemed like ages to Pat before the trio showed up, and he was greatly relieved when he saw the boat finally coming downriver. Though he couldn't see who was in the boat, he immediately recognized the *Flavell* was riding low in the water. As the three men pulled their boat to shore, Pat was "weak with relief."

The four men turned the *Susie R* right side up. Pat had lost both his running oars, but the boat's one spare was still tied securely in place. The hatch covers had stayed mostly watertight, with only about a quart seeping in. With the one spare oar from the *Susie R*, and one of the two spares from the *Flavell*, the *Susie R* was ready to go. The river runners loaded up and headed on downriver.

Within a mile after their launch, the ever-alert Joe Szep spied one of the two missing oars floating in an eddy. Pat was so glad when Joe retrieved the oar that he kissed the oar. There was much ribbing of Pat in camp that night at South Canyon, including the threat of telling Susie that Pat had taken to kissing his oars. Pat had good reason to show such affection, as each boat now had only one spare oar. They still had a safety margin, albeit a thin one.

Split-twig figurine from Stanton's Cave, June 24, 1959.Courtesy Joe Szep

The following morning, the men walked upriver and climbed up into the cliffs to view the headless skeleton. Over the eleven years since Moulty had first seen the skeleton, the remains had deteriorated noticeably. From here, the four headed back toward the boats, making a stop at Stanton's Cave along the way. While in the cave, Carl discovered a small animal-shaped figurine made of wood twigs. Pat took the split-twig figurine and later delivered it to the Park Service for radiocarbon dating. It would turn out that the split-twig figurines, first noticed by members of a river trip in 1934 and at the time thought to be children's play toys, were roughly 4,000 years old.

The rest of the day was spent in a casual and uneventful float to Little Nankoweap for camp. The next morning, the canyoneers broke camp and floated the short distance to the mouth of Nankoweap Creek to fill their canteens from the fresh flowing stream. The group hiked up to the ancient granaries at the base of the towering Redwall Limestone cliffs. Pat noted in his log that the trail to the granaries was "becoming quite well worn." The view downstream from the granaries was as stunning then as it is today, with the river heading off to the south around the next corner and out of sight. The river runners saw many large sandy beaches, any one of them capable of serving as a great campsite, lining both sides of the river channel.

Back on the water, the men headed downriver to scout Kwagunt Rapid. The run was made with ease, with Pat and Moulty rowing the boats.

The Colorado River flows just under 35,000 cfs downstream from Nankoweap Canyon, June 25, 1959. Courtesy Joe Szep

After a stop for a swim in the clear blue waters of the Little Colorado River, they proceeded to the mouth of Lava Canyon where Pat wanted to camp for the night. On arriving, the group found a disgusting mess of used toilet paper adorning the shoreline mesquite trees. Dock later acknowledged his trip was the responsible party. In a letter to Pat in August, he feared "we were responsible for the dirty camp at 65. We stopped there two nights but not according to plan. I discovered the fouling too late to do anything about it." That evening, Pat, who had been closely watching Carl at the oars, told him that Moulty would be rowing the big rapids to come. If Carl was irritated by having the oars taken away from him, he didn't show it.

In the five years they had boated together, Pat had only rowed the *Gem* a thousand feet or less. On this 1959 trip, Moulty had a chance to row the *Flavell* through a number of rapids, and to compare boats. On rowing the *Flavell*, he wrote it "handled better than the Nevills type but in no way compared to the *Gem*."

The following morning, Pat did not feel well. He ached all over and had no appetite. He rested in the shade while Carl and Joe hiked up Lava Canyon. By mid-morning Pat was feeling well enough to move on, so the party headed downriver. Shade from the large willow trees just below

the mouth of Cardenas Creek attracted the river runners about noon. After lunch and a siesta, they scouted both Unkar and 75 Mile rapids, finally pulling into camp at the top of Hance a little before 6:00 p.m. There was a slight breeze blowing when the river runners fell asleep that night. As the night wore on, the wind speed increased, so much so that the second half of the night was a veritable sandstorm.

On Saturday, June 27, 1958, the four men emerged from their sand traps and shook as much sand out of their ears and sleep gear as possible. With breakfast done and packed away, the four walked down to look at Hance. Pat didn't see a way through the rapid, even at 32,000 cfs, so he decided to line his boats. The *Flavell* was let down along the left shore first, and only took about an hour. Things seemed to go fairly easy, so Pat decided to line the *Susie R* as well. Unfortunately, the crew was a little overconfident, and maybe a little careless. The *Susie R* lurched at one point, and Carl, who was on the *Susie R*, was hurled into the rough water. He was immediately swept downstream along the rocky shore. After tumbling over a series of boulders, he finally caught hold of one. Pat ran down the shore and helped Carl out of the river while Moulty and Joe held the *Susie R* in place. Carl's unintentional swim in shallow water resulted in a number of nasty bruises and abrasions.

The lining of the fiberglass boats along the rocky shoreline took a serious toll on Pat's boats, but the truth was that the boats were already leaking water into their hatch areas before the lining even began. The river runners, mostly Carl and Pat, spent the rest of the day repairing the boats. As Pat filed down the *Susie R*'s chines to prepare the fiberglass for patching, he suddenly realized he had filed off five years of patches and had gone clear through the chine! There was literally no fiberglass left for a good *ten feet* in the middle of each chine, where the floor of the boat met the boat's side.

On top of this, the 1958 "ghost boat" run from Lava Falls to Lake Mead had allowed water to work its way into the "waterproof" air chambers. While painting the *Susie R* earlier in the spring, Pat had heard water sloshing in the boat as he turned it over. He had also noticed the steel in the frame was rusting, and the wooden cross-members were rotting. With the basic structure of the boats greatly weakened, Pat had a new "issue" to worry about as he filed into mushy fiberglass in the hot sun at the foot of Hance Rapid. Just downstream awaited Sockdolager and Grapevine. These rapids, along with Horn Creek, Hermit, Upset, and 205 Mile, could put enough stress on either boat to cause a sudden catastrophic failure of the fiberglass. Pat kept his thoughts to himself. Carl's accident and the repairs that day, while covered in Joe's journal, didn't even merit a single word in Pat's record of the trip.

With the boats finally patched up, the group had dinner. The wind had blown all day and picked up speed again after dark. Fortunately, the wind was blowing upriver and onto the beach, so the sand load was greatly reduced. The river runners had a much-needed peaceful night's sleep.

On Sunday the 28th, the boaters were up at dawn. There was much to do, and right after breakfast the boats were turned upright, moved back to the water, and repacked. The group was on their way before 8:00 a.m., with stops to scout Sockdolager, then Grapevine. Pat and Moulty piloted the two boats under the black bridge and to the boat beach just before noon. The trip was at least "on-schedule" as Pat had reserved a cabin at Phantom Ranch for the night.

The afternoon was spent swimming in the Phantom Ranch pool. Joe received a letter from his wife, Winnie, but he couldn't reach her on the phone. Pat was luckier with the phone, and had a good chat with Susie. The river runners noted that while the pool was in better shape than they had seen it in years past, the quality of the food was not.

Patching twenty-seven holes in the two glass boats, at the foot of Hance Rapid, June 27, 1959. Courtesy Joe Szep

On Monday, June 29, with fresh provisions and water, the group pulled out of Phantom at 9:00 a.m. just as the mule packers crossed the black bridge. The boaters and the packers waved at one another. Little did Pat realize it would be his group's gear the packers would be hauling out of the Canyon in the next day's load.

The river distance from Bright Angel Rapid to Pipe Creek is only about a mile. About half way between Bright Angel and Pipe Creek, the river takes a hard turn to the left, with a wicked eddy on the right. While there are many eddies on the Colorado River in the Grand Canyon that can catch river runners and pull them toward shore and back upriver, there are few eddies that are real traps. This eddy is one of those few.

Ever true to maintaining running order, Pat headed downriver first, piloting the *Susie R* into mid-river, with Moulty following in the *Flavell*. As Pat approached the bend with the keeper eddy, out of nowhere a large boil formed around the *Susie R* and abruptly turned into a whirlpool four to five feet deep and twelve feet across. The whirlpool sucked the *Susie R* down, and water poured over the sides of the boat into the cockpit and passenger area. At the same time, a heavy lateral developed and Pat strained at the oars, fighting for control of the swamped boat as it slid into the eddy. Suddenly Pat's right oar snapped with a loud *crack*.

Pat worked the *Susie R* as best as he could with one oar as the whirlpool disappeared. Then he set his only spare oar into place and rowed the *Susie R* to the right shore in the middle of the eddy. He and Joe bailed out the boat, while Moulty and Carl, seeing Pat in distress, cut left of the bad spot and landed the *Flavell* on the opposite side of the river.

At this point, Pat must have realized that the many years of wear and tear on his two boats had finally caught up to him. With only one spare oar left between the two boats, a spare with a bad crack in it no less, Pat realized that he would be jeopardizing himself and his friends if he headed downriver without extra oars. He had seen how well the Smokers had worked for Moulty but had not made the effort to purchase better oars.

With the *Susie R* bailed out, Pat and Joe worked the boat up the shore to the top of the eddy, where Pat thought he could row across the river without getting trapped again. He rowed Joe across the river and landed at the mouth of Pipe Creek, where the Bright Angel Trail meets the Colorado River. Moulty and Carl pushed the *Flavell* back into the current and rowed downriver to join Pat and Carl.

The group talked things over and had lunch. Pat knew that if they left the boats to go get extra oars, any passing hiker could attempt to run the boats on downriver. At the same time, Pat knew that to head on without any spare oars was folly as well. He decided then and there to scuttle his fleet.

That afternoon Pat walked up the trail to the telephone located at the River House just a short way up the Pipe Creek drainage. He called Chief Ranger Coffin, and explained the situation. Coffin offered to arrange for mules to pick up the expedition's gear the following morning, and Pat accepted the offer.

The four river runners then removed all their gear and most of the hardware off the two boats, exchanging their river running supplies, latches, and oarlocks for some large rocks that were nearby. Pat took a geology pick and knocked holes into the main compartments of each boat, and punched holes through the boats' decks and floor. Many years later, Joe Szep recalled his surprise at how easily the rock pick knocked holes through the fiberglass shells.

Pat shoved the *Flavell* off first, into the fast moving river at the top of Pipe Creek Rapid. The *Flavell* hesitated a moment at the foot of the rapid and, already riding low in the water, rounded the bend out of view. The *Susie R* was next, and went through Pipe Creek Rapid as if Pat was at the oars, taking the laterals at the perfect angle. The *Susie R* followed the *Flavell* around the corner and out of sight. Neither boat has ever been seen since.

Joe started up the Bright Angel Trail about 3:00 that afternoon, and topped out at the South Rim five hours later. After getting a hot meal, he checked on lodging for the night. Unfortunately, all the hotel rooms were booked, so he walked over to the campground and tried to sleep on the ground. The cold kept him awake, so at one point he hiked back to the Bright Angel Lodge, where the night watchman let him sleep in the lounge. The next day Joe was able to hitchhike all the way to Art Greene's, pick up Pat's truck and trailer, and make it back to the South Rim mule stables by

6:30 that evening. There he found Carl with all the baggage the packers had hauled out that day. The two men loaded up the pickup and headed to the campground where they found Moulty. On returning to the South Rim train station, Carl said goodbye to his friends, and boarded the southbound train for home. A short time later, Pat cleared the top of the trail. After a good meal at the Bright Angel, the three men spent the night at the campground.

The next day the trio drove to Lee's Ferry where they met Gaylord Staveley, who had purchased Mexican Hat Expeditions from Frank Wright after the 1957 season. Moulty observed that Gay had made no changes to the design of the sadiron, noting they were the "Same old trucks!!!" On the evening of Friday, July 3, 1959, Moulty caught the Santa Fe Chief to Chicago and arrived in Muncie late on Sunday afternoon.

Moulty wrote Pat a few weeks later that even with the difficulties the trip encountered, he had enjoyed the journey. He wrote it was "with a sad feeling that I watched the *Susie R* and the *Flavell* start out on their last ride on the afternoon of June 29th. They were fine boats – made for the big river – and given to the river at their finale!!" Moulty also imagined that he had "pulled my last oar in the big canyon." He thanked Pat for the six years of attempted river trips, 1954 being a dry run. Moulty noted "To them and to you I "take off my hat" and bow graciously and with a thankful heart." Like all river trips, Moulty noted "The various experiences have made life a little richer and more meaningful."

After the river trip, Moulty also wrote to Dock Marston, recounting the flip at 24½ Mile and the sinking of the boats at Pipe Creek. Moulty noted that this year, like the last two, the river runners only managed to traverse about ninety miles of the Canyon. Dock wrote back that he had not heard a word about the trip from Pat and was amazed when he read Moulty's letter. Dock noted oars were available in Phoenix by two-day delivery, and the boats could have been pulled out of the river below Pipe Creek Rapid where no one would see them. But it was all too late, as the two boats were gone. Besides, Dock had missed the point. Pat was looking for a way to get rid of his boats as they were "in discouragingly bad shape." Sinking the boats at Pipe Creek was Pat's way of freeing himself of the wrecks.

In July, Moulty received news that he had been inducted into the Society of Fellows of Physical Education. With only fourteen active members in the U.S. and Canada, he was only the third Hoosier in history to receive the honor. Moulty received congratulations on his induction from the husband of a local Muncie girl, another river runner who had also boated with Norm Nevills, Arizona Senator Barry Goldwater. Moulty wrote back to Goldwater and included a few photos of the *Gem*. Goldwater replied that while he had helped Norm build the boats used in the 1940s, they were difficult to spin if "one wanted to avoid rocks or make a quick change of position." Senator Goldwater went on to note that Moulty's boat "with the uplift in the stern indicates it would handle nicely in these maneuvers."

In August and September of 1959, correspondence between Moulty and Pat included the question of building new boats. Pat was for it if Moulty would do the same, but if Moulty was not going to do it, Pat would look elsewhere. There was a lot involved, not just in building boats, but the myriad behind-the-scenes details of putting a river trip together. Moulty was as non-committal as ever and wanted to see how the *Eva L* performed before considering building again. With the *Moja* and the *Sausage*, Moulty had a fleet of boats capable enough for the San Juan, and he was considering a shakedown cruise with Guy's boat on the Juan, along with a possible Yampa run in 1960. Both Moulty and Pat were still sitting on the boat-building fence at the end of 1959.

Of note for the 1959 river season was the journey from Lee's Ferry to Phantom Ranch by two other Hoosiers in August. College students John Morgan and Ken Stroud used canoe paddles to steer their small yellow army surplus rubber life raft. They flipped their tiny raft multiple times, but repeated practice taught them how to right it and keep on going. Morgan had done the food pack, and many of the men's meals required clear water for cooking. The muddy river water was a poor substitute, and the pair would fill their canteens at clear water sources whereever they found them. The duo's matches eventually got wet, and so there was no way to heat their food. Their cameras were also soaked.

Morgan and Stroud arrived at Phantom Ranch after four days on the river and attempted to resupply missing and damaged provisions. Their intent was to replace a lost canteen used to carry cooking and drinking water, get more matches, and head on downriver. After making enquiries at Phantom Ranch about replacing equipment, the two were approached by Ranger Dan Davis who informed them they were under arrest and had twenty-four hours to hike to the South Rim. The two rolled up their raft and made arrangements to carry out their belongings and have their boat mailed back to Indiana. Chief Ranger Coffin was waiting for the exhausted men as they arrived at the top of the trail. Coffin cited the two for failure to obtain a permit to run the river. Morgan attempted to explain that they had applied for a permit but had not heard back from the NPS. Coffin said their permit had been denied as the two had not demonstrated they had adequate equipment or skill to run the river.

After receiving their citations, the two had something to eat, then went to the Bright Angel Lodge front desk where they were informed the hotel was fully booked. Fortunately, a sympathetic park guest overheard the conversation and allowed Morgan and Stroud to stay the night on the floor of her hotel room. This same guest drove them to Lee's Ferry the next day where they retrieved their car and began their journey back to Indiana.

Later that year, they were summoned to Federal Court in Indiana, to face charges for entering Grand Canyon National Park by boat without a permit from the Department of Interior. The permit had been denied as the river was running too low, and the rubber raft the two proposed to use was deemed inadequate. After reviewing the charges, Federal Court Judge Cale Holder suggested the case be dismissed. Holder noted the very fact that Morgan and Stroud had made it from Lee's Ferry to Phantom Ranch was reason enough to give the two young men medals of valor.

When the suggestion for dismissal reached the prosecutor's office in Phoenix, United States Attorney Jack D. H. Hays objected. The NPS legal team presented the judge with a full-sized photo of the sign posted at Lee's Ferry, the very sign Moulty Fulmer had seen that summer prohibiting unauthorized river running. The two men did not deny running the river without a permit. When asked about the sign, they admitted they had driven right past it. Holder cited them for a misdemeanor, charging them each with a $25 fine and court costs. In 1960, using the same "inadequate" rubber raft, Morgan and Stroud would go on to run the Snake River through Hell's Canyon, the Middle Fork, and Main Salmon rivers.

The issue at hand was not one of low water or an inadequate raft, but one of control. In this instance, the Park Service had won. It only made sense that the NPS should have the final say in who would be able to travel the river, be they the do-it-yourself public who sought to challenge themselves in traversing the mighty Colorado River in the Grand Canyon, or anyone who wanted some assistance from a commercially guided company to run the river.

17

New Boats, a New Dam, and a New River

1960 and beyond

Moulty celebrated Christmas and ushered in the New Year, 1960, flat on his back. The knee tendon he had injured on the 1958 trip had continued to bother him, and a handball-sized Baker's cyst had developed as well. He had surgery just before the holidays, and was instructed not to walk at all for three weeks, then to use crutches for six weeks after that. By mid-February, Moulty was back in the gym strengthening his knee, and by the end of February, he was able to engage in vigorous exercise.

The 1960 Summer Olympic Games were to be held in Rome, and Moulty, now fifty-four, was given the opportunity to attend by the YMCA Board of Directors, with pay. Janice was allowed vacation time, so Moulty added a two-week European vacation onto the front end of the trip. While planning the European travel itinerary, Moulty was also exchanging letters with Pat about a possible San Juan run. Pat wanted to attempt a number of Grand Canyon hikes and fit a five-day raft trip into his hikes, even though he had no boats. Moulty, who had the *Moja* and *Sausage*, wanted to take a ten-day cruise during the sixteen days of vacation he had in June. Needless to say, their plans did not mesh.

In the end, Moulty ran the San Juan into Glen Canyon for ten days in June from Bluff, Utah, to the take-out at Kane Creek. A road had been constructed to the Colorado River well upstream of the Glen Canyon Dam construction site, and all downstream boat traffic had to exit at Kane Creek. Guy Taylor brought the *Eva L*, Moulty rowed the *Sausage*, and Roy Elton of Muncie came along for the ride. It was a good trip and Moulty ran the *Sausage* through every rapid except 13-Foot. The flow was a respectable 6,600 cfs for most of the trip. At the put-in, Deputy Sheriff Max King almost stopped the river runners from launching. Moulty had to convince Deputy King they knew what they were doing. Moulty figured the deputy, who clearly knew "nothing of the river and the rapids," might have been stopping all do-it-yourself river traffic in order to "drum up business" for the local river guiding company.

While Moulty, Roy, and Guy were floating the San Juan, Dock was cruising on the Grand. This time, he was in a new type of boat, one driven not with a propeller but by a powerful jet of water shot out the back of the boat. Called a jet boat, Marston's trip had four of these craft. Two were eighteen-footers named the *Wee Red* and *Wee Yellow*, and there were two twenty-four-footers, *Big Red* and *Big Yellow*.

Dock's group launched from Lee's Ferry, on June 16, 1960 depositing caches of gasoline along the route. At Lava Falls, with the river running at roughly 39,000 cfs, Dock and Bill Austin headed down through Lava in *Big Red*. Bill was driving, and powered into the foaming rapid at a high rate of speed. At one point the boat was airborne, and on impact Bill shattered his left femur. He was evacuated by helicopter the next day, June 24. At Lake Mead, the two larger jet boats were replaced by two more eighteen-foot jet boats, the *Kiwi* and *Dock*, as the large boats had proved too big to make it up some of the harder rapids.

After overhauling the equipment and resupplying, an uprun of the river began on July 4, 1960, on about 18,000 cfs. Not surprisingly, Lava Falls proved the most difficult rapid, but a New Zealander with jet-boat experience named Jon Hamilton was able to pilot all four boats up through the falls by the end of the day on July 6. The cheers of the shore-side observers could not be heard over the din of the V-8 Gray Marine 188-HP

TurboJet engines. All seemed to be going well until the up-runners reached Grapevine Rapid on July 10. On starting into the rapid, the *Wee Yellow*'s deck suddenly separated from the boat's hull and the craft sank at once. The three remaining boats, the *Kiwi*, the *Wee Red*, and the *Dock* made it up to Lee's Ferry on July 12.

After more then twelve years of trying, Dock Marston had finally completed the up-run of the Grand Canyon. It had taken almost 2,500 gallons of fuel, scattered in caches throughout the entire length of the Canyon, and had cost the river runners the loss of a boat and a badly broken leg. The up-running party encountered two groups coming downriver, Georgie White's group at Elves Chasm and Gay Staveley's Mexican Hat Expeditions trip in the flatwater below Grapevine Rapid.

The National Park Service quickly banned all up-running above Diamond Creek. Entrusted by the American people with preserving such resources as wilderness and natural quiet, up-running introduced an artificiality that detracted from the wilderness experience of the Canyon. The Park Service also considered these watercraft to be exceedingly loud, and by 1966 had identified a desired river experience as "the slow float trip in small parties without power." While downstream river travel went with the flow, upstream travel overcame the river. Safety was also an issue. When upstream travelers encountered downstream traffic, especially in a rapid, accidents would be inevitable.

Another "first" occurred five days after Dock's jet boats headed downriver from Lee's Ferry. Walter Kirschbaum launched his homemade fiberglass kayak on the Colorado River for a run through the Grand Canyon launching June 21. The thirty-four-year-old was the first paddler to kayak the entire Canyon and run all the river's rapids. He had learned to kayak in his German homeland, and in 1953 he had won the Kayak Slalom World Championship. Kirschbaum came to America in 1955 to compete in kayak races at Salida, Colorado, and settled in Carbondale, Colorado, soon after. Once there, he discovered he enjoyed exploring remote rivers more than racing.

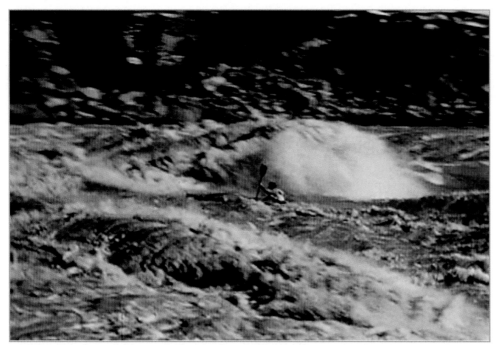

Walter Kirschbaum paddles Lava Falls at a flow of about 40,000 cfs, June, 1960. Courtesy Dr. Yuji Oishi

Obtaining a permit to paddle the Grand Canyon required, as Kirschbaum put it, "rather rugged methods," including a thirty-minute shouting match between Grand Canyon National Park River Ranger Dan Davis and Kirschbaum's attorney friend, Tyson Dines. One of Davis's requirements was that Kirschbaum kayak Cataract Canyon first. After successfully running Cataract, which Kirschbaum noted required "more skill in dodging rocks than any rapid in the Grand Canyon at 40,000 second feet," he received the permit from Davis to kayak the Colorado River through the park.

Accompanying Kirschbaum on the six day trip were Dines in his Peterborough freight canoe with an 18-HP outboard, Bus Hatch's son Ted, running a motorized pontoon boat, along with eight other people. In order to keep up with the motor boats, Kirschbaum would head out of camp before the others, and would not always wait for their company at major rapids.

While making a right to left run in Hance Rapid, all went well until Kirschbaum was rolled over in the rapid's tailwaves. Sucked out of his kayak and stripped of his paddle by a powerful whirlpool, he swam through the "pleasantly warm" river water to his kayak where he retrieved his spare paddle off the back of his boat. With spare paddle in hand, Kirschbaum steered his upside-down kayak to a small beach where he bailed out his boat, then gave chase for his lost paddle. Once he retrieved it, he pulled to shore and waited for the other two boats.

Dan Davis had specifically instructed Kirschbaum to portage Lava Falls, but Kirschbaum ran it left of the Ledge Hole, and found it an easier run than "many another rapid in the Grand." What concerned him most was eating his way through all of his food by day three. The rest of the trip members invited him to dine with them after that. Amazingly, Kirschbaum's boat had no foot or thigh braces, and no seat, as he believed that to use more than what he considered the minimum of equipment was a sacrilegious insult to the natural purity of the canyons he so loved.

Far away from the Grand Canyon, Moulty and Janice had a wonderful time in Europe, and Moulty greatly enjoyed the Summer Olympic Games in Rome. That winter, Pat Reilly suggested to Moulty that he and Brick Mortenson might like to build new boats. Reilly wanted to know if Moulty would build again. While not averse to the idea, Moulty didn't see how it could happen in 1961, although he thought 1962 was a possibility. Once again, Pat suggested a May run, but Moulty's vacation time was in June. As the spring of 1961 turned into summer, Pat had not built a boat. Moulty took three friends from Muncie and ran Glen Canyon in late July with the *Moja* and *Sausage*. The flow of the Colorado River dropped from 8,000 cfs to 5,000 cfs during their eight-day run of 120 miles between White Canyon and Kane Creek. The uneventful trip included a hike up to Rainbow Bridge.

The 1961 Glen Canyon crew in Indiana. From left to right: Bob Carpenter, Moulty Fulmer, John Kinsinger, and Joe Whitman. Courtesy Fulmer Collection, reproduced by permission, Utah State Historical Society, all rights reserved

That summer, Martin Litton was traveling in Oregon and happened to attend the McKenzie River White Water Boat Parade. Martin had a chance to row a constant-rocker double-ender. He really liked how the boat handled, and wrote to Pat that they should try these boats for a run down the Grand Canyon. The boats would need to be just a little longer and wider, to haul enough passengers to make the trip pay for the boats. Pat agreed, except he wanted to build the boat's storage compartments and decks himself. Martin contacted boat builder Keith Steele of Leaburg, Oregon, and ordered two boats, one just a hull, the other, fully decked with gear compartments already built in. Pat spoke to Brick, who immediately started to build his own boat from scratch.

Pat wrote to Moulty in early August, saying he was considering writing a book about Grand Canyon boat design. Pat noted "A bloke by the name of Fulmer will have considerable space." Pat asked for the dimensions of the *Moja*, including "rake, materials, where you got the idea, and full photos." He also wanted Moulty to explain "why you departed from the lines of the *Moja* when you built the *Gem*." Pat also asked him to explain "the reasons the *Eva L* was inferior to the *Gem*." Pat mentioned in the letter that if he built again, his new boat would have more rocker than the *Flavell*. He noted that flattening her rocker when building her "was the worst thing I did, and made her handle like a scow."

Moulty's reply in mid-August was complete and telling. He went through the dimensions of the *Moja*, including the twelve-inch rocker, overall length, beam at the chine and gunwale, side panel length, basically describing Woodie Hindman's McKenzie River double-ender dory hull design. Moulty then described his afternoon with Woodie back in 1945, including how he had disturbed Woodie from his after-lunch nap. The letter recounted how the two had discussed rough water boats and how he and Woodie had agreed that a wider beam in a double-ender steep-rocker design "could be the rough water boat of the future."

Moulty then explained how he altered the hull design of the *Moja* when he built the *Gem* for a better Grand Canyon boat, with more beam. "I added about 14-15 inches" and for rocker "I added 1½ inches." He built the *Gem* intending it to be a double-ender like the *Moja*, but noted that as he "was afraid I might split the plywood trying to bend it from the bow to stern, I made the 20 inch square stern." He noted that the blunt end didn't hinder the boats maneuverability and "may be an asset in some kinds of rough water over the pointed stern." In the same letter, he noted the *Eva L* was much inferior to the *Gem* as it had a decreased rocker and a decreased beam.

While Pat was gathering information about Moulty's hull designs, retirement was on the Hoosier's mind. Moulty was back out to Arizona in September, flying out for a long weekend. He traveled with Janice, and the couple quietly looked at property at a new development called Sun City, just northwest of Phoenix. The couple was sure they had seen enough of the cold Indiana winters to know they did not want to stay in Muncie after Moulty's departure from his job at the Muncie Y.

In the winter of 1961-1962, as Steele worked on the construction of the boats Litton had ordered, Pat started to become concerned about what Steele was doing. Pat was worried that an eighty-four-inch "beam at the gunwales is too damn wide for one man to handle. Moulty's *Gem* turned out to be 76" at gunwales and that seemed as wide as I would want when I ran her in Hance." He then went on to compare the flare of the side of the new boat with the *Gem*, *Flavell,* and *Susie R.*

While Pat fretted, Brick began building the *Flavell II* in February. The boat would have the same lines as the first *Flavell*, but would have removable side compartments that could be taken out of the boat and up to a river camp kitchen. Brick built the *Flavell II* with his loss of the *Flavell* in 1958 in mind. The compartments at the very bow and stern of Brick's boat were filled with empty plastic Clorox bottles sealed tight and encased in closed-cell foam. This guaranteed the boat would be practically unsinkable. The boat also had a flotation device on the back with 200 feet of cord attached to the boat. The idea was that a swimmer could take the flotation unit off the boat and swim to shore, pulling the boat into shore as well.

In March, Martin visited Steele's boat shop in Oregon and took some photos of the new boats which he sent to Pat. Martin wrote that the hulls were "6 inches wider than standard McKenzie" and explained that the bottom of the new boats would be flat. Not only flat from side to side, but also from front to back. The two men had just floated straight into the contentious theoretical rough-water world of Pacific Northwest dory design.

Litton summed up the flat hull argument well when he wrote to Pat:

> Bottom is flat for a ways to give higher flotation than continuous rocker shape would. Theory is that deeper curve than this would mean center of boat would be deeper in water and would present more resistance to pivoting. Platter shape is supposed to float whole boat higher (as it obviously will) and more of bow and stern are tharafore [sic] supposed to remain clear of water than would with continuous rocker form.

On hearing from Martin, Pat wrote back that he was sitting on a couple of questions, hoped Steele would keep his due date, and wished the boat was seventeen feet long instead of sixteen. Pat also commented on the flat bottom, noting it was "only after I ran Moulty's *Gem* in Hance that I found out it pivoted much easier than my boat and Moulty said it was built on a constant radius."

Nevertheless, when Steele finished the boats, Martin picked them up and trailered them back to California in April, where he dropped off the open boat at Pat's. For Pat, it was not love at first sight. After beginning to add storage and seating to the hull, Pat noted he "would be lucky to get these boats empty through Grand Canyon." He noted that the wide "79.5 inch beam could be surmounted if we did not have that flat area in the middle. I can't see these boats having enough maneuverability to get thru without lining most of the big ones and some not so big." He went on to note he would have been better off to have "obtained the small McKenzie boat with full rake and counted on a maximum of two passengers each." He was so despondent he wrote Dock "I am thinking seriously of kissing this boat off and getting a jet boat." Dock wrote back that jet boats run about $3,500. It was a lot of money, and while Pat may have had little faith in the new boats, he kept building.

Pat also wrote to Moulty in late April that he, Brick, and Martin would be making another Canyon run, and he included a tentative trip itinerary. Pat had not invited Moulty to join in a new build, and it is very possible Moulty would not have participated if offered the chance. Pat knew that after the 1956 trip, neither of the two, Martin or Moulty, cared to travel together again. On hearing of the poor relations between Martin and Moulty, Dock wrote to Pat that the "Martin-Moulty feudin[sic] is news but the long record of feudin on the river suffices to prevent surprise."

In early May, Martin wrote to Pat that to abort the trip "would literally sink me, as the fares are the only way I have to keep my head above water." Martin noted that had they purchased standard McKenzie hulls they would have spent less and saved much delay. He postulated that there should be no difference in pivoting between the new boats' "pancake" hulls and Moulty's rocking-chair hull. While nicknamed the "monsters," officially Pat named his boat the *Susie Too*, and Martin named his the *Portola*. The doubter's misgivings about their boat hulls echoed those of Moulty in 1945. Pat and Martin would learn about their boats just as Moulty had, once the boats were on the water.

In June 1962, Moulty, Janice and their niece Priss went out west. They took along the *Sausage* and did a day run on the San Juan from Bluff to Mexican Hat. While they did not see Deputy King, they did run into a San Juan commercial guide, who refused to even speak with them. From there it was on to hike rim to rim, starting in a snow flurry at the North Rim on June 16. While Janice drove around to the South Rim, Moulty and Priss reached the Cottonwood Campground for the night. The next day they hiked past Phantom Ranch, on their way to spend the night at Indian Garden. By midmorning on the third day they reached the South Rim.

On June 26, Janice was driving as they crossed a one-lane bridge over the San Rafael River on Highway 24 just out of Green River, Utah. Suddenly, a truck came careening at them as they were just about to exit the bridge. The trio sustained some minor bruising and small cuts from broken glass, while the truck driver was arrested on the spot. Moulty used a highway patrolman's wrecking bar to bend the fenders away from the wheels and limped into Green River. A check at the local garage showed the car to be roadworthy, and the three drove back to Indiana.

While the Fulmers were driving across Utah, the Reilly-Litton-Mortenson river trip launched from Lee's Ferry on June 25, 1962. The Colorado was running at 52,000 cfs, and Pat was the trip leader. Other members of the trip included Susie Reilly, Brick Mortenson, his son Dave, Martin Litton, his son John, and Joe Szep. On arriving at 24½ Mile Rapid on day two, Pat insisted the boats should be lined around the rapid. This was the same rapid where Pat had flipped in 1959, and he was taking no chances. The lining job turned into a portage and took all afternoon. It was the first time Pat had lined any rapid in Marble Canyon.

Flavell II, *Portola* and *Susie Too* at the foot of 24½ Mile Rapid, June 27, 1962. Courtesy Joe Szep

A few days later, the river party lined Hance Rapid on the left, and arrived at Phantom Ranch on July 2, with the river holding at 51,500 cfs. A sandstorm at Hermit Camp made for poor sleeping, and the party remarked on the trash left at Elves Chasm, labeling it the messiest location they had seen. At Stone Creek, a large dune of sand completely trapped the running stream in the side canyon, making a very large pool of clear water for swimming. The river runners lined Lava on the left, and Carl Pederson towed them out across Lake Mead.

At the end of his river trip, Pat could not say enough about the two dories. He wrote Keith Steele, thanking him for the boats, stating they were "the first McKenzie River dories ever to run the Grand Canyon section of the Colorado." Pat also wrote Moulty to say as much, and mistakenly wrote that the boats he and Martin had used were built by Prince Helfrich of Vida, Oregon.

Another trend the river runners had noticed, that of increasing amounts of trash and charcoal along the river, had not gone unnoticed by Grand Canyon Chief Ranger Coffin. In a late season letter to "Boat Operators," in 1962, Coffin directed the operators to review the new boating regulations, instructing river runners to burn or bury their trash. Coffin noted the park might soon be forced to require all river trips to pack out all their trash.

The letter also made mention of increased requests for river trips. These were from "persons we felt were not qualified, and therefore, were not issued a permit." Coffin went on to note the number of unauthorized attempts to float the river "was below past years." Off the record, Coffin had told Pat when the two had visited that summer that Coffin's office had been "swamped with requests from the kayak boys for permits but had turned them down." Coffin had also mentioned that every permit request from "experienced boatmen" was granted.

In the fall, winter, and spring of 1962-1963, Moulty was busy at the Muncie YMCA, working on a major renovation of the swimming pool. This included replacing the pool's antiquated filter system with a new one. Moulty came up with the idea of digging a large hole in the alley by the Y, and cutting through the side of the building. In a letter to Pat that fall, Moulty noted that "Old knucklehead came up with the idea," and if the building had fallen down in the process, he would have come "to Burbank to get a sweeper job at Lockheed."

Meanwhile, in far-off and remote northern Arizona, on January 21, 1963, Bureau of Reclamation engineers began to take control of the Colorado River. The intake gates in the right diversion tunnel, routing the free-flowing Colorado River around the Glen Canyon Dam site, began to slowly close. The gates were fully closed two days later, and the mighty river's flow decreased to 700 cfs. The river quickly pooled behind the dam, and within two more days had risen high enough to begin flowing through the left diversion tunnel. The outlet gates in the left tunnel were left wide open until 2:00 p.m., March 13, 1963. It was then that outlet gates 1 and 3 were fully closed in the left diversion tunnel, and gate No. 2 was opened only enough to allow 1,000 cfs to escape. Water in the reservoir immediately began to back up into Glen Canyon.

With Glen Canyon starting to slowly fill, Moulty took one last opportunity to explore its stunning canyons before they were drowned. With two companions, he rented a small motor boat and explored the Escalante River and hiked thirty-three miles in two days to Gregory, Barker, and Broken Bow arches. Moulty took the small boat up the San Juan arm, past 13-Foot Rapid, which was already underwater. He also explored Hidden Passage, Music Temple, Oak, Davis, and Aztec canyons, which would all eventually be flooded by the lake.

After the exploration of Glen Canyon, the trio visited Arches National Monument, then Moulty and his friends parted ways, and he ran Cataract Canyon on a commercial trip operated by John Cross Jr. and Larry Davis. The party launched on July 1 in a twenty-eight-foot-long neoprene raft with two rowing stations and a 15-HP motor. The flow was near record low, at just over 4,000 cfs. The rubber raft hung up on rocks in two of the rapids, and hit "dozens of others" on the way. Moulty spent a little time on the twelve-foot long oars, but wrote to Dock that is was "hard pulling as I worked them on several occasions." Moulty doubted he would want to ride "a big neoprene raft again – not much fun." He was also disappointed with the Cataract trip, partly by the speed at which the party made the transit, taking a day and half to get through Cataract and past Dark Canyon. He also noted that except "for a couple of spots it is a fairly dry canyon, and the color wasn't what I thought it might be."

Moulty had been back in Muncie for almost a month when Dock and Bill Belknap left Lee's Ferry August 6 for a twenty-six-day Grand Canyon cruise to Lake Mead. With the concrete plug upstream only releasing 1,000 cfs, Dock had to abandon motorized river transport and return to oar power, a mode of propulsion he had not used since running with Norm and Moulty in 1948. For this extremely low-water run, the craft of choice was a Sportyak, a bathtub-sized plastic boat with four-and-a-half-foot-long oars. The river had never been run at such low water levels, and they encountered many rapids that did not exist at higher water.

Such was the supreme control that Glen Canyon Dam exerted on the Colorado River. A number of people, including Dock Marston, were predicting what the long-term effects of the dam would be. In a letter to Chief Ranger Coffin a year earlier, Dock surmised that the lack of seasonal fluctuations in the river would eliminate "most of the sand beaches as the willow and tamarisk will grow into a jungle as it does along many of the bars in Glen Canyon and the upper part of Lake Mead." Dock also assumed the river would be overrun with trout, kayakers, and trash, which would force the Park Service to require that all trash be removed by the river runners who generated it. Another change Dock foresaw was the hardening of riverside campsites by excessive use, "like at the mouth of Aztec Creek in Glen Canyon."

Glen Canyon Dam caused immediate changes. Without an inflow of water, the level of Lake Mead dropped precipitously. Between July 1962 and July 1964, the reservoir level dropped over 100 feet. Ironically, it was this effect of the dam on Lake Mead that led to the discovery of the *Gem*. Dock wrote to Moulty that the *Gem* had really been found this time, as the discoverer, Park Naturalist Ted Whitmoyer, had called Dock on the morning of September 30, 1964, to report the find. Moulty wrote right back. He was glad, after six-and-a-half years, to learn where the *Gem* had snuck off to, having never fully convinced himself that the boat had sunk. Moulty noted that this concluded "the last unsolved and unfinished chapter in the life of the *Gem*."

On October 14, Dock wrote to Moulty that the *Gem* was being towed in for use in a historical museum and that "Whitmoyer is in charge." As soon as he had them, Dock sent Moulty some photos of the *Gem* as it lay in God's Pocket. Moulty was greatly appreciative, and noted the bottom and the chine still looked to be in fairly good condition, and were the "strongest points from a construction standpoint."

The same month the *Gem* was discovered in God's Pocket, President Lyndon Johnson signed the Wilderness Act, in an attempt to save some of the last great places in America from development. On signing the bill, President Johnson noted "If future generations are to remember us with gratitude rather than contempt, we must leave them something more than the miracles of technology. We must leave them a glimpse of the world as it was in the beginning, not just after we got through with it." Almost all of Grand Canyon National Park, including the Colorado River, qualified for wilderness protection. The NPS at Grand Canyon began work on designating the river and backcountry as wilderness by 1968, and would continue to work on the wilderness issue while guided motorized river trips in the Canyon, clearly inconsistent with the Wilderness Act, greatly increased.

Having only rarely corresponded with Pat in the last few years, in January, 1965, Moulty sent Pat a letter asking if he was ready to tackle the Grand with lightweight rubber boats. If Pat was willing, Moulty wanted to go along. Pat was not keen on the idea, and later that summer sold his dory, the *Susie Too*, to Martin Litton for $350. Brick also sold the *Flavell II* to Martin that same year. Martin repainted the *Susie Too*, and renamed her *Music Temple*. Ten years later, Martin donated the boat to Grand Canyon National Park, and Pat's wish of having one of his boats at the South Rim of the Grand Canyon was achieved at last.

In the summer of 1965, Moulty and Guy Taylor took a road trip out to the Grand Canyon. Their trip included backpacking into Havasu Canyon. While their packs were heavy, they "thought it one of the most beautiful spots we had ever seen." From there it was on to a warehouse in Boulder City, Nevada, to look in on the *Gem*, and then the two headed out to visit with John Riffey and gaze down towards Lava Falls from the Toroweap Overlook. Moulty and Guy clowned around at the edge, as many travelers do. Back behind the wheel, it was on to the Lee's Ferry put-in, to watch the boat-rigging activities, before driving on to Moab for a quick run on the Colorado above Moab in the *Sausage*. Finally, the two headed to Canyonlands National Park and on out to Dead Horse and Grandview points, before heading back to Muncie.

That winter, Moulty had some serious sinus difficulties. His doctor advised him that spending the winter in a drier, warmer climate might be beneficial to his health. While the couple had planned for this, leaving Muncie for the "Land of the Sun" was nothing they wanted to rush into. So it was a shock to the community when the May 22, 1966, *Muncie Star* ran a half-sheet article announcing Moulty's pending retirement from the Y in October. After thirty-seven years as physical director at the Muncie YMCA, it was time to do what Moulty had always tried to do, quit while he was ahead. Moulty was at the top of his game, and his physical fitness program at the Y was taxing the capacity of the Y's facilities as never before. Janice, after many years serving as receptionist at Warner Gear Plant No. 3, would be retiring as well.

An article ran in the *Muncie Star* that summer in Bob Barnet's column "After the Ball," in which the reporter recalled playing tennis with Moulty:

> Let's say you are playing Old Mole on a sunny afternoon and you get lucky and catch him half a step out of position back there on the baseline and ram the ball past him with your very best forehand. Well sir, you stoop to tie your shoe before winning the next easy point and when you straighten up you take a look at some fleecy white clouds high in the sky and while you are looking you hear a whirring noise and it is the ball heading for the right hand corner, where it kicks up dust just inside the line. The thing that has just happened is that Moulie ran the ball half way to Losantville, fell down, rolled over twice, and hit it past you while lying flat on his back. He was a hard man to beat in any game, a real fighter and a real gentleman. It has been a pleasure to have known him and worked with him through the years. He made Muncie a better place.

The Board of Directors of the Muncie YMCA held an appreciation dinner for Moulty October 4, 1966. Over 300 members of the community were in attendance, as Muncie had a chance to offer the Fulmers a heartfelt "well done!" With board president John Cardle acting as master of ceremonies, ten speakers honored Moulty in various ways. Reverend William Wagner, General Superintendent of Friends Church in Indiana, gave the opening invocation. Jack Peckinpaugh, Vice President of the Muncie YMCA Board of Directors, honored Moulty with the gift of a silver plate inscribed:

Moulton B. Fulmer

Leader of Men and Boys

Superb Athlete

Christian Gentleman

With our sincere gratitude for 37 years of devoted

Service to others through the Muncie YMCA

YMCA State Chapter President Russell Hulse presented Moulty with a green baseball cap. At one point, Hulse asked Moulty what his hat size was, and Moulty shot right back "Pretty big tonight!"

Jim Kaat, pitching at that time for the Minnesota Twins baseball team, spoke to the audience about Fulmer's positive mental attitude. Edmund F. Ball, President of the glass manufacturing company Ball Corporation, noted, "The character and reputation of a community is the composite and reputation of its citizens. Few have done as much as Moulton Fulmer to enrich the image of the Muncie community."

Ray Gribble, Chairman of the YMCA physical department committee, presented Moulty with a check to assist with travel to the following year's Olympic Games in Mexico City. Finally, it was Moulty's turn to speak. He approached the podium to a standing ovation, and addressed the crowd "I'm sure I have fallen a little short and my record is not as good as it should be. When you honor me, you honor an individual and an institution. The individual is my wife, Janice Fulmer, and the institution is the YMCA on a local, state, and national basis."

And with that, the Fulmers sold their lawnmower, leaf rake, snow shovel, and home, and headed to Sun City. Moulty's eighty-five-year-old step-father, George, who had been living with the couple for a few years, went as well. Arriving at their new Arizona home in the fall of 1966, Moulty found it difficult for his new community to grasp his name. If you asked for Moulty Fulmer back in Muncie, people would immediately direct you to the YMCA. If you asked for Steve Fulmer, they would politely say they didn't know the man. In Arizona, Moulty was a difficult name for people to understand. Fulmer dropped Moulty and became Steve with his new acquaintances. He was Stephen Moulton Babcock Fulmer after all, and had a little more leeway in the name department than most folks. Janice, not to be left out, became Jan. While it was a lot easier for Steve's new neighbors, the dual names confused and alienated some of the family back in Indiana, as well as some of the couple's river running friends.

While there were huge changes in the Fulmers' lives, there were also monumental changes happening on the Colorado River in the Grand Canyon. One huge difference on the new dam-controlled river was the daily tides in the water released from the dam. Glen Canyon Dam furnished "peak" hydropower, and as electrical demand rose in the morning, so did the discharge of water through the dam's electricity-generating turbines. At night, when demand for electricity dropped off, the dam needed to generate less electricity and the water flow through the turbines was decreased.

The 1967 summer flows varied between low flows around 7,500 cfs to high flows around 13,500 cfs every day except when something needed to be tweaked at the new dam. Then flows might drop unexpectedly to 7,000 cfs, or go up to 19,000 cfs. River runners had to expect the unexpected with the new dam-controlled flows. As the reservoir continued to fill behind the dam, these tides would continue in an ever-increasing swing, in a rather unpredictable manner. The highest flows were now not far above the all-time, pre-dam, lowest peak natural summer runoff flows. Following a very dry winter, the highest flow of 1934 produced a maximum 25,300 cfs on May 16. Following a peak flow test in early 1965, the Colorado River below the dam would not see a flow as high as the 1934 peak flow until 1968.

The lack of high springtime flows coursing through the heart of the Grand Canyon had dramatic effects on some of the rapids. Formerly, the Canyon's rapids grew larger and more constrictive after side canyons delivered massive slurries of boulders and water, called debris flows, into the main river channel. The debris would largely be washed away downriver in the large late spring runoff from Rocky Mountain snowmelt. But the lower flows released by Glen Canyon Dam stopped this seasonal scouring of the river channel. In 1966, a freak storm sent a torrent of rocky debris down Crystal Creek causing a major rapid to develop. Crystal Rapid still provides a challenge for today's river travelers.

Moulton and Janice Fulmer, about 1960. Courtesy Priss Becker

The river's water temperature also changed. The water released through the dam's turbines is drawn from the cold depths of the reservoir. The water was cool in the first years of post-dam flows as the reservoir filled, but once the lake was full, the water at the base of the dam became much colder, averaging a chilly forty-eight degrees. The dam also served as a sediment and driftwood filter, as these materials sank to the bottom of the flooded Glen Canyon well over 100 miles upstream of the dam. It was indeed a new Colorado River, based on the new Glen Canyon Dam.

Immediately after the dam became operational in the spring of 1963, there was so little water being released that only one trip went down the river that year, Dock's Sportyak traverse. In 1964, while the dam was still impounding water and releasing very low flows, the river saw a little more traffic. When the dam started producing electricity in the fall and winter of 1964, flows were once again at a more runnable level. Demand to participate in river trips skyrocketed. In 1966, more people ran the Colorado River than had done so from the time of James White's 1867 float through the end of the 1960 river running season. More people would cruise the Canyon in 1967 than the total number of pre-dam river runners combined.

The Park Service continued to give commercial companies all the river trips they wanted. There were nineteen trips in 1965 and thirty-nine in 1966. The number of commercial companies flourished. If you wanted to run the Grand Canyon a lot, after your first trip, you could start a company and receive all the permits you asked for. There was no limit on the number of passengers a company could take. One of the largest commercial trips in 1966 had "15 pontoon rafts with 150 mostly high school students."

For do-it-yourself river runners who wanted to challenge themselves by running the river without a guide, the Park Service also continued the now-standard practice of denying the vast majority of requests for river permits. There were more than fifty applications for self-guided river trips in 1966, and only three were allowed, down from four the year before. To those denied permits, the Park Service simply suggested they seek out commercially guided trips for access to the river.

Another change brought about by the dam was the disappearance of small hard-hulled outboard motor boats and an explosion in the number of large neoprene motorized baloney boats. Additionally, with the increased number of river trips through the Canyon, lining boats around the large rapids for safety became a thing of the past. If a river party was in trouble because they flipped a boat in a big rapid, chances were good another trip was just downstream to catch the miscreant boat, while the next trip upstream would show up to offer assistance.

Dories, like the ones used by Moulty, then Pat and Martin, were still making the cruise in small but growing numbers. In May of 1968, *Sunset* magazine published an article on dories written by Martin Litton. In that article, he very succinctly identified what he called the "Dory Formula." He wrote:

> There are no precise dimensions that make a boat a dory – and indeed some Western boatmen resist the use of the term "dory" for what they prefer to call Rogue River boats, McKenzie boats, or drift boats. However, all these craft embody the principles that make the dory the most maneuverable of all boats and the most stable of all keelless boats. In general, there is only one shape a dory can have. It is wide amidships and pointed or narrow at both ends (the squared-off end is a concession to the outboard motor, but it remains narrow; rowing dories are often double-enders). The bottom is perfectly flat in cross-section, but markedly rocker-shaped when viewed from the side; ideally, its longitudinal profile is a segment of a circle. The secret (no secret, really) of a dory's "spin" – its instantaneous response to either oar – is that because of this curve or "rake" it presents little resistance to turning; only the middle of the boat is in contact with the water, while the two ends are up in the air. The broad beam (often 6 feet or more at the gunwales amidships) gives the oars hefty leverage. The stability of the dory is related to its maneuverability. It can teeter like a rocking-horse fore and aft, but rare is the wave that can come over its flared, buoyant bow or stern. The sides slant outward about an inch for every two inches of height; the resulting angle is the "flare".

While Martin had described both the *Moja* and *Gem* to a tee, the boats he and Pat had used in 1962 were missing that longitudinal profile being the "segment of a circle" as the hulls of the Steele boats were flat from front to back for about four-and-a-half feet. Martin mentioned later in the article that two "oversize, decked-over McKenzie dories" had been introduced to the Grand Canyon in 1962, "fleet and responsive as no other Grand Canyon craft had ever been." Except one. It had shown up in 1955, owned by someone Martin didn't particularly like.

After Martin started Grand Canyon Dories in 1969, the brochures he produced mentioned the 1962 river trip using "larger, decked over, compartmented boats for the Grand Canyon in 1962." To Martin's credit, the brochure didn't say the 1962 trip was the first to do this. Also, in the summer of 2008, during a long conversation about his recollections of the 1950s river trips, out of the blue Martin said "Moulty had a little dory called the *Gem*, not like Pat's boats, his was a dory design."

Martin Litton acknowledged what Moulty had done, but Pat Reilly never cited Moulty's seminal meeting with Woodie and the influence that meeting had on Moulty's boat-building career. In the late 1970s, Pat wrote a short paper on the historic boats at Grand Canyon for John O'Brien, Grand Canyon National Park Chief of Interpretation. In his write up of the *Gem*, Pat recounted Moulty's having run with Nevills in the 1940s, and mentions the *Moja* without providing any dimensions. Of the *Gem*, Pat noted its beam "was 64 inches at the bottom, which flared in true dory style, to 76 inches at the oarlocks. The bottom had a rake of 15 inches and was a constant radius forward to aft." Pat went through the rest of the *Gem*'s dimensions, listed the boat's river runs, and then recounted the *Gem*'s loss in 1958. Throughout the entire review of the boat and the boat builder, Pat failed to mention Woodie Hindman's influence.

While Moulty's boat building accomplishments were being overlooked, Moulty, Janice, and George settled quickly into their new Arizona home and continued to explore the Southwest they loved so much. In 1967, Moulty ran the Rogue River and attempted to climb to the top of Mount Whitney in the California Sierra. He was turned back after climbing to an elevation of 12,000 feet. Undaunted and all the wiser after the first attempt, Moulty summited Whitney the next year. He also returned to Havasu twice, and hiked down Soap Creek to the river. The local Phoenix YMCA held a "Run For Your Life" program, and Moulty received a trophy for running over 250 miles. In June of 1968, Moulty took his now eighty-seven-year-old stepfather George on the San Juan from Bluff to Mexican Hat in the trusty *Sausage*. George was thrilled by the run, and talked about it until his passing four years later.

Regrettably, Dock Marston's wife Margaret passed away September 19, 1968, after a long illness. The seventy-six-year-old had lived the last forty years of her life in Berkeley, California, where she had started a symphony orchestra for youth. Margaret was also instrumental in seeing that the local Police Department began hiring women to serve as police officers. Moulty sent his sympathies to Dock, noting he would "never forget the wonderful trip we had on the Yampa in 1950."

Things were still changing fast in the Grand Canyon. While there were nine commercial operators in 1966, there were eleven in 1968, and twenty-one by 1971. In the winter of 1971-1972, the NPS changed the commercial operators to twenty-one concessions contracts. To this day, the only way new businesses can enter the commercial river business is to purchase an existing contract. In 1970, a whopping 9,935 river travelers ran the river, and almost twice that number, 16,432, would make the cruise just two years later.

From the three do-it-yourself river trips allowed in 1966, that number had risen to forty-four trips of 550 people in 1972, while the commercial operators had 520 trips carrying just under 16,000 people. In 1973, the NPS divided the permit process into two components, the river concessions and the do-it-yourself river runners. In order to continue to limit do-it-yourself demand, there was a two-year no-repeat rule imposed in 1973. This rule was not imposed on the river concessions passengers. That rule was dropped in 1976, but re-emerged as a one-year no-repeat rule for all do-it-yourselfers, along with concessions passengers, beginning in 2006.

Today the NPS estimates there are about 14,385 commercial passengers (not including crew) on 476 river trips in the summer months. In the same time period, 2,270 do-it-yourself river runners participate on 185 self-guided river trips. In the spring and fall, 3,221 commercial passengers participate on 122 river trips and 2,926 do-it-yourselfers participate on 199 river trips. In the dead of winter, there are no concessions river trips and the NPS allows 1,855 do-it-yourself river runners to travel on 120 river trips. While an incredible improvement over the 1960s and 1970s, this discrepancy in access between the commercial companies and do-it-yourself river runners has been litigated three times. The most recent litigation over this issue occurred in 2006, and failed to bring about the needed reforms in recreational access between the different use groups. This issue still vexes river runners as well as river managers up and down the Colorado River today, from the Grand Canyon to the San Juan, Desolation, Yampa and Lodore canyons.

Group sizes were established for the first time in 1972, with fifty-five passengers being allowed in any one party camping together at the end of the day. That was decreased in 1973 to forty passengers on commercial trips, and sixteen on do-it-yourself trips, a level that would remain for the next thirty-three years. Today, group sizes are capped at thirty-two people for concessionaire summer trips, while do-it-yourself trips are limited to either sixteen or eight.

Throughout the 1960s and 1970s, the proliferation of motorized boats for guided tours led the Park Service to attempt to transition the commercial operators from motorized to motor-free watercraft in order to follow the legal requirements of the 1964 Wilderness Act. A telling letter from Grand Canyon National Park Superintendent Merle Stitt in 1975 noted management of the Colorado River in Grand Canyon "will probably have more impact on wilderness proposals for Grand Canyon than all other issues and studies combined."

Indeed, his words proved tragically visionary. The commercial river companies pushed back, using the Western River Guides Association, the trade organization Colorado River Outfitters Association, and assistance from a few members of Congress, in an attempt to keep their fast motorized trips. In 1980, the river concessionaires prevailed in blocking the phase out of motorized tour boats and wilderness designation for Grand Canyon. The Park Service has yet to regain momentum in ushering motor-free wilderness river management back into Grand Canyon National Park, and as of this writing there is no congressionally designated wilderness anywhere in Grand Canyon National Park.

One of the few but important successes the Park Service realized was Chief Ranger Coffin's 1962 threat to require all waste be removed from the river. This finally became mandatory policy, along with the transition from building fires on the beach to using cook stoves and fire pans, by 1979. The policy was a direct result of four years of research from 1972 to 1976, along with environmentalist pressure, including litigation by the Sierra Club, demanding the NPS do more to protect the river resource. Today all river runners carry out their trash, including all their solid human waste.

While river traffic continued to expand, the late 1960s were a busy time for the Fulmers. Moulty won the first Sun City Tennis Club tournament, taking both the men's singles, and the doubles, paired with Blake Stewart. Moulty learned lapidary and silversmithing, and in 1967 Janice and Moulty rode a boat on the Inside Passage to Alaska. Moulty climbed Mount Lassen along the way. In 1969, lacking any river running friends who were going to run the Grand Canyon themselves, he went on a commercial oar trip through the Canyon.

The 1970s were both a difficult and then busy time for the Fulmers. Moulty developed ever worsening low back pain and eventually he could not walk 100 yards. In 1975 he had lumbar surgery to relieve compressed nerves, and it gave him a new lease on life. Pat and Susie Reilly moved to Sun City in 1972, after Pat took early retirement. Yet, even living in the same town, the Reillys and the Fulmers saw little of each other.

Harvey Butchart, the famed Grand Canyon hiker, and his wife Roma, moved from Flagstaff to Sun City in 1976. The Fulmers and Butcharts became fast friends, and played scrabble and bridge together, while Harvey and Moulty gave each other exhausting workouts on the tennis court. When he was seventy and the country celebrated the bicentennial, Moulty joined a commercial oar-powered river trip for another run through the Grand Canyon. He went with a rowing-only company called OARS. As the trip made its way through the Canyon he loved so much, Moulty's river running history became known among the crew and passengers. Moulty was given the oars and he rowed North Canyon, Kwagunt, 75 Mile, Walthenberg, 205 Mile, and 217 Mile rapids.

Feeling confident after his recovery from surgery, Moulty backpacked by himself down the Hermit Trail all the way to Hermit Rapid in 1977. From there he headed east to Monument Creek, down to Granite Rapid, and then out to Indian Gardens and the South Rim. In 1978, Moulty hiked the Boucher Trail to the river, then worked his way west down to Slate Creek to get photos of Crystal Rapid. Given the unpredictable swings in river flows, Moulty saw Crystal at a decreased river flow of 1,200 cfs. Later that year, he hiked through the narrows of Paria Canyon in four days.

Moulty Fulmer at the oars below Lava Chuar, always the ham, 1978.
Courtesy Plez Talmadge Reilly Collection, Cline Library,
Northern Arizona University

That same year, Moulty was off for another run through the Canyon with OARS on a thirteen-day trip from Lee's Ferry to Diamond Creek. Moulty rowed some of the rapids as well, the biggest being Hermit. There were six oar boats on the trip, and one flipped in House Rock with "one shoe, two hats, and one pair of sunglasses the only casualties."

After the Grand Canyon run, Moulty and Janice drove to Muncie in September. It was good to be home to visit with relatives and friends. There was a reason far beyond a family visit that brought Moulty back to Muncie. He was inducted into the Ball State University Athletic Hall of Fame.

A year later, Moulty was inducted into the Delaware County Athletic Hall of Fame as well. On the first of June in 1979, Moulty and Janice took the *Sausage* out for one last high water spin on the San Juan. It had only been thirty-two years since their 1947 *Moja* run, and how the time had flown by. The *Sausage* was now leaking like a sieve, and Janice spent a lot of time pumping, trying to keep air in the leaky raft. The San Juan was running at 14,500 cfs, down 1,100 cfs from its peak for the year just three days earlier.

While Moulty and Janice were rigging their boat, another much-younger couple drove up. Avid river runners Dan and Linda Lindeman saw the older couple and were curious who they were. Dan asked the old-timers what they were doing. On hearing about the many San Juan runs Moulty had made, Dan and Linda asked if they could join the Fulmers, who quickly agreed. The two couples had a nice but quick trip, taking about five hours to make the twenty-seven-mile run.

In 1980, Moulty made one more river trip, a three-day trip on the Tuolumne River in California. Moulty, now seventy-four, noted the Tuolumne trip "was real hairy." And there it was, gone, the last trip, with the last rapid coming up.

Dock Marston, the Grand Old Man of the River, passed away August 30, 1979. Friends for over thirty years, Moulty took the opportunity to recognize Dock in a letter a year before Dock's passing, when he wrote "Harvey probably is one of the greatest of Canyon hikers, but you have no peers when it comes to history of the world's greatest canyon – the GRAND."

Moulty did not leave us with many thoughts of his 1940s and 1950s river running compared to his 1969 through 1978 Grand Canyon river trips. In a 1984 interview, the ever-reserved river runner commentd that he wasn't "very keen on the large, rubber boats now used in running the Colorado. In a smaller boat, you get an intimate view of the river as you're down in it."

While Moulty may not have left us many thoughts on the changes in river running he had seen, Pat did. In 1982, Pat and Susie were invited guests on a commercial motorized pontoon boat. After the trip, Pat wrote in a letter to Joe Szep that there had been some changes on the river. Pat was surprised to see about "150 people depart Lee's Ferry each day and the Colorado is just like the John Muir Trail in that one is seldom out of sight of another rig." He was also surprised to note there were "few beaches left and often there is a scramble for camps." He noted that where there had been nice beaches there were now "cobble fields." Pat also observed that the water had dropped to such a low flow that it was a big deal when it rose above 12,000 cfs.

There were good boatmen, he wrote, along with "some incompetent ones with inadequate training." He also was not pleased with the speed of the trips, going 280 miles in eight days. Pat was not impressed with the passengers who started drinking in the morning and saw most of the river while in a drunken stupor. He reported seeing "7½ nudists," and his final note was that commercialism "had brought Coney Island to the Canyon. Glad we went – but never again." Pat summed it all up in one sentence: "The old days of river running are as dead as the endless buffalo herds on the Great Plains, and neither will return."

Then it was Moulty Fulmer's turn. After a short battle with cancer on July 20, 1989, forty-one years to the day from leaving Phantom Ranch to head west on big water in little boats, Moulty took his final breath. Janice Fulmer died in January of 1996. A few river runners scattered the couple's ashes together into the waters of the Colorado River in the heart of the Grand Canyon the summer after Janice's passing.

Epilogue

Colleen unlocked the padlock on the rickety door. It was a mild July day at the South Rim in 2006. The constant chatter of nearby tourists washed over us. The 100-year-old Kolb Studio perched on the rim of the Grand Canyon was only a stone's throw away. The door stuck, and then, with an extra push, the rusted overhead rollers creaked down their track. We stepped into cool darkness. A cat hissed, and then scrambled out a small hole in the back of the garage. The floor was covered with a thick layer of leaves, dust, and years of accumulated dried woodrat droppings. In the far corner of the garage was the outline of a boat. I had just been introduced to the *Gem*.

When I contacted Colleen Hyde at Grand Canyon National Park's Museum Collection asking about the boat, she told me the *Gem* was in a garage next to the Kolb Studio. "You really don't want to see it" she said. "Why not?" I asked her. "You'll see when you see it," she laughed. Colleen was right. We stepped closer to the wreck of the boat, and I couldn't help chuckling, given how this had all started. I thought back to the day I met Dave Mortenson and his daughter, Cecelia, standing on a tiny beach about a mile below Upset Rapid, deep in the heart of Grand Canyon National Park.

I had been exploring the Grand Canyon on foot and by boat since the 1960s, and was now working as a physical therapist in the medical clinic at the South Rim. A group of us were on a thirty-day Grand Canyon rafting trip in the early spring of 1996. We did an awful lot of hiking on that trip. My climbing partner and I had been high up in the Redwall Limestone above 140 Mile Canyon earlier in the day. Sitting on a ledge at the highest point we were willing to climb up to, he pulled a copy of Harvey Butchart's *Grand Canyon Treks* from his pack. One of a handful of highly accomplished Grand Canyon climbers, my partner began reading about the Cranberry Canyon Route, a route we had a great view of from our perch across the river. Harvey mentioned the route had been discovered by a guy named Dave Mortenson and his friend. We both wondered out loud who Mortenson was. He didn't live in Flagstaff, we were pretty sure of that. And who was "his friend?"

Later that same afternoon, we were rowing to a camp called Ledges, and were the last boat in our group. Suddenly, I saw some backpackers up in the limestone cliffs above the river. One of them was heading down to the small beach just downstream of us. Pulling to shore, we were stunned to see a gorgeous young woman asking us for a beer. "What's your name?" must have sounded a bit informal out there in the middle of nowhere, but Cece Mortenson handled the request with a smile. Mortenson? We looked at each other. "And who's that guy up there?" I asked, pointing at the guy sitting by his pack a few hundred feet up the slope from us. "That's my dad, Dave," came Cece's cheerful and quick reply.

From Dave Mortenson's perspective up on the limestone bench above his daughter, something was going seriously wrong. One of the river runners was now boulder-hopping up toward him. Cece was supposed to get a beer or two, and now one of those folks was coming his way. Worse yet, the tall wiry guy advancing toward him up the rocky slope was calling out "Are you Dave Mortenson and who is your friend?"

After a brief introduction, Dave admitted he was the guy who had discovered the Cranberry Canyon Route, along with Arnie Richards, his long-time hiking partner and close friend. I invited Dave, Cece, and her two lady friends to join us for dinner that night. Our group was fourteen men and one woman. Adding Dave and the trio of twenty-two-year-old women to our camp for the evening would certainly change that ratio. To my surprise, Dave said "Sure."

That night after dinner, while the party on shore was warming up, Dave and I chatted by the river. He told me the most amazing stories of his father, Brick, running the Grand Canyon in the 1950s on do-it-yourself river trips. That was before the construction of Glen Canyon Dam, back when Ledges Camp was sometimes called Reilly's Roost after river runner Pat Reilly. Dave told me about one of the river runners named Moulty, and how he lost his boat in a complicated series of events on a Grand Canyon river trip in the late 1950s.

Over the next several years, I had the great fortune to get to know Dave's dad, Brick, before his passing in 2000, and to hike the backcountry of the Grand Canyon with Dave, Cece, and Arnie Richards. While Pat Reilly passed away the same year I met Dave, I had the chance to visit with Susie Reilly in 2000, a year before she died in April 2001. The story of Moulty and the *Gem* still had not grabbed my attention.

That changed in 2005, when I asked Dave why anyone would want to be called Moldy, as in moldy cheese. Dave corrected me. "It's not Moldy, but Moulty, as in Molten, like lava." Dave casually mentioned that Brick, before his passing, had said Moulty's boat, the *Gem*, was supposedly somewhere on the South Rim. Dave suggested I look for the boat. And here we were, Colleen and I, standing in the Kolb Garage looking at the *Gem*, or what was left of it.

Ellsworth Kolb arrived at the South Rim of the Grand Canyon in 1901, and by 1903 had set up a small photography studio right on the rim of the Canyon with his brother Emery. The Kolb brothers decided to try a river run through the Canyon, taking motion pictures as they went. In the fall of 1911 the Kolbs launched on the Green River at Green River, Wyoming. They floating down the Green to the Colorado, and went on to successfully complete the seventh documented river trip on the Colorado River through the Grand Canyon in January 1912. The Kolbs, on a do-it-yourself river trip, were the first to take motion pictures of their journey through Grand Canyon. They also wrote a book of their adventures, *Through the Grand Canyon from Wyoming to Mexico*, first published in 1914. The brothers began showing their film to tourists at their studio, which soon expanded to include a theater. Business was good, and in 1927 an automobile garage was built adjacent to the studio. After Emery's death in 1976, the Kolbs' studio and garage became the property of the National Park Service.

How the *Gem* ended up in the Kolb garage was another bit of magic. Ted Whitmoyer had moved on in his NPS career soon after recovering the *Gem* in 1964. Before he left, Whitmoyer had hoped to have a boat museum at Lake Mead and had stored the *Gem* in a warehouse at Boulder City, Nevada. In 1979, Park Service officials at Lake Mead had contacted John O'Brien, Chief of Interpretation at Grand Canyon National Park, asking if O'Brien was interested in the wreck. If O'Brien didn't want it, the Lake Mead maintenance crew knew of a landfill that would take it. O'Brien was indeed interested, and in October of 1979, the *Gem* was moved to Grand Canyon.

Museum Collections Curator Colleen Hyde and the wreck of the *Gem* in the Kolb garage, Grand Canyon National Park, July 2006. Tom Martin photo

The *Gem*'s sturdy floor held the boat together through thick and thin. Kolb garage, Grand Canyon National Park, 2007. Tom Martin photo

The *Gem* on its temporary cradle, Kolb garage, May 2008. Tom Martin photo

Once in the Kolb garage, the *Gem* had been placed on a sheet of plywood and covered with a stout tarp. The tarp had been draped over a wooden framework to hold it up off the boat. Someone eventually realized the woodrats were happy to have a tarp over their nests, and the tarp was pulled off the *Gem* and heaped up about the bow of the boat. Cleaning this all up was going to take some work.

In subsequent visits to the garage, I was allowed to volunteer for the park and slowly sweep up, clean the animal and plant debris out of the boat, and build a temporary wooden cradle under the *Gem*. After years in the deep waters of Lake Mead, the *Gem*'s red, white, and blue paint scheme was just visible; now, fifty years after it had last seen fresh paint, most of the colors were long gone, leaving a flat, dirty-white primer exposed over the boat's outer surface. Unfortunately, no supports had been placed under the front or back of the boat while it rested on the flat plywood. As the years went by, gravity pulled the *Gem* to the floor, splitting the sides of the boat. Still, as I worked on cleaning up the boat over the next two years, it became clear to me that the bottom of the *Gem* was built very solidly. It was the strength of this floor that had held the rest of the boat together all these decades.

Once the *Gem* was cleaned up and on a temporary cradle, I realized there were a lot of things I needed to learn. Who was this guy named Moulty? What were the river trips like back then? Finally, I needed to find out what had happened to this boat. It took a little research. Okay, it took a lot of research.

The research had its ups and downs. Like the time the phone was hung up with a definitive "this call is terminated" click. I hadn't even gotten to mention looking for information on Moulty Fulmer. Maybe this was a wrong number and I was bothering someone in Indiana for nothing. In 2007, in the Utah State Historical Society archives, I had found the name of Moulty's niece, Priss Becker, and the name of the school where she had worked as a young woman. A phone call to the Shambaugh Elementary School in Fort Wayne, Indiana, connected me with the longest standing staffer at the school. Yes, she had worked with Priss many years earlier. There were two listings for Becker in the phone book and she kindly gave me both numbers.

I waited thirty seconds and called back. This time I quickly said I was looking for the family of Moulty Fulmer. There was a long silence, and then a woman's voice asked "Who wants to know?" Two hours later, Moulty's niece Priscilla had filled in so many gaps in the story my head was spinning. Even though some of her family thought I might be a scam artist, Priss was kind enough to entertain a visit. She had, after all, been in the Grand Canyon with her uncle in 1957, and no one had asked her a thing about her 1957 river trip for fifty years.

A year later, my wife Hazel and I drove historic Route 66 to Indiana. As we drove the four-lane highway through miles of corn fields, I wondered what it must have been like pulling a wooden boat on a trailer from Indiana to the Grand Canyon every year on what was then a two-lane road with a lot more traffic. What we had thought would be an afternoon's visit turned into a three-day crash course on Stephen Moulton Babcock Fulmer. As Hazel and I finally drove away, and Priss and her husband John stood on the porch waving, John turned to Priss and said in his low Midwest drawl "Looks like we've been scammed." Indeed, we had gotten away with the story of Moulty Fulmer!

Moulty Fulmer's Smoker oar, Utah State Historical Society, 2009. Tom Martin photo

It turned out Moulty's story was scattered all over the West. The Huntington Library had all of his correspondence with Dock Marston. Joe Szep answered the phone when I called him out of the blue, and in a subsequent visit to his home in California, he was very generous with access to many hundreds of his photos. Scattered in tiny pockets, like at the Plez Talmadge Reilly collection at Northern Arizona University and the Norm Nevill's collection at the University of Utah, were photos of Moulty's early boats. Then there was the oar. One of Moulty's oars from the *Moja* was in the collection at the Utah State Historical Society in Salt Lake City, Utah, along with all the correspondence between Moulty and Pat. Once the story started to become clear, there was one more thing I needed to do. It would require a little carpentry and a life jacket.

With the encouragement of Dave Mortenson, in the fall of 2008, I figured it would be a good idea to build a full-sized replica of the *Gem*. It took a few months to find a garage where construction could take place. Luckily, a young and talented boat builder named Kyle Frye introduced me to Bob and Beth Goforth. The Goforths owned a large garage in Parks,

Ladder frame construction allows for correct alignment of the bulkheads, placement of the keelson, chine, and gunwale, 2009. Tom Martin photo

Arizona, and were kind enough to let me build a full-sized replica of the *Gem* there. While I had built houses in my past, I had never built a boat. Fortunately, the remains of Moulty's *Gem* at the South Rim were there to guide me. Kyle was also building a dory in the Goforth garage, and I looked over his shoulder as he built his boat and plied him and Bob with many questions as I worked on the *Gem* replica.

It is unclear just how Moulty built his *Gem*. Pacific Northwest dories today are either built off a structure laid out on the ground called a ladder frame, or are built using a stitch-and-glue technique. I chose the ladder frame method. This technique requires cutting out the bulkheads and positioning them upside down along the frame. Once set in place, the bulkheads are attached one to another by the chine and gunwale strips. I used two sixteen-foot-long, 1½ x ¾-inch strips of pine laid one on top of the other for these corner pieces. While Moulty had used a sixteen-foot-long 1 x 6 inch oak board down the center of the floor, called a keelson, I used a pine board of the same dimension. Once all set, this inner structure was covered with the outer plywood skin of the boat. Moulty used the keelson as a center anchor point to attach two sheets of sixteen-foot-long by four-foot-wide plywood for the floor. I would use four sheets, each eight feet long.

It was while I was skinning the boat by bending the plywood onto the boat frame that I heard the snapping of plywood just as Moulty had fifty some years earlier. Moulty had the dimensions as tight as the plywood would bend. With the original boat to compare to, it was a relatively easy build and I followed the *Gem*'s dimensions as closely as I could. Historic photos of the *Gem*, along with Moulty's correspondence, also came to my assistance.

The replica *Gem* was finished in the fall of 2009. It was easy to relate to Moulty's excitement in wanting to get the *Gem* on the water somewhere. Meanwhile, in the Pacific Northwest, Dave Mortenson was talking with Ian Elliot about building replicas of the other boats that had accompanied

Moulty Fulmer's *Gem* in the Kolb garage on the left, and the *Gem* replica on the right, 2009. Tom Martin photo

Moulty when he had run the Grand in the 1950s. Maybe we could get all three boats on the river together since Dave had a non-commercial permit to run the Grand in the spring of 2011. That was a long way off. In the meantime, Hazel and I were invited by friends to run the Grand with them in December of 2009 for thirty days. Given the scarcity of do-it-yourself river trip permits, we jumped at the chance!

The twenty-nine-night river trip, going almost 300 miles, would cost us $900 each, right in keeping with Georgie's "Share The Expense" trip costs fifty years before. Georgie sold her company to Western River Expeditions just before she died in 1992. Last time I checked, Western charged $500 per person a night for their five-night river trip, and that's only 187 river miles from Lee's Ferry. The days of low-cost, shared-expense river trips in the concessions world are long gone.

The question that kept running through my mind was how the replica would handle one rapid we would encounter on the trip.

Lava Falls. Vulcan. Whatever you call it. Water gone mad. Water rolling back on itself, curling together, shooting in the air and pounding over boulders, making an unavoidable severe drop stretching bank to bank across the river. The sound hits you first, long before you actually see the river disappear in a horizon line only a few hundred yards away. A horizon line punctuated with the occasional froth of white water dancing for the sky. The sound of a low roar, seeping through your very bones, is unavoidable. It is Vulcan taking a drink after making thunderbolts on his anvil.

Ken and I stood alone at the scout rock on the right side of Lava. It was a cold January day in 2010. We watched the rest of our group take their rafts through the left side of Lava, one by one making the run. A raft or two went a little too close to shore and hung up momentarily on a few boulders, but then they were through. Hey, better safe than sorry. It was those boulders that had Ken and me on the right side of Lava, scouting a line with fewer rocks, but more water. Big water. As we looked at the churning water below us, I tried not to remind myself that our little replica *Gem*, like the original, had never actually run Lava Falls with anyone at the oars.

We pushed away from shore and Ken climbed into the passenger seat behind me. We floated along the right side of the river, making a few oar stroke adjustments as we drifted ever closer to the edge. The few ripples I had identified as guide markers from the scout rock were not reassuring down here. They were after all, just wrinkles in the water that led to a sudden horizon.

At the edge, it was clear we were where we needed to be. A chute of water led us into the first wall of water, a low wall at that. An easy pull on the oars and we were straight into what is known as the "V Wave," where a much larger wall of water pounded us with gay abandon. I had ducked as we hit the V and now looked up to see the next wave approaching. Hey, we were still right side up!

The next wall of liquid madness rolled over us and the footwells where Ken and I sat were now completely full of water. From oarlock to oarlock the little boat had become one with the river. Ken and I were helpless as we headed into the last big drop, where one final wave rolled right over us… and we were through! And still right side up! Vulcan had let us through!

As the boat bobbed up out of the water, scuppers draining, I grinned from ear to ear. Moulty was right! He had written to Dock in 1958 that he "thought" there was a run through the big water of Lava in his little boat. And he was spot-on. It only took fifty-two years to prove it could be done.

One good trip deserves another. In 2010, I took the *Gem* through the Canyon, and again the boat handled like a dream. That same year, we took the replica boat to the McKenzie River Wooden Boat Festival. It was here that I learned the definition of a Grand Canyon dory had been limited solely to the huge dories used on commercial trips and designed to carry four passengers and a guide. That definition was devoid of even a mention of Moulty Fulmer, and completely ignored the smaller, sportier, decked Grand Canyon dories like the Gem, popular to this day among self-guided river runners.

The replica *Gem* in Granite, 2010. Courtesy Barb Vinson

In February of 2011, Dave Mortenson's permit finally came up. By then, Ian Elliot had constructed replicas of Pat Reilly's two boats. It was time to take the three replicas down the Canyon together, with Ian rowing the *Susie R* and Cece Mortenson rowing the replica *Flavell*, following the footsteps of her grandfather. Arnie Richards was also on the trip, and rowed his first trip through the Canyon. Also on the trip was Dave's granddaughter, Natalie.

Natalie was always watching. And she was only nine. When doing her homework out on the boats, she was doing her sums, but she was watching what the grownups were doing too. And she was smiling, always smiling. When she fought her way into her cold drysuit in the early morning, when there was ice an inch thick in the footwells, she was always smiling. When hit in the face with a wave of freezing water over the bow of the boat, she was not only smiling, she was laughing. My heavens, but it was cold that winter, and she didn't mind at all. She liked best of all to ride with her Aunt Cece.

Natalie "got it" as we re-matched the old photos, and watched patiently as we scratched our heads trying to figure out where the 1957 high water line was. If there was someone practicing a yoga pose, she'd try it too. If someone was sketching or filming, she'd watch in silence. And if you sang to her, she'd laugh yet again.

She slept on the boat if we'd let her, and once the boat was back home in the garage, she still slept on it. She snoozed all snug in her sleeping bag just fine on the *Susie R* hatches. If anyone tried to do a cartwheel in Redwall Cavern, Natalie would try too. The sand would fly, so look out. When the old men sat around the fire, and the sparks would sputter up into the black night sky, she looked with wide eyes and listened to their stories with a keen ear. She would never fail to ask, as we were finishing up with dinner, "So Tom, what are we going to do tomorrow?"

If Hazel asked her to "hold on tight!" in big water she would hold on like she would never let go. When told it was time to go to bed, she was off to brush her teeth. You'd think that after thirty days of this, she would have cried, or sulked, or pouted, maybe once... but it never happened. Even when Grandpa walked her around Vulcan. By the way Gramps, you won't get away with that next time!

Natalie is Brick Mortenson's great-granddaughter after all, and she has fourth-generation Grand Canyoneer coursing through her veins. She has the best spirit of Moulty Fulmer's YMCA there can ever be, the concept of working for the team, for the greater good, and giving it her all. May she find the Canyon a place of inspiration and solace, as her forefathers have.

Brick Mortenson's great-granddaughter Natalie, a fourth generation Grand Canyoneer, following in the wake of those who rowed before her, Grand Canyon National Park, February, 2011. Courtesy Cindy McDonald

Acknowledgements

This small work on Moulton Fulmer would never have come about without the generous assistance, encouragement, and friendship of a very large number of people. Please be sure that if I left anyone out, it was simply due to my forgetfulness and not your lack of aid in this project.

The Kolb Garage Crew was so helpful in providing electricity to the garage and included Bill Brookins, Ginny Martin, and Helen Ranney of the Grand Canyon Association. Thanks to Bill Allen and Tim Beale of Grand Canyon National Park Trail Crew, with Pablo Garza of Grand Canyon National Park Maintenance, for the *Gem* rescue. Thanks to Hazel Clark and Jim McCarthy for assistance in cradle construction.

I am very appreciative for all the assistance from the archivists that helped in this book. They include *Muncie Star Press* archivist Breena Wysong; the Huntington Library's Dr. Bill Frank and Juan Gomez; Dickinson College Archivist Jim Gerencser; Lake Mead National Recreation Area staff Rosie Pepito and Susan Warner; Doug Misner and his crew at the Utah State Historical Society; Krissy Giacoletto, Stan Larson and Roy Webb of the University of Utah Marriott Library Special Collections; Talela Florko at Glen Canyon National Recreation Area; Oregon Historical Society archivists Scott Daniels and Scott Rook; and Northern Arizona University Special Collection's Karen Underhill, Peter Runge, Richard Quartaroli, and Jess Vogelsang. Thanks to Janeen Trevillyan at the Sedona Historical Society, Dr. Tom Myers and Mary Wyatt for assistance with information on the Elmer Purtymun river trip and pointing the way to Dale Slocum. Special thanks to Kim Besom, Colleen Hyde, and Mike Quinn at Grand Canyon National Park Special Collections, and Brynn Bender, Senior Conservator, *National* Park Service Western Archaeological and Conservation Center, who have all done so much for this project. I am ever in your debt. Research assistance was provided by Al Ainsworth, Marcy Demillion, and Hazel Clark.

The replica boat-building questions team included "Windy" Jon Aldrit, www.woodenboatpeople.com webmaster Randy Dersham, Roger Fletcher, Kyle and Lincoln Frye, Larry Hedrick, and Doug Ross. A very special "Thank You" to Bob and Beth Goforth for the use of your dream garage and to Duwain Whitis for the dream trailer.

Then there is the group of folks who floated through the Grand Canyon before Glen Canyon Dam, or were contemporaries with those who did. You are the real Grand Canyoneers. Your logs, letters, photos, stories and friendship made this book happen. Joe Szep was most instrumental here. Thank you Joe! The same goes for Priss and John Becker, Loel Buckley, Amrette Butler, Bruce Dines, Walter Furen, Dick Griffith, Edward Hudson, Ruth Kirschbaum, Martin and Esther Litton, the "Grand Old Man of Muncie" John Llewellyn, Brick Mortenson and his son Dave, Bill Mooz, Joan Nevills-Staveley, Neal Newby, Dr. Yuji Oishi, Earline Pederson, Ellen Reynolds, Bob Rigg, Maradel Marston Rowlands, Dale Slocum, Ken Stroud, Jorgen Visbak, Chuck Warren, Edith Woodring, Marge Woodroof, Ted Whitmoyer, and Buzz and Loie Belknap for starting me on the trail to find Ted Whitmoyer, Bevan Wright, and Otis Wright.

The Canyoneers' children and younger friends helped out too. Thanks so much to Debbie Woodroof; Muncie YMCA contacts Don Stetson and Debbie Todd; Guy Taylor's children Bob Taylor and Barbara Crookston; along with Carl Pederson's children Joann Maxson and Marilyn Koch; and Bret Reynolds.

So many additional folks helped in so many additional ways. Thanks to Bruce Bergstrom and Richard McKinney at Sawyer Paddles and Oars, Alistair Bleifuss and Ann Cassidy, Dan Cassidy, Jim David, Mathew Larsen, Betty Leavengood, Dan Lindemann, Dick McCallum, Dove Menkes, Grand Canyon National Park Chief of Interpretation John C. "Jack" O'Brien, Lily Richards, Richard "Dicky" Romero, Doug and Phil Smoker, Aaron Tomasi, and Jim Vaaler.

Special thanks to the following river trip crews, you all are the BEST!

2009: Mrill Ingram and Ken, Emlyn and Isaiah Agnew, James Bronzan, Peter Brown, Hazel Clark, Kimi Eisele, Torsten Johnson, David Long, Ken Loving, James Machin, Sara Mullett, Myles O'Kelly, Barbara Vinson, Anne Walker, and Duwain Whitis.

2010: Barbara Vinson and Duwain, Elliot, Grace, and Leah Whitis, Hazel Clark, Susan Langsley, and Kele Thrailkill.

2011: Dave, Pam, Cece, and Leif Mortenson with Yoshie Koboyashi and Natalie Mortenson, Chris Alstrin, Brynn Bender, Conan Bliss, Hazel Clark, Kathy Darrow with Tom and Orion Pendley, Ian Elliot, Marion Gonzales, Jeff Ingram, Sabette Jutras, Cindy McDonald, James "Q" Martin, Maria Coryell-Martin, Arnie Richards, Gus and Sandra Scott, Mike Splendor, Jason Wesley, and Craig Wolfson.

My heartfelt thanks to the manuscript reviewers including Kim Besom, Bill Bishop, Hazel Clark, Kathy Darrow, Randy Dersham, Dan Driskill, Helen Fairley, Roger Fletcher, Greg Hatten, Kim Holland, Rosie Houk, Edward Hudson, Jeff Ingram, Jo Johnson, Murphy Johnson, Maurya and Maeve Kaarhus, Jules Lund, Dave Mortenson, Dr. Tom Myers, Wayne Ranney, Ellen, Bret and Laurie Reynolds, Arnie Richards, Jim Sanders, Doug Sherman, Mike Splendor, Joe Szep, Chuck Warren, John Weisheit, Duwain Whitis, Debbie Woodroof, and Bevan Wright.

This book never would have happened without the help, encouragement, corrections and support from two folks, Hazel Clark and Dave Mortenson. I am indebted to you both.

Citation Key

GRCA is the Museum Collection at Grand Canyon National Park, AZ
Marston collection is the Otis R. "Dock" Marston collection housed at the Huntington Library, San Marino, CA
NAU is the Special Collections and Archives at Northern Arizona University, housed at the Cline Library, Flagstaff, AZ
Nevills collection is the Norman D. and Doris Nevills collection housed at the Marriott Library, University of Utah, Salt Lake City, UT
USHS is the Utah State Historical Society archives housed at the Rio Grande Depot, Salt Lake City, UT

Notes

Page

Chapter 1 The *Gem* in God's Pocket (1964)

13	"The National Park…" Belknap photo collection NAU
13	"Extremely low water…" USBR Lake Mead water resource information http://www.usbr.gov/lc/region/g4000/hourly/mead-elv.html
13	"Had the boat…" 2007 personal site visit Tom Martin
13	"Ted Whitmoyer, Chief…" Sep 30, 1964 Marston to Fulmer, Box 74, Marston collection
13	"As Whitmoyer eased…" NAU.PH.96.4.50.17 Reilly collection NAU
14	"It had been…" Reilly Grand Canyon log, 1955, Box 13-209, Reilly collection NAU
14	"And that Fulmer…" NAU.PH.96.4.113.41 Belknap collection NAU
14	"As Belknap took…" Reilly Grand Canyon logs, 1955-1959, Box 13-209 and 212, Box 34-5, 7 and 8, Reilly collection NAU
14	"God had certainly…" Oct 25, 1964, Marston to Belknap letter, Box 17, Marston collection

Chapter 2 The Midget Champion (1906-1941)

15	"In his mid…" Enlisted Record and Report of Separation, Priss Becker collection
15	"The policemen informed…" May 31, 1943 Fulmer to Nevills, Box 8, Nevills collection
15	"When his elder …" Moulton Fulmer birth certificate, Priss Becker collection; Daughters of the American Revolution application, Priss Becker collection; Priss Becker 2008 personal interview
16	"Moulty's father, Francis…" Priss Becker 2008 personal interview
16	"A Union soldier…" Daughters of the American Revolution application, Priss Becker collection
16	"Francis graduated from…" 1926 newspaper clipping, ID unknown, Priss Becker collection; Wisconsin Historical Society Babcock collection
16	"After graduation, Francis…" 1926 newspaper clipping, ID unknown, Priss Becker collection
16	"Francis met a…" Daughters of the American Revolution application, Priss Becker collection
16	"The couple's first…" May 22, 1966 *Muncie Star*
16	"In 1915, Moulty's…" newspaper clipping, ID unknown, Marge Woodroof collection
16	"Divorce in the…" Marge Woodroof 2008 personal interview
17	"On enrollment at…" May 20, 1966 *Muncie Star*; Priss Becker 2008 personal communication
17	"Coached by H.J…" May 22, 1966 *Muncie Star*
17	"Moulty captained the…" Ibid
17	"Basketball aficionados will…" Ibid
17	"After graduating from…" Ball Teachers College is now Ball State University, Priss Becker 2008 personal communication
17	"In his freshman…" Aug 15, 1978 Ball State University paper
17	"Besides college basketball…" Photo of 1978 Ball State Hall of Fame plaque, Fulmer collection USHS
17	"He lettered all…" Ibid

Page

17   "The Muncie Young…" John Llewellyn 2008 personal communication
17   "Though he was…" John Llewellyn 2008 personal communication
18   "In 1929 Moulty…" May 22, 1966 *Muncie Star*
18   "As if college…" May 22, 1966 *Muncie Star*
18   "Moulty also played…" John Llewellyn 2008 personal communication
18   "While playing for…" John Llewellyn 2008 personal communication; newspaper clipping ID unknown, Priss Becker personal collection
18   "A young woman…" Priss Becker 2008 personal communication++
18   "Janice and Moulty…" 1920-1942 Cass County Marriage Records, Ft Wayne Library; Apr 30, 1942 Fulmer to Nevills, Box 8, Nevills collection
18   "The couple attended…" Marge Woodroof 2008 personal interview
18   "About that time…" Priss Becker 2008 personal interview
18   "Many years later…" Nov 21, 1975 *Sun City News*, Priss Becker personal collection
19   "Even after the…" newspaper clipping, ID unknown, Marge Woodroof collection
19   "In the summer…" Marston Grand Canyon log, 1948, Box 286, Marston collection
19   "The couple rode…" Jun 21, 1941 Rainbow Bridge National Monument Guest Register, Glen Canyon National Recreation Area Special Collections
19   "At a showing…" newspaper clippings, ID unknown, Marge Woodroof collection
19   "Interestingly, Norm had…" Jun 8, 1941 Rainbow Bridge National Monument Guest Register, Glen Canyon National Recreation Area Special Collections

Chapter 3 The River Bug Bites (1942)

21   "An oil boom…" Chronology of Norman Davies Nevills, Box 20, Reilly collection NAU
21   "In October of…" Ibid; Bio, Nevills collection
21   "Norm was hired…" Ibid
21   "Clover and Jotter…" Box 32, Marston Collection; Apr 14, 1982, Fletcher to GRCA, 1752 Fldr 28, GRCA
21   "In April 1942…" Apr 7 and Apr 11, 1942 Fulmer to Nevills, Box 8, Nevills collection
21   "In that letter…" Apr 30, 1942 Fulmer to Nevills, Box 8, Nevills collection
21   "Janice was hesitant…" Nov 21, 1975 *Sun City News*, Priss Becker personal collection; Apr 30, 1942 Fulmer to Nevills, Box 8, Nevills collection
22   "The San Juan…" www.waterdata.usgs.gov
22   "The plan was…" Fulmer San Juan log, 1942, Box 8, Nevills collection
22   "Norm would row…" Ibid; Apr 30, 1942 Fulmer to Nevills, Box 8, Nevills collection
22   "Moulty noted the…" Fulmer San Juan log, 1942, Box 8, Nevills collection; Frank Wright, *Life Story of John Franklin Wright*, Vishnu Temple Press 2012
22   "The group of…" Fulmer San Juan log, 1942, Box 8, Nevills collection
22   "After lunch, the…" Whitis and Martin *Guide to the San Juan River*, Vishnu Temple Press, 2005, pg. Map 7-Map 11
22   "The next morning…" Fulmer San Juan log, 1942, Box 8, Nevills collection
23   "The next day…" Ibid
23   "Up early on…" Ibid
23   "After Moulty did…" Ibid
23   "Regretfully, Moulty boarded…" www.waterdata.usgs.gov
24   "Later that evening…" Fulmer San Juan log, 1942, Box 8, Nevills collection
24   "Since college, Moulty…" Priss Becker 2008 personal interview
24   "In late June…" Jun 26, 1942 Fulmer to Nevills, Box 8, Nevills collection
24   "Drawing large crowds…" Jul 17, 1942 Fulmer to Nevills, Box 8, Nevills collection
24   "The river journey…" Jun 26, 1942 and Jul 17, 1942 Fulmer to Nevills, Box 8, Nevills collection
24   "When Norm passed…" Aug 3, 1942 Fulmer to Nevills, Box 8, Nevills collection
24   "Norm replied in…" Sep 1, 1942 Nevills to Fulmer, Box 8, Nevills collection
24   "In September 1942…" Sep 10, 1942 Fulmer to Nevills, Box 8, Nevills collection

Chapter 4 Indiana Boating in a *Tub* (1942-1943)

25   "The first boat…" Fulmer Photo collection USHS; Sep 10, 1942 Fulmer to Nevills, Box 8, Nevills collection; Jul 31, 1959 Fulmer to Reilly, Box 1, Fulmer collection USHS
26   "Operated with a…" Sep 10, 1942 Fulmer to Nevills, Box 8, Nevills collection
26   "The *Tub* cost…" Ibid; Jul 31, 1959 Fulmer to Reilly, Box 1, Fulmer collection USHS

Page
26   "There was some…" Jul 31, 1959 Fulmer to Reilly, Box 1, Fulmer collection USHS
26   "Moulty requested a…" Jan 29, 1943 Fulmer to Nevills, Box 8, Nevills collection
26   "In February, Norm…" Feb 5, 1943 Nevills to Fulmer, Box 8, Nevills collection
26   "Moulty went right…" Feb 12, and Apr 6, 1943 Fulmer to Nevills, Box 8, Nevills collection
26   "Moulty had gone…" Feb 5 and 12, 1943 Fulmer to Nevills, Box 8, Nevills collection
27   "Unfortunately, keeping the…" Ibid.
27   "By mid-May…" May 31, 1943 Fulmer to Nevills, Box 8, Nevills collection; www.waterdata.usgs.gov
27   "Moulty was out…" May 31, 1943 Fulmer to Nevills, Box 8, Nevills collection
27   "After reading Moulty's…" Aug 20, 1943 Nevills to Fulmer, Box 8, Nevills collection
27   "Moulty wanted to…" Sep 9, 1943 Fulmer to Nevills, Box 8, Nevills collection
27   "The train from…" May 31, 1943 Fulmer to Nevills, Box 8, Nevills collection
28   "With little time…" Ibid
28   "Back in Muncie…" Ibid; Jul 31, 1959 Fulmer to Reilly, Box 1, Fulmer collection USHS
28   "The sides were…" Feb 4, 1944 Fulmer to Nevills, Box 8, Nevills collection
28   "Norm again wrote…" Jan 26, 1944 Nevills to Fulmer, Box 8, Nevills collection

Chapter 5 The Boating Soldier Meets a Boat Builder (1944-1945)

29   "Having failed to…" Feb 4, 1944 Fulmer to Nevills, Box 8, Nevills collection
29   "While Moulty found…" Feb 4, 1944 Fulmer to Nevills, Box 8, Nevills collection
29   "During this time…" Feb 4, 1944 Fulmer to Nevills, Box 8, Nevills collection
29   "Sadly, a furlough…" Aug 12, 1944 Fulmer to Nevills, Box 8, Nevills collection
29   "In January 1945…" Jan 5, 1945 Fulmer to Nevills, Box 8, Nevills collection
30   "On January 21…" Jan 22, 1945 Fulmer to Nevills, Box 8, Nevills collection
30   "In the spring…" May 8, 1945 Fulmer to Nevills, Box 8, Nevills collection
30   "Norm had run…" Aug 18 and Sep 5, 1950 Fulmer to Marston, Box 74, Marston collection
30   "The filming party…" Aug 18 and Sep 5, 1950 Fulmer to Marston, Box 74, Marston collection; Fulmer San Juan log, 1945, Box 370, Marston collection
32   "On the train…" Jul 6, 1945 Fulmer to Nevills, Box 8, Nevills collection
32   "Norm was pleased…" Aug 13, 1945 Nevills to Fulmer, Box 8, Nevills collection
32   "The filming went…" Jan 10, 1947 Fulmer to Nevills, Box 8, Nevills collection
32   "Moulty shipped out…" Jul 6, 1945 Fulmer to Nevills, Box 8, Nevills collection
32   "The McKenzie River…" Fletcher, Roger, *Drift Boats and River Dories*, Stackpole Books, 2007, pg. 5
32   "Construction of the…" Fletcher, Roger, *Drift Boats and River Dories*, Stackpole Books, 2007, pg. 18
32   "Plywood, thin veneers…" www.apawood.org
32   "As an aside…" Sep 5, 1959 Marston to Reilly, Box 4, Marston collection
33   "It wasn't long…" Fletcher, Roger, *Drift Boats and River Dories*, Stackpole Books, 2007, pg. 28-75; *Sunset* magazine April, 1956 pg. 60-63, Dave Mortenson collection
33   "At the southern…" Fletcher, Roger, *Drift Boats and River Dories*, Stackpole Books, 2007, pg. 28-39; Maurya Kaarhus 2011 personal communication; Randy Dersham 2011 personal communication
34   "The classic Hindman…" Fletcher, Roger, *Drift Boats and River Dories*, Stackpole Books, 2007, pg. 249
34   "Camp Adair happened…" May 17, 1954 Fulmer to Marston, Box 74, Marston collection
34   "The two talked…" Aug 16, 1961, Fulmer to Reilly, Box 1, Fulmer collection USHS
34   "Moulty told Woodie…" Aug 16, 1961, and Sep 10, 1962 Fulmer to Reilly, Box 1, Fulmer collection USHS
34   "The exact boats…" Fletcher, Roger, *Drift Boats and River Dories*, Stackpole Books, 2007, pg. 33; Aug 17, 1945, Fulmer to Nevills, Box 8, Nevills collection; Mar 2, 1954 Fulmer to Frost, Mar 2, 1954, Box 74, Marston collection; May 17, 1954 Fulmer to Marston, Box 74, Marston collection

Chapter 6 Eating Sand Waves with the *Moja* (1945-1947)

35   "In October 1945…" Dec 7, 1945 Fulmer to Nevills, Box 8, Nevills collection
35   "In November, Norm…" Ibid
35   "Moulty wrote right…" Ibid
35   "Moulty settled into…" Mar 20, 1945 Fulmer to Nevills, Box 8, Nevills collection

35   "In the summer…" May 15, 1946 Fulmer to Nevills, Box 8, Nevills collection

35   "Moulty used drawings…" Mar 2, 1954 Fulmer to Frost, Box 74, Marston collection

35   "The new boat…" May 15, 1946 Fulmer to Nevills, Box 8, Nevills collection; Mar 25, 1954 Fulmer to Frost, Box 74, Marston collection; Aug 16, 1961 Fulmer to Reilly, Box 1, Fulmer collection USHS; Jan 10, 1947 Fulmer to Nevills, Box 8, Nevills collection

35   "Access to the…" Sep 11, 1959 Fulmer to Reilly, Box 1, Fulmer collection USHS

35   "The ¼-inch plywood…" Mar 2, 1954 Fulmer to John Frost, Box 74, Marston collection

35   "Moulty noted the…" Sep 11, 1959, Fulmer to Reilly, Box 1, Fulmer collection USHS

36   "The boat was…" Priss Becker 2008 personal interview

36   "They happened to…" Original Smoker oar from *Moja*, Fulmer collection USHS

36   "The Smoker Lumber…" Don Smoker 2008 personal interview

36   "He and Janice…" Jan 10, 1947, Fulmer to Nevills, Box 8, Nevills collection

36   "Norm wrote back…" Jan 13, 1947 Nevills to Fulmer and Fulmer to Nevills Jan 27, 1947, Box 8, Nevills collection; Nevills Chronology by Reilly, pg. 8, Box 20, Reilly collection, NAU

36   "Before heading to…" Apr 29, 1947 Fulmer to Nevills, Box 8, Nevills collection

37   "Plez Talmadge Reilly…" Nov 17, 1950, Reilly to Marston, Box 3, Reilly collection USHS; PT Reilly Interview, USHS Oral History Project; Apr 1, 1953 Reilly to Marston, Box 3, Reilly collection USHS

37   "While attending Los…" PT Reilly Interview, USHS Oral History Project; Elizabeth "Susie" Reilly by Dave Mortenson, Grand Canyon Pioneer Vol. 5, No. 5, May, 2001; Norm D. Nevills as I Knew Him by PT Reilly, Box 1, Reilly collection USHS; Apr 20, 1953 Reilly to Marston, Box 3, Reilly collection USHS

37   "The couple stopped…" Susie Reilly Interview, 2000, GRCA

38   "For the first…" www.waterdata.usgs.gov, Marston photographic collection; Susie Reilly Interview, 2000, GRCA

38   "Though George was…" Susie Reilly Interview, 2000, GRCA; Apr 1, 1953 Reilly to Marston, Box 3, Reilly collection USHS

38   "Ruth was also…" Dave Mortenson 2008 personal communication

38   "A man doesn't…" Nov 25, 1986 Interview with Stephen Moulton Babcock Fulmer, Box 1, Fulmer collection USHS

38   "They pushed off…" Warner Gear-O-Gram Vol. IV No. 9, Feb 1948, pg. 6, Priss Becker collection

39   "With two weeks…" Jan 1, 1948 Fulmer to Nevills, Box 8, Nevills collection

39   "This was all…" Jul 7, 1947 Fulmer to Doris Nevills, Box 8, Nevills collection

39   "Moulty ran 13…" Warner Gear-O-Gram Vol. IV No. 9, Feb 1948, pg. 7, Priss Becker collection; Aug 15, 1947, Fulmer to Nevills, Box 8, Nevills collection

39   "The weather was…" Jul 7, 1947, Fulmer to Doris Nevills, Box 8, Nevills collection

39   "Returning from a…" Feb 28, 1953, Fulmer to Marston, Box 74, Marston collection; Aleson Bio, USHS; White Bio, NAU; Dick Griffith 2011 personal communication

39   "The *Moja* had…" Aug 15, 1947 Fulmer to Nevills, Box 8, Nevills collection

39   "Sadly, Janice's father…" Jan 30, 1948 Fulmer to Nevills, Box 8, Nevills collection

39   "Janice took a…" Jan 30, 1948 Fulmer to Nevills, Box 8, Nevills collection; Warner Gear-O-Gram Vol. IV No. 9, Feb 1948 pg. 7

39   "With the new…" Jan 1, 1948 Fulmer to Nevills, Box 8, Nevills collection

39   "Norm wrote back…" Jan 14, 1948 Nevills to Fulmer, Box 8, Nevills collection

40   "That kind of…" Current Population Reports, U.S. Department of Commerce, February 14, 1950, Series P-60, No. 6 pg. 1 on-line report

40   "By the end…" Jan 30, 1948 Fulmer to Nevills, Box 8, Nevills collection

40   "In March, Moulty…" Mar 4, 1948 Fulmer to Nevills, Box 8, Nevills collection

Chapter 7 The Grand at Last (1948)

41   "While Moulty was…" Apr 1, 1953 Reilly to Marston, Box 3, Reilly collection USHS; Joe Szep 2008 personal interview; PT Reilly Interview, USHS Oral History Project

42   "Back at Lockheed…" PT Reilly Interview, USHS Oral History Project

42   "By 1948, twenty…" Chronology section, index, Marston collection; Richard Quartaroli, Dock's Data of Navigational Numbers: The First 100 Grand Canyon River Runners, BQR Vol. 22 number 2, 2009

42   "Ten people from…" Otis Marston Grand Canyon log, 1948, Box 286, Marston collection

42   "Wayne and Lucile…" Garth Marston Grand Canyon log, 1948, Box 286, Marston collection

42   "Bestor was a…" Farquhar, Francis P., History of the Sierra Nevada, University of California Press, Berkeley, 1965, Sierra Club on-line archives; Jeff Ingram 2011 personal communication

42   "Another passenger making…" Dickinson College Special Collections; Advisory Board on National Parks, Historic Sites, Buildings and Monuments, Council members, Grand Canyon National Park Administrative Record Vol. 3, 49-50

42   "The Robinsons would…" Garth Marston Grand Canyon log, 1948, Box 286, Marston collection

42   "Doerr had just…" www.NPS.gov archives

42   "Also joining the…" Garth Marston Grand Canyon log, 1948, Box 286, Marston collection; BQR Vol 11 Number 2, 1998

42   "Rosalind had participated…" *Desert* magazine, November 1947 pg. 6

42   "Another addition to…" Roy Webb, *High, Wide and Handsome*, Utah State University Press, 2005, pg. 158, 176; Brad Dimock, *The Very Hard Way: Bert Loper and the Colorado River*, Fretwater Press 2007 pg. 420

42   "The four boatmen …" Otis Marston Grand Canyon log, 1948, Box 286, Marston collection

42   "Frank Wright had …" Otis Wright 2011 personal conversation; Wright, Frank, *Life Story of John Franklin Wright*, Vishnu Temple Press 2012

43   "Otis Marston and…" Roy Webb, *High, Wide and Handsome*, Utah State University Press, 2005, pg. 121

43   "The elder Marston…" Chronology of Norman Davies Nevills, Box 20, Reilly collection NAU

43   "Otis Reed Marston…"Mar 17, 1964 Marston Bio, Box 2, Reilly collection USHS; Loel M. Buckley 2011 personal communication

43   "During his submarine…" Otis R. "Dock" Marston interview, Jul 8, 1964, by PT Reilly, Box 2, Reilly collection USHS

44   "There were four…" Otis Marston Grand Canyon log, 1948, Box 286, Marston collection; Wright, Frank, *Life Story of John Franklin Wright*, Vishnu Temple Press 2012

44   "All four were…" Brief History of Boats at Grand Canyon Visitors Center, Box 8, Reilly collection NAU

44   "When the rower's…" Ibid

44   "The group pushed…" www.waterdata.usgs.gov

44   "The trouble is…" Roy Webb, *High, Wide and Handsome*, Utah State University Press, 2005 pg. 122

44   "As Dock entered…" Otis Marston Grand Canyon log, 1948, Box 286, Marston collection

45   "The next day…" Ibid

45   "The group stopped…" Garth Marston Grand Canyon log, 1948, Box 286, Marston collection

45   "A few large…" Otis Marston Grand Canyon log, 1948, Box 286, Marston collection

45   "On the fifth…" Ibid

45   "After lunch, Dock…" Dove Menkes 2010 personal communication

45   "The threesome hightailed…" Otis Marston Grand Canyon log, 1948, Box 286, Marston collection

45   "Garth went over…" Fulmer Grand Canyon log, 1948, Box 286, Marston collection

46   "In August 1869…" Michael P. Ghiglieri, *First Through Grand Canyon*, Puma Press, 2003, pg. 208

46   "Early river runners…" Nov. 7, 1957 David Rust to Harry Aleson, Box 12, Aleson collection USHS

47   "As the river…" Otis Marston Grand Canyon log, 1948, Box 286, Marston collection

47   "During the first…" Moulton Fulmer Grand Canyon log, 1948, Box 286, Marston collection

47   "While at the…" Garth Marston Grand Canyon log, 1948, Box 286, Marston collection

47   "At Hermit Rapid,…" Fulmer Grand Canyon log, 1948, Box 286, Marston collection

47   "Four years and…" Tessman, Norm, *Falling into a Hole of Some Sort*, Pittsburgh History Vol 80 Number 3, pg. 93-103; Tessman, Norm, *The Rescue of the Liberator 107 Crew*, Arizona Highways , 73(7): 12-15; Tom Martin personal hikes in this area; Original messages, Box 21, Reilly collection

49   "The party ran…" Otis Marston Grand Canyon log, 1948, Box 286, Marston collection

50   "Here they found…" Roy Webb, *High, Wide and Handsome*, Utah State University Press, 2005, pg. 226; Otis Marston Grand Canyon log, 1948, Box 286, Marston collection

50   "Norm and Dock…" Otis Marston Grand Canyon log, 1948, Box 286, Marston collection

50   "The *Ross* was…" Box 121, Marston collection

51   "When the 1948…" Otis Marston Grand Canyon log, 1948, Box 286, Marston collection

51   "The river runners…" Ibid

51   "Moulty was thrilled…" Fulmer Grand Canyon log, 1948, Box 286, Marston collection

51   "They reached Bedrock…" Fulmer, Otis and Garth Marston Grand Canyon logs, 1948, Box 286, Marston collection

51   "July 25, 1948,…" Fulmer Grand Canyon log, 1948, Box 286, Marston collection

51   "Camp was on…" Roy Webb, *High, Wide and Handsome*, Utah State University Press, 2005, pg. 230; Otis Marston and Fulmer Grand Canyon logs, 1948, Box 286, Marston collection

52   "One of the…" Otis Marston Grand Canyon log, 1948, Box 286, Marston collection

52   "The next day…" Fulmer and Otis Marston Grand Canyon logs, 1948, Box 286, Marston collection

Page

52   "Six years earlier…" Otis Marston Grand Canyon log, 1942, Box 286, Marston collection; "Ed" Hudson hated his given name Egbert and is called Ed in this text, Edward Hudson 2011 personal communication
52   "Hudson then went…" Box 95, Marston collection
53   "After looking at…" Fulmer and Otis Marston Grand Canyon logs, 1948, Box 286, Marston collection
53   "The next day…" Ibid
53   "Early the next…" Ibid

Chapter 8 Tragedy and Gasoline (1949-1950)

55   "Moulty was buried…" Oct 1, 1948 Fulmer to Nevills, Box 8, Nevills collection
55   "There was a…" Mar 28, 1949 Fulmer to Nevills, Box 8, Nevills collection
55   "And travel they…" Aug 8, 1949 Fulmer to Nevills, Box 8, Nevills collection
55   "He did some…" Oct 11, 1949 Fulmer to Marston, Box 74, Marston collection
55   "While the Fulmers…" Aug 8, 1949 Fulmer to Nevills, Box 8, Nevills collection; Roy Webb, *High, Wide and Handsome*, Utah State University Press, 2005 pg. 247, 300
55   "A new boatman…" Bob Rigg 2011 personal communication
55   "The previous winter…" Edward Hudson 2010 personal interview
56   "In the 1940s…" Box 285, Marston collection
56   "As the two…" Apr 18, 1950, Reilly to Marston, Box 3, Reilly collection USHS; PT Reilly Interview, USHS Oral History Project
56   "Hudson picked up…" Ibid
56   "While Dock and…" Norm D. Nevills as I Knew Him by PT Reilly, Box 1, Reilly collection USHS; Reilly Grand Canyon log, 1949, Box 13, Reilly collection NAU
56   "The July 1949,…" Ibid
56   "Just a few…" Reilly Grand Canyon log, 1949, Box 13, Reilly collection NAU; Brad Dimock, *The Very Hard Way: Bert Loper and the Colorado River*, Fretwater Press 2007 pg. 425-430
58   "That night, Norm…" Aug 12 and Dec 26, 1950 Reilly to Marston letters, Box 3, Reilly collection USHS
58   "Hearing about the…" Jan 5, 1951 Marston to Reilly letter, Box 3, Reilly collection USHS
58   "The group spent…" Reilly Grand Canyon log, 1949, Box 13, Reilly collection NAU
58   "The term "river …" Aug 16, 1950 and Aug 16, 1953 Marston to Reilly, Box 3, Reilly collection USHS; Marston Grand Canyoneers 101-206, Dick Griffith collection
58   "It had "seemed"…" Dec 16, 1949, Marston to Reilly, Box 3, Reilly collection USHS; Mar 21, 1950, Reilly to Marston, Box 3, Reilly collection USHS; Nov 14, 1952 Marston to Reilly and Nov 20, 1952 Reilly to Marston, Box 3, Reilly collection USHS
58   "These differences between…" Mar 24, 1950 Marston to Reilly, Box 3, Reilly collection USHS
58   "Even Frank Wright…" Frank Wright, *Life History of John Franklin Wright*, Vishnu Temple Press 2012
58   "After the 1949…" Sep 14, 1949 Nevills to Reilly, Box 18, Nevills collection
58   "In the fall…" Nov 4, 1949 Fulmer to Marston and Jan 31, 1950 Marston to Fulmer, Box 74, Marston collection
59   "Dock, on hearing…" Dec 4, 1949 Marston to Fulmer, Box 74, Marston collection
59   "Rubber boats first…" Box 25, Marston collection
59   "Soon after the…" Jan 22, 1950 Reilly to Marston, Box 3, Reilly collection USHS
59   "A month later…" Feb 22, 1950 Reilly to Marston, Box 3, Reilly collection USHS
59   "Only moments after…" Bob Rigg 2011 personal communication
59   "Of Doris and…" Oct 17, 1949 Marston to Fulmer, Box 74, Marston collection
59   "However, by 1970…" www.canyoneers.com
59   "After Norm's death…" PT Reilly Interview, USHS Oral History Project; Frank Wright, *Life History of John Franklin Wright*, Vishnu Temple Press 2012; Bob Rigg 2011 personal communication
59   "Frank and Jim…" Feb 14, 1950 Frank Wright and Jim Rigg to Dear River Friends, Joe Szep collection
60   "Moulty wrote to…" Jan 27, 1950 Fulmer to Marston and Jan 31, 1950 Marston to Fulmer, Box 74, Marston collection
60   "Moulty wrote Frazier…" Feb 17, 1950 Frazier to Fulmer, Box 74, Marston collection.
60   "Dock wrote back…" Mar 26, 1950, Apr 20, 1950, Marston to Fulmer, Box 74, Marston collection
60   "Moulty responded that…" Apr 24, 1950, Fulmer to Marston, Box 74, Marston collection
60   "On May 16…" May 16, 1950 Lyons to Marston, Box 74, Marston collection

Page

60 "With the trusty…" 1986 Reilly interview of Fulmer, Box 1, Fulmer collection USHS

60 "While Moulty and…" Hudson-Marston Colorado River Trip, 1950, William Belknap Jr. Notes, Edward Hudson collection; Motorboat Traverse of the Grand Canyon 1950, Otis Marston, Edward Hudson collection

61 "Shortly after departure…" Edward Hudson 2011 personal interview; Marston Grand Canyon log, 1950, Box 287, Marston collection; Hudson-Marston Colorado River Trip, 1950, William Belknap Jr. Notes, Ed Hudson collection

62 "Willie's good-natured humor…" Jorgen Visbak 2010 personal interview

62 "Meanwhile, Hudson was…" Aug 15, 1950 Marston to Reilly, Box 3, Reilly collection USHS

62 "The bend in…" Box 287, Marston collection; Martin and Whitis *Guide to the Colorado River in Grand Canyon*, 4th edition, 2008, Vishnu Temple Press, Map 18

62 "By all accounts…" Aug 18 and 29, 1950, Fulmer to and from Marston, Box 74, Marston collection; Marston Yampa log, 1950, Box 287, Marston collection

63 "Almost a month…" E.M. Reilly 1950 diary, Box 14, Reilly collection NAU; Otis Wright 2011 personal interview; Aug 12, 1950 Reilly to Marston, Box 3, Reilly collection USHS

64 "Frank made it…" Bevan Wright, 2011 personal interview; Aug 12, 1950 Reilly to Marston, Box 3, Reilly collection USHS

65 "After a day…" E.M. Reilly 1950 diary, Box 14, Reilly collection NAU

65 "At Lava Falls…" Ibid

65 "When the party…" Ibid

65 "In late May…" *Rainbow Bridge Register* pg. 285, Glen Canyon National Recreation Area special collections; Box 95, Marston collection

66 "At the end…" Sep 5, 1950 Fulmer to Marston, Box 74, Marston collection

66 "Dock was encouraging…" Feb 13, 1951 Marston to Fulmer letter, Box 74, Marston collection

66 "The river called…" Nov 18, 1951 and Aug 1, 1959, *Muncie Star;* Priss Becker 2008 personal communication; Nov 21, 1950 Fulmer to Marston, Box 74, Marston collection

66 "On hearing the…" Ibid.

Chapter 9 More Practice and the *Gem* (1951-1952)

67 "The trip planning…" Roy Webb, *High, Wide and Handsome*, Utah State University Press, 2005, pg. 63, 188; Ellen Reynolds 2010 and 2011 personal interview; Oct 20, 1982 *Green River Star*

67 "Dock wrote to…" May 22, 1951 Marston to Fulmer, Box 74, Marston collection

67 "Dock called this…" Box 288, Marston Collection; Bill Sanderson, BQR Vol. 18, Number 3, Fall 2005

67 "The group met…" Fulmer and Marston Desolation Canyon logs, 1951, Box 3, Reilly collection USHS

68 "In 1951, this…" Ibid

68 "On day three…" Ibid

68 "As Moulty arrived…" E. Reilly Grand Canyon log, 1951, Box 14, Reilly collection NAU

68 "A month earlier…" Jun 12, 1951 *Los Angeles Times*, Box 2, Reilly collection USHS

69 "For sheer speed…" BQR Vol 11 Number 1, 1997

69 "Also on the…" E.M. Reilly Grand Canyon log, 1951, Box 14, Reilly collection NAU; Tad Nichols *Glen Canyon, Images of a Lost World,* 1999 MNM Press; Tad Nichols, BQR Vol 13 Number 2, 2000

69 "In those days…" E.M. Reilly Grand Canyon log, 1951, Box 14, Reilly collection NAU

70 "This group, like…" Ibid

70 "The river runners…" Ibid

70 "Dock would count…" Aug 16, 1953 Marston to Reilly, Box 3, Reilly collection USHS; Marston Grand Canyoneers 101-206, Dick Griffith collection

71 "The party had…" Griffith Grand Canyon log, 1951, Dick Griffith collection; Dick Griffith 2011 personal interview

73 "What he had…" Aug 16, 1961 Fulmer to Reilly letter, Box 1, Fulmer collection USHS

74 "The McKenzie River …" Randy Dersham, Tatman Boats, 2011 personal communication

74 "Holding all this…" Aug 21, 1959 Fulmer to Reilly, Box 1, Fulmer collection USHS

74 "With the basic…" Oct 4, 1951 Fulmer to Marston, Box 74, Marston collection

75 "Dock was pleased…" Oct 15, 1951 Marston to Fulmer, Box 74, Marston collection

75 "Dock wrote back…" Nov 23 and Dec 17, 1951 Marston to Fulmer, Box 74, Marston collection

75 "In February, Moulty…" Mar 12, 1954 Fulmer to Reilly, Box 1, Fulmer collection USHS

75 "Eight days later…" Mar 18, 1952 Marston to Fulmer; April 7 and 28, 1952 Fulmer to Marston, Box 74, Marston collection

75 "On May 11…" May 12, 1952 and Feb 28, 1953 Fulmer to Marston, Box 74, Marston collection

75 "Moulty sent a…" May 25, 1952 Marston to Fulmer, Box 74, Marston collection

75   "In May 1952…" May 10, 1952 Marston to Reilly, Box 3, Reilly collection USHS
75   "The summer of…" Jun 30, 1952, Feb 28, 1953, Feb 16, 1960, Fulmer to Marston, Box 74, Marston collection
77   "While Moulty was…" Dec 4, 1952 Marston to Reilly and Dec 9, 1952 Reilly to Marston, Box 3, Reilly collection USHS
77   "As the party…" Frank Wright, *Life Story of John Franklin Wright*, Vishnu Temple Press 2012; Bob Rigg 2011 personal communication
77   "In the winter…" Feb 28, 1953 Fulmer to Marston, Box 74, Marston collection

Chapter 10 A Hell of a Good Time (1953)

79   "1953 was not…" Apr 20 and Jul 21, 1953, Fulmer to Marston, Box 74, Marston collection
79   "In the spring…" Aug 2, 1953 Reilly to Marston, Box 3, Reilly collection USHS; Reilly Grand Canyon log, 1953, Box 14, Reilly collection NAU; Apr 12, 1953 A.K. Reynolds to Reilly, Box 8, Reilly collection USHS
79   "Pat thought he…" Ellen Reynolds, 2010 personal communication; Aug 2, 1953 Reilly to Marston, Box 3, Reilly collection USHS
79   "Making up the…" Aug 27, 1953, *Los Angeles Times*, Los Angeles Adventurers Club archives
79   "Gerald "Lug" Larsen…" Mathew Larsen and Edith Woodridge, 2011 personal communication; Apr 23 and May 18, 1953 A.K. Reynolds to Reilly, Box 8, Reilly collection USHS
80   "A.K. and Ellen…" Ellen Reynolds, 2010 personal communication; Aug 2, 1953 Reilly to Marston, Box 3, Reilly collection USHS
80   "Trouble between A.K.…" May 18, 1953 A.K. Reynolds to Reilly, Box 8, Reilly collection USHS; Ellen Reynolds, 2010 personal communication
80   "The river runners…" Reilly Grand Canyon log, 1953, Box 14, Reilly collection NAU
80   "Both Ellen and…" Ellen Reynolds, 2010 personal communication
81   "With the river…" Reilly Grand Canyon log, 1953, Box 14, Reilly collection NAU
82   "First thing on…" Aug 2, 1953 Reilly to Marston letter, Box 3, Reilly collection USHS; Reilly Grand Canyon log, 1953, Box 14, Reilly collection NAU
82   "The boaters-turned-climbers…" Ellen Reynolds, 2010 personal communication
83   "It was a…" Ibid
83   "The party finally…" Aug 2, 1953 Reilly to Marston, Box 3, Reilly collection USHS; Reilly Grand Canyon log, 1953, Box 14, Reilly collection NAU
83   "As they were…" Feb 25, 1954 Reilly to Marston, Box 3, Reilly collection USHS
83   "There was a…" Aug 2, 1953 Reilly to Marston letter, Box 3, Reilly collection USHS; Reilly Grand Canyon log, 1953, Box 14, Reilly collection NAU
84   "George was very…" Aug 2, 1953 Reilly to Marston, Box 3, Reilly collection USHS; Reilly Grand Canyon log, 1953, Box 14, Reilly collection NAU
84   "The bad news…" Ellen Reynolds, 2010 personal communication; Reilly Grand Canyon log, 1953, Box 14, Reilly collection NAU
85   "Up to 1953…" Aug 27, 1953, *Los Angeles Times*, Ellen Reynolds collection
86   "Dock wrote back…" Aug 16, 1953 and Mar 1, 1954 Marston to Reilly, Box 3, Reilly collection USHS
86   "Five weeks later…" Sep 24, 1953 Fulmer to Marston, Box 74, Marston collection
86   "Moulty did a…" Jan 14, 1961, Fulmer to Reilly, Box 1, Fulmer collection USHS
86   "Dock encouraged Moulty …" Oct 8, 1953 Marston to Fulmer, Box 74, Marston collection
87   "Dock met up…" Feb 6, 1954 Marston to Fulmer, Box 74, Marston collection
87   "In February, Pat…" Feb 25, 1954 Reilly to Marston, Box 74, Reilly collection USHS
87   "So once again…" Mar 1, 1954 Marston to Reilly, Box 3, Reilly collection USHS
87   "Dock then wrote…" Mar 8, 1954 Marston to Fulmer, Box 74, Marston collection
87   "On March 16…" Mar 16, 1954 Fulmer to Reilly, Box 1, Fulmer collection USHS

Chapter 11 The Trip That Never Left Lee's Ferry (1954)

89   "By early March…" Mar 8, 1954 Marston to Fulmer, Mar 16, 1954 Fulmer to Marston, Box 74, Marston collection
89   "Indeed, the peak…" www.waterdata.usgs.gov
89   "After Moulty's outreach…" Mar 24, 1954 Reilly to Fulmer, Box 1, Fulmer collection USHS
89   "Moulty described his…" Mar 16, 1954 Fulmer to Reilly, Mar 24, 1954 Reilly to Fulmer, Box 1, Fulmer collection USHS
90   "Moulty wrote back…" Mar 29, 1954 Fulmer to Reilly, Box 1, Fulmer collection USHS; Mar 29, 1954 Fulmer to Marston, Box 74, Marston collection
90   "By mid-March…" Mar 16, 1954 Fulmer to Marston, Box 74, Marston collection
90   "Dock wrote back…" Mar 31, 1954 Marston to Fulmer, Box 74, Marston collection
90   "Toward the end…" Apr 22, 1954 Reilly to Marston, Box 3, Reilly collection USHS
90   "Using ⅛-inch…" Jan 14, 1988, Utah State Historical Society Oral History Project interview of PT Reilly, pg. 9
90   "Five friends had…" Ibid

90   "For the first…" Mar 12, 1954 Fulmer to Reilly, Box 1, Fulmer collection USHS (This letter appears to be misdated, as it would predate Fulmer's first letter to Reilly by 4 days, and fits with late March correspondence.); Jan 27, 1955, Fulmer to Reilly, Box 1, Fulmer Collection USHS

90   "On April 24…" Apr 24, 1945 Reilly to Fulmer, surprisingly this was in the Marston collection, Box 74

91   "On that same…" Bruce Dines and Chuck Warren 2010 and 2011 personal communication

91   "Ty talked a…" Ibid; Webb, *Riverman*, Labyrinth Publishing, Rock Springs, WY, 2nd edition, 1990, pg. 68, 129-130

91   "Ty had rafted…" Ibid

92   "In letters to…" Mar 13, 1954 Reilly to Marston, Box 3, Reilly collection USHS; May 17, 1954 Fulmer to Reilly, Box 1, Fulmer collection USHS

92   "On May 17…" May 17, 1954 Marston to Reilly, Box 3, Reilly collection USHS

92   "Regardless of the…" Jorgen Visbak interview December 13, 2010

93   "Meanwhile, in California…" May 24, 1954 Reilly to Marston, Box 3, Reilly collection USHS

93   "On June 19,…" Jan 2, 1958 Fulmer to Aleson, Box 1, Fulmer collection USHS

93   "Pat was towing…" Nov 11, 1985 Reilly to Topping, Box 1, Reilly collection USHS

93   "Retained from the…" Cataract boat construction plans, Ellen Reynolds collection

93   "The boat that…" Boat beam dimension from replica reconstruction Dave Mortenson and Ian Elliot

93   "His next stop…" Nov 21, 1975, *Sun City News*, Priss Becker collection

93   "In a late…" Jun 27, 1954 Marston to Reilly, Box 3, Reilly collection USHS

93   "By the end…" Fulmer Lodore Canyon log, 1954, Box 289, Marston collection

93   "The Green River…" www.waterdata.usgs.gov

93   "On the second…" Fulmer Lodore Canyon log, 1954, Box 289, Marston collection

95   "With a little…" Sep 2, 1954 Fulmer to Marston, Box 74, Marston collection

95   "In August, Moulty…" Aug 24, 1954 Fulmer to Reilly, Box 1, Fulmer collection USHS

95   "As the last…" Dec 8, 1954 Reilly to Marston, Box 3, Reilly collection USHS

95   "Throughout the 1950s…" Dan Davis Sr. Interview, Grand Canyon River Guides Oral History Collection, Interview No. 53.16, NAU

95   "In that first…" Butler and Myers, *Grand Obsession: Harvey Butchart and the Exploration of Grand Canyon*, Puma Press, Flagstaff, AZ, 2007, pg. 120; Dan Davis Sr. Interview, Grand Canyon River Guides Oral History Collection, Interview No. 53.16, Northern Arizona University Special Collections; *Arizona Daily Sun* Jun 21 and Jun 24, 1954; *Arizona Republic*, Aug 22, 1954, Dale Slocum collection; Dale Slocum 2011 personal communication

97   "The Park Service…" Jun 28, 1955 Superintendent Patraw to Marston, Box 333, Marston collection

97   "While requiring prior…" Jun 24, 1955 Marston to Patraw, Box 333, Marston collection

97   "Indeed, the park…" Grand Canyon National Park Noncommercial River Trip Regulations, revised April 19, 2011, pg. 5

97   "Until the park…" Westways Magazine, Mexican Hat Expeditions Advertisement, February 1960, Box 23, Reilly collection NAU

Chapter 12 Only One Flip (1955)

99   "After the previous…" Jan 24, 1955 Reilly to Fulmer, Box 1, Fulmer collection USHS

99   "When Pat approached…" Brick Mortenson 2000 personal interview

100   "Two other Lockheed…" Earline Pederson 2011 personal communication

100   "In February, Pat…" Feb 27, 1955 Reilly to Larsen and Mar 7, 1955 Larsen to Reilly, Box 9, Reilly collection USHS

100   "Then there was…" Martin Litton Interview, Oct 10, 1992 NAU Special Collections

100   "He then left…" Feb 16, 1955 Interoffice memo, *Sunset* magazine, Box 13, Reilly collection NAU

100   "It was Martin…" May 13, 1954, Reilly to Marston, Box 3, Reilly collection USHS; Feb 21, 1955 Reilly to Litton, Box 13, Reilly collection NAU

100   "Pat began giving…" Mar 29, 1955 Reilly to Litton, Box 13, Reilly collection NAU; May 5, 1955 Reilly to Fulmer, Box 1, Fulmer collection USHS; Earline Pederson 2011 personal communication

100   "In researching the…" Ian Elliot 2009 personal communication

100   "By early May…" May 5, 1955 Reilly to Fulmer, Box 74, Marston collection

100   "Pat had seen…" Dave Mortenson 2006 personal communication

101   "The colors Goff…" Reilly Grand Canyon log, 1955, Box 13, Reilly collection NAU

101   "In April, Dock …" Apr 20, 1955 Reilly to Marston, Box 4, Reilly collection USHS

101   "Pat was so…" Ibid

101   "Besides, Pat thought…" Feb 16, 1955 Interoffice memo, *Sunset* magazine, Box 13, Reilly collection NAU; Feb 25, 1955 Reilly to Litton, Box 4 Reilly collection NAU

102   "Pat filled out…" May 5, 1955 Reilly to Fulmer, Box 74, Marston collection; Boating Permit, Box 2, Reilly collection USHS

102   "All the myriad…" Jun 11, 1955 Western Union Telegram, Box 13, Reilly collection NAU; Brick Mortenson 2000 personal interview

102   "Pat strode over…" Brick Mortenson 2000 personal interview

102   "With the *Gem* …" Priss Becker 2008 personal communication

102   "With the constraints…" Joanie Staveley 2011 personal communication; Evelyn Greene interview 2001, NAU

102   "Meanwhile, Brick, Pat…" Reilly Grand Canyon log, 1955, Box 13, Reilly collection NAU; Mortenson Grand Canyon log, 1955, Box 13, Reilly collection NAU; Fulmer Grand Canyon log, 1955, Box 1, Fulmer collection USHS

103   "The group stopped…" Reilly Grand Canyon log, 1955, Box 13, Reilly collection NAU; Mortenson Grand Canyon log, 1955, David Mortenson collection

103   "Moulty was using…" Fulmer Grand Canyon log, 1955, Box 1, Fulmer collection USHS; Oct 11, 1955 Fulmer to Reilly, Box 1, Fulmer collection USHS

104   "While Moulty had…" Reilly Grand Canyon log, 1959, Box 14, Reilly collection NAU

106   "Less than a…" Butler and Myers, *Grand Obsession: Harvey Butchart and the Exploration of Grand Canyon*, Puma Press, 2007, pg. 145-148

107   "Boyd Moore's body…" Jul 31 and Aug 14, 1955 Reilly to Marston, Box 4, Reilly collection USHS

108   "Moulty ran the…" Fulmer Grand Canyon log, 1955, Box 1, Fulmer collection USHS; Jul 21, 1955 Fulmer to Marston, Box 74, Marston collection

108   "It was an…" Fulmer Grand Canyon log, 1955, Box 1, Fulmer collection USHS; Jul 21, 1955 Fulmer to Marston, Box 74, Marston collection; Sep 10, 1955 Fulmer to Reilly, Box 1, Fulmer collection USHS

111   "The roar of…" Nancy Brian, *River To Rim: A guide to place names along the Colorado River in Grand Canyon from Lake Powell to Lake Mead*, Earthguest Press, 1992, pg. 92 for discussion of Waltenberg and Walthenberg spellings.

115   "Meanwhile, Martin, Esther…" Esther Litton 2008 personal communication

118   "In 1955, the…" http://www.usbr.gov/lc/region/g4000/lakemead_line.pdf; Reilly Grand Canyon log, 1955, Box 13, Reilly collection NAU; Fulmer Grand Canyon log, 1955, Box 1, Fulmer collection USHS

118   "At trip's end…" Jul 21, 1955 Fulmer to Marston, Box 74, Marston collection; Jul 31, 1955 Reilly to Marston, Box 4, Reilly collection USHS

119   "Within five weeks…" Aug 11, 1955 Fulmer to Marston, Box 74, Marston collection

119   "Pat was considering…" Aug 14, 1955 Reilly to Marston, Box 4, Reilly collection USHS

119   "The 1955 river…" Jul 31, 1955 Reilly to Marston, Box 4, Reilly collection USHS; Georgie Trip Schedule, 108601, Folder 23, GRCA

119   "Also of note…" Jul 31 and Aug 14, 1955 Reilly to Marston, Box 4, Reilly collection USHS, Mar 6, 1956 Litton to Reilly, Box 13, Reilly collection NAU; Box 290, Marston collection; Bill Beer *We Swam the Grand Canyon*, Mountaineers Press, 1988, 15 Minute Press, 1995

119   "Another portent of…" Sep 7, 1955 Harris to Marston, Box 333, Marston collection

Chapter 13 The Perfect Run, Almost (1956)

121   "There was a…" Feb 2 and 15, 1956 Fulmer to Marston, Box 74, Marston collection

121   "Pat wrote Martin…" Feb 19, 1956 Reilly to Litton, Box 13, Reilly collection NAU

121   "On March 5…" Mar 6, 1956 Litton to Reilly, Box 13, Reilly collection NAU

122   "Meanwhile, in the…" Feb 2, 1956 Fulmer to Marston, Box 74, Marston collection; Mar 6, 1956 Litton to Reilly, Box 13, Reilly collection NAU

122   "Pat responded only…" Mar 11, 1956 Reilly to Marston, Box 4, Reilly collection USHS

122   "Dock didn't see…" Mar 14, 1956 Marston to Reilly, Box 4, Reilly collection USHS

122   "On returning from…" Mar 21, 1956 Marston to Reilly, Box 4, Reilly collection USHS; May 16, 1956 Reilly to Litton, Box 13, Reilly collection NAU; May 17, 1956 Reilly to Marston, Box 4, Reilly collection USHS

122   "Dock was not…" May 23, 1956 Marston to Reilly, Box 4, Reilly collection USHS

122   "When the Hisers…" Bob Taylor 2008 personal communication; Barbara Crookston 2011 personal communication

122   "In early March…" Mar 6, 1956 Litton to Reilly, Box 4, Reilly collection NAU

123   "Pat wrote back…" Mar 11, 1956 Reilly to Litton, Box 13, Reilly collection NAU

123   "Amrette Ott, also…" May 3, 1956 Litton to Reilly, Box 13, Reilly collection NAU; Amrette Butler 2009 and 2010 personal interview

123   "Martin rented a…" Apr 19, 1956 Reilly to Litton, Box 13, Reilly collection NAU; Dec 23, 1956 Reilly to Marston, Box 4, Reilly collection USHS

123   "As for the…" Apr 19, 1956 Reilly to Litton, Box 13, Reilly collection NAU

123   "Pat had purchased…" May 7, 1956 Reilly to Watson, Box 24, Reilly collection NAU

123   "William "Bill" McGill…" Jun 1, 1956 Reilly to Litton, Box 13, Reilly collection NAU; Jul 21, 1956 Reilly to Chapman, Box 4, Reilly collection NAU

124   "While the Reilly-Fulmer…" Sep 22, 1956 Marston to Fulmer, Box 74, Marston collection; Canyoneers List, Reilly collection NAU;   www.waterdata.usgs.gov

124   "Nine days after…" Reilly Grand Canyon log, 1956, Box 13, Reilly collection NAU

128   "It was here…" Ibid; Aug 6, 1956 Reilly to Marston, Box 4, Reilly collection USHS; Apr 7, 1956 Reilly to Litton, Box 13, Reilly collection NAU [Though this is the date on the letter, the letter is discussing incidents from the June 1956 river trip and also mentions an Aug 6, 1956 letter from Litton to Reilly]

128   "The show that..." Aug 12, 1956 Watson to Reilly, Box 24, Reilly collection NAU; Jul 15, 1956 Ott to Reilly, Box 24, Reilly collection NAU;   Aug 6, 1956 Litton to Reilly, Box 13, Reilly collection NAU

129   "On June 25..." Reilly Grand Canyon log, 1956, Box 13, Reilly collection NAU, www.waterdata.usgs.gov ; Nancy Brian, *River To Rim: A guide to place names along the Colorado River in Grand Canyon from Lake Powell to Lake Mead*, Earthguest Press, 1992, pg. 92

130   "Once onshore, Pat..." Reilly Grand Canyon log, 1956, Box 13, Reilly collection NAU; Dec 21, 1988 Reilly to Topping, Box 1, Reilly collection USHS

132   "Pat continued on..." Aug 5, 1956 *Los Angeles Times*, Box 10, Reilly collection NAU

132   "As the boatmen..." Danny R. Driskill, 2008 and 2011 personal interview, Martin and Whitis Guide to the Colorado River in Grand Canyon, 4th edition, 2008, Vishnu Temple Press, Map 11

135   "The letters reveal..." Reilly Grand Canyon log, 1956, Box 13, Reilly collection NAU; Jul 15, 1956 Ott to Reilly, Box 24, Reilly collection NAU; Jul 22 and Aug 12, 1956 Reilly to Fulmer, Box 74, Marston collection; Aug 6, 1956 Litton to Reilly, Box 13, Reilly collection NAU; Apr 20, 1963, Reilly to Marston, Box 5, Reilly collection USHS

135   "The drive back..." Jul 16, 1956 Fulmer to Marston, Box 74, Marston collection; Apr 7, 1956 Reilly to Litton, Box 13, Reilly collection NAU [This letter is most likely from Aug 7, as it talks about incidents from the July 1956 trip]

135   "Susie, Jean, Ruth..." Reilly Grand Canyon log, 1956, Box 13, Reilly collection NAU; Jul 18, 1956 Susie Reilly to Hildegarde Chapman, Box 4, Reilly collection NAU

135   "Within a week..." Ibid; Jul 26, 1956 Chapman to Reilly, Box 4, Reilly collection NAU

135   "Pat wanted Brick..." Jul 21, 1956 Reilly to Chapman and Jul 26, 1956 Chapman to Reilly, Box 4, Reilly collection NAU

136   "With funding for..." Jul 30, 1956, Chapman to Reilly, Box 4, Reilly collection NAU

136   "Within forty-eight..." Aug 4, 1956 telegram Chapman to Reilly, Aug 6, 1956 Reilly to Greene and Reilly to Coffin, Aug 22, 1956 Reilly to Coffin, all Box 4, Reilly collection NAU

136   "While Pat was..." Neal Newby 2010 personal interview; Neal Newby, Lost in the Grand Canyon, The Ol' Pioneer, Vol. 22: Number 4

137   "The last thing..." Danny R. Driskill, 2008 and 2011 personal interview

137   "Two other events..." Aug 6, 1956 Reilly to Marston, Box 4, Reilly collection USHS; Nov 26, 1956, Marston to Fulmer, Box 74, Marston collection; www.usbr.gov

Chapter 14 To Phantom on 126,000 cfs and We're Hiking Out (1957)

139   "Over the winter..." Dec 7, 1956 and Mar 4, 1957 Fulmer to Marston, Box 74, Marston collection

139   "Pat was looking..." Dec 4 and 23, 1956 Reilly to Marston, Box 4, Reilly collection USHS

139   "As in previous..." Dec 23, 1956 Reilly to Marston, Box 4, Reilly collection USHS

139   "By mid-February..." Feb 15 and Mar 4, 1957 Fulmer to Marston, Box 74, Marston collection; Feb 20, 1957 Marston to Fulmer and Reilly, Box 4, Reilly collection USHS

139   "In early April..." Mar 22 and Apr 2, 1957 Fulmer to Marston, Box 74, Marston collection

139   "On April 17,..." Apr 10, 1957 Marston to Reilly, Box 196, Marston collection

139   "Moulty replied to..." Apr 23, 1957 Fulmer to Marston, Box 74, Marston collection

140   "The drive out..." Priss Becker 2008 personal communication

140   "Plans changed somewhat..." Reilly Grand Canyon log, 1957, Box 13, Reilly collection NAU

140   "Moulty headed out..." Ibid; Dave Mortenson 2008 personal communication

141   "One of the..." Reilly Grand Canyon log, 1957, Box 13, Reilly collection NAU; Wayne Ranney 2011 personal communication

142   "Finally, launch day..." Reilly, Mortenson and Szep Grand Canyon logs, 1957, Box 13, 14, and 27, Reilly collection NAU

143   "Moulty was surprised..." Dec 7, 1957 Fulmer to Marston, Box 74, Marston collection; Call of the Canyon 16mm film, Priss Becker collection

146   "When their party..." Topping, Schmidt and Vierra, *Computation and Analysis of the Instantaneous-Discharge Record for the Colorado River at Lee's Ferry, Arizona—May 8, 1921, through September 30, 2000* USGS Professional Paper 1677, pg. 18, 29; www.waterdata.usgs.gov

146   "Since flow records..." Ibid

146   "Another flood was..." www.waterdata.usgs.gov

147   "Even with the..." Reilly and Mortenson Grand Canyon logs, 1957, Box 13 and 14, Reilly collection NAU

148   "As Priss and..." Priss Becker 2008 personal communication

150   "Susie spoke alone..." Szep Grand Canyon log, 1957, Box 27, Reilly collection NAU; Dec 7, 1957 Fulmer to Marston, Box 74, Marston collection

151   "Moulty had asked..." Jul 19, 1957 Fulmer to Marston, Box 74, Marston collection; Szep Grand Canyon log, 1957, Box 27, Reilly collection NAU

153   "Moulty wondered why..." Dec 7, 1957 Fulmer to Marston, Box 74, Marston collection

154   "After dinner, Moulty ..." Dec 7, 1957 Fulmer to Marston, Box 74, Marston collection

155   "While Pat was …" Szep and Mortenson Grand Canyon logs, 1957, Box 27 and 14, Reilly collection NAU

155   "What none of…" Dec 12, 1957 Marston to Fulmer, Box 74, Marston collection

155   "Indeed, Dock had…" Jul 22, 1957 Marston to Fulmer, Box 74, Marston collection; Marston Grand Canyon log, 1957, Box 3, Reilly Collection USHS

155   "On the 19th…" Reilly Grand Canyon log, 1957, Box 13, Reilly collection NAU; Dec 7, 1957 Fulmer to Marston, Box 74, Marston collection

156   "In August, Moulty…" Aug 28, 1957 Fulmer to Reilly, Box 1, Fulmer collection USHS; Sep 9 and Sep 26, 1957 Tidball to Aleson, Box 12, Aleson collection USHS

156   "Harry was in…" Nov 7 and Nov 11, 1957 Rust to Aleson and Aleson to Rust, Box 12, Aleson collection USHS

156   "Harry also corresponded …" Nov 11, 1957 Marston to Fulmer, Box 74, Marston collection

156   "Somewhere amidst the…" *Muncie Star*, May 9, 1957

156   "Another river trip…" Apr 28, 1965 Beck to Reilly, Box 8, Reilly collection USHS; Peter Huntoon 2011 personal communication

Chapter 15 A Race to Temple Bar Without Boats (1958)

159   "The snow fell…" www.waterdata.usgs.gov

159   "Dock had already…" Mar 4 and Mar 19, 1958 Marston to Fulmer, Box 74, Marston collection

159   "Pat wanted to…" Jan 2 and Feb 24, 1958 Fulmer to Marston, Box 74, Marston collection

159   "A few days…" Mar 29, 1958 Fulmer to Aleson, Box 12, Aleson collection USHS

159   "In the end…" Apr 10, 1958 Reilly to Fulmer, Box 74, Marston collection

159   "Moulty and Guy…" May 6, 1958 Fulmer to Marston, Box 74 Marston collection

159   "Meanwhile, from the…" Szep Grand Canyon log, 1958, Szep collection

160   "Moulty already had…" May 24, 1958 Aleson to Dock, Box 12, Aleson collection USHS

160   "Georgie was motoring…" Dick Westwood, *Woman Of The River: Georgie White Clark, Whitewater Pioneer*, Utah State University Press, pg. 63; Jim David 2008 personal communication; John Weisheit 2011 personal communication

161   "Arriving at the…" Szep Grand Canyon log, 1958, Szep collection; Mortenson Grand Canyon log, 1958, Mortenson collection, Reilly Grand Canyon log, 1958, Box 14, Reilly collection NAU

161   "The run downriver…" Ibid

166   "Having watched all…" Mortenson Grand Canyon log, 1958, Mortenson collection; Call of the Canyon 16mm film, Priss Becker collection

168   "From the *Gem*…" Fulmer Grand Canyon log, 1958, Box 293, Marston collection; Szep Grand Canyon log, 1958, Szep collection; Mortenson Grand Canyon log, 1958, Mortenson collection; Reilly Grand Canyon log, 1958, Box 14, Reilly collection NAU; Jul 7, 1958 Fulmer to Marston, Box 74, Marston collection

169   "Moulty told him…" Jun 4, 1958 Fulmer to Aleson, Box 12, Aleson collection USHS

169   "Pat was worried…" Jul 7, 1958 Fulmer to Marston, Box 74, Marston collection; Jul 22, 1958 Reilly to Fulmer, Box 74, Marston collection

170   "At 7:00 in…" Joe Szep 2008 personal communication

171   "On Wednesday morning…" Western Union Telegram, Reilly collection NAU

172   "On righting the…" Sep 4, 1958 Fulmer to Marston, Box 74, Marston collection

172   "On the long…" Jun 3, 1958 *Muncie Morning Star*; Jun 23, 1958 Fulmer to Reilly, Box 1, Fulmer collection USHS

172   "Moulty had the…" Jun 6, 1958 Fulmer to Marston, Box 74, Marston collection

172   "In June, Pat…" Jun 20, 1958 Schulz to Reilly, Box 12, Reilly collection NAU

173   "The boats ranged…" Berger, *Reflections of Grand Canyon Historians*, Grand Canyon Association, Grand Canyon, AZ, 2008, pg. 26

173   "Georgie made another…" Jul 9, 1958 Reilly to Norton, Box 23, Reilly collection NAU

173   "In early winter…" Nov 29, 1958 Bundy to Reilly, Reilly collection USHS; Jan 16, 1959 Reilly to Fulmer, Box 1, Fulmer collection USHS

173   "On receiving the…" Jan 20, 1959 Fulmer to Reilly, Box 1, Fulmer collection USHS

173   "In the winter…" Jan 20, 1959 Fulmer to Marston, Box 74, Marston collection

Chapter 16 The Sinking of the Reilly Fleet (1959)

175   "In mid-December, Pat…" Dec 14, 1958 Reilly to Fulmer, Box 74, Marston collection

175   "Moulty was as…" Dec 5, 1958 Fulmer to Marston, Box 74, Marston collection

175   "There was something…" Mar 10, 1959 Fulmer to Marston, Box 74, Marston collection

175   "The new boat…" Jul 31, 1959 Fulmer to Reilly, Box 1, Fulmer collection USHS

175   "In the latter…" Mar 19, 1959 Reilly to Fulmer, Box 74, Marston collection

175   "Moulty was uncertain…" Apr 20, 1959 Fulmer to Marston, Box 74, Marston collection

176   "Pat wrote to…" May 15, 1959, Fulmer to Marston, Box 74, Marston collection
176   "Coordinating his schedule…" May 25, Jul 29, 1959 Fulmer to Marston, Box 74, Marston collection
176   "Moulty was back…" Szep Grand Canyon log, 1959, Joe Szep collection
176   "The Colorado River…" United States Bureau of Reclamation Technical Paper, *Glen Canyon Dam and Powerplant: Technical Record of Design and Construction*, Denver Colorado, 1970, pg. 39-42
177   "Pat had heard…" Nov 24, 1958 Reilly to Marston, Box 4, Reilly collection USHS
177   "Arriving at Lee's…" Reilly Grand Canyon log, 1959, Box 14, Reilly collection NAU; Szep Grand Canyon log, 1959, Joe Szep collection
181   "It would turn…" Emslie, Mead and Coats, *Split-Twig Figurines in Grand Canyon, Arizona: New Discoveries and Interpretations*, Kiva, Vol. 61, N0. 2, 1995; Box 88, Marston collection
182   "On arriving, the…" Aug 23, 1959 Marston to Reilly, Box 4, Reilly collection USHS
182   "That evening, Pat…" Jul 14, 1959 Fulmer to Reilly, Fulmer collection USHS
182   "In the five…" Jul 29, 1959 Fulmer to Marston, Box 74, Marston collection
183   "The lining of…" Sep 2, 1959 Reilly to Marston, Box 4, Reilly collection USHS
184   "On top of…" Ibid; Szep Grand Canyon log, 1959, Joe Szep collection
185   "Many years later…" Joe Szep 2008 personal communication
186   "The next day…" Jul 29, 1959 Fulmer to Marston, Box 74, Marston collection; Frank Wright, *Life Story of John Franklin Wright*, Vishnu Temple Press 2012; Otis Wright 2011 personal communication; www.canyoneers.com
186   "Moulty wrote Pat…" Jul 14, 1959 Fulmer to Reilly, Box 1, Fulmer collection USHS
187   "After the river…" Jul 29, 1959 Fulmer to Marston, Box 74, Marston collection; Sep 2, 1959 Reilly to Marston, Box 4, Reilly collection USHS
187   "In July Moulty…" Aug 1, 1959, *Muncie Star*
187   "Moulty received congratulations…" Aug 14, 1959 Fulmer to Reilly, Box 1, Fulmer collection USHS; Aug 20, 1959 Goldwater to Fulmer, Box 74, Marston collection
187   "In August and…" Aug 9, 1959, Reilly to Fulmer, Box 74, Marston collection; Sep 2, 1959 Reilly to Marston, Box 4, Reilly collection USHS
187   "With the *Moja* …" Sep 11, 1959, Fulmer to Reilly, Box 1, Fulmer collection USHS
187   "Both Moulty and…" Dec 8, 1959, Fulmer to Marston, Box 74, Marston collection
187   "Of note for…" Ken and Angela Stroud 2011 personal communication
187   "Coffin cited the…" Aug 1959 Superintendents Report, page 2 and 7, GRCA
187   "Later that year…" United Press International and Associated Press reports, Box 294, Marston collection

Chapter 17 New Boats, a New Dam, and a New River (1960 and beyond)

189   "Moulty celebrated Christmas…" Dec 8, 1959, Jan 29, and Feb 26, 1960, Fulmer to Marston, Box 74, Marston collection
189   "The 1960 Summer…" Apr 8, 1960 Fulmer to Marston, Box 74, Marston collection
189   "In the end…" Jun 23, 1960 and Feb 16, 1962 Fulmer to Marston, Box 74, Marston collection
189   "While Moulty, Roy…" Marston 1960 Grand Canyon log, Box 295, Marston collection
189   "After overhauling the…" Ibid; Aug 13, 1960 Marston to Reilly, Box 4, Reilly collection USHS
190   "It had taken…" http://www.gcrg.org/docs/gtslib/50th_anniversary-jet_boat_up_run.pdf
190   "The National Park…" Preliminary Wilderness Proposal, 1973, Grand Canyon National Park Wilderness Administrative Record, Vol. 3, GRCA
190   "Entrusted by the…" Mar 4, 1975 Kerr to Marston, Box 333, Marston Collection
190   "Another "first" occurred…" Ruth Kirschbaum 2010 personal communication; Dr. Yuji Oishi 2010 personal communication; April 14, 1982, Fletcher to GRCA, 1752 Fldr 28, GRCA; Kirschbaum, *"Grand" Adventure*, American Whitewater Journal, Vol 6, No. 3, November, 1960, pg. 5-10; RRFW Riverwire 50th Anniversary of Kirschbaum Kayak Run, www.rrfw.org
191   "That winter, Pat…" Jan 14, 1961 Fulmer to Reilly, Box 1, Fulmer collection USHS
192   "That summer, Martin…" Fletcher, Roger, *Drift Boats and River Dories*, Stackpole Books, 2007, pg. 86-87
192   "Pat wrote to…" Aug 6, 1961 Reilly to Fulmer, Box 197, Marston collection
192   "Moulty's reply in…" Aug 16, 1961 Fulmer to Reilly, Box 1, Fulmer collection USHS
192   "Moulty was back…" Nov 26, 1962 Fulmer to Marston, Box 74, Marston collection; Sunday, May 22, 1966 *Muncie Star*
192   "In the winter…" PT Reilly Interview, USHS Oral History Project; Mar 10, 1962 Reilly to Marston, Box 5, Reilly collection USHS; Fletcher, Roger, *Drift Boats and River Dories*, Stackpole Books, 2007, pg. 86-87
192   "Pat was worried…" Jan 31, 1962 Reilly to Litton, Box 13, Reilly collection NAU
192   "While Pat fretted…" Dave Mortenson 2006, 2008, and 2011 personal communication; PT Reilly Interview, USHS Oral History Project

Page

192   "In March, Martin…" Mar 28, 1962 Litton to Reilly, Box 13, Reilly collection NAU

193   "On hearing from…" Apr 1, 1962 Reilly to Litton, Box 13, Reilly collection NAU

193   "After beginning to…" Apr 29, 1962 Reilly to Litton, Box 13, Reilly collection NAU

193   "He was so…" Apr 28, 1962 Reilly to Marston, Box 5, Reilly collection USHS

193   "Dock wrote back…" Apr 30, 1962 Marston to Reilly, Box 5, Reilly collection USHS; May 20, 1962 Reilly to Marston, Box 5, Reilly collection USHS

193   "Pat also wrote…" May 1, 1962 Fulmer to Marston, Box 74, Marston collection; Apr 20, 1963 Reilly to Marston, Box 5, Reilly collection USHS

193   "Pat had not…" Apr 20, 1963 Reilly to Marston, Box 5, Reilly collection USHS

193   "On hearing of…" Apr 22, 1963 Marston to Reilly, Box 5, Reilly collection USHS

193   "In early May…" May 7, 1962 Litton to Reilly, Box 13, Reilly collection NAU

193   "In June 1962,…" Oct 18, 1962 Fulmer to Marston, Box 74, Marston collection

193   "While the Fulmers…" PT Reilly Interview, USHS Oral History Project; Szep Grand Canyon log, 1962, Szep collection

194   "At the end…" Jul 21, 1962 Reilly to Marston, Box 5, Reilly collection USHS

194   "He wrote Keith…" Jul 28, 1962 Reilly to Steele, Box 13, Reilly collection NAU

194   "Pat also wrote…" Aug 26, 1962 Reilly to Fulmer, Box 1, Fulmer collection USHS

195   "Another trend the…" Oct 9, 1962 Coffin to Marston, Box 333, Marston collection

195   "Off the record…" Aug 21, 1963 Reilly to Marston, Box 333, Marston collection

195   "In the fall…" Sep 10, 1962 Fulmer to Reilly, Box 1, Fulmer collection USHS

195   "Meanwhile, in far…" United States Bureau of Reclamation Technical Paper, *Glen Canyon Dam and Powerplant: Technical Record of Design and Construction*, Denver Colorado, 1970, pg. 416

195   "With two companions…" Nov 19, 1963 Fulmer to Marston, Box 74, Marston collection

195   "After the exploration…" Ibid; December 2, 1963 Fulmer to Marston, Box 74, Marston collection

195   "Moulty had been…" Marston Grand Canyon trip log, 1963, transcribed by Jirge and Weisheit, www.riverguides.org

195   "Such was the…" Nov 14, 1962 Marston to Coffin, Box 333, Marston collection

196   "Glen Canyon Dam…" http://www.usbr.gov/lc/region/g4000/hourly/mead-elv.html

196   "Dock wrote to…" Sep 30, 1964 Marston to Fulmer, Box 74, Marston collection

196   "Moulty wrote right…" Oct 2, 1964 Fulmer to Marston, Box 74, Marston collection

196   "On October 14…" Oct 14, 1964 Marston to Fulmer, Box 74, Marston collection

196   "As soon as…" Jan 6, 1965 Fulmer to Marston, Box 74, Marston collection

196   "The same month…" Congressional Record, House Volume 152, Jul 24, 2006; Mar 15, 1968 Superintendent Stricklin to Southwest Regional Director, Grand Canyon National Park Wilderness Administrative Record, Vol. 1, GRCA

196   "Having only rarely…" Jan 16, 1965 Fulmer to Reilly, Box 1, Fulmer collection USHS

196   "Pat was not…" Reilly collection NAU

196   "Brick also sold…" Nov 11, 1985 Reilly to Topping, Box 1, Reilly collection USHS

196   "In the summer…" 16mm film, Barbara Crookston collection; Aug 10, 1965 Fulmer to Marston, Box 74, Marston collection

196   "That winter, Moulty…" May 22, 1966 *Muncie Star*

197   "An article ran…" Jun 13, 1966 Bob Barnet *Muncie Star*

197   "The Board of…" Oct 4, 1966 Program, Priss Becker collection; Oct 5, 1966 *Muncie Star*

197   "Arriving at their…" Priss Becker 2008 personal communication

198   "One huge difference…" www.waterdata.usgs.gov

199   "Immediately after the…" Myers, 'River Runners and the Number Game,' Boatman's Quarterly Review, Winter 1996-1997, Vol 10, No. 1, pg. 23; Nov 11, 1985 Reilly to Topping, Box 1, Reilly collection USHS

199   "The Park Service…" Ingram, *Hijacking A River*, Vishnu Temple Press, 2003, pg. 11

199   "In May of…" Litton, 'The Dory Story,' *Sunset* magazine, May 1968, pg. 88, Mortenson collection

200   "After Martin started…" Grand Canyon Dories brochure, Box 13, Reilly collection NAU

200   "To Martin's credit…" Martin Litton 2008 personal communication

200   "In the late…" Brief History of Boats at Grand Canyon Visitor's Center, Box 2, Reilly collection NAU

200   "In 1967, Moulty…" Fulmer oar with river trips listed, USHS; Sep 18, 1968 *Muncie Star*; Jan 24, 1969 Fulmer to Marston, Box 74, Marston collection

200   "In June of…" Jan 24, 1969 Fulmer to Marston, Box 74, Marston collection

200   "Regrettably, Dock Marston's…" Sat Sep 21 1968 *Independent Journal*, Box 5, Reilly collection USHS; Jan 24, 1969 Fulmer to Marston, Box 74, Marston collection

Page

200   "While there were…" Ingram, *Hijacking A River*, Vishnu Temple Press, 2003, pg. 19, 35; River Use Plan, 1972, Grand Canyon National Park Wilderness Administrative Record, Vol. 2, GRCA

200   "In 1970, a…" Myers, 'River Runners and the Number Game,' Boatman's Quarterly Review, Winter 1996-1997, Vol 10, No. 1, pg. 23; Feb 1979 Final Environmental Statement, Proposed Colorado River Management Plan, II-42, GRCA; 2006 Colorado River Management Plan Record of Decision, pg. 7, GRCA

200   "Today the NPS…" 2006 Colorado River Management Plan Record of Decision, pg. 3, GRCA; http://www.rrfw.org/grand-canyon-litigation

201   "Group sizes were…" River Use Plan, 1972, Grand Canyon National Park Wilderness Administrative Record, Vol. 2, GRCA; Final Environmental Statement, Proposed Wilderness Classification, 1973, Grand Canyon National Park Wilderness Administrative Record, Vol. 2, GRCA; Preliminary Wilderness Proposal Draft Environmental Statement, 1976, Grand Canyon National Park Wilderness Administrative Record, Vol. 3, GRCA

201   "Today, group sizes…" Noncommercial Operating Requirements and Commercial Operating Requirements, 2011, GRCA

201   "Throughout the 1960s…" Ingram, *Hijacking A River*, Vishnu Temple Press, 2003, pg. 266, 350; Preliminary Wilderness Proposal Draft Environmental Statement, 1976, Grand Canyon National Park Wilderness Administrative Record, Vol. 3, GRCA; Nov 18, 1975 Stitt to Denver Service Center, Grand Canyon National Park Wilderness Administrative Record, Vol. 3, 55-1, GRCA

201   "This finally became…" Ingram, *Hijacking A River*, Vishnu Temple Press, 2003, pg. 234

201   "Moulty won the…" Nov 21, 1975 *Sun City News*, Priss Becker collection; Nov 1, 1970 *Muncie Star*

201   "Moulty developed ever…" Aug 31, 1978 Fulmer to Marston, Box 74, Marston collection

201   "Pat and Susie…" Aug 1, 1991, Reilly to Linthacum, Box 10, Reilly collection NAU

201   "Harvey Butchart, the…" Butler and Myers, *Grand Obsession: Harvey Butchart and the Exploration of Grand Canyon*, Puma Press, 2007, pg. 328-329

201   "When he was…" Aug 31, 1978 Fulmer to Marston, Box 74, Marston collection

202   "A year later…" May 10, 1979 Fulmer to Paul Schafer, James Vaaler collection

202   "On the first…" Jun 6, 1979 Fulmer to Marston, Box 74, Marston collection; Dan Lindeman 2009 personal communication

202   "In 1980, Moulty…" Sep 24, 1984 *News-Sun*, Priss Becker collection

202   "Dock Marston, the…" Aug 31, 1978 Fulmer to Marston, Box 74, Marston collection; Otis Reed Marston info prepared 3-17-64 for F. Farquhar, Box 2, Reilly collection USHS

202   "Moulty did not…" Sep 24, 1984 *News-Sun*, Priss Becker collection

202   "In 1982, Pat…" Jul 22, 1982 Reilly to Szep, Box 27, Reilly collection NAU

203   "Pat summed it…" Jul 18, 1982 Reilly to Denoyer, Box 2, Reilly collection NAU

203   "Then it was…" Jul 21, 1989 *Muncie Star*; Priss Becker and Marge Woodroof 2008 personal interviews; Dec 21, 1988 Reilly to Topping, Reilly collection USHS

Epilogue

205   "Colleen unlocked the…" 2006 personal site visit Tom Martin

205   "Harvey mentioned the…" Harvey Butchart, *Grand Canyon Treks*, Spotted Dog Press 1998, pg. 191

206   "Ted Whitmoyer had…" Oct 14, 1964 Marston to Fulmer, Box 74, Marston collection; Ted Whitmoyer 2009 personal interview

206   "In 1979, Park…" Rosie Pepito LMNRA archives 2008 personal interview; John O'Brien 2008 personal interview; *Gem* Accession report, GRCA

207   "In subsequent visits…" personal site visits 8-06, 1-07, 9-07, 4-08 Tom Martin

207   "Unfortunately, no supports…" Aug 21, 1959 Fulmer to Reilly, Box 1, Fulmer collection USHS

210   "The twenty-nine-night river…" http://www.westernriver.com

211   "It was here…" Fletcher, Roger, Drift Boats and River Dories, Stackpole Books, 2007, pg. 89

Photographs next to chapter headings

Courtesy Priss Becker
Chapter 2: Roscoe, Thelma, Emma and Moulty in late 1920s; Chapter 4: Priss Ratican about to drive over her favorite uncle Moulty;
Courtesy Los Angeles Adventurers Club
Chapter 6: Pat Reilly at end of 1949 Grand Canyon river trip
Courtesy Edward Hudson
Chapter 8: *Esmeralda II* in Hermit, 1950; Chapter 9: *Esmeralda II* and *Hudson* at Phantom Ranch, 1950
Courtesy Tom Martin
Prologue: View downcanyon from Royal Arch, Grand Canyon National Park; Chapter 5: McKenzie River Wooden Boat Festival 2010; Epilogue: Priss Becker in her original 1957 life jacket, 2008
Courtesy Neal Newby
Chapter 13: Neal Newby and Frank Moltzen launching at Paria beach, 1956
Courtesy Carl Pederson
Chapter 1: Tow across Lake Mead, 1955
Courtesy Joe Szep
Foreword: 22 Mile camp, 1957; Chapter 3: Norm Nevills rowing punt on 1948 San Juan trip; Chapter 7: Moulty Fulmer in Marble Canyon, 1957; Chapter 10: Pat Reilly filling canteens, Vasey's Paradise, 1957; Chapter 12: Brick Mortenson attaching camera to *Flavell,* 1958; Chapter 14: *Susie R* at Nankoweap, 126,000 cfs, 1957; Chapter 15: Duane Norton at Randy's Rock, 1958; Chapter 16: *Susie R, Gem* and *Flavell* at top of Hance, 1957; Chapter 17: *Susie Too, Portolla* and *Flavell II* at foot of 24.5 Mile Rapid, 1962
Courtesy Chuck Warren
Chapter 11: A rare photo of the first bridge pontoon *Millipede* in Grand Canyon, 1954

Please, if you know of any photographs, logs or journals of river trips in the Grand Canyon before 1963 in your family's possession, get in touch with the author via Vishnu Temple Press at the address on the copyright page at the front of this book.

Index

12.5 Mile Camp 69, 80, 143, 144

13-Foot Rapid 23, 31, 39, 76, 189, 195

21 Mile Rapid 104

22 Mile Camp 125, 145, 146

24½ Mile Rapid 58, 104, 124, 147, 178-180. 187, 193, 194

25 Mile Rapid 147, 178, 179

75 Mile Rapid 45, 81, 107, 128, 153, 183, 201

83 Mile Rapid 154

138 Mile Rapid 168

140 Mile Canyon 123, 131, 165, 168, 169, 205

205 Mile Rapid 52, 116, 134, 184, 201

217 Mile Rapid 52, 53, 65, 116, 201

220 Mile Camp 52

224 Mile Rapid 116

232 Mile Rapid 53

234 Mile Rapid 53

Aleson, Harry 39, 52, 56, 103, 156, 159-161, 163

Allen, Smuss 91

Anasazi Canyon 23

Arches National Monument 195

Ashley 79, 82, 83, 85

Atherton, Ballard 155

Atkinson, Dale 119

Austin, Bill 189

Aztec Canyon 195

Aztec Creek 71, 196

B-24 Liberator 47-49, 58, 62

Babcock, Stephen Molton 16

Badger Rapid 44, 60, 80, 103, 125, 137, 143, 178

Ball State University 16, 17, 27, 202

Ball Teachers College 16, 17, 18 see also Ball State University

baloney boats 137, 140, 199

Barker Arch 195

Barnet, Bob 172, 197

Bass Camp 51

Bass Tramway 129, 130

Bass, William 51

Bat Cave 117, 118, 135

beam 6, 28, 33-35, 44, 58, 66, 86, 89, 93, 100, 192, 193, 199, 200

beaver 115, 134, 161

Becker, John 208

Becker, Priscilla Ratican 76, 139, 140-142, 145, 147-149, 151, 153-156, 193, 208

Beck, George 156, 157

Bedrock Rapid 51, 83, 86, 92, 111, 112, 130, 139, 163

Beer, Bill 119, 137

Belknap, Bill 8, 13, 14, 102, 118, 195

Bertram, Jack 160

bighorn sheep 112

Big Joe Rapid 62

Big Red 189

Big Yellow 189

Birdseye Expedition 146

Blanding, Utah 42

Bluff, Utah 35, 36, 39, 75, 76, 159, 189, 193, 200

boat lining 7, 52, 65, 73, 82, 84, 86, 108, 114, 115, 119, 133, 134, 141, 150, 153, 183, 193, 199

boat portaging 7, 52, 94, 137, 141, 153, 164, 191, 193

Boo 67

Boo Too 142, 155

Boucher Camp 47, 49, 58

Boucher Canyon 129

Boucher Rapid 47, 83, 111

Boucher Trail 201

Boulder City, Nevada 13, 124, 171, 172, 196, 206

Boulder Landing 65

Boulder Narrows 139, 141, 142, 144, 145, 178

Brennan, Jack 70, 140, 176

Bridge Canyon Dam 9, 53, 116, 135

Bright Angel Campground 128, 155

Bright Angel Creek 46, 108, 156

Bright Angel Trail 58, 82, 150, 185

Broken Bow Arch 195

Brower, David 9, 42

Brown, Frank 178

Brown's Park 93

Brown's Riffle 178

Bryant, Harold C. 27, 28

Buck Farm Canyon 45, 58

Bundy, Chet 161, 172, 173

Bureau of Reclamation 8, 53, 67, 195

Burg, Amos 59

burros 51, 52, 134, 137

Butchart, Harvey 106, 201, 202, 205

Butchart, Roma 201

Butler, Amrette Ott 123, 125-128, 130, 131, 133-135

Cactus 142, 155

Camp Adair, Oregon 31, 32, 34

canteens 49, 50, 126, 147, 148, 172, 181, 187

Canyonlands National Park 42, 196

Cape Royal 141

Cape Solitude 135

Cardinals 17

Cardle, John 197

Carpenter, Bob 191

cataract boats 14, 44, 51, 53, 56, 58, 59, 65, 67-69, 79, 83, 86, 89, 93, 100, 118, 119, 186

Cataract Canyon 7, 39, 66, 73, 190, 195

catfish 108, 126

Cave Canyon 53

Cave Springs Rapid 179, 180

Cessna airplanes 123

Chapman, Everett 135, 136

Chapman, Hildegarde 135

Charles Russell 50

Charlie 59

Chase, Frank 203

chine 6, 35, 44, 74, 76, 93, 104, 115, 119, 128, 135, 153, 192, 196, 209

Chris Craft 60, 62, 67, 76

Christmas Tree Cave 131

Clackamas River 32

Clayton, Fred 135

Clear Creek Rapid 108, 154

Cliff Dwellers, Arizona 71, 102, 124, 140-142, 155, 176

Clover, Elzada 21

Coffin, Lynn 135, 137, 140, 185, 187, 195, 201

Collegiate All-State 17

Colorado River 7-9, 11-15, 19, 21, 23, 24, 28, 31, 39, 42, 43, 45, 46, 48, 51-53, 56, 58, 60, 62, 64, 66, 76, 80, 86, 89, 93, 99, 100, 101, 103, 114, 121, 123, 133, 134, 136, 140, 141, 143, 146, 149, 156, 157, 159, 165, 173, 174, 176, 177, 182, 185, 188, 189, 190, 191, 193-196, 198, 199, 201-203, 206

Colorado River Outfitters Association 201

Colter, Mary Jane 46

Columbia River 32

Columbine Falls 53, 54, 118, 172

Comanche Creek 151

Copper Canyon 21

Corvallis, Oregon 32

Cox, Tommy 100, 103, 105, 106, 110, 112, 116, 117

Cross, John Jr 195

Cruickshank, Maurice "Moe" 48, 49, 62

Crystal Creek 49, 198

Crystal Rapid 49, 83, 129, 198, 201

Curtis, Larry 66

Daggett, John 119, 137

Dark Canyon 195

Davis, Dan 95, 97, 155, 187, 190, 191

Davis, Larry 195

Day, Norman 123, 125, 126, 130, 135

Dead Horse Point 196

DeColmont, Bernard 21

DeColmont, Genevieve 21

Deer Creek Falls 51, 113, 131, 165-167

Deer Creek Narrows 51, 84

Deer Spring 51

Dellenbaugh, Frederick 24, 27, 58

Desert magazine 37

Desert Watchtower 60

DeSeyne, Antoine 21

Desloge, Joe 61, 67

Desolation Canyon 68, 71, 73, 201

Deubendorff Rapid 51, 84, 112, 130, 139, 164

Diamond Creek 11, 52, 53, 58, 85, 116, 135, 146, 157, 190, 202

Dines, Bruce 91

Dines, Tyson "Ty" 91, 190

Disaster Falls 71, 93

Disney, Walt 100

Doerr, John "Little John" 42, 49-51, 54

Domino 28, 29, 34, 39

Doris Rapid 168

dory 6, 7, 32-35, 39, 69, 95, 103, 118, 170, 192, 196, 199, 200, 209

double-ender 32, 34, 73, 74, 89, 93, 192

dragonflies 130

driftwood 7, 8, 11, 13, 27, 45, 49, 51, 56, 58, 61, 64, 70, 76, 82, 84, 107, 114, 115, 125, 126, 133, 135, 141, 144, 146, 153, 155, 160, 163, 165, 166, 172, 178, 180, 199

Driftwood Bay 13

Dripping Springs 140

Dunn, William 53

eagles 130, 133

East Rim Drive 140

Echo Park 60, 62, 73, 94

Eddy, Clyde 26, 27

Eisaman, Josh 124

elephant rig 160

Ellingson, Malcolm "Moki Mac" 119

Elliot, Ian 100, 209, 212

Elton, Roy 189

Elves Chasm 51, 83, 111, 112, 129, 130, 162, 163, 190, 194

Ely, Northcutt 9

Embanks, Royce "Roy" 48, 49, 62

Emerald Rapid 83

Emery, Walt 91

Escalante River 195

Esmeralda Elbow 62

Esmeralda II 52, 55, 56, 60-65, 68, 124

Espejo Creek 151

Eugene, Oregon 34

Eva L 175, 187, 189, 192

Evinrude outboards 52, 67, 92

fake oar 128

Fall Canyon 85

Federal Bureau of Investigation 137

Fern Glen Camp 114, 132, 133, 168

Fern Glen Canyon 114, 169

Fern Glen Rapid 114

fiberglass 14, 89, 90, 92, 93, 100, 113, 115, 118, 128, 134, 136, 148, 151, 153, 164, 165, 172, 175, 177, 183, 184, 185, 190

Finally 66

fish eye 44, 134

Fishtail Rapid 168

flare gun 49, 50, 51

Flavell 100, 101, 103-105, 110, 112, 114-116, 119, 125, 126, 128, 134, 135, 139, 140, 142, 143, 147, 151, 153, 154, 161, 163, 166, 168, 169, 171, 172, 176, 177, 180-183, 185, 186, 192, 212

Flavell, George 101

Flavell II 192, 194, 196

Folbot 93, 94

Forbidding Canyon 23, 31, 39

Forcier, Guy 61, 67

Forster Rapid 63-65

Fort Wayne, Indiana 27, 75, 76, 156, 208

Fox, Twentieth Century 30, 32

Frazier, Russell 60

Fred Harvey Company 46

Freeman, Lewis 24

Frye, Kyle 208, 209

Fulmer, Conrad 16

Fulmer, Emma Greenwood 15, 16, 18, 19, 75, 79

Fulmer, Francis Burton 15-18, 27, 29

Fulmer, Jacob 15, 16

Fulmer, Janice Zehring 18, 19, 21-29, 31, 32, 35-39, 42, 51, 52, 55, 60, 71, 75, 79, 95, 108, 118, 121, 122, 139, 140, 154-156, 189, 191-193, 196-198, 200-203

Fulmer, Jennie 15

Fulmer, Roscoe 16-19

Fulmer, Stephen Moulton Babcock "Moulty" 1, 7-9, 12, 14-19, 21-32, 34-47, 49-56, 58-60, 62, 66-69, 71, 73, 77, 79, 86, 87, 89, 90, 92-95, 97, 99-113, 115, 116, 118, 119, 121-125, 128-132, 134, 135, 139-151, 153-156, 159-162, 164, 166, 168-178, 180-189, 191-193, 196-203, 206-212

Fulmer, Thelma 15-18, 75

Furen, Mildred 94

Furen, Walter 93, 94

Galloway, Nathaniel 50

Galloway 67, 79, 80, 82, 84, 93, 94

Gandy, Jack S. 132

Gates of Lodore 56

Gem 5-7, 13, 14, 75-77, 86, 87, 90, 93-95, 101-104, 106, 108-113, 115, 116, 118, 119, 121, 122, 124-126, 128, 130, 134, 135, 140, 142, 145, 150, 151, 153-156, 159, 160-162, 164, 168-173, 175, 182, 187, 192, 193, 196, 199, 200, 205-212

Glen Canyon 19, 21-23, 25, 38, 39, 52, 69, 70, 76, 137, 173, 175-177, 189, 191, 195, 196, 199

Glen Canyon Dam 8, 9, 11, 13, 45, 69, 114, 137, 146, 163, 173, 176, 177, 189, 195, 196, 198, 199, 206

Glenwood Springs 66

God's Pocket 5, 13, 172, 173, 196

Goff, Ralph Harper 100, 101

Goforth, Beth 208, 209

Goforth, Bob 208, 209

Goldblum, Charles "Goldie" 48, 49, 50, 62

Goldwater. Sen. Barry 187

Government Rapid 22, 30, 76

Grand Canyon 58, 126, 148, 149

Grand Canyon Dories 200

Grand Canyoneer 12, 58, 70, 173, 212

Grand Junction Daily Sentinel 19, 21

Grandview Point 196

Grand Wash Bay 118, 135, 173

Grand Wash Cliffs 42, 43, 53, 87, 92

Granite Gorge 128

Granite Narrows 165, 166

Granite Rapid 47, 58, 82, 97, 110, 129, 139, 161, 201, 211

Granite Springs Rapid 52

Grapevine Camp 81

Grapevine Rapid 45, 108, 128, 137, 154, 184, 190

Gray Canyon 68, 73

Gray Marine 55, 189

Great Thumb 140

Greene, Art 102, 103, 124, 125, 135, 136, 140, 142, 176, 177, 185

Green River 24, 55, 56, 60, 67, 69, 79, 93, 94, 206

Green River, Utah 21, 39, 67, 68, 73, 91, 193

Green River, Wyoming 28, 39, 56, 60, 67, 71, 73, 79, 93, 101, 206

Gregg Basin 172

Gregory Arch 195

Gribble, Ray 197

Griffith, Dick 71-73

Griffith, Isabelle 71-73

Gromer, Julian 172

Grua, Kenton 69

gunwale 6, 35, 44, 81, 93, 172, 173, 192, 199, 209

Hakatai Canyon 129, 130

Hamilton, Jon 189

Hance Camp 107, 108, 128, 153, 183, 184

Hance Rapid 7, 45, 81, 96, 107, 108, 117, 119, 128, 137, 152, 153, 157, 183, 184, 191-194

Hansbrough, Peter 179

Harding Hole 62

Harris, Don 70, 119, 140, 179

Hatch, Don 97

Hatch, Frank 91

Hatch, Robert Rafael "Bus" 91, 92, 97, 190

Hatch, Ted 190

Havasu Canyon 51, 56-58, 62, 65, 84, 113, 114, 133, 157, 196, 200

Hays, Jack D.H. 188

headstands 14, 23, 30

Heale, Naomi 70

Helfrich, Prince 194

helicopters 9, 62, 150, 151, 189

Hell's Canyon 188

Hell's Half Mile 94

Hemenway Harbor 73

Hermit Camp 27, 28, 194

Hermit Creek 28, 47, 111

Hermit Rapid 27, 28, 40, 47, 58, 61, 83, 107, 111, 129, 139, 161, 162, 184, 201

Hermit Trail 27, 28, 40, 52, 97, 140, 201

Hidden Passage Canyon 23, 31, 39, 195

Hidden Passage 22, 30

Hindman, Wood Knoble "Woodie" 32-34, 74, 118, 192, 200

Hiser, Lucile 42, 43, 46, 54, 122

Hiser, Wayne 42, 46, 51, 54, 122

Hite, Utah 7, 39, 73

Holder, Cale 187, 188

Holmes, Burton 30

Holmstrom, Haldane "Buzz" 59

Honaker Trail 21, 30

Hoover Dam 52, 53

Horn Creek Rapid 14, 47, 81, 82, 86, 97, 108, 109, 117, 118, 122, 129, 139, 161, 176, 184

House Rock Rapid 44, 137, 144, 178, 202

House Rock Wash 125

Howland, O.G. & Seneca 53

Hudson, Ed Jr 52, 55-57, 62

Hudson, Ed Sr 8, 52, 55-58, 60, 61-66

Hudson 60, 62, 67

Hulse, Russell 197

hummingbirds 130, 133, 165

Hyde, Bessie 21

Hyde, Colleen 205, 206

Hyde, Glenn 21

I'Anson, J. E. "Ed" 95, 97

Iceberg Canyon 13, 155, 172

impingement wall. See Granite Narrows

Indian Gardens 82, 193, 201

Ingram, Jeff 9

Jensen, Reed 119

Jensen, Utah 56, 60

jet boats 189, 190, 193

Joan 44, 51-53

Johns Canyon 38, 76

Johnson, Jo 12

Johnson outboards 91

Johnson, Pres. Lyndon 196

Johnson, Rosalind "Ros" 42, 47, 50, 53, 54

Johnson, Willis 59

Jones Hole 94

Jordan, Jimmy 67, 178

Jotter, Lois 21

June Bug 67

Kaarhus, Torkel "Tom" 33, 34, 74

Kaat, Jim 197

Kaibab Suspension Bridge 46, 81, 154, 184, 185

Kaibab Trail 46, 70, 155, 159, 160

Kanab Canyon 132

Kanab Creek 112

Kanab Rapid 169

Kanab, Utah 140

Kane Creek 189, 191

Keyhole Natural Bridge 132, 140, 165

King, Max 189, 193

kingsnakes 153

Kinsinger, John 191

Kirschbaum, Walter 190, 191

Kolb, Ellsworth 206

Kolb, Emery 28, 37, 146, 156, 160, 206

Kolb Studio 28, 37, 205, 206

Kuhne, Jack 30

Kwagunt Rapid 61, 81, 106, 151, 181, 201

Labyrinth Canyon 73

Lake Mead 8, 13, 14, 21, 39, 45, 52, 53, 55, 57, 59, 65, 67, 71, 73, 85, 102, 116, 118, 154, 155, 157, 159, 170-174, 184, 189, 194-196, 206, 207

Lake Powell 8, 69, 76, 146

Larsen, Gerald "Lug" 79-81, 83-86, 93, 94, 100

Lauck, Paul "Zeke" 11

Lava Canyon Rapid 107

Lava Chuar Canyon 45, 60, 81, 107, 128, 151, 155, 202

Lava Falls 7, 11, 14, 52, 58, 65, 72, 73, 77, 84, 114, 115, 133, 134, 139, 146, 155, 157, 169-171, 173, 184, 189, 190, 191, 194, 196, 211

Lava Falls Trail 169, 170

Lavender, David 7

Laws, Ed 49

Layton, Jim 108

Leaburg, Oregon 192

Ledges Camp 84, 114, 133, 205, 206

Lee's Ferry, Arizona 5, 8, 23-25, 32, 35, 36, 38, 39,

41-45, 53, 55, 56, 60, 61, 66-69, 71, 73, 76, 77, 80, 86, 90-93, 95, 99, 100, 102, 119, 122-124, 137, 140-142, 146, 151, 156, 157, 159, 175, 177, 180, 186-190, 193, 195, 196, 202, 203, 210

Lehman, Chubby 30

Lewiston, Idaho 35

life jackets 44, 51, 69, 82, 84, 85, 89, 97, 102, 106, 112, 119, 137, 179, 208

Lily Park 60, 62

Lindeman, Dan 202

Lindeman, Linda 202

lining 7, 52, 65, 73, 82, 84, 86, 108, 115, 119, 133, 134, 141, 146, 150, 153, 181, 183, 193, 199

Little Colorado River 45, 81, 96, 106, 114, 118, 127, 128, 133, 146, 150, 151, 157, 182

Little Nankoweap Camp 149, 181

Little Nankoweap Creek 149, 151

Litton, Esther 100, 103, 106, 110, 113, 115, 117, 121-123

Litton, Martin 7, 77, 100, 102, 103, 105, 110, 111, 113, 115, 117, 121-123, 125, 126, 128-132, 134, 135, 173, 192-194, 196, 199, 200

Llewellyn, John 203

Lockheed Corp. 37, 41, 42, 79, 89, 90, 99, 100, 102, 123, 132, 135, 136, 140, 159, 195

Lodore Canyon 60, 71, 73, 79, 80, 91, 93-95, 201

Lodore 67, 79-83, 93, 94

Long Tom River 32

Loper, Bert 7, 50, 56, 58, 126, 127, 148, 149

Los Angeles Adventurers Club 79, 85

Los Angeles Times 100, 132

Loving, Ken 211

Lower Lava Camp 85, 115, 134

Lower Lava Rapid 115, 134

Lower Tuna Camp 62

Lower Tuna Rapid 62

Lyons, John 60

MacLean, Mary Elizabeth "Bee". *See* Reilly, Susie

MacRae, Alan 49

Malagosa Crest 183

Mantle Ranch 62

Marble Canyon 37, 42, 80, 93, 96, 101, 135, 141, 149, 193

Marble Canyon Dam 9, 126

Marble Canyon Lodge 24, 32, 36, 38, 42, 102

Marston, Garth 42-47, 49, 51, 53, 54, 124

Marston, Maradel 67-69

Marston, Margaret 60, 62, 67, 122, 200

Marston, Otis Reed "Dock" 8, 42-47, 50-56, 58-62, 66-68, 70, 74, 75, 77, 79, 83, 86, 87, 90, 92, 93, 95, 97, 99, 101, 117-119, 121-124, 137, 139-144, 149, 154-156, 159, 165, 173, 175, 176, 178, 182, 187, 189, 190, 193, 195, 196, 199, 200, 202, 208, 211

Marston, Shirley 53

Martin, Paul S. 11

Masland, Frank 42-46, 49, 50, 51, 53, 54, 56, 92

Mather Campground 155

Matkatamiba Canyon 113, 132

Maumee River 75, 76

May, Sam 140

McConkie, Wayne 30-32

McGill, Bill 123-126, 128, 130-132, 134, 135

McKenzie River dory 7, 14, 32-35, 39, 58, 74, 93, 95, 103, 118, 170, 192-194, 199, 200

Mercury 94, 95, 102, 159

Mexican Hat, Utah 21, 24, 25, 27, 30, 35-39, 41-44, 55, 59, 76, 77, 159, 193, 200

Mexican Hat Expeditions 59, 69, 76, 77, 86, 186, 190

Mexican Hat II 44, 51, 52

Midgets 17

Milam, Fred 48, 49

Millipede 91, 92

Moja 5, 35-39, 55, 58, 60, 62, 66-69, 73, 75, 76, 86, 87, 175, 187, 189, 191, 192, 199, 200, 202, 208

Moltzen, Frank 136, 137

Montez, Ramon 101

Monument Valley 19, 24, 38

Moonshine Rapid 62

Moore, Boyd 106, 107

Moore, Buck 117

Morgan, John 187, 188

Mortenson, Bonnie 141, 143, 155

Mortenson, Cecelia "Cece" 205, 206, 212

Mortenson, Dave 147, 148, 193, 205, 208, 209, 212

Mortenson, Natalie 212

Mortenson, Vernon "Brick" 99, 100, 102-108, 111-118, 121, 123, 135, 139-145, 147-149, 151, 153-155, 159, 161-166, 168, 169, 171, 172, 191-193, 196, 206, 212

Motorcade, Marston Grand Canyon 67, 68, 178

mountain lions 13, 134

Muncie Central Bearcats 17

Muncie Central High 17

Muncie, Indiana 15-19, 24-28, 32, 35-37, 39, 40, 42, 55, 66, 68, 75, 94, 122, 135, 140, 155, 159, 172, 175, 186, 187, 189, 191, 192, 195-197, 202

Music Temple Canyon 195

Music Temple 30, 196

muskrats 104

Mystery Canyon 23

Nankoweap Canyon 44, 45, 137, 149, 154, 182

Nankoweap Creek 126, 150, 181

Nankoweap granaries 45, 106

Nankoweap Trail 150

National Canyon 169

National Geographic 24

National Park Service 8, 12, 13, 42, 49, 57, 97, 102, 106, 135-137, 155, 177, 181, 187, 188, 190, 196, 199-201, 206

National Park Service Advisory Committee 42

Navajo Bridge 96, 143

Navajo Dam 173

Navajo Mountain 19, 31

Navajo Sandstone 177

Nelson, Jim 91

Nelson, Louis 75, 76

Nevills, Doris 21, 32, 36, 39, 45, 47, 58, 59, 168

Nevills Expedition 21, 37, 42, 56, 58, 59, 67, 68, 86, 93

Nevills, Joan 30

Nevills, Mae "Mo" 21, 59

Nevills, Norm 19, 21-32, 34-47, 50-56, 58, 59, 67, 71, 85-87, 102, 116, 173, 187, 195, 208

Nevills, William "Billy" 21

Newby, Neal 136, 137

Nichols, Edward Tatnall "Tad" 69, 70

Nixon Rock 49

Norm 68

North Canyon Rapid 80, 86, 104, 125, 137, 145, 201

North Rim 46, 49, 137, 141, 156, 193

Norton, Duane "Nort" 140-142, 147, 153, 155, 159, 160, 161, 163, 165, 166, 168, 169, 171

Oak Canyon 195

oar block 75, 76, 87, 103, 104, 107, 119, 163, 166

oarlock 6, 22, 28, 34, 35, 44, 51, 58, 62, 66, 75, 76, 90, 93, 103, 104, 107, 108, 118, 119, 122, 125, 161, 163, 165, 185, 200, 211

OARS 201, 202

O'Brien, John 200, 206

Olo Canyon 84

Ott, Amrette *See* Butler, Amrette Ott

Ouray, Utah 67

Outlaw Cave 23

Padre 71, 72

Paiute Farms 31

Palisades Canyon 60

Panthon 101

Parashant Canyon 52, 85, 115, 134

Paria beach 41, 56, 70, 136, 137

Paria Canyon 201

Paria Riffle 32, 56

Paria River 140-143

Parks, Arizona 208

patching 64, 80, 85, 105, 113, 115, 118, 128, 134, 147, 148, 153, 154, 165, 183, 184

Patraw, Preston 97

Peach Springs, Arizona 157

Pearce Ferry 52, 56, 63, 68, 85, 118, 135, 172

Peckinpaugh, Jack 197

Pederson, Carl 99, 100, 103, 107, 108, 110, 112-117, 122, 159, 175-178, 180-186, 194

Pederson, Earline 100, 175

Pederson, John 95, 97

Pelican Brand oars 104, 153

permits 8, 97, 102, 136, 137, 177, 187, 188, 190, 195, 199, 200, 210, 212

Petschek, Rudi 69

Pettijohn, H.J. 17

Pfeiffenberger, Matt 91, 92

Phantom Ranch 5, 8, 21, 24, 42, 45-47, 56, 58, 59, 63, 69, 70, 81, 95-97, 107, 108, 112, 119, 128, 135-137, 146, 150, 153-157, 159, 160, 161, 165, 177, 184, 185, 187, 193, 194, 203

Pierce, Elgin 77

Pieroth, Ruth 38, 69, 70, 79, 80, 83, 85, 118, 135,

140, 141, 144, 145, 147, 153, 155

Pipe Creek 58, 185-187

Pipe Creek Rapid 185, 187

Piper airplanes 36, 59

Plateau Point 37, 176

plywood 25, 28, 32, 33, 35, 44, 58, 60, 73, 74, 89, 90, 149, 156, 173, 175, 192, 207, 209

pontoon boats 91, 119, 137, 160, 190, 199, 202

Portola 193, 194

postage stamp 166

Powell, John Wesley 26, 46, 53, 128

President Harding Rapid 58, 70, 105, 124, 126, 149

Pumpkin Spring 134

punt, San Juan 22, 23, 30, 32, 34, 38, 41, 56, 71

Purtymun, Elmer 95-97

Queen 72, 73

Quigley, David 70, 149

Quist, Goddard 50

Rainbow Bridge 19- 21, 23, 31, 32, 39, 191

Rainbow Lodge 19

rake 6, 34, 35, 192, 193, 199, 200

rattlesnakes 153

Rattlesnake 142, 155

Recapture Creek 39

Red Canyon 153

Red Slide 134

Redwall Cavern 43, 60, 80, 105, 124-126, 148, 149, 157, 212

Redwall Limestone 45, 84, 125, 130, 149, 181, 205

Reek, Edmond 30, 31

Reilly, Plez Talmadge "P.T." "Pat" 8, 14, 37, 38, 41, 42, 55, 56, 58, 59, 63-65, 68-70, 75-77, 79-87, 89, 90, 92, 93, 95, 97, 99-119, 121-132, 134-136, 139-156, 159-166, 168, 169, 171-187, 189, 191-196, 199, 200-203, 206, 208, 212

Reilly's Roost 133, 206. *See also* Ledges Camp

Reilly, Susie 37, 38, 41, 42, 58, 59, 63-66, 68-70, 79, 80, 82, 85, 87, 99, 102, 103, 106, 107, 112, 114-117, 123-125, 128, 130, 131, 135, 136, 140, 141, 142, 146, 147, 149-151, 154, 155, 159, 161, 171-173, 181, 184, 193, 201, 202, 206

Renthrop, Esther 70

Reynolds, Adrian 67

Reynolds, Adrian Kenneth "A.K." 67, 68, 79, 80-86, 93, 94

Reynolds, Ellen 79, 80, 82-86, 93, 94

Reynolds, George 79-86

Reynolds, Helen 67

Reynolds, Steve 69

Richards, Arnie 205, 206, 212

Richards, Henry 179

Riffey, John 114, 123, 150, 169-172, 196

Riffey, Laura 114, 123

Rigg, Bob 63-65, 68-70, 104

Rigg, Jim 55, 56, 58, 59, 63-65, 68-70, 76, 79, 97, 104, 119

River House Ruin 76

Robinson, Bestor 42-46, 55-57

Robinson, Florence 42, 43, 46

rocker 6, 26, 32, 34, 35, 44, 66, 73, 93, 192, 193, 199

Rogue River 75, 93, 199, 200

Rose Poly 17

Ross Wheeler 50, 51

Route 66 38, 102, 135, 208

Rowe, Willis "Cappy" 79, 80, 82, 85

Royal Arch Canyon 130

Royal Order of Colorado River Rats 53, 58, 70, 85, 116, 135

Royal Order of Drift Wood Burners 45, 51, 70

rub rail 6, 35, 93

Ruby Rapid 83

Rumel, Hall 30, 31

Russell-Ball All-Stars 18

Russell, Charles 7

Rust, David 46, 156

Salmon River 34, 42, 75, 188

Sanderson, Rod 67

Sandra 44, 50, 51, 52, 69, 71

sand waves 36, 39, 76, 87, 118

Sandy Point 172

San Juan River 21-25, 30, 31, 34-39, 41-43, 52, 55, 58, 69, 71, 72, 75, 76, 79, 87, 103, 140, 159, 173, 175, 176, 187, 189, 193, 195, 200, 201, 202

San Juan 30

San Rafael River 193

Santiam River 32

Sapphire Rapid 83

Satran, Mr. 155

Sausage 75, 187, 189, 191, 193, 196, 200, 202

Schlump, John 71, 73

Schmidt, George 18, 19, 35, 75, 197, 200

Schulz, Paul 172, 173

scupper 6, 90, 211

Separation Canyon 53, 116, 135

Serpentine Rapid 83, 86

Sheer Wall Rapid 104, 137, 144, 178

Shinumo Creek 51, 83, 111, 129

Shiprock, New Mexico 36-38, 42, 71, 72, 173

Shirley, Robert F. 132

side flare 34, 35, 44, 75, 192, 199, 200

Sierra Club 9, 42, 201

Signature Cave 62

skeletons 45, 125, 181

Slate Creek 201

Slickhorn Canyon 22, 30, 39

Slickhorn Rapid 76

Slocum, Dale 95-97

Smoker oars 36, 76, 86, 103, 153, 185, 208

Snake River 42, 188

Soap Creek Rapid 44, 80, 103, 104, 137, 143, 178, 200

Sockdolager Rapid 108, 128, 137, 139, 154, 184

South Bass Trail 50

South Canyon 45, 104, 105, 118, 125, 149, 156, 180, 181

South Rim 27, 37, 40, 46, 55, 65, 82, 97, 128, 135, 136, 137, 140, 155, 156, 159, 160, 171, 176, 177, 185-187, 193, 196, 201, 205, 206, 209

Specter Rapid 51, 129, 130, 163

Spencer Canyon 53, 85, 116

spillways 146

Split Mountain 56, 60, 67, 73, 80, 94

split-twig figurine 181

Sportyaks 8, 195, 199

Spring Canyon 115, 134

Springfield, Oregon 34

Stairway Canyon 51

Stanton, Robert Brewster 26, 179

Stanton's Cave 181

Staveley, Gaylord 186, 190

Steele, Keith 192-194, 199

stem 6, 173

Stevens, Larry 11

Stewart, Blake 201

Stillwater Canyon 73

St. Joseph River 75

St. Mary's River 75

Stitt, Merle 201

Stone Creek 130, 164, 194

Stone, Julius 26, 27, 50, 173

Stone 173

Stover, Smokey 91

Streator, Nancy 42, 47, 50, 51, 54, 56

Stroud, Ken 187, 188

Studio City, California 37, 42, 92, 135, 159

Sun City, Arizona 79, 192, 197, 201,

Sunset 101

Sunset magazine 100, 102, 121-123, 199

Surprise Valley 84, 113, 131, 166

Susie R 101, 103, 108, 112-116, 119, 125, 126, 128, 132, 134, 135, 140, 142, 144, 145, 147, 148, 150, 151, 153, 154, 162, 163, 164, 166, 168, 169, 170, 172, 174, 176-179, 181, 183-186, 192, 212

Susie Too 193, 194, 196

Swanson, Marian 141, 143

sweep boatman 7, 103, 161

Syncline Rapid 23, 39, 76

Szep, Joe 41, 140, 142, 144, 149, 153, 155, 159, 161, 164, 166, 168, 169, 171, 172, 175-184, 193, 202, 208

Szep, Winnie 41, 184

Tadje, August 50

Tanner Camp 45, 70

Tanner Rapid 45, 107

Tanner Trail 150

Tapeats Creek 62, 64, 66, 91, 112, 113, 130, 165

Tapeats Narrows 131

Tapeats Rapid 51, 84, 131, 165

Tapeats sandstone 48, 50, 51, 113

Taylor, Guy 122, 123, 124, 125, 126, 130, 131, 132, 134, 135, 159-161, 166, 168, 169, 171, 172, 175, 187, 189, 196

Taylor, Willie 52, 55-57, 61, 62, 67, 123, 124

Temple Bar 5, 11, 14, 118, 122, 124, 135, 140, 143, 155, 169, 171-173

ten-man boats 71, 73, 77, 91, 92, 95, 156

Tequila Beach. *See* Lower Lava Camp

Terry, Helen 79

Terry, Paul 79, 81, 83, 85, 86, 92, 93, 99, 100, 103, 106, 107, 116, 117, 177

Thompson, Utah 30

Three Fords Camp 67

Three Springs Canyon 134, 135

thrill craft 160

Thunder River 113, 130

Thunder Spring 91, 113

Tidball, Dean 140, 156

Tonto Platform 47-50, 62, 82

Toroweap Overlook 114, 123, 196

Toroweap Point 114

Towne, Bill 95, 97

transom 6, 34, 74

Trans World Airlines 132, 135, 136, 137, 151

trash 8, 135, 163, 165, 194-196, 201

Travertine Canyon 116, 135

Travertine Falls 53, 85

Triplett Falls 93, 94

trout, rainbow 32, 34, 51, 113, 165, 196

Tub 5, 15, 25, 26, 27, 28, 34, 39, 87

Tuckup Canyon 65

Tuna Creek 47, 48, 49, 58, 61

Tuna Rapid 48, 62

Tuolumne River 202

Tusher Wash Diversion Dam 68, 69

Tuweep 114, 123, 169

Twin 67

Uinta Basin 67, 68, 73

United Airlines 132, 135, 137, 151

United States Geological Survey 27, 46, 108, 140, 146, 156, 160

United States Geological Survey Board of Geographical Names 132

Unkar Delta 81, 108

Unkar Rapid 107, 117, 128, 141, 153, 183

Up Lake 52

Upset Rapid 51, 73, 84-86, 89, 112, 113, 118, 122, 132, 139, 184, 205

Van Deren, Don 95-97

Vasey's Paradise 43, 45, 80, 105, 125, 139, 149

Vernal, Utah 91, 94

Vida, Oregon 194

Vishnu Creek 81

Vulcan Rapid 52, 115, 211, 212. *See also* Lava Falls Rapid

Vulcan's Anvil 115, 211

Wagner, Rev. William 197

Waldes, Milo 93, 94

Waldes, Rosalie 93, 94

Walker, Preston 22, 23, 31

Walker Special 22, 23

Walthenberg Rapid 112, 201

Warner Gear 18, 39, 60, 140, 196

Warren, Chuck 91

Watson, Bob 123, 125, 126, 128, 130

Wee Red 189, 190

Wee Yellow 189, 190

Weisheit, John 9, 12

Welty, Howard "Cowboy" 42, 50, 51, 54, 56

Wen 44, 50, 52, 173

Western River Expeditions 210

Western River Guides Association 119, 201

Westwater Canyon 66

whirlpools 85, 116, 128, 149, 150, 151, 185, 191

White Canyon 191

White, Georgie Clark 8, 39, 77, 103, 107, 119, 121, 128, 139, 160-162, 169-173, 175, 177, 190, 210

White, James 199

White River, Indiana 15, 25-29, 36

Whitman, Joe 191

Whitmore Wash 52, 77, 116, 173

Whitmoyer, Ted 13, 14, 196, 206

Wilderness Act 9, 196, 201

Willamette River 32

Willamette Valley 32-34

Willie's Necktie 62

Wilson, Bill 19

Wilson Camp 31

Wilson, Mel 203

Wind River Range 60, 159

Wing, George 38, 41

Wooden, John 18

Woodruff, Burton 74-76

Wright, Dora 42

Wright, Frank 41-46, 50-56, 58, 59, 63-65, 68-70, 79, 97, 102, 119, 186

Wright, Helen 70

Wright, Paul 70

Wyckoff, Jean 69, 70, 118, 135

Yampa River 55, 60, 62, 91, 94, 175, 187, 200, 201

Yavapai Point 156

Young Men's Christian Association (YMCA) 16-18, 27, 35, 39, 55, 66, 122, 159, 189, 195-197, 200, 212

Ziess, Ray 30

Zoroaster Rapid 108, 154

About the Author

Tom Martin is a physical therapist, working at the Grand Canyon Clinic at the South Rim, Grand Canyon National Park, since 1996. He has written two books, *Day Hikes from the River*, and with co-author Duwain Whitis, the popular *Guide To The Colorado River In The Grand Canyon, Lee's Ferry To South Cove*, which won the 2007 National Outdoor Book Award. A hiker and river runner in the Grand Canyon since the 1960s, he currently volunteers as co-director of River Runners for Wilderness, as Secretary of the Grand Canyon Historical Society, and as an executive committee member for the Grand Canyon Sierra Club chapter.